MW00813016

FILLING IN THE SEAMS
THE STORY OF TRENTON THUNDER BASEBALL

CHRISTOPHER T. EDWARDS

The Middle Atlantic Press
Moorestown, New Jersey

Manufactured in the United States of America

1 2 3 4 5 99 98 97

Library of Congress Cataloging-in-Publication Data

Edwards, Christopher T.
    Filling in the seams : the story of Trenton Thunder baseball /
Christopher T. Edwards.
        p.   cm
    ISBN 0-912608-97-8 (alk. paper)
        1. Trenton Thunder (Baseball team)—History.   2. Minor league
baseball—New Jersey—Trenton—History.   I. Title.
    GV875.T74E38   1997
    796.357'64'0974966—dc21   97-16802

Photos copyright © 1997 by David M. Schofield.
Cover and interior design by Robert Lebrun.
Thunder team logo on cover used by permission of the Trenton Thunder.

For information write:

The Middle Atlantic Press
10 Twosome Drive
P.O. Box 600
Moorestown, NJ 08057

To Sunshine, the true Thunder in my life

Acknowledgments

The idea for *Filling in the Seams* originated during the spring of 1994 as I began covering the Trenton Thunder. Over the last three years, the project gradually assumed a character of its own.

There are so many people whose help has been invaluable. Edward Jutkowitz, my editor, believed enough in the book to make it happen. I thank him for his patience and prompt attention to all of my questions as a first-time author.

I would like to thank all of my friends in the Trenton Thunder front office and ownership, including Garden State Baseball Limited partners Sam Plumeri, Sr. (as gentle and kind a man as you'll ever meet) and his wife, Josephine, Joe Caruso, the late Jim Maloney, Joseph Plumeri, Joe Finley, and Thunder General Manager/Chief Operating Officer Wayne Hodes. Assistant General Manager Tom McCarthy has been a valued friend and fellow baseball lover. In addition, my gratitude is extended to former Thunder Assistant General Manager Brian Mahoney, Director of Marketing and Merchandising Eric (Pookie) Lipsman, Director of Business Operations Todd Pae, Director of Ticket Sales John Fierko, Broadcaster Andy Freed, Director of Public and Community Relations Rick Brenner, Controller John (Bean) Coletta, Merchandising Manager Andrea Bunney, Ticket Manager Scott Gross, Group Sales Manager Adam Palant, 1996 intern Kate McKenna, and last but certainly not least, Waterfront Park sound coordinator Bart Mix and public address announcer Brandon (Horse) Hardison.

Two others who have provided hours of laughter are Paul (a.k.a. Boomer the Mascot) and team photographer Dave Schofield, who illustrated this book.

So many great people collaborated to make minor-league baseball in Trenton a reality, and to them I extend sincere congratulations. My thanks go to Mercer County Executive Robert D. Prunetti, Executive Director of Mercer County Park Frank Ragazzo, Lee Millas, Trenton Mayor Douglas Palmer, New Jersey Governor Christine Todd Whitman, and Waterfront Park Head Groundskeeper Jeff Migliaccio.

Any book based on history is only as entertaining as the characters who bring it to life. To that end, I'm grateful for 1994 Thunder Manager Tom Runnells and 1995-96 skipper Ken Macha. To "Mock," I submit that your entertaining quotes and undying patience with the press made many long nights so much more lively. Thanks for your insight into the game—and into life. To the almost 150 players who passed through the Trenton clubhouse between 1994 and 1996, I salute your talent and your dreams.

I also owe a huge debt of gratitude to my newspaper colleagues at *The Times of Trenton*. Publisher Richard Bilotti, Editor Brian Malone, Metro Editor Pete Callas, Executive Sports Editor Jim Gauger, and Assistant Sports Editors Phil Coffey, Bill Kennedy, and Craig Haley gave me unlimited access to the information needed to write this book. To fellow writers John Nalbone, Rick Freeman, Jed Weisberger, and *Trentonian* Thunder beat man Larry O'Rourke (who was also with the team from day one), I extend my hand in thanks.

Finally, the will to persevere comes from those closest to you. To my mother-in-law, Audrey Meredith, I say thanks for letting me take over your computer room for almost two years (I promise I'll clean up). To my wife, Tracey, I say thanks for believing in me. To my family, Dr. and Mrs. Richard T. Edwards and siblings Clarissa, Jocelyn, and Evans, I say thanks for putting me through Princeton.

See ya at the ballpark . . .

Contents

Introduction

> "The good news is that we've got a stadium, we've got a ball team, we've brought baseball back to Trenton and Mercer County, and I think it has probably, in terms of attendance, exceeded all of our expectations. Fan reaction from every standpoint that we can see has been very, very positive, and growing, which I think is significant. We've accomplished several objectives with this stadium, and we're well on our way to accomplishing some others. First of all, we wanted to show that a professional sports franchise could work in this area. It has, to this point. We wanted to show that we could change the image of the city of Trenton, both from within, the spirit from within, and the perception of the city of Trenton from outside. We wanted to demonstrate that if we brought class acts to this town, people would frequent them."
>
> —MERCER COUNTY EXECUTIVE ROBERT D. PRUNETTI, AUGUST, 19, 1994

Late August 1994. There is only one game in Trenton, New Jersey, one place where people congregate night after night to watch minor-league baseball. Each time the Trenton Thunder (then the Double-A affiliate of the Detroit Tigers) takes the field, overflow crowds of more than 7000 fill Mercer County Waterfront Park, a $17.3 million facility that officially seats only 6400. Fans who don't have assigned seats, which cost between $5 and $7 depending on their location, pay $3 to stand along the main concourse above the grandstand. The Thunder franchise is an infusion of life and excitement for Trenton, which is a metropolitan hybrid blending cultural influences from New York to the north and Philadelphia to the south. Suddenly, with the Thunder in town, Trenton is more than just an Amtrak stop on the Northeast Corridor rail line. Inside the first-year municipal playground, which was hastily completed during late April 1994 following one of the Delaware Valley's most inclement winters of the 20th century, patrons enjoy the full pageantry that has made minor-league baseball one of America's fastest-growing family entertainment options of the 1990s.

Throughout Waterfront Park's gently curving concrete-and-brick layout, among its forest-green folding seats, Thunder fans visit with acquaintances they haven't seen for years, and new friendships develop out of the bonds formed by the game of baseball. They purchase a variety of reasonably priced ballpark favorites like soft pretzels, french fries, pizza, and hamburgers from state-of-the-art concession stands, which weren't fully operational until 3 months after the Thunder began playing in the new stadium. The concessions also offer a unique Trenton delicacy—the pork roll sandwich—which is made from thin-sliced pork processed by a local business since the early 1900s. Pork roll is to Trenton what cheesesteak is to Philadelphia. In right field, thick smoke from the outdoor grill lingers over the matted natural grass playing surface like early morning fog. All present breathe in the crisp, late summer air as an orange sunset descends beyond the western horizon, framing a glorious backdrop for the national pastime. The Delaware River meanders south just several yards beyond the right-field fence, offering a spectacular view for fans and an inviting target for home-run hitters. Occasionally, foul balls sail over the stadium's right-field concourse, only to find a home in the muck.

Quite simply, the 1994 season revitalized the New Jersey capital area, harnessing an excitement and a spirit of community athletic pride not experienced by local residents since 1950, when the Trenton Giants and their star outfielder, a 19-year-old phenom named Willie Mays, played their final season at rickety, 3500-seat Dunn Field. Since that unforgettable season, Trenton's population decreased from 128,009 to 88,675 (the 1990 census figure) as a suburban exodus gradually changed the socioeconomic make-up of the area. Minor-league baseball brought many of those suburbanites back to the city, even if only for one evening's entertainment.

"It's been a tremendous boon for the community," said Waterfront Park architect John Clarke. "There's nothing else that brings hundreds of thousands of people, most of whom are coming from the suburbs, back into town."

Also in late August 1994, Major-League Baseball is on strike, having walked out at midnight on August 12. The shutdown marks yet another work stoppage in a continuing litany of labor tension over the last two decades. Big-league fans everywhere are fed up with the game and its millionaire stars, and many supporters pledge never to return to big-league parks when the matter is finally resolved. Philadelphia's Veterans Stadium and the Bronx's Yankee Stadium are dark. There are no pennant races to follow, although the Yankees were well on their way to capturing the American League East when labor strife halted their pursuit. For those in need of a baseball fix, there is only Trenton and other minor-league venues like Skylands Park in the North Jersey community of Augusta, where the Single-A, short-season New Jersey Cardinals (a St. Louis affiliate) play before sold-out crowds in a brand-new, 4340-seat stadium. While the Cardinals are en route to the Single-A, short-season New York–Penn League championship during their inaugural season, the Thunder, battling nightly to stay out of the Eastern League's Southern Division cellar, bask in the spotlight of baseball's diverted attention. Each Saturday night, New Jersey Network television crews broadcast the team's home games. Some of the highlights appear on national sports network ESPN as stations search desperately to fill the void created by the major-league strike. All 142 Thunder games are heard on Trenton AM radio station WTTM as the broadcasting team of Tom McCarthy and Nick Simonetta call the action.

None of the huge crowds seem too concerned with the Thunder's final 55-85 record (a dismal .393 winning percentage), worst in the 10-team Eastern League. They come to see the team's big blue furry mascot, Boomer, as he parades around the stadium in his yellow-beaked bird uniform, water gun in hand. They laugh as he races little children around the bases, finding innovative ways to lose each time. They listen intently to computerized sound effects, which run a wide gamut from a chainsaw (for strikeouts) to a breaking window (for foul balls) to a splash of water (for balls hit toward the Delaware). The sounds are complemented by a $200,000, kelly green scoreboard in right-center field that is topped by an arching "Trenton Thunder" sign. Waterfront Park's visual showpiece and the personal coup of team general manager Wayne Hodes, who custom-ordered it from DAK Electronics, the scoreboard supplies graphics for every aspect of the game, from a player's statistics to a video-simulated version of children's television hero Barney being struck in the head by a foul ball. "I love you. You love me. . . ." The purple dinosaur falls backward as youngsters all over the park cheer robustly. Few people know that the scoreboard was temporarily delayed in South Dakota during March 1994, when a trucker's strike halted its journey east. Like everything else about the stadium, it has a story, a hidden saga. In its shadow, children flock to the railing beside the home dugout to beg the players for their autographs. They linger, baseball cards in hand, until all the young men in uniform disappear up the tunnel.

Above the stadium's main seating area is an upper level of luxury that includes 16 corporate suites and an 88-seat restaurant behind home plate. Viewed from one of the suites, Waterfront Park is a minor league marvel with all-inclusive creature comforts, a big-league ambience scaled down to Double-A dimensions. Within weeks of their offering, the luxury boxes were sold out. Leased at a cost of $15,000 each for the season, they provide a different perspective from which to view the franchise's immense popularity.

By August 1996, nothing had changed except for the status of major-league baseball, which canceled the '94 World Series only to return to work in the spring of '95 without a labor agreement. That matters little to New Jersey minor-league fans. Overflow crowds of more than 7000 continue to jam Waterfront Park to watch the Thunder, now affiliated with the Boston Red Sox, run away with the EL Southern Division pennant, Trenton's first unshared minor-league championship since 1947. Over the first three Thunder seasons, more than 1.2 million patrons passed through the Waterfront turnstiles. In the process, the Thunder became the first EL franchise to surpass 435,000 fans 2 years in a row (454,225 in '95 and 437,446 in '96) . During the 71 home games of the '96 season, the Thunder compile a league-best 49-22 record (86-56 overall). The novelty of on-field promotions has been bolstered by a winning product. Along the way, stadium regulars have learned a great deal about the game of baseball. They've watched 20-year-old Thunder pitching sensation Carl Pavano throw a 94-mph fastball. They've marveled as Trenton sluggers Adam Hyzdu, Tyrone Woods, and Todd Carey smashed baseballs over the outfield fence. They've been entertained by players with charismatic nicknames like "Pork Chop," "Doobie," "Whiskey," "Soup," "Stumpy," and "Rosie." They've witnessed the major-league ascents of opposing players like the New York Yankees' Derek Jeter, the Florida Marlins' Charles Johnson and Edgar Renteria, the

New York Mets' Paul Wilson and Alex Ochoa, the Philadelphia Phillies' Scott Rolen and Ricky Bottalico, and the Baltimore Orioles' Rocky Coppinger and Armando Benitez. Somehow, they've felt like a part of their development. In all, they've seen 14 players appear in a Thunder uniform and subsequently make their major-league debut. Furthermore, seven of the franchise's players were promoted directly from Trenton to Boston during the '95-'96 seasons. Others will follow in the years to come.

During Waterfront's first three seasons, there have been marriage proposals, career-threatening injuries, and dying wishes that could be fulfilled only by an evening at the ballpark. There have been business deals, heart-to-heart father-son conversations, and first dates. On July 8, 1996, a stadium-record crowd of 8369 joined an ESPN2 national television audience to celebrate the sixth-annual Double-A All-Star Game. On that glorious evening, which showcased everything that the Thunder franchise had worked so diligently to build, Pavano was the starting pitcher and Carey the third baseman. In addition, Thunder manager Ken Macha was the skipper for the American League affiliates and catcher Walt McKeel a back-up.

Also in late August 1996, Trenton has signed on for 2 more years as a Boston affiliate. The Thunder are in town to stay, because minor-league baseball in the 1990s has become more than just a training ground for pampered big-league athletes. It is entertainment. It is marketing. It is an opportunity to catch a foul ball within shouting distance of the player who hit it. It is a chance to be part of the action. Perhaps nowhere was that joyous truth more evident than Waterfront Park.

"In a way, it's like a microbrewery," Clarke said of Waterfront's universal appeal to patrons young and old. "You can have Miller and Budweiser, and they are like Veterans Stadium and Yankee Stadium, but there is also the issue of a smaller place that has an identity in people's lives. One doesn't necessarily exclude the other, but what this shows is that cities like Trenton can make good things happen."

In a very real sense, minor-league baseball in the mid-1990s is a microcosm of life. Nowhere is that more evident than the Double-A level, considered by most baseball officials to be "the proving ground for future major leaguers." Prospects arrive in Trenton knowing that their careers hang in the balance. Some thrive and move on. Others quickly realize that they have reached the end of the line. Dreams die hard. Lives are shattered. It is Social Darwinism scaled down to a 23-man baseball roster. Change is inevitable. Faces come and go like the tidal waters of the Delaware. Nobody ever said the process was fair.

The tales and experiences that come out of any minor-league baseball season are unforgettable, however. They include unforeseen relationships. They grow from idle time spent together in a dugout or a crowded bus. They showcase personalities and superstitions. Inevitably, they underscore the reality that baseball is a game of repetition, routine—and failure. As Thunder outfielder Trot Nixon once said, "In baseball, a .300 batting average is considered good, but that still means you're out seven out of 10 times you go up to the plate. That's a hard thing to accept."

The Thunder franchise infiltrated every fabric of the Delaware Valley by August 1996. Schoolchildren flock to the park on field trips. Businessmen play hooky to enjoy the team's occasional afternoon games. The novelty of minor league-baseball in the New Jersey capital has given way to tradition, a tradition molded by the people and events that have brought Waterfront Park to life. It is a tradition that must be preserved for future parents to enjoy with their sons and daughters on a warm summer evening. This is the story of the '94-'96 Trenton Thunder, their travels, trials, and triumphs.

CHAPTER 1

The Days Before
the Thunder

> "'Say Hey' Willie Mays is the dominant figure in Trenton baseball. He was in the majors the year after he played here in 1950, with only a brief, blazing stop at Triple-A Minneapolis. He played with the New York and San Francisco Giants and New York Mets from 1951 through 1973, 22 seasons. He hit over .300 ten times, finished third in career home runs (with 660), and was a Gold Glove center fielder from 1957 through 1968. He was elected to the Hall of Fame in 1979."
>
> —COLLEGE OF NEW JERSEY JOURNALISM PROFESSOR ROBERT COLE

Trenton's first official "minor-league" team began play in the Interstate Association in 1883, less than 20 years after the Civil War. According to sports historians, the first organized game of baseball took place in 1846 at the Elysian Fields in Hoboken, New Jersey. It didn't take long for the sport to filter south to Trenton, which was home to more than 40 iron businesses by the 1890s. In 1859, John A. Roebling moved his wire-rope factory to Trenton. Before his death in 1869, he planned the Brooklyn Bridge, which was built with Roebling cable. The Roebling Company employed a large number of Italian and Slavic immigrants, many of whom learned baseball in Trenton.

During the years immediately following the Civil War, many amateur teams appeared in the city, eager for competition. Industrial leagues throughout the area became a breeding ground for the game, as did independent, barnstorming teams. In fact, baseball became so popular during these years that even disabled veterans formed their own league. By the time baseball players began earning money for their play during the late 19th century, Trenton was at the forefront of that professional movement.

In 1884, after moving to a new league, the Eastern League (an early predecessor of the Thunder's current 10-team league), Trenton won the pennant almost by default. The other three teams left the circuit, leaving the capital city club—known simply as "The Trentons"—to survive and be crowned the champion. The team's influential owner, Patrick Thomas Powers, grew up in Trenton's postwar amateur leagues and went on to manage the major-league New York Giants in 1892. Twenty-three years later, he became co-owner of the only major-league team in New Jersey history, the Newark Peps of the 1915 Federal League. During the interim, Powers was named president of minor-league baseball's governing body, the National Association of Baseball teams. In that role, he was forced to regulate tension between the majors and the minors, but by the time he resigned his presidency in 1909, the minors had more than doubled in size to 52 leagues.

The 1884 Eastern League championship team moved to Jersey City in 1885, and Trenton was forced to wait until 1889 for another minor-league entry. That club, the all-black Trenton Cuban Giants (a generic name to conceal that they were black), finished second in the 13-team Middle States League behind pitchers William Whyte (26-5) and William Selden (23-6) and top hitter Frank Gant (.313). Opportunities for black players disappeared following that glorious 1889 season, however, as a result of racial attitudes of the time. In 1897, Trenton fielded an entry in the New Jersey State League, but this ill-fated league disbanded after one season. The city would have to wait until 1907 for another minor-league team to call its own.

During the second half of the 19th century, businessmen had discovered that good money could be made by charging admission to the games. Naturally, competition for the best players quickly became part of that equation. In 1883, a document called the National Agreement had been created to both govern minor-league ball and to protect team owners. By the turn of the century, that agreement was coming apart. The American League, a new major-league circuit, was not bound by the National Agreement; as a result, it could lure players away from the minor leagues. Facing the American League threat, the older National League renounced the agreement, too.

On September 5 and 6, 1901, at Chicago's Leland Hotel, minor-league baseball representatives formed the National Association of Professional Baseball Leagues (NAPBL). Today, almost a century later, the NAPBL is headquartered in St. Petersburg, Florida, and remains the governing body of minor-league baseball, overseeing leagues at all levels, from the short-season rookie classification to Triple-A. Under Powers' direction, the NAPBL set up league classifications (which didn't change until 1963), roster and salary limits, and a system for drafting players. Between 1902 and 1905, the number of minor leagues grew from 15 to 34.

Under the 1901 classification system, A was the highest level, followed by B, C, and D. In the classification restructuring of 1963, all class B leagues were moved to class A. This is significant because most of Trenton's minor-league entries between 1907 and 1950, when the Trenton Giants played their final season at Dunn Field, competed in class B leagues. From 1907 through 1914, Trenton was a member of the Class B Tri-State League, and from 1940 through 1950, the capital city fielded a team in the Class B Interstate League.

In 1907, the Tri-State League began play with eight teams—including the Trenton Tigers—under President Charles F. Carpenter. Williamsport, Pennsylvania, ran away with the pennant (86-38), finishing eight games ahead of Harrisburg (79-47). The Trenton Tigers compiled a 70-54 record, which was good for fourth place, 16 games behind Williamsport. The following year, Trenton finished a dismal 28 games behind the first-place team, at 54-73, or sixth place in the Tri-State League, which once again was won by Williamsport (82-45). The situation worsened for the Tigers in 1909 as they limped to a seventh-place, 43-

71 season, 32 games behind Lancaster (75-39). In 1910, Trenton improved to
58-52 but could get no closer than 14 games behind league-champion Altoona
(72-38). That winning ledger was a sign of things to come, however, as the 1911
Tigers not only finished second, nine games behind Reading (74-37) with a 65-
46 mark, but also boasted the league batting champion, John Davis, who hit
.363 as Trenton fell short of the pennant by nine games.

The 1912 Trenton Tigers showcased Charlie Johnson, who led the league
with a .403 average and 161 hits as his team finished third behind Harrisburg
(75-37) with a 61-51 mark. Johnson's batting record remains unequaled in
Trenton minor-league history, even by legendary players Maurice "Mo" Cunningham and Mays. (Consider that 1995 Thunder first baseman Ryan McGuire
led the club with a .333 average, second in the league.) At the time Johnson exceeded the magical .400 barrier, however, his career was on the way down, having reached its zenith with the 1908 Philadelphia Phillies. He would never
make it back to the majors. The Tigers' 1913 season ended with a 50-61, fifth-
place finish in a Tri-State League that had been pared down to six clubs. In
1914, Pop Foster led the circuit with a .388 batting average, but the Tigers finished 22 games behind pennant-winner Harrisburg with a 44-66 ledger. Following the 1914 season, conflict between the NAPBL-outlawed Federal League
(which encouraged minor-league players to jump their contracts) and the
major leagues as well as US participation in World War I spelled the end of
minor-league baseball in Trenton until 1936, with the Great Depression and
the advent of motion pictures and automobiles pushing baseball further into
the recesses of national consciousness.

THE FIRST REVIVAL

Finally, during the 1936 Class A New York–Penn League season, York, Pennsylvania, owner and laundry tycoon Joe Cambria returned minor-league baseball
to Trenton for the first time since World War I. Lured by the promise from one
of the players, Trenton native and outfielder George Case, Jr., of a modern ballpark, Cambria packed up the York stadium's light fixtures and headed east with
his team, the White Roses. George's brother, W. Clifford ("Cliff") Case, prepared Trenton for the new team, which would be called the Senators due to its
affiliation with Washington's major-league club. Dunn Field, which was located on Brunswick Circle at US Route 1 on a site that now houses the New Jersey Lottery Building, was owned by the Catholic Diocese of Trenton and originally used as Trenton Cathedral High School's athletic field. It had a wooden
grandstand that seated 3500 but rarely was filled to capacity. Its dimensions
were 350 feet down the foul lines and 385 to straightaway center, making it a
challenging park for most hitters. "It was very deep, and it certainly wasn't a hitter's paradise," recalled 1950 Trenton Giants catcher Len Matte. Cambria spent
$5000 upgrading the facility, but there were no dugouts (players sat on benches
along each side) and no lights until they arrived from York several weeks after
the team relocated (the Senators played all day games until that time). Once in
their new home, the 1936 Senators finished with a woeful, last-place, 40-99

record, 41 games behind Binghamton, New York. Nonetheless, one of the more colorful players on manager Charles ("Bud") Shaney's roster was a former prisoner named Alabama Pitts, whom Cambria signed out of New York's Sing Sing Prison in 1935.

In 1937, despite pitcher Joe Krakauskas' league-best 184 strikeouts, the Senators tied Albany for the worst record on the circuit at 54-80, behind pennant-winner Elmira, New York, by 29 1/2 games. Nonetheless, George Case was destined for major-league stardom. At the end of the 1937 New York–Penn campaign, he was promoted to Washington. He played 11 seasons in the majors and hit .290 or better during seven of them. He also led the majors in stolen bases a record five straight seasons from 1939 to 1943. In 1943, he recorded 61 thefts. Case remains one of just two Trenton natives to play minor-league ball both in the New Jersey capital and the majors. The other was third baseman Edgar Leip, who was called up during the 1939 season but did not have the same impact as Case on the majors. During the inaugural 1994 Trenton Thunder season, Case was one of the original two inductees into the Trenton Baseball Hall of Fame, joining '47-'50 Trenton Giants radio broadcaster, Trenton sports journalist, and National Baseball Hall of Fame member Harold "Bus" Saidt, who passed away in 1989. Ironically, George Case died in Lower Makefield, Pennsylvania, also in 1989.

Accepting Case's Trenton Hall of Fame plaque at Waterfront Park was his son, George Case III, who said, "My dad claimed that although he loved Trenton, he thought Dunn Field was the worst field he played on in his life." As an example, during the late 1930s, an Albany outfielder named Como Cotelle became a minor-league conversation piece when he carried a lantern to center field. Hoping to aid his pursuit of the ball in Dunn's shadowy reaches, he was instead ejected from the game by one of the umpires.

Continuing to play under Dunn Field's dingy lighting, the Senators compiled a 62-77 record in 1938, finishing in seventh place of the Class A Eastern League, 24 games behind Binghamton. Both the '37 and '38 clubs were managed by Spencer Abbott, who compiled the second-longest managing career in minor-league history—34 seasons. Following the 1938 season, however, Cambria moved his team to Springfield, Massachusetts, paving the way for Trenton's move to the Class B Interstate League 1 year later. During the first three Thunder seasons of the mid-1990s, replica Trenton Senators wool hats became a popular item in the Waterfront Park Dugout Store. The blue hats with a red "T" were manufactured by Ebbets Field Flannels and sold for $27.

Before the 1939 season, the Interstate League was organized at the urging of Trenton semipro manager Frank Spair. After the league received NAPBL approval, it was administered by President Harold Hoffman, who served as governor of New Jersey from 1935 to 1938. The '39-'41 Trenton Senators (the city kept the name of Cambria's teams) were led by Goose Goslin, a player-manager who had spent 18 major-league seasons as an outfielder with the Washington Senators, the St. Louis Browns, and the Detroit Tigers. Like Mays and Saidt, Goslin is enshrined in the Hall of Fame in Cooperstown, New York. Born in the South Jersey community of Salem, Goslin continued to play during his Trenton days only because he loved the game so much. Well-liked by his players both for his major-league accomplishments and his scrappy nature, he was the first manager in Interstate League history to be thrown out of a game for fighting. His 1939 team compiled a 51-51 record, three games behind first-place Allentown. Pitcher Russ Bailey led the four-team circuit with a 3.11 ERA. In 1940, the Interstate League doubled in size to eight teams, and Goslin led the Senators to a second-place finish (68-52), four games behind Reading (which today remains an Eastern League rival of the Thunder). Trenton's 35-year-old George ("Three-Star") Hennessey led the league with 18 victories, but the Senators fell to Reading, three games to none, in a best-of-five semifinal playoff series.

Meanwhile, New Jersey's other minor-league entries—Newark and Jersey City of the Class AA International League—were attracting phenomenal crowds just up the road from Trenton. On May 22, 1938, 23,610 showed up in Newark to watch the Bears play, and on April 20, 1939, the largest crowd in minor-league annals to that time, 45,112, packed Roosevelt Stadium to watch Jersey City lose a home game to Buffalo (3-2). Crowds at Dunn Field weren't nearly as sensational, but Goslin's 1941 club finished the regular season 11 games over .500, at 68-57. In the playoff semifinals, the Senators swept Hagerstown, Maryland, three games to none. In the best-of-seven championship series, however, Trenton fell agonizingly short, losing four games to three to Harrisburg.

In 1942, Cliff Case purchased the team and renamed it the Packers, after his meat-packing business. (A billboard advertising Taylor Pork Roll was one of the first placed on the outfield wall at Waterfront Park during the 1994 season, and pork roll sandwiches are sold at the ballpark for $4.50.) The '42 Packers struggled to last place with a 56-82 record, although pitcher Jack Casey had the dubious distinction of no-hitting Hagerstown only to lose the game (3-2), on walks and errors. In 1943, with the Philadelphia Phillies providing the talent and financial support, the Packers (64-73) finished fifth in the six-team league, 18 1/2 games behind Lancaster. The star of that club was outfielder Del Ennis, who hit .346, with 37 doubles, 16 triples, 18 homers, and 93 RBIs. Following a 2-year stint in the Navy, Ennis played 14 years with the Phillies.

As World War II continued and gasoline rationing limited minor-league travel, the Interstate League forged ahead with Trenton as one of its hubs. The league would be one of only nine to operate continuously through the war. In 1944, future Brooklyn and Los Angeles Dodgers manager Walter Alston became the Packers' player-manager. Undoubtedly the most famous skipper in Trenton's minor-league history in terms of his subsequent accomplishments, Alston went on to lead the Dodgers to seven pennants and their first four World Series championships. He, too, is permanently enshrined in the Baseball Hall of Fame. During the '44 Packers season, he hit .350, with several homers, but at 32 years old, he would never make it back to the majors as a player. His only big-league plate appearance was a strikeout—back in 1936. Alston's 1944 club was led by pitcher Harold Kelleher, first in the league with a 2.53 ERA. The Packers finished in last place that year, however, with a 63-75 mark. His 1945 team, renamed the Spartans and affiliated with the Brooklyn Dodgers, climbed to third place—one game over .500, at 70-69—but fell to Lancaster, four games to three, in the playoffs. Trenton's Maurice Santomauro paced the circuit with

117 RBIs, while pitcher Lester Studener had a league-high 191 strikeouts. Kelleher had the best ERA for the second consecutive year at 2.58.

THE GIANTS OF DUNN FIELD

In 1946, the New York Giants purchased the Trenton team. That postwar season included Jackie Robinson's historic shattering of organized baseball's color barrier on April 18, 1946, during an International League game between Montreal and Jersey City. In Interstate League competition, the Trenton Giants struggled to a seventh-place, 60-78 record, 24 games behind first-place Wilmington. Then, in 1947, the parent New York club suddenly began to assemble a minor-league powerhouse in Trenton under the direction of Hall of Fame manager Bill McKechnie, who also became the team's principal stockholder.

At the end of May 1947, the Giants were mired in last place, nine games behind Harrisburg. By mid-July, they had improved to sixth place in the eight-team league. What followed over the season's final 2 months was the most torrid stretch of success in Trenton's minor-league history. The Giants won 52 of their last 62 games, sprinting down the stretch to capture Trenton's first minor-league pennant of the 20th century and completing the season with an 88-50 record, 9 1/2 games ahead of Wilmington. Led by pitcher Andy Tomasic's career-topping year (18 wins, 278 strikeouts, 2.48 ERA—all league bests) and Hal Bamberger's .333 average, manager Tommy Heath's Giants attracted 99,115 patrons to dilapidated Dunn Field, including a record 7126 for the last game. During that historic summer, fans ringed the outfield fence. Bamberger led all minor leaguers with 24 triples, but the Giants were eliminated in the first round of the playoffs, four games to two, by third-place Allentown.

Heath's success with the Giants continued in 1948. Behind Mo Cunningham, who set a team record with 25 homers, Trenton tied Wilmington for the pennant with an 82-56 record and rolled to the capital city's first playoff championship by edging Sunbury four games to three in the first round and sweeping York four games to none in the final. Attendance for the historic season totaled 97,389, an average of almost 2000 per game. Also in 1948, the Trenton Schroths won the city's only American Legion World Series crown as future major-league pitcher Al Downing led the team to national prominence.

From 1947 through 1950, when the Giants left Trenton for Salisbury, Maryland, and Dunn Field was razed, all of the team's action was chronicled on WBUD-AM by Bus Saidt, who spent long evenings poring over the games with the team's managers and coaches. Opened in January 1947, WBUD provided a valuable link to Trenton fans and was the predecessor of WTTM's Trenton Thunder broadcasts of the mid-1990s with personalities Tom McCarthy, Nick Simonetta, and Andy Freed.

In 1949, Saidt watched Cunningham lead the Interstate League with 101 RBIs as manager Hugh Palond's Trenton club rallied from a fourth-place regular season (73-66) to defeat Wilmington and Harrisburg for its second consecutive playoff crown. Attendance had dwindled to 67,604, however, and there were grumblings that old Dunn Field wouldn't be able to support the team much longer. What remained was one unforgettable season that showcased the precocious talents of 19-year-old center fielder Willie Mays, who made his Trenton Giants debut on June 24, 1950, in Hagerstown, Maryland. Ironically, he was picked up at the Trenton train station and driven to the game by Bus Saidt.

In 81 games for Trenton manager Chick Genovese, Mays hit .353 and served notice of his remarkable ability as an outfielder. Signed by the New York Giants from the Birmingham Black Barons of the Negro Leagues, Mays had already honed many of his skills by the time he reached New Jersey. His 1950 Trenton teammates still recall a bare-handed catch that he made to prevent a homer during his 3-month Interstate League stint. On June 25 of that year, during his second minor-league game, he beat out two infield hits, his first two with the Giants. Three days later, during a 21-8 rout of Sunbury, he produced his first organized ball homer—a grand slam. Before he earned the nickname "Say Hey," Willie Mays was called "Junior" by his Trenton teammates. He was popular at Dunn Field and responsible for bringing a new, black clientele to the stadium, although the Giants drew only 48,354 during the 1950 season, a considerable dropoff from the gates of '47 and '48.

According to Trenton Thunder owner Sam Plumeri, Sr., Mays wasn't the only attraction at Dunn Field during the facility's heyday. Plumeri vividly recalls that a black peanut vendor named Spader entertained crowds with his antics. Spader often crouched behind the plate and begged opposing pitchers to throw the ball in as hard as they could. He would then catch the ball bare-handed. "Never saw him flinch," Plumeri insisted. The colorful vendor also tossed change to his customers as he trolled the bleachers. In many ways, he was the direct ancestor of Thunder mascot Boomer, who patrols Waterfront Park half a century later.

Following the 1950 season and Willie Mays' brief stint in the New Jersey capital, the Giants sold the franchise to George Smith, who had run the concessions at Dunn Field during the 1940s. Despite two passed referenda to build a new stadium in Trenton (a dream finally brought to fruition 4 1/2 decades later), Smith took the franchise to Salisbury, Maryland—and the lights at Dunn Field went dark. What ensued was a painful, 44-year hiatus for minor-league baseball in Trenton.

THE CHANGING FACE OF THE MINORS

By 1994, as new stadiums and colorful team logos sprung up across the United States, minor-league baseball had become big business. The first three seasons of Thunder baseball coincided with the most significant increase in the popularity of minor-league baseball since the post–World War II years, when Cunningham and Mays roamed the basepaths at Dunn Field. Between 1993 and 1994—Trenton's first-ever Double-A season—Eastern League attendance increased from 1,699,822 to 2,554,570, an improvement of more than 50 percent. In 1995, the league's appeal and fan-interactive atmosphere helped produce a final attendance figure of 3,057,051 (or 4529 per game), an improvement of 19.7 percent over the previous season's unprecedented total.

With a structure that is the equivalent of a developmental ladder, encompassing six ascending rungs from short-season, Single-A rookie ball to Triple-A, which is one level below the majors, the minor leagues were established as a strict breeding ground for big-league prospects. During the early 1960s, as minor-league attendance continued to plummet from an all-time high of 39,782,717 in 1949 to less than half that figure in 1962, the major-league clubs realized that their farm systems had to be protected or their talent pools would suffer devastating consequences. To that effect, on May 19, 1962, Major-League Baseball instituted the Player Development Plan, which guaranteed that at least 100 minor league clubs would survive. It also abolished the B, C, and D classifications that had been designated in 1901, blanketing them under the classification Single-A. Three Double-A leagues—the Eastern, the South Atlantic, and the Texas—were designated, and two Triple-A leagues—the International and the Pacific Coast—remained intact. Furthermore, it stipulated that of the required 100 teams, at least 20 would belong to Triple-A, 20 to Double-A, and 60 to Single-A. Major-League Baseball also agreed to pay all Triple-A salaries above $800 per month and all but $150 of Double-A salaries. In the process, the minor leagues became the direct property of the major-league affiliates, a bond that remains intact today.

When Detroit moved its Double-A franchise from Labatt Stadium in London, Ontario, to Trenton's Waterfront Park before the 1994 season, the Tigers had six farm teams in their minor-league system. The lowest level was the Bristol (Tennessee) Tigers of the rookie Appalachian League, followed in ascending order by the Single-A, short-season Jamestown (New York) Jammers of the New York–Penn League, the Fayetteville (North Carolina) Jammers of the Single-A South Atlantic League, the Lakeland (Florida) Tigers of the Single-A Florida State League, Trenton, and Toledo of the Triple-A International League. The Detroit farmhands were paid according to their level, with 1994 salaries ranging from a paltry $800 a month at Bristol to approximately $2000 a month at Toledo. The average Thunder salary was in the $1400 to $1600 range, or barely enough to make ends meet in the Delaware Valley economy.

During the '95 and '96 seasons, following the Thunder's September 1994 affiliation switch from Detroit to Boston, the six Red Sox farm teams were located in Fort Myers, Florida (rookie Gulf Coast League); Utica, New York ('95), and Lowell, Massachusetts ('96), of the Single-A New York–Penn League; Battle Creek, Michigan, of the Single-A Midwest League; Sarasota of the Florida State League; Trenton, and Pawtucket of the Triple-A International League. According to '95-'96 Thunder pitcher and Australian native Brett Cederblad, Waterfront Park was "the Mercedes of the Red Sox organization." Salaries in the Boston organization were comparable to the checks received by the Detroit farmhands. The Red Sox players were paid twice a month (the 15th and the 30th), making it imperative that an athlete manage his funds judiciously.

The light at the end of the minor-league tunnel, however, was a bright and alluring one. The major-league *minimum* salary during the 1996 season was

$109,000, which breaks down to approximately $18,000 per month. As a minor leaguer chases his goal, that figure is permanently etched in his mind. For some, it makes the monotony and repetition of life "down on the farm" ultimately worth the sacrifice.

When a Double-A team takes to the road, often for a week to 10 days at a time, players are given $16 a day for meal money. (By comparison, the major league "per diem" was $60.50 during the 1996 season.) Visiting clubhouse dues are a minimum of $2.50 a day, so that must be deducted right off the top. Tipping is optional, but many young prospects are left with thin wallets and hungry stomachs. Frequent stops at inexpensive sandwich shops like Subway are the norm.

How quickly can a player expect to rise through the Single-A levels en route to the Eastern League during the 1990s? For most, the road to Double-A is a rigorous process that requires an average of three to five seasons. If a prospect signs a contract directly out of high school at 17 or 18 years old, he can realistically hope to reach Trenton by the age of 22 or 23 if he excels at the various Single-A stops. Most prospects spend one summer in a rookie league; one summer in a short-season, Single-A league; one summer in a low-level Single-A league; and one summer in an advanced Single-A league. The most talented players often are promoted through the ranks several times within a season. As a result, the funneling process into Double-A is intense, making the competition in the Eastern League some of the best in professional baseball. "This is the make-or-break league, the prospect's league, and we want all of our players to spend one year in Double-A," said Boston Minor-League Coordinator Bob Schaefer.

The core of professional baseball's developmental process is the annual amateur draft, which is conducted each June. Professional scouts spend countless hours researching the talent pools and reporting back to the respective major-league front offices. There is no room for error. A top prospect often is labeled a "five-tool" player, meaning he can: 1) hit for average; 2) hit for power; 3) field his position with excellence; 4) run the bases well, and 5) throw with accuracy and power. Based on the five tools, scouts grade each prospect from 1 (the bottom of the scale) to 8 (exceptional skill).

During the 1990s, first-round selections in the draft have routinely been rewarded with six- or seven-figure signing bonuses. As the rounds descend, players are offered less and less to sign. In addition, most organizations are willing to take a chance on undrafted free agents, particularly raw Hispanic talents from areas like Puerto Rico, the Dominican Republic, and Venezuela.

The first three Trenton Thunder teams showcased several first-round "bonus babies," including '94 first baseman Tony Clark, '94 pitcher Rick Greene, '95 shortstop Nomar Garciaparra, '95-'96 outfielder Trot Nixon, '95 outfielder Greg Blosser, '96 pitcher Reggie Harris, and '96 outfielder Adam Hyzdu. Clark received an $800,000 bonus to sign with Detroit as the No. 2 pick overall in 1990 following a storied scholastic career in El Cajon, California. Greene received $750,000 in 1992 when he was signed out of Louisiana State University. In 1994, the flashy Garciaparra received a then-Boston-record bonus of $895,000 following his junior year at Georgia Tech. In 1993, Nixon signed for

$890,000 out of New Hanover High School in Wilmington, North Carolina, rather than accept a full scholarship to play quarterback at North Carolina State University. At the time, Nixon was labeled "the best high school athlete to come out of North Carolina since Michael Jordan."

While most first-round draft picks are given every opportunity to make it to "The Show," others must fight their way up the ladder. Being a Double-A ballplayer is not the most glamorous lifestyle. The sellout crowds that filled Waterfront Park during the Thunder's first three seasons only served to disguise that reality for the franchise's players. "Most of these people think we're there [in the big leagues]," said Carey. "We're not there yet. We're still working to get there. But I guess if you're going to play Double-A baseball, you want to play here. The atmosphere is just unbelievable. The fan support is amazing."

Added '95-'96 pitcher Shawn Senior, a native of Cherry Hill, New Jersey, whose local ties made him a fan favorite at Waterfront, "A lot of people come to the park at 7 o'clock to see us play in front of 7000 people and it looks great. And it is . . . most of the time. But those people aren't getting an accurate picture of what it's all about. It's that mental thing, day in and day out."

THE DAILY GRIND

As Senior or any of the other 142 players who appeared in a Thunder uniform between 1994 and 1996 would readily admit, minor-league baseball is tediously repetitive. At every level, from rookie ball through Triple-A, the daily activities are carefully regimented. They vary subtly depending on whether a team is at home or on the road, but by and large, the four hours leading up to game time include stretching, bullpen work (for pitchers), batting practice (for hitters), infield practice, and pregame meetings. For a normal 7:05 night game at Waterfront, players begin arriving in the home clubhouse between 2 and 3 PM. Out of necessity, almost all minor leaguers are nocturnal creatures who eat a lot of late-night dinners and sleep until the late-morning hours. The clubhouse invariably is filled with sarcastic chatter about the previous night's game, the major leagues, the girl somebody picked up last night, or the daily fan mail (which is distributed by the front office). Thunder players have received everything from female lingerie to love poems to marriage proposals via the US Postal Service. Some of the packages are quite comical, and many carry a thick essence of perfume.

In the center of the Thunder clubhouse is a "spread" table offering snacks like peanut butter and jelly, fresh fruit, bubble gum, sunflower seeds, and crackers. After donning their practice jerseys, the players take the field for 15 minutes of stretching. The exercises are supervised by the team trainer (the first three Thunder trainers were Lon Pinhey, '94; Chris Correnti, '95; and Terry Smith, '96). Once the players are loose, they splinter into groups. Infielders, catchers and outfielders head to the batting cage in groups of four or five; the pitchers make their way to the home bullpen along with the pitching coach. Starters throw a "side day" either 2 or 3 days before their next scheduled appearance. Side days usually consist of 40 to 50 deliveries. In the background, relievers run conditioning laps around the warning track, which is approximately 200 yards from the right-field foul pole to the left-field pole. Accordingly, these sprints are known as "poles." One of the most amusing sights of the first three Thunder seasons was watching '95-'96 pitcher Jared Fernandez run poles. The 6-foot-2, 230-pound Fernandez was nicknamed "Twinkletoes" for his unique running style. "I'm cat-quick when I need to be," Fernandez said.

Meanwhile, the batting practice pitcher usually is the manager or one of the assistant coaches. He throws from behind a protective screen. During the first three Thunder seasons, managers Tom Runnells and Ken Macha made thousands of deliveries. They were complemented by '94 coaches Kevin Bradshaw, Rich Bombard, and Dan Raley; '95 coaches Al Nipper, Rick Peterson, and Rico Petrocelli (the well-known Boston Red Sox shortstop of the 1960s and early 1970s); and '96 coach Gomer Hodge. "Taking BP from Nip is like going to the drive-thru at McDonald's," said '95-'96 infielder Lou Merloni. "A fastball, a change-up, and a slider on the outside corner—to go."

During a normal batting practice, each group spends 15 to 20 minutes in the cage on a rotating basis. Youngsters gather around the outfield fence to chase souvenirs as they clear the wall. On the field, there are clearly defined roles that must be observed. The next day's starting pitcher shags balls behind a second-base screen. Giant bucket in hand, he returns the balls to a basket on the pitcher's mound. Simultaneously, a pair of relief pitchers hit groundballs to the infielders from either side of the batting cage. At times, all of the divergent activity resembles a pinball machine during a multiball bonus. For that reason, caution and awareness are a necessary part of any batting practice.

After both teams complete batting practice, the batting cage is dragged by tractor to a concealed corner of the stadium, and the home team conducts a brief, 10-minute infield practice. The manager hits groundballs to the perimeter players and concludes with a few towering pop-ups to the catchers. Throughout the pregame preparation, one face is conspicuously absent—that evening's starting pitcher. He is the only player granted a 1-day exemption from the routine. He is free to follow his own personal preparation and arrive at the ballpark as late as 1 hour before the first pitch. Once at the stadium, he usually sits in front of his locker for a while, pondering his approach. The clubhouse is closed to the media 45 minutes before game time. Some players head to the field early to sign autographs along the railing adjacent to the dugout, and children line the rails for a few seconds of contact. The starting pitcher limbers up in the outfield before beginning his warm-up pitches in the bullpen. The managers exchange line-up cards with the umpires 10 minutes before the first pitch. That exchange is followed by the National Anthem and the home-plate umpire's command to "Play ball!"

CHAPTER 2

Waterfront Park Takes Shape

"Our goal was to make Waterfront Park more of a traditional structure than some of the other minor-league parks. I think the architecture helps to keep the intimacy. In many ways, Waterfront was the right facility in the right place at the right time."

—WATERFRONT PARK ARCHITECT JOHN CLARKE

At 12:30 PM on September 29, 1993, during a ceremony that included Bob Prunetti and New Jersey Gov. James Florio, ground was broken on the cozy, 13-acre tract that became Waterfront Park and its adjacent parking lot. The groundbreaking was an odd political configuration as Florio, a Democrat, and Prunetti, a Republican, dug their respective shovels into the ground. On the other hand, it represented the first physical step in the creation of Trenton's state-of-the-art municipal melting pot. During the summer of 1993, Florio had promised Prunetti and Mercer County $4 million in grant money from the New Jersey Economic Development Authority. The grant represented a significant portion of the stadium's originally projected $11.4 million cost. The balance would come from a multimillion-dollar municipal bond issue.

In early October, when site work and steel framing began under the direction of Lawrenceville, New Jersey, contractor Scozzari, Inc., the stadium plot was little more than an undeveloped field of dirt and overgrown weeds bordered by US Route 29 and Cass Street to the east, the Delaware River to the west, and the Riverview Executive Plaza to the north. A pile of rotting wood had been pushed to one corner, where right field eventually would be located. Remnants of an old steel mill foundation lay buried beneath layers of mud. Contractors would excavate countless truckloads of debris from the site by the time the stadium was completed 7 months later. For decades, local youngsters had referred to the unoccupied playground as "The Gully." The mill was long gone, and generations of Trenton schoolchildren had used the open space for pick-up games. It also provided an opportunity to fish from the steep riverbank. One of those youngsters was 1971 Trenton High graduate Brandon Hardison, who became the Thunder's public address announcer in 1994.

Before each Waterfront Park game, Hardison imparted a bit of his childhood to the crowd. His trademark welcome became, "Welcome to beautiful and always versatile Mercer County Waterfront Park, along the banks of the historic Delaware River, where tonight the capital city's motto, 'Trenton Makes, The World Takes,' unfolds another chapter in its illustrious sports history." The ad-libbed introduction was borrowed from a nearby bridge that shuttles traffic over the river to Morrisville, Pennsylvania. The phrase "Trenton Makes, The World Takes" originally was coined in 1910 as the winning slogan in a contest "to capture the pride of this industrial city." It later was attached to the south side of the bridge in bright red neon lettering. As a result, locals refer to the bridge as "The Trenton Makes."

"I remember playing in the dirt field that used to be here [on the stadium site]," Hardison recalled. "And we could see the Trenton Makes bridge off in the distance. Back then, Trenton was a factory town, and we watched all these people come to Trenton from all these faraway places that we wanted to get to." In a very real sense, that desire was mirrored by the optimistic young baseball prospects who passed through Waterfront Park during the mid-1990s.

When Prunetti took office as Mercer County Executive in January 1992 following his November 1991 election, he quickly targeted the southern Trenton site as the most attractive location to build a minor-league stadium, selecting it over an abandoned freightyard on northern Trenton's Olden Avenue and another site near the Mercer County Airport in Ewing. In 1987, the riverfront tract had been purchased from the USX Corporation by Trenton developer Michael LaMelza for $940,000. Between 1987 and the September 29, 1994, stadium groundbreaking, LaMelza had torn down several decaying buildings and performed an environmental clean-up of the plot. He claimed the site had a real estate value "in excess of $5 million."

From the moment he took office, Prunetti knew that Trenton desperately needed a new economic/entertainment venue. During the late 1960s and early 1970s, the 7.65-square-mile New Jersey capital had been altered drastically by socioeconomic changes that precipitated urban flight on a massive scale. Rather than remain in a city whose neighborhoods were being torn apart by violent conflict and changing attitudes that reflected the larger urban problems of the time, many native Trentonians moved to the suburbs of Hamilton, Lawrence, Princeton, West Windsor, and Bucks County, Pennsylvania, located directly across the Delaware River.

A 1989 survey of Mercer County per-capita incomes revealed that Trentonians made $11,018, which was significantly lower than per-capita incomes in the surrounding townships of West Windsor ($30,761), Hamilton ($17,635), Ewing ($18,102), and Lawrence ($23,605). Furthermore, 15,348 of Trenton's 88,675 residents (17.3 percent) lived below the national poverty line. As a result, Trenton's minor-league baseball market would be geared toward the outlying municipalities. Most Trentonians simply didn't possess enough disposable income to spend $15 a night at a baseball game. However, Prunetti and prospective Thunder owners Joe Caruso, a South Jersey investment banker, and Sam Plumeri, Sr., a former Trenton City Commissioner and local businessman, felt that many of the 325,824 Mercer County residents counted in the 1990 census would be grateful for a new form of entertainment. After all, baseball's roots ran deep in Trenton's history.

The quest to acquire a minor-league team also was a race against time. The Trenton contingent faced competition from Atlantic City, its southern New Jersey neighbor. Atlantic City Mayor James Whalen was anxious to build a stadium as well, and Prunetti knew it. When the Atlantic City council hesitated to move forward with stadium plans, Prunetti and Mercer County moved to the forefront.

As word began to spread that Trenton might become the home of a multi-million-dollar minor-league baseball stadium, the first (and most immediate) concerns quite naturally became, "Who would attend the games, and would they be safe parking their cars at night in one of the city's oldest and most run-down neighborhoods?" Those questions represented the biggest challenge the new franchise eventually had to face. How would they coax suburbanites back to the city? Trenton's 1990 crime index of 81.5 (per 1000 population) was more than twice that of West Windsor (30.3) and Hamilton (27.9), and it was considerably higher than Ewing (50.7) and Lawrence (71.0).

LAYING THE GROUNDWORK

Aside from selecting the most optimum site, one of the first design priorities for Prunetti and the county was to make the new ballpark aesthetically pleasing while including modern amenities like corporate luxury boxes and spacious clubhouses for the players. During the Waterfront planning stages, the county executive consulted with Maryland entrepreneur Peter Kirk, chairman of the Maryland Limited Baseball Partnership and co-owner of the Single-A Frederick and Double-A Hagerstown franchises (and later co-owner of Double-A Bowie). From the moment he heard of Prunetti's effort to build a ballpark and lure a team to southern Trenton, Kirk insisted that the location, with the river providing a scenic backdrop, "would be one of the most stunning in all of minor-league baseball."

In September 1992, when his name first surfaced as a prospective minor-league owner, Joe Caruso explained his interest in bringing minor-league baseball to Trenton as more than a wise investment. "It is good family entertainment," he said. "Seats are so much cheaper than at major league games. I love the Yankees and I love going to Yankee Stadium, but man, it's a hassle. In a minor-league park, you're much closer to the field. You can see the expression on a batter's face when he swings, and you can smell the grass."

Throughout the summer of 1993, debate raged about the financial prudence of such a huge project. "It's destined to become a white elephant," argued some. "It's been so long since Trenton's had minor league baseball; it'll never catch on," insisted others.

On April 14, 1993, Mercer County officials estimated the cost of the proposed 6300-seat stadium at $7 million, not including the cost of the land. By June 7, a joint project estimate by two Trenton-based architectural firms—Clarke and Caton, and Fariday, Thorne, Fraytak—raised that figure to $9,047,000, again not including the land. The architects were asked by Prunetti, Caruso, Plumeri, and fellow partner/legal counsel James F. Maloney to design a "third-generation stadium," which would be closely patterned on the vastly popular Single-A Carolina League facilities completed in Frederick, Maryland, in 1991 and Wilmington, Delaware in 1993. During the '93 season, 300,968 fans passed through the turnstiles of Frederick's 5400-seat Harry Grove Stadium (an average of 4777 per game), and 358,766 showed up at Wilmington's 5911-seat Frawley Stadium (an average of 5200 per game). With blueprints of both facilities in hand, the Trenton officials wanted a larger version with "wider, more open" concourses to accommodate standing-room-only patrons and allow unimpeded access to concession/souvenir stands and public restrooms. Once Waterfront was completed, the result was a massive demand for $3 general admission tickets that allowed fans to stand along the concourse railing with an unobstructed view of the action. The $3 tickets also produced crowd figures that routinely exceeded the stadium's official 6300-seat capacity.

Within a frenzied span of 6 months, the project architects completed the stadium plans. As a youngster, Clarke had attended Dodger games at Brooklyn's Ebbets Field. He wanted Waterfront Park to have a similar cozy, neighborhood feel, but by September 29, as Prunetti and Florio smiled for the cameras at the groundbreaking, "the emotion was one of exhaustion" according to Clarke.

"The permitting for the project is enormously complicated because the site is on the river," Clarke added. "It could easily have taken a year to get everything in order, but Bob Prunetti went to the state and pushed everything through. I guess this was one case where bureaucracy worked."

On August 12, 1993, moments after the Mercer County Park Commission voted 6-0 to approve the Caruso and Plumeri–owned Garden State Baseball Corporation's bid for a 20-year lease of the stadium, the architects revealed colorful renderings of the ballpark that incorporated a long list of specifications required by Major-League Baseball as a result of their 1990 agreement. At the top of the facility's red brick facade and sloping green metal roof was an open turret with a flagpole extending skyward. The design was both stunning and humbling. Initial plans also showed parking lots that could accommodate 1800 cars. Additional lots across Route 29 would hold another 476.

Throughout the public wooing process, Prunetti lined up corporate and private support for the stadium project. His efforts were tireless as he staked his political career on the project and implored Mercer County taxpayers to believe that the park was an investment in their future. A $237,000 economic study conducted in 1993 indicated that a Double-A franchise would funnel at least $9 million a year directly into the Mercer County economy. That estimate was based on a season attendance figure of 290,000 for 71 home dates, or an average crowd of just over 4000 per game. To reach that figure, the Thunder would have to fill the stadium to 64 percent of its capacity.

During late August 1993, the Mercer County Board of Chosen Freeholders voted 6-1 to approve a $12 million bond issue for the "Waterfront" stadium construction budget, including the cost of the land. The lone dissenting vote was cast by Freeholder Carolyn Bronson. Ironically, Bronson was a Republican. During June, she had asked the county to conduct an opinion poll on the stadium because "there still is a sizable number of people with uncomfortable doubts. The purpose [of an opinion poll] is to see if we build it, will they come? If they're not going to come to Trenton, we'd better know that now."

On September 21, 1993, eight days before the official groundbreaking, Prunetti asked Mercer County officials to file condemnation papers officially seizing the lot from LaMelza, who "owned" the property but also owed considerable back taxes on it. As a result, the site was condemned for a price of $1.35 million. The county paid for the land by withdrawing funds from a $6 million Open Space Preservation Fund raised by Mercer County taxpayers, who contributed an extra 1 cent on their annual property taxes.

On September 28, the Mercer County Improvement Authority (MCIA) authorized the sale of up to $13 million in bonds to finance the ballpark. The figure was larger than previously anticipated "to provide a cushion in case of unforeseen costs." Over the next 20 years, the money would be paid back to the county through a small property tax increase (which ranged from $1.62 per year on a Trenton residence assessed at $64,900 to $8.35 for a Princeton Borough home assessed at $167,000) and a $1 donation for each ticket sold to the team's games. Through the first three Thunder seasons, the ticket kickback totaled almost $1.2 million. The county also received $1 for each parking ticket sold.

Some Mercer County residents were outraged that Prunetti's original stadium bond issue projection of $6 million had ballooned to $13 million. "I consider it a mistake if you use taxpayers' money to build a stadium to have this team," said West Windsor resident Irwin Goldberg. "The market is not particularly large, and commuters will stay in New York or Philadelphia to watch a game. I want to go on the record to say you're making a mistake."

Despite these dissenting voices, Prunetti and the MCIA forged ahead with the project. "I have thought from the very beginning that it really is time for the county to be involved in the revitalization of Trenton," said Democratic Freeholder Wendy Benchley. Benchley pointed to Wilmington's first-year success in a very similar market. "They had many of the same hesitations that Mercer County has, and they have not proven to be true. The Wilmington stadium has provided thousands of hours of family entertainment and redevelopment dollars flowing into the area surrounding the stadium, and they are getting local benefit from having minor-league players in town."

Democratic Freeholder Joseph Yuhas made a more emotional plea for the stadium project. "When that site was a steel mill, my dad worked there. He was put out of work when the plant closed, along with the other workers who mostly lived in the surrounding neighborhood. This isn't just a governmental decision for me. It's an emotional decision, too."

THE ANTICIPATION BUILDS

By November 22, 1993, the stadium's dull-red structural steel began forming a skeletal outline alongside the Delaware River. By Christmas, project contractor Donald Burris and his crew placed a holiday pine tree atop the highest piece of metal. By the new year, all of the steel work had been completed; however, the estimated cost of the stadium project had been increased to $15.65 million due to the overtime and rush orders that would be required to complete the facility in just 4 months.

"I remember one morning feeling particularly low about something or other," Prunetti said. "And I was driving to work along Route 29 and I saw the first crane lifting a piece of steel, and that just changed my whole attitude. I have said from the beginning, 'Any city that is a real city has a professional baseball franchise—major or minor, whatever.' You've gotta have professional sports. It's not going to change the make-up of this city overnight, but long term, it's going to have a tremendous impact."

To that end, Prunetti and the prospective Trenton ownership (Garden State Baseball) negotiated throughout 1993 a franchise transfer with the Tigers of London, Ontario (Detroit's '93 Double-A affiliate). The Tigers played the '93 season in 4500-seat Labatt Park, the oldest professional baseball park in North America. Detroit was eager to upgrade its Double-A facility by relocating. Garden State Baseball paid approximately $3.5 million to purchase the franchise from the London ownership.

From the outset, Prunetti's minor-league pursuit involved constructing the publicly funded stadium first and then worrying about which major league affiliate would occupy it. At 11:30 AM on December 20, 1993, news arrived that the county executive's build-it-and-someone-will-come approach had been rewarded. Major League Baseball had officially approved the relocation of the London franchise from Canada to the Garden State capital. It was the final step in a series of approvals that also included blessings from the Eastern League and the National Association of Professional Baseball Leagues.

"It's sort of anticlimactic in a way," Prunetti said of the early Christmas present. "I fully expected this, but I guess what came to me when I heard the news was a tremendous sense of achievement. For the city of Trenton, the team itself is great, but the most significant thing is that we've shown the rest of the world—developers, business people, whomever—that things can happen in Trenton. Now, it's sort of a clue for them to get on board and take advantage of the opportunities that are going to be there."

Throughout his courtship of the London officials, including partners Dan Ross and Dick Stanley (who became a minority Thunder owner following the transfer), Prunetti had a little fun veiling his intentions for local reporters. On the shelf behind his office desk, he placed three major-league baseball caps. The middle one belonged to Detroit. Later, he claimed that each time he was interviewed in his office, the answer to questions about which major-league affiliate would be in Trenton was staring them right in the face.

Another amusing aspect of Prunetti's negotiations with the London contingent was the insistence by Stanley and Ross that they had no knowledge of Trenton or its attempt to lure a minor-league franchise to town. At one point, Stanley was quoted as saying that he "didn't know who PINETTI was," implying that he couldn't even pronounce the county executive's name so he must be telling the truth. As a Mercer County official read the quote in a local paper, however, Stanley was meeting with the Trenton contingent in an adjacent room. The whole situation was comical.

During his January 20, 1994, State of the County address, Prunetti trumpeted the Thunder's arrival as the most significant event of the decade for the Mercer County region. "Enthusiasm for the Thunder's descent has been overwhelming," he said. "From the groundbreaking through all the various announcements along the way, people's interest has grown in the team and the stadium it will call home. In fact, I wouldn't be surprised if by next year we hear variations of Yogi Berra's famous declaration, 'Nobody goes there anymore— it's too crowded.' "

By late January, the first phase of the stadium's electrical work was completed. Workers shielded themselves from the elements with a giant plastic tarp as they toiled in the bowels of the concrete-and-brick structure. Outside, a sheet of ice and snow at least an inch thick covered the frozen surface that would become the playing field. "We're still OK to be ready for the [scheduled April 16 stadium] opening, but obviously this frigid weather doesn't help," said Executive Director of Mercer County Park Frank Ragazzo, the man directly responsible for overseeing the Waterfront Park field completion. "We can't take much more of it, but in Wilmington they prepared the field and laid the sod in about 4 weeks."

In early April, the first-ever Thunder roster was finalized, and the prospects had a look at their new stadium. Manager Tom Runnells had visited the construction site during February, and at that time, he made a mental note that the workers had a major challenge before them. On the evening of April 6, one night before the team departed for Harrisburg for its season-opening, three-game series against the Senators, Runnells again toured Waterfront Park. To his considerable dismay, he observed that the facility was nowhere near being ready for baseball. None of the sod had been laid. Without causing much of a commotion, Runnells thought to himself that it would be a miracle if the Thunder played a home game by the end of the month. And if they did play on a hastily thrown-together surface, would the decision to take the field before it was ready place his players in danger? Ultimately, his team would be the only concern in such matters of judgment. What was best for the 23 young men with whom the Detroit Tigers had entrusted him?

Ironically, the situation was exactly the opposite for Prunetti and the Mercer County officials. For them, the players were almost incidental, in the sense that if the stadium and field weren't completed, it wouldn't matter who was on the roster. Every passing day put more pressure on the county.

CREATURE COMFORTS

By May 9, 1994, when the Thunder finally opened Waterfront Park after two delays, most of the structural work had been completed. The gently curving, red-brick facade facing Route 29 welcomed patrons through the park's main portals and up the stairs to the main concourse. The facility had three levels: one on the ground, one on the main concourse, and one private area above the grandstand. In mid-May, 1994, the unfinished details included the 16 luxury boxes on the stadium's upper level, the 88-seat stadium restaurant (also on the top level), the Thunder offices (on the ground level), and the permanent concession stands on the concourse level. The luxury boxes and concession stands were completed by the final month of the inaugural '94 season. The Thunder Dugout Shop, situated between the concession stands on the concourse with three large glass windows facing the stadium's welcoming plaza, was not finished until after the inaugural season; throughout the first year, Director of Marketing and Merchandising Eric Lipsman and his staff shuttled merchandise back-and-forth from the Thunder's temporary offices in the 200 Building of the Riverview Executive Plaza with hand-trucks. The team offices were completed in September 1995, and the Thunder management team moved into its new quarters shortly thereafter.

Despite the inconveniences associated with temporary concession and merchandise stands, the product that the Thunder offered was an immediate success. The careful planning that went into Waterfront's fan-friendly design played a large part in that warm public reception. In the weeks after the stadium opened, news of the franchise spread through the Trenton metropolitan area by way of the media, and most significantly, word of mouth. "Have you been down to the stadium yet?" was the question repeated in shopping malls, restaurants, and bars. By the end of the '96 season, Waterfront Park was "the single biggest attraction in Trenton" according to Sally Lane, director of the Trenton Convention and Visitors Bureau.

Access to the stadium was aided immeasurably by the December 1994 opening of the $400 million Trenton Complex road network, a series of highways that included Route 129. The new road connected Interstates 195 and 295 to US Route 1. In fact, the Cass Street exit on Route 129 led motorists past the imposing brick walls of the Trenton State Prison (which were painted with a giant baseball mural during the '95 season) and directly to Waterfront Park. Cass Street was renamed "Thunder Road" and colorful banners were hung from the thoroughfare's lamp posts. Furthermore, rush-hour traffic on Route 129 was alleviated considerably by the Trenton Complex network. For many suburbanites who wanted to get into the city to watch a game and leave as soon as it was over, the Route 129 opening was a godsend.

During the inaugural season, tickets to a Thunder game ranged in price from $5 (terrace seats) to $7 (for club and pavilion seats). Children from 3 to 14 years of age and senior citizens received a $2 discount. Those prices remained unchanged through the first three seasons. From any of the park's 6300 seats, the on-field action is clearly visible, and fans in all sections of the grandstand are likely to have at least one foul ball hit in their direction during the game. Perhaps the biggest appeal of an intimate minor-league facility like Waterfront is its proximity to the action. "When you're on the concourse waiting in line for a beer, you're still involved in the game," Clarke observed.

The outfield fence, which varies in distance from 330 feet to the foul poles and 407 feet to straightaway center, includes 84 billboard spaces that range from three 8-foot tiers in left field to one 8-foot level in right. During the first three seasons, many of these spaces changed hands as advertisers came and went. One of the most memorable billboards was the giant, two-tiered head of health care spokesman and former Philadelphia Eagles head coach Dick Vermeil that appeared in left-center field during the 1995 season. During the inaugural '94 season, a local dentist's billboard prompted an outcry from many players. The billboard featured a white tooth that actually made the baseball difficult to see as it came out of the pitcher's hand. The challenge was especially difficult for left-handed batters, who complained vociferously that the sign was taking points off their average. Several Thunder players threatened to cover the tooth with black electrical tape. Early in the '95 season, it was moved and painted neon green, but at least a few members of the '94 Thunder roster probably blame the end of their careers on Dr. Paul Kost, who offered free dental work to the Trenton front-office employees in exchange for the advertising space.

Another one-of-a-kind billboard was sponsored by downtown Trenton's Byer's Men's Shop, which offered the promotion, "Hit the Sign! Win a Suit!" Owner Mark Byer said the inspiration for the 8-by-16-foot sign came from Ebbets Field. In fact, the company that leased the Ebbets Field billboard had reversed its financial fortunes by advertising at the ballpark. During three seasons, five Thunder players took advantage of the enticement and were rewarded with free clothing—a result of home runs that bounced off the third-tier billboard in left field. The lucky quintet included Tony Clark ('94), Clyde "Pork Chop" Pough ('95), Nomar Garciaparra ('95), Adam Hyzdu ('96), and Andy Abad ('96).

During the '94 season, a local automobile dealership also sponsored a billboard promotion that featured a 4-by-4 vehicle with a tiny hole in it. For hitting a homer through the small opening, a player could win a Geo Tracker. First baseman Mike Rendina came the closest, smashing a 1994 line-drive homer just over the top of the advertisement.

In billboards, there also was humor. During the '96 season, outfielder Trot Nixon slammed into a right-field billboard and injured himself. The next day, a giant Band-Aid was attached to the sign where Nixon made his impact. Only in the minors.

Also befitting the minor-league atmosphere, Waterfront concession prices were scaled down to meet family budgets. During the '96 season, a 12-ounce soda cost $1.50, while a 32-ounce soda cost $2.75. Other items sold by Aramark, the company in charge of stadium concessions and the employer of more than 100 hourly personnel, included cheeseburgers, pizza, hot dogs, nachos, french fries, peanuts, ice cream sandwiches, and pork roll sandwiches.

In addition to the two permanent stands located along the first- and third-base sides of the main concourse, Waterfront has several specialty cart vendors that sell Italian water ice, fresh-squeezed lemonade, funnel cakes, gourmet ice cream, and premium bottled beers. For health-conscious patrons, fresh fruit salad also is available (for $4.50). A speed-pitch booth is located on the right-field side as well. In many ways, the stadium's spacious concourse justifies the architects' original mandate. Indeed, the park is an open-air carnival on any given night.

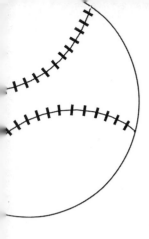

CHAPTER 3

Nightly Pageantry

"Waterfront Park's appeal is part baseball, part social, and part entertainment, not necessarily in that order."

—THUNDER CO-OWNER JOE CARUSO, FOUNDER AND PRINCIPAL OWNER OF OMNIFIRST CAPITAL CORPORATION

"We're almost like Great Adventure—we add a couple rides a year."

—THUNDER BROADCASTER AND DIRECTOR OF PUBLIC AND MEDIA RELATIONS TOM McCARTHY

In the months following the Waterfront Park groundbreaking, the Thunder laid the foundation for immediate success through a carefully executed series of steps that included announcement of the team name, the key front-office executives, the team logo, and the franchise's first publicly offered merchandise. That gradual, choreographed process began on October 20, 1993, less than 1 month after construction of the stadium began. During a press conference at the Hyatt Regency Princeton, the name *Thunder* was officially selected from a contest pool of four finalists that also included the Mud Puppies (a reference to the Detroit Tigers' Triple-A affiliate, the Toledo Mud Hens), the River Cats, and the Capital Clippers.

Said Prunetti, as the 80-year-old Plumeri looked on proudly, "The name Thunder connotes strength and power. It was by far the most appealing name." Appropriately for the new franchise, which would appeal particularly to young fans, the winning name was submitted by 10-year-old West Windsor, New Jersey, elementary school student Lindsay Maschino, who chose Thunder for the new baseball club because she "thought they'd be a really good team, so they would get a lot of thunderous applause." In retrospect, the choice of Thunder over the other three options was a stroke of genius by the Trenton ownership. The name gave the franchise a great deal of flexibility in creating merchandise. Following mixed initial reaction, it quickly caught on with the public and gained an identity all its own.

HODES TAKES OVER

On November 22, 1993, during a press conference inside the lobby of Hamilton Hospital, 29-year-old Wayne Hodes (pronounced Ho-DESS) was introduced by Prunetti as the Thunder's Chief Operating Officer (COO). In Hodes, the franchise owners had selected a young, hungry executive with a vision for the stadium that was rising alongside the Delaware River and the product it would showcase. More significantly, though, they had chosen a man with a definitive plan, a blueprint for minor-league success in the 1990s. A native of Watchung Hills, New Jersey, with an undergraduate degree from Tulane University and a master's in sports administration from Montclair State, Hodes had served as assistant general manager of the Single-A Rancho Cucamonga Quakes of the California League during the '93 season. That magical summer, the Quakes played before sell-out crowds in the brand-new, 6300-seat Epicenter. As a result, Hodes was familiar with the pitfalls of opening a new facility. As he addressed the Trenton media on that late fall afternoon, he was ready to meet the challenge of Waterfront Park head on.

By returning to the Garden State, he was taking a long-awaited step up in a minor-league administrative career that began during the 1980s as an intern for the New York Mets' Triple-A affiliate in Tidewater, Virginia. Like minor-league players, minor-league executives often are weeded out and promoted in an upward path. Wayne Hodes had no intention of failing. In Trenton, he would make most of the decisions that shaped the Thunder's ultimate impact on the Delaware Valley. His job was part administration, part public relations, part business, and part marketing.

"I went out to California for a couple of years, but my interest obviously lies in the state of New Jersey, and being able to bring professional baseball back to my home state was something that was very important to me," he said after taking over the day-to-day operations of the new franchise. "I couldn't have written a better script for my career."

Ironically, the Thunder ownership (a.k.a. Garden State Stadium Corporation at the time that Hodes was hired) wasn't the only group to pursue Hodes' services before the '94 season. Another fledgling New Jersey minor-league team, the Single-A, short-season New Jersey Cardinals of the New York–Penn League, made him an offer to run their Sussex County franchise. Although Hodes declined the Cardinals' job offer because he wanted to move up to the Double-A level and explore the huge (over 3 million residents within a 35-mile radius) market that gradually would become Trenton's fan base, the Cardinals opened play in June 1994 at 4340-seat Skylands Park. Unlike Waterfront, Skylands was a privately funded facility. Built in a cornfield some 80 minutes from New York City, Skylands was received with an enthusiasm that rivaled that for the Thunder and Waterfront Park. In 1994, a New York–Penn record total of 156,447 fans packed Skylands to watch the Cardinals capture the league's McNamara Division pennant with a 43-32 record. The '94 Cardinals went on to sweep the Auburn Astros, two games to none, in the playoff championship.

After Hodes accepted the Thunder COO position, he insisted that the team ownership let him bring 26-year-old Brian Mahoney on board as the assistant general manager. In Rancho Cucamonga, the pair had formed a lasting bond, and Hodes knew how important it would be to have a trusted assistant who also was familiar with the inner workings of minor-league baseball. Mahoney, a 1991 graduate of Hobart College, immediately bolstered the Thunder staff. During the '93 season in Rancho Cucamonga, he had served as Director of Ticket Sales, overseeing the general operation of the ticket office while establishing a new ticket system. His expertise would be invaluable to the Thunder in dealing with its new marketing base.

Also on hand during Hodes' introduction was 25-year-old Tom McCarthy, the Thunder's new radio broadcaster and Director of Public and Media Relations. A 1990 graduate of Trenton State College, McCarthy had a background in sports journalism as a former sportswriter for the *The Times* of Trenton. By leaving that career, he was making an ambition-based decision that the Thunder would find a niche in the Trenton community. Universally well-liked, the outgoing McCarthy had an enthusiasm for the Thunder venture unparalleled by anyone, except for perhaps Prunetti and Hodes. In many ways, the franchise was his personal stake in the Trenton community. He believed the concept of minor-league baseball would succeed in the Delaware Valley. Ultimately, he was willing to go to any length to make the players—many of whom were his age or even older—feel comfortable in their new surroundings. Many times during the first three seasons, he was the direct liaison between the team and front office.

McCarthy would be joined in the broadcast booth by 35-year-old Nick Simonetta, a 1984 graduate of Rutgers-Camden Law School who abandoned a career as counsel to the Bank of Manhattan to pursue his love of radio play-by-play. Simonetta, like Hodes, Mahoney, and McCarthy, was staking his livelihood on the Thunder's success.

Also named to the Thunder front-office staff was Director of Business Operations Todd Pae. A 1986 graduate of Pennsbury High in Fairless Hills, Pennsylvania, Pae was a former high-school baseball player who amused reporters at his introductory press conference by promising, "I'm going to be the first to hit a ball into the Delaware." In many ways, that statement let everyone know that minor-league baseball was just around the corner for the Thunder.

THE THUNDERBIRD RISES

Working out of temporary offices in the 400 Building of the Riverview Executive Plaza adjacent to the stadium construction site, Hodes, Mahoney, Pae, and McCarthy were joined by Director of Marketing and Merchandising Eric Lipsman. Before joining the Thunder, Lipsman worked with the '93 Wilmington Blue Rocks during their inaugural season. Nicknamed "Pookie" by his Thunder front-office colleagues, Lipsman recognized that the Thunder could be a merchandising gold mine. Before caps and T-shirts could be sold, however, the team needed a distinctive logo, something that would capture the public eye.

On January 11, during a crowded press conference inside the New Jersey Lottery Building on Trenton's Brunswick Circle, the Thunder logo was unveiled. In

1950, the New Jersey Lottery Building did not exist; rather, the site was the left-center field of the old Dunn Field, where the Trenton Giants and Willie Mays played their final professional season. As a room full of reporters and cameramen awaited their first glimpse at the logo, a symbolic bridge had been built to Trenton's minor-league past. There was silence as Prunetti revealed the new symbol—a blue, two-headed Thunderbird with yellow lightning shooting from each mouth superimposed atop a kelly green "T."

"This logo is going to represent our area, not only its past but also its future," the county executive proclaimed as flashbulbs exploded around him. "For Indians who lived along the Delaware Valley, the Thunderbird was a mythical bird that would rise up and create thunder and lightning by beating its breast with its wings to connote power." Explaining the curious-looking twin heads, Prunetti added in his distinctive New Jersey accent, "One head is looking backwards to represent the past, a rich heritage. Most importantly, though, the other head is looking toward the future, at what we see as a vision for Trenton and our region, the vitality and strength."

The logo was designed by Hamilton, New Jersey, graphic artist Alexander Ladnyk, president of Excalibur Graphics, Inc. Ladnyk had been asked to create a logo that would appeal particularly to children. "That's the trend in professional sports," Ladnyk explained while fielding questions about his creative inspiration for the two-headed Thunderbird.

On January 19, a bitterly cold midwinter day, green adjustable baseball caps with the new logo went on sale inside the Thunder's temporary offices. At a cost of $18 apiece, they were an immediate hit. Curious fans flocked to the Riverview Plaza—many on their lunch breaks—to be among the first to own the new merchandise. Two styles of Thunder T-shirts—one gray and one black, each with a distinctive, screened print on the front—also were made available at $14 each. For Lipsman, it was the beginning of a merchandising bonanza that ultimately would evolve into the award-winning Thunder Dugout Shop on the second level of Waterfront Park. "We let them wait in the lobby because we didn't want them freezing outside," Lipsman recalled of the chaos surrounding the franchise's first-ever merchandise sales. "And they were just buying everything."

By late January, less than 1 month after the transfer of the London, Ontario, franchise to Trenton had been approved by Major League Baseball, the Thunder had received orders for more than 1000 season tickets. The franchise had reached out to the community through advertising, networking at business functions, and old-fashioned door-to-door cold-calling. Hodes quickly established a standard of hard work that he expected each and every one of his employees to follow.

"There was a lot of skepticism during January and February [1994], more because of the weather than anything else," McCarthy recalled. "And the fans were wondering, 'Were the players we would be getting like college players, or were they a notch higher?' There were so many unanswered questions, and everything was so new at that point."

Over the ensuing eight months, many of the blanks would be filled in.

BOOMER

Hodes arrived in Trenton with fond memories of his stay in Rancho Cuca-monga. During the inaugural '94 Thunder season, he referred to the California franchise with a great deal of nostalgia, a sentiment he shared with Mahoney. Both young executives wanted desperately to harness the same dynamic that had made the Epicenter a special place and transfer it to Waterfront Park. To that end, they needed a unique, lovable mascot to entertain the Delaware Valley crowds during games. In Rancho Cucamonga, the mascot was named "Tremor." Tremor was a puffy, teal-blue dinosaur who exuded personality and provided immediate identification with the Quakes' franchise. Hodes realized the Thunder would be fortunate to create a mascot equally as appealing as the ubiquitous California dinosaur he left behind. By May 13, 1994, however, when the Thunder mascot was first presented to the public, he was extremely pleased with the reaction.

"Boomer," the giant blue Thunderbird who is a direct extension of the two-headed franchise logo, was designed by Morrisville, Pennsylvania, artist Bill Pae, the father of Todd Pae. With his son's involvement in minor-league base-ball, he had plenty of opportunity to study mascot prototypes. "The idea for Boomer hit me real fast," Pae explained. "You know . . . Thunder, Boomer. I've done a lot of caricature work, and I did some sketches. I wanted something that wouldn't be too frightening to kids." The friendly, one-toothed expression on the mascot's face is a result of that concern.

Loosely basing his work on the major-league Philadelphia Phillies' popular Phanatic, Pae created a giant blue creature with a huge yellow beak. While col-laborating with the Thunder front office and ownership, he—like Hodes—knew the mascot would be one of the keys to the Trenton franchise's public ac-ceptance. Like any baseball fan, he also knew, "You're going to have games that drag on. That's when a mascot has to do some of his best work."

In the 1995 Thunder yearbook, Boomer's biographical information con-tained the following tidbits:

Height: 6′4″
Weight: 320 pounds
Hat size: Haven't found a tape measure big enough
Width: Robust around the waistline
Color: Royal blue with a bright yellow beak. Green sneakers and purple sun-glasses
Bats/Throws: Poor/even worse
Closest Known Relatives: Big Bird, Foghorn Leghorn, and Tweetie
Favorite Foods: Rally the Raven, Slugger the Sea Dog, Tater the Gator

Ironically, on the cool spring evening of Boomer's debut—which was wit-nessed by a curious Waterfront Park crowd of 3909—Bill Pae was in China on a business trip. Needless to say, he anxiously awaited word of the mascot's recep-tion. In large part, that depended on the man inside the suit, a 29-year-old ele-mentary school teacher and kid-in-adult-body named Paul (his last name must remain anonymous not to ruin his alter-identity).

Inside the costume, which reads "BOOMER 00" on its back, Paul has a distinctive strut as he strolls through the main concourse and the 16 luxury boxes above, always in search of mischief. On steamy summer nights, he douses patrons with 100-foot jets of water from a "Super Soaker" toy machine gun. During the 1996 season, he added a yellow go-kart to his repertoire. Before each home game, he sped around the warning track to the theme song from the cartoon *Speed Racer*. "He's going to tip that thing over," several observers predicted.

Once he reaches the seating area, Boomer is entirely unpredictable. When a Thunder player hits a home run, he drops to his knees and begins bowing reverently. He tussles people's hair and tosses their hats into the next row. He is the object of incessant youthful adulation. Children punch him. They tug at him. They have their picture taken with him. They gleefully scream his name as he approaches their seat with an assistant in tow (to make sure that he isn't inundated by admirers). They duck as he shoots strand after strand of Silly String toward their faces from a small metal canister. They laugh and smile as he spends a moment with them.

As the most visible nonplaying representative of the franchise, Boomer's creativity mirrored the Thunder's efforts to reach out to the Delaware Valley community. Because Paul rarely missed a night, even during the 95-degree heat of mid-summer, he gave the character a continuity. As a student of the mascot craft, he frequently made trips to other minor-league stadiums to watch his costumed compatriots in action. As a result, he routinely concocted new and hilarious ways to make fans laugh at Waterfront. During one 1995 series against Portland, he tied a plastic dog bone to the end of a retractable toy fishing rod and dangled it over the lip of the visitor's dugout, teasing the Sea Dog players until the bone was finally ripped from its line. Each time the Norwich Navigators came to Trenton, he dragged an inflatable green alligator around the outfield, taunting the opposition. Most of the visiting players went along with his antics, knowing they were all in good fun. Once during the '96 season, however, Boomer was flesh-piled by a group of seven Navigators, recalling, "I said, 'Uh, oh,' because I knew it was time to get out of there." Often before games, he's used a giant slingshot to fire water balloons at the visiting players as they stretched in left field. Some of the players tried to bat the balloons out of the air as the gradually filling stadium applauded. Frequently, he plays an impromptu game of wiffle ball with youngsters in the seats near the Thunder dugout.

"You can have a great mascot costume and design, and if the person in there isn't good at portraying the character, it's not going to work," Bill Pae said, adding that he thinks Paul is one of the best in the business at evoking a mascot personality. "I think a lot of it has to do with the way you move."

During the '95 and '96 seasons, Boomer hosted his annual birthday party. The guests of honor were mascots from other Eastern League teams like Rally the Raven (New Haven) and characters representing other organizations like the Baltimore Oriole, Winger the Washington Capital, and the University of Delaware Blue Hen. Before each party, Paul became particularly excited about the potential for organized mayhem. During the festivities, the assembled mascots played musical chairs to the chicken dance. (Boomer won, of course.) Because the Boomer costume absorbed so much wear and tear during a season, it was replaced each year. In 1995, that allowed Thunder officials to dress up the old costume to look like Boomer's mother. The big question from onlookers during the 1995 birthday party became, "Who's inside Boomer's mother?"

The answer? Thunder Group Sales Manager Adam Palant.

During the '96 season, Boomer received the ultimate mascot compliment when he was tossed out of a game by home-plate umpire Bill Welke. After making several crude, pelvic-thrusting gestures atop the visitor's dugout, Boomer was given the heave-ho. Emotionally wounded by the ouster, Paul retreated to his dressing quarters and donned the Boomer's mother outfit. Resplendent in pill-box hat, metal-rimmed glasses, and scarf, he sashayed through the stands. Hodes encouraged the re-emergence because he wanted to make a statement to the perturbed umpire that he might want to spend a little more time watching the game and a little less worrying about the mascot. After all, minor-league baseball is about fun, too. It was a triumphant moment for Paul, a rare opportunity to buck the wide-ranging authority granted to the men in blue who work Double-A games for approximately $2500 a month (1996 salary).

On March 21, 1996, Bill Pae was honored during a display of gifts at the Smithsonian Institution in Washington, D.C. On hand for the ceremony, which celebrated the achievements of the last 12 U.S. Presidents, were President Bill Clinton and First Lady Hillary Clinton. The exhibit featured artists from around the country, and Pae was invited for his contributions to the Thunder franchise's success.

NIGHTLY PROMOTIONS

During any Thunder game at Waterfront Park, the action between half-innings is rigidly scripted to provide nonstop entertainment. Some of the promotions are unique to the Trenton franchise, while others are borrowed or derived from other minor-league teams. Of course, Boomer has an oversized hand in most of the Thunder's activities. When play began at the new stadium in early May 1994, one of the first promotions was "The Corner Inn Pizza Giveaway." During the second inning, a representative of The Corner Inn (a nearby restaurant/tavern) and a "fuzzy helper" (Boomer) delivered "a hot, fresh tomato pie" to a lucky fan. Another popular staple of the first three seasons was "the Boomer race." During each game, Thunder staffers selected a youngster to race the mascot around the bases. Invariably, Boomer found a new and innovative way to lose the contest. Sometimes, he was tripped or held by an opposing player. Occasionally, he was disqualified for making a wrong turn. Sometimes, he was beaten at the last second as he mysteriously slowed to a walk and hung his head in defeat to make it look convincing. During the '95 and '96 seasons, the prize for winning the Boomer race was a 10-pound Nestle's Crunch bar, which always elicited a reaction from the crowd. The candy bar often was too heavy for the youngster to carry unassisted. "What are we going to do with that?" more than one parent was overheard wondering. Boomer's only recorded victory came on the final day of the inaugural '94 season, when he edged an opponent who had been instructed to take a dive. Afterward, a trio of Thunder staffers triumphantly carried the mascot off the field atop their shoulders.

While some promotions fizzled during the first three Thunder seasons—a golf putting game, a giant dice toss sponsored by an Atlantic City casino—another mainstay was the STS Car Service Center dizzy bat race. As Boomer looked on from one side, a pair of contestants placed their foreheads on the top of an upside-down bat and spun around at least 15 times. The result was a loss of equilibrium that produced some very entertaining spills, particularly by adult patrons who had enjoyed some liquid refreshments during the early innings. The dizzy bat race was always a crowd pleaser. Occasionally, a contestant strayed into the field of play as the visiting team warmed up between innings.

During the '96 season, the Thunder added another fan favorite, the Great Adventure "Let's Make a Deal" promotion. The idea came from similar promotions run in Harrisburg and Reading. During the fourth inning, McCarthy left the Trenton radio booth with an assistant who carried a large banner. Wireless microphone in hand, McCarthy walked into the stands and inquired, "Who wants to play?" Amidst yelps and pleas, he selected a contestant who could choose either the prize in McCarthy's possession or the prize in a small gold box near the Thunder on-deck circle. Invariably, manager Ken Macha stopped by to inspect the contents of the box. One of the prizes was something valuable, such as 1996 All-Star Game tickets or a gift certificate to the Thunder Dugout Shop, and the other was a gag gift/boobie prize. Once, the gag gift was 20 gallons of maple syrup (the good prize was dinner with Ken Macha). Other gags included two tokens to cross the Route 1 toll bridge into Pennsylvania, a band-aid from McCarthy's head, and a cacophonous rendition of "You've Lost that Loving Feeling" by Thunder staffer Adam Palant. Where did McCarthy come up with ideas for the gag gifts? "I just walked around the office and it would come to me," he said.

SIGHTS AND SOUNDS

During each game, the action was carefully orchestrated by public address announcer Hardison, computer sound effects wizard Bart Mix, and the scoreboard graphics operator, who controlled the video board in right-center field. Hardison's daily script is repeated 71 times a season. At specific intervals, he narrates the on-field promotions, delivers corporate advertisements, and makes player introductions. Perhaps no Eastern League franchise puts more effort into its corporate-sponsored giveaways than the Thunder. Of the team's 71 home dates during the '96 season, 52 were accompanied by some type of free merchandise. Over the course of the season, fans can accumulate a slew of items, including foam can holders, minibats, garment bags, team card sets, beach towels, sport bottles, first-aid kits, seat cushions, kid's caps, and magnetic schedules. Of course, all of these free souvenirs are decorated with the Thunder logo and the corporate logo of the game's sponsor. In addition to the bulk giveaways, which usually are offered to the first 2000 to 3000 fans entering the stadium, the Thunder offered special promotional opportunities that included free airline tickets, free jewelry, a free cruise, a free trip to the next season's spring training, and even a free car (presented during the last regular-season game).

In addition to the giveaways and on-field promotions, the Thunder scheduled annual appearances by the Phillie Phanatic, Sport (Dave Raymond, who used to be the Phillie Phanatic), and the Blues Brothers. During the '94 season, the Thunder players donned replica uniforms of the 1947 Trenton Giants for a game billed as "Turn Back The Clock" night. In both 1995 and 1996, the "Turn Back The Clock" uniforms were patterned after the 1939 Trenton Senators. Both sets of uniforms provided a tangible link to the capital city's minor-league baseball past.

Mix, a junior-high teacher in the Trenton School District, was hired by the Thunder before the inaugural season to handle the computerized sound effects that accompany all of the Waterfront action. The 31-year-old Mix immediately became notorious for his devious use of the Apple Macintosh "click effects" system. Produced by a company called Sound Creations, the click-effects program was in use at baseball parks throughout the country by the mid-1990s due to its wide range of sound capabilities and easy operation (Mix learned to use the system in one training session). The computer can reproduce any number of sounds, from music to shattering glass when a foul ball is hit over the stadium roof to the inane musings of MTV cartoon characters Beavis and Butt-head. When a Thunder player slides safely into second with a stolen base, the loudspeaker proclaims, "We're there, dude!" Possessed with a mischievous personality, Mix tirelessly authored a litany of well-timed sound bites that satirized the players and their exploits.

During a 1996 game, Portland Double-A All-Star center fielder Todd Dunwoody tagged third base and scored on a sacrifice fly, tripping as he crossed the plate. Without hesitation, Mix reached for the computer mouse and played a sound bite from the helpless old lady in the recent television commercial who muttered, "I've fallen, and I can't get up." Early in the '95 season, wacky right-handed Thunder relief pitcher Glenn Carter nicknamed himself "Wild Thing." Naturally, Mix had The Troggs' rock-and-roll hit of the same name programmed into the computer within days. Once, when Carter unleashed a pick-off attempt to first base and the ball sailed wide into the Thunder bullpen, Mix played the song at a most inopportune time. Seconds later, Thunder pitching coach Al Nipper was on the top step of the dugout, glowering toward the press box. The scene was reminiscent of the final home game of the inaugural season, when Guilfoyle threw a ball over the second baseman's head into center field. Mix was ready, playing "Never mind" as the record crowd of 7869 cackled en masse. When 1994 Harrisburg star shortstop Mark Grudzielanek came to the plate, Mix played "Huuuuhhhh" in reference to the elongated pronunciation.

In a word, Mix was incorrigible. One of those dubious moments occurred during an extra-inning game on May 1, 1995, when Reading infielder Jason Moler suffered the first serious injury in Waterfront history, breaking his leg while sliding into second base. As paramedics attended to the fallen player, Mix played the chicken dance over the loudspeaker. The players in the Phillies dugout and much of the remaining crowd of 4669 were appalled. (The next day, Moler's leg was surgically repaired at Trenton's St. Francis Medical Center.)

Mix also could be cruel with his selections. When '94 Thunder first baseman Mike Rendina returned in April 1996 as a member of the Harrisburg roster, the sound man was waiting. During his Thunder days, Rendina had complained incessantly about the white tooth billboard located directly to the left of the green center-field hitting backdrop. By 1996, although the tooth had been painted lime green and moved to the other side of the backdrop, Mix serenaded the infielder with Billy Joel's "She's Always a Woman To Me" each time he came to bat. Quipped Rendina, "Nothing's changed. That's the same way they treated me when I played here."

During prolonged arguments between opposing managers and umpires, Mix selected all types of sounds, including babies crying and high-pitched shrieks. Lines from the hit television cartoon *The Simpsons* also were among his favorites. During Hardison's pregame concession announcements, Homer often was heard muttering, "Mmmmm. . . Beer."

With virtually unlimited sound capabilities at their disposal, Mix and the Thunder front office encouraged players to select their own personalized music, which was played before each plate appearance. During the inaugural season, some of the more memorable choices included Naughty By Nature's "Hip Hop Hooray" (Tony Clark), "The Monster Mash" (outfielder Justin Mashore), and The Knack's "My Sharona" (catcher Joe Perona). Because it rhymed so perfectly with his name, Perona's song had shadowed him through three minor-league seasons by the time he arrived in Trenton. "I wish I had a dollar for every time I've heard that at the ballpark," he grumbled. One evening, Mix played "My Sharona" for all nine players in the Thunder lineup. Perona was not amused.

The most memorable songs of the '95 season included slugger Pork Chop Pough's "Tomahawk Chop," infielder Lou Merloni's "Louie, Louie" by The Kingsmen, and outfielder Abad's favorite, the theme from the television show *Cops*. ("Bad boys, bad boys, what you gonna do? What you gonna do when they come for you?") Because Abad's name was unique, he also heard George Thorogood's stuttering "Bad to the Bone" on occasion. ("B-B-B-B-Baaaad to the Bone.")

By 1996, as the Thunder's performance improved, so did the level of musical creativity. While second-year Double-A player Merloni was stuck with the Kingsmen and a mooing cow that elicited choruses of "Looouuuu!!!" shortstop Donnie Sadler selected rap music. Nixon picked country music. Designated hitter Woods opted for the theme song from the 1970s sitcom *Sanford and Son*. Outfielder Adam Hyzdu wanted Mozart. Catcher Walt McKeel asked for the theme song from *The Dukes of Hazzard*. Outfielder Paul Rappoli wanted U2's "Desire." When Norwich visited Waterfront late in the '96 season, Japanese pitcher Katsuhiro Maeda and his interpreter, a colorful gentleman named "Pancho," were greeted with a string of jibberish and a clanging gong that Mix sounded with gleeful pride. Maeda, who dyed his hair pink earlier in the season, laughed aloud at the noises even though he wound up losing the game 6-0.

Aside from Pough's ubiquitous "Tomahawk Chop," the biggest musical craze of the first three Thunder seasons was reserved for Macha. By 1996, the Latin dance song "Macarena" by the group Los del Rio was sweeping baseball stadiums across the county. Ironically, the hit tune's chorus, though spelled differently, rhymed with the Thunder manager's name. So, naturally, each time Macha visited the mound, Mix cued up the Macarena and arms throughout the grandstand flailed to the rhythm. Once, however, Mix forgot to play the song as the manager walked from the dugout to the field. Pausing as if to indicate something was wrong, Macha simply gestured toward the press box with upturned palms. Within seconds, the Macarena commenced.

As Prunetti predicted during his efforts to jumpstart the stadium project, Waterfront became more than just a venue for Thunder games. During the '95 season, while the team was on the road, more than 7000 people showed up on July 4 to enjoy a concert and a fireworks display. Several high-school baseball teams rented the facility for games. (During a Mercer County American Legion All-Star Game, one of the left-handed participants hit a home-run ball into the river.) The stadium also hosted an annual business exposition, and toward the end of the '96 season, the Thunder formed their own concert promotion company. An annual Jazz Festival drew hundreds of patrons to the park. And, of course, the '96 season was memorable for the week-long Thunderfest leading up to the Double-A All-Star Game, which included tours of the stadium and the clubhouses, a chance for patrons to see their name on the scoreboard, and an appearance by the 1996 U.S. Olympic Baseball team. Head coach Skip Bertman's amateur squad defeated Korea 7-2 on July 5 before a standing-room-only crowd of 7065. The game was part of the NationsBank Team USA Baseball Tour, a pre-Olympic tour that stopped at several top minor-league venues. The U.S. Olympians went on to win a bronze medal in the Atlanta Olympics.

CHAPTER 4

First Spring Training

"My teammates are all curious about Trenton. I have to keep them in check because they're all wondering, 'Ah, what's it going to be like up there, horrible?' I just kinda let 'em know, 'Hey, don't worry about it. I'll take care of it.' Basically, I'm going to feel like a tour guide."

—1994 THUNDER PITCHER AND BAYONNE, NEW JERSEY, NATIVE MIKE GUILFOYLE

On Monday morning, March 13, 1994, as the boiling central Florida sun rose over Tigertown, the Detroit Tigers' spring training facility in Lakeland, a new chapter was being authored in the athletic and cultural history of Trenton, some 1000 miles north of baseball's Grapefruit League. Inevitably, the snow and ice that gripped the Northeast during the winter of 1994 wouldn't last forever. When the thaw began, baseball—and its attendant pageantry— would soon follow. As spring approached, anticipation surrounding the Thunder's arrival rose to a fever pitch.

The Thunder franchise's transfer from Canada, where the Tigers' farmhands had played at London's Labatt Stadium since 1990, was a business transaction that benefited both parties. The Tigers hadn't been able to draw a steady gate in Ontario, and Trenton—which had drawn crowds in excess of 1000 for Little League games during the early 1990s—was desperate for a minor-league team. Knowing that its Double-A prospects would benefit from playing in front of larger crowds and becoming the focus of a new town's adulation, Detroit was pleased with the move. After all, the London Tigers had averaged less than 2000 fans per game in 1993.

On March 13, the Thunder's first scheduled game (April 16) at Trenton's Waterfront Park remained a mirage on the flat, hazy landscape of spring training. One by one, the Tigers' Double-A roster hopefuls emerged from the Tigertown minor-league dressing compound. Greeting the players with their first glimpse of the Thunder home uniform, a white jersey and pants with kelly green pinstripes and the name "THUNDER" emblazoned across the chest in green letters, were Lipsman and team photographer Dave Schofield.

One by one, the prospects stepped to a green picnic table beside the dressing compound to have their headshots snapped. Most of them wiped sleep from their eyes as Lipsman and Schofield tried to match their 1993 baseball trading cards with their faces. Among the first to arrive was 22-year-old outfielder Justin Mashore, a blond California native with a friendly smile and a full complement of questions. Throughout the '94 season, Mashore—Detroit's fifth selection in the June 1991 amateur draft—would frequently speak his mind without regard for the consequences. "What is Trenton like?" he asked Lipsman. "Is the stadium going to be ready in time? Is it expensive to live there? Will my wife be able to find a job? She's a manicurist, you know."

During the previous off-season, Mashore had married his high-school sweetheart, Melissa. They attended rival high schools in the Concord, California, area, where Mashore was a four-sport star at Clayton Valley. In addition to his abilities as a baseball player, he was a star tailback on the football team, a talented track and field competitor, and a varsity basketball player. His father, Clyde, was a former major-league player with the Cincinnati Reds and Montreal Expos, and his brother, Dustin, was a minor-league prospect climbing through the levels of the Oakland A's farm system. Baseball ran deep in Mashore's genes. The '94 Thunder season would be his first experience at the Double-A level.

"You've gotta take what they can give you," Mashore said about the uncertainties of life in the minors. "Some places, you can't afford everything you want. I've slept on floors and done things just so I could stay in nicer places. Right now, I've got my wife with me and I've got to do what's best for her. I can't just camp out anywhere like before. Besides, you can get along a lot easier if you have somebody around to talk to that doesn't care about baseball."

By May, the Mashores would be expecting their first child.

Also emerging from the locker area that bright March day to pose in the new Thunder duds—designed by the same man who had conceived the Thunder logo, Alexander Ladnyk—was team manager Tom Runnells. Runnells' assignment: to mold a Double-A team from the varied personnel Detroit had assigned to him and his staff. It would be one of the biggest challenges of the 38-year-old Runnells' life, tougher in many ways than managing a major-league club, which he did for the National League Montreal Expos from June 3, 1991, to May 22, 1992.

Looking trim and eager to get on with his assignment, Runnells modeled the whimsical pinstripe suit for Schofield. "How do you like the uniform?" the photographer inquired. Runnels replied, "This is the second time I've worn it. I tried it on at a press conference in the Trenton area last month. The uniforms are nice."

The uniforms, from a baseball purist's standpoint, were a bit comical. They reflected the growing trend toward marketing in minor-league circles. The Thunder's three hats (a kelly green base with a two-headed, blue, black, and gold Thunderbird for home games; a black base with the same logo and a blue brim for away games; and a white base with the logo and a kelly green brim for home Sundays) elicited a wide variety of questions, not the least of which was, "What is it [the logo]?"

In any case, the uniform numbers that Runnells modeled for Schofield on March 13 resembled a computer font that had merged several types of print into one illegible mass. Throughout the season, fans, broadcasters, and writers would mistake "3" for "8" and "1" for "7." At the 1994 Double-A All-Star Game in Binghamton, New York, on July 11, Thunder pitchers Mike Guilfoyle and Ken Carlyle were the subject of their American League peers' clubhouse abuse because their uniforms looked "like a Little League team." One Eastern League general manager, New Haven's Charlie Dowd, deemed the gray and green Thunder road uniforms (which used the same barbaric numerical font) "the ugliest uniforms in the history of professional sports." Not surprisingly, the numbers were redesigned before the '95 season.

As Schofield captured Runnells' smiling face that March morning, uniforms were the least of the manager's concerns. Like his players and the whole Detroit organization from general manager Joe Klein down through Director of Minor League operations Dave Miller, Runnells' mandates were: 1) to put a competitive team together in 3 short weeks of exhibition play, and 2) to make sure that the new, palatial facility in which that team would play was up to Double-A specifications.

One after another as the sun mounted the sky, the players introduced themselves to Lipsman and Schofield. "Hi, I'm Mike Rendina, first baseman." "I'm Darren Milne, outfielder." "I'm Joe Perona, catcher." "I'm Kelley O'Neal, second baseman." "I'm Dean Decillis, third baseman." "I'm Brian Edmondson, pitcher." Each face had a story behind it. Each player had a different agenda to pursue and, ultimately, a dream of playing major-league baseball, although a precious few would ever ascend to that level. All expressed a certain degree of trepidation about the Tigers' Double-A move to Trenton.

Through 95-degree heat, the Tigers farmhands labored on the practice diamond. Runnells spent the mornings drilling fundamentals, hitting groundballs, and throwing batting practice. He chattered nonstop, challenging his players, driving himself to get them into playing shape. By his side through each workout were Thunder assistant coaches Kevin Bradshaw and Rich Bombard. Bradshaw, a diffident young former minor leaguer with Midwestern roots, would spend 2 months of the season with the Thunder before Detroit promoted him to manager of the Tigers' rookie club in Bristol, Virginia. Bombard, a no-nonsense Texan, would spend the entire '94 journey entrenched as Runnells' pitching coach and right-hand man.

THE SKIPPER

During a break in one of the morning practices, Runnells sat on a bench behind the minor-league fields. The manager removed his blue Detroit Tigers' cap and wiped the perspiration from his forehead. During his 38 years, he had achieved much more than most career baseball men his age. An 8-year minor-league infielder who originally was signed as an undrafted free agent by San Francisco in 1977, he toiled in the Giants' farm system for six seasons until he was acquired by Cincinnati in 1983. A highly regarded second baseman/shortstop, his near-decade of minor-league persistence finally paid off in early August 1985. As a 30-year-old rookie, he was summoned from the Triple-A Denver Zephyrs to the big-league Cincinnati Reds—on the same day Major League

Baseball went on strike to solve one of its many labor disputes. The impasse was resolved in just 2 days, however, and Runnells joined the Reds in the midst of a pennant-race against the Los Angeles Dodgers. When Runnells arrived in Los Angeles, a limousine shuttled him to the Beverly Hills Hotel, where his first encounter was with Reds' star Dave Parker. "What's up, Runnells Wrap?" Parker bellowed at the stunned infielder.

While with Cincinnati, Runnells played with baseball's all-time hit leader, Pete Rose, who recorded 4256 safeties during his illustrious career. In fact, he was in the lineup when Rose eclipsed Ty Cobb's career record for hits with his 4192nd. (During 1994 spring training, Rose showed up at Cleveland's Winter Haven, Florida, minor-league facility to watch his son, Pete, Jr., play an exhibition game against the Thunder.) Runnells' first major-league at-bat was against the Dodgers' Fernando Valenzuela on August 10, 1985, and his first major-league hit was recorded against the Dodgers' Jerry Reuss 1 day later. He appeared in 40 games with Cincinnati over the next two seasons, hitting .200 (8-for-46) with two doubles and four runs scored. The stint was little more than a cup of coffee, but it motivated him to return to the big leagues for a more-prolonged experience. He knew that would require becoming a manager or coach.

Therefore, in 1987, Runnells became a minor-league manager for the first time at the age of 31. His Cincinnati-affiliated, Double-A Vermont team compiled a 73-67 record and advanced to the best-of-five championship series of the Eastern League playoffs, where it lost to Harrisburg, three games to one. The next year, Cincinnati switched Double-A leagues and Runnells moved to Chattanooga of the Southern League, where his Lookouts won the championship, finishing the regular season with an 81-61 mark and sweeping Greenville in three games for the playoff title. After two seasons as a manager, his career was very much on the ascent. He signed with Montreal before the '89 season to manage the Expos' top farm team, the Triple-A Indianapolis Indians. The Indians ran away with the league championship, finishing 87-59 and defeating Omaha, three games to two, in the playoffs. Runnells was named the International League Manager of the Year.

On June 3, 1991, after 3 months as a Montreal coach, Runnells was named manager of the Expos, completing his coveted professional baseball double: big-league player, big-league manager. Runnells received the call to report to Houston: "We want you to take over for Buck Rodgers," Montreal officials told him. As photographers chronicled the moment, he entered the visiting manager's office in the Astrodome, bringing with him a bold sense of conviction, a disciplinarian style, and a spartan work ethic that had worked so well at the minor-league level for 4 1/2 years.

Aged 36 at the time of his appointment, he was the youngest manager in the major leagues. Many of the volatile motivational tactics he used with young prospects were useless with veteran players, however, some of whom were almost the same age. He managed 112 big-league games during the remainder of the 1991 season, compiling a 51-61 record. He was rehired for the '92 season but lasted only 37 games before losing his job to Felipe Alou. When he was fired on May 22, 1992, the Expos were 17-20. His overall record as the Montreal skipper was 68-81. "He was extremely harsh with the players, always screaming at them after a loss, and I think that had a lot to do with the firing," said one Montreal coach who spent the '91 season as part of Runnells' staff.

Naturally, the dismissal left Runnells unfulfilled. As his Tigers' minor-league hopefuls worked in the background one morning, he discussed his bittersweet major league tenure in Montreal. "Oh yeah, I'd like to get back there," he said candidly. "I'm like halfway through the book, and it was like somebody took the book from me, so I'll never know how it ended. I think if I wouldn't have made it to the majors as quick as I did the first time, my patience might be tried right now, but I've already been there."

The Thunder manager might as well have been speaking for everyone who dedicates their adult life to the game of baseball, to everyone who spends March through September traveling on minor-league buses chasing a dream. "I've wanted to be in baseball since I was five or six years old," he said. "It's pretty much everything that I enjoy. You don't compete once a week in this game. You compete daily, but I am so competitive that I have a tendency to lose patience sometimes. I don't lose patience in the fact that I'm ever giving up on kids, but sometimes I just take for granted they should know certain things about the game."

Runnells knew that dealing with minor leaguers and accomplished major-league stars who make millions of dollars a season were two very different challenges.

"I'm one of the luckiest men in the world," he insisted. "I was one of very few men to ever get an opportunity to manage in the big leagues. I'm very, very thankful for that opportunity, and if it never comes around again, I'll be tickled that I got that chance. I guess because of being so competitive, I guess that I could snap at some point, and I have. I think that keeps just enough of the edge." Several times during the '94 season, the Thunder experienced the dark side of that edge, and it left the players with blank expressions of humility. Runnells liked to call those tirades "airing them out." They had been a staple of his managerial philosophy during his brief Montreal stint.

THE FIRST ROSTER TAKES SHAPE

While Runnells' Double-A hopefuls practiced on the minor-league fields (in the shadow of Lakeland's Joker Marchant Stadium and the Tigers' big-league exhibition games), 6-foot-8 first baseman Tony Clark was working out with manager Sparky Anderson and the major leaguers. "Big Tony," a gentle giant who was the Tigers' first-round pick in the June 1990 amateur draft (he was drafted second overall behind Atlanta's Chipper Jones), entered the '94 season as something of a project. The first three seasons of his professional career had been tainted by injuries, everything from a herniated disk to a torn ligament in his right wrist, but Clark's assignment to Double-A (and Trenton) was a formality. The Tigers' brass knew it. Runnells knew it. And Tony—T.C. to his teammates and coaches—probably knew it, too.

Clark, an El Cajon, California, native and former college basketball player at the University of Arizona and San Diego State, spent a couple of precious weeks with Detroit stars Cecil Fielder, Alan Trammell, and Kirk Gibson before he and outfielder Brian DuBose (a streetwise, 53rd-round draft pick from Detroit) were sent to the minor-league camp for reassignment. In professional baseball, a player who is on the major league 40-man roster—as both Clark and DuBose were during the spring of 1994—must be optioned to the minors before joining the minor-league club.

On the day they were optioned to the Thunder from the Tigers' active roster, Clark and DuBose were no-shows for Runnells' Double-A practice. The volatile skipper was not impressed.

"Hell, those guys are practically on scholarship to Double-A anyway," Runnells jabbed. The next day, both players showed up on time, ready to go to work. Not a day passed before Runnells had Clark taking extra ground balls at first base and honing his swing with extra cuts in the batting cages next to the dressing complex. The manager would make the huge man field 100 balls in a row without a bobble or the count would begin again.

Partly because of Runnells' constant shepherding, Clark would turn out to be the inaugural Thunder season's brightest light. His personality, combined with his emerging talent, pointed his career in a direct line to Tiger Stadium alongside Fielder and the rest. And from day one of his assignment to the Double-A roster, he was Runnells' No. 1 project. To wake Tony from his professional slumber (during which he had never played more than 36 games in a season) was another in a long line of very personal challenges. He knew that Detroit officials would be monitoring his progress on a daily basis.

A strained arch in Clark's left foot, suffered during a March workout, hindered his ability to run during spring training and the early portion of the season, but speed was not his calling card anyway. The signature part of his game was power, the type of slugging force that sends balls screaming over the outfield fence.

"It's just the type of thing that if I continue to play and I continue to improve and progress the way everybody hopes I will, somewhere in the future I'll be able to reach the big leagues," T.C. said after joining the Double-A roster. During spring training, the switch-hitting Clark amazed Detroit officials by hitting baseballs out of the park from both sides of the plate. This feat was all the more impressive because he did it off a rubber hitting tee.

THE FETZER HILTON

Unlike many major-league organizations, which house their minor-league players in cheap motels near their spring training facilities, the Tigers had an on-site dormitory to accommodate all 160 of their minor leaguers. It was a no-frills, three-story, military-type barracks called Fetzer Hall. Many of the players, particularly the veterans, sarcastically called it the "Fetzer Hilton." Like the minor-league developmental ladder, Fetzer had its own hierarchy of privilege. The younger players lived on the top floor, three to a room. The second floor was filled with players who had some experience in the organization, also three to a room. On the first floor were Double-A and Triple-A prospects, privileged characters who were allowed some breathing room by living only two to a suite. As a player moved up the Tigers' chain, he moved down Fetzer Hall toward the ground-floor quarters.

"It was worse than a college dorm, smaller than that," said Perona, who was also a 1991 graduate of Northwestern University. "All it had in the rooms was a closet and two beds. It didn't even have a desk. There were no bathrooms in the rooms, and only one bathroom on each hall. And there were three phones for [more than] 150 guys."

Runnells' wife, Kathy, loved to tell stories of the Fetzer Hall telephones and the primitive system she had to use to contact her husband during 1993 spring training. "Somebody would answer the hall phone and I would ask, 'Is T.R. around?' " she said, adding that occasionally the person on the other end of the line didn't speak English. "I would hear the person yelling down the hall, 'Has anybody seen T.R.?' Sometimes I would get in touch with him; sometimes I wouldn't."

There were other, unseen perils to Detroit dormitory life. Added Perona, "There was something in the Fetzer pipes, because every year you come down—they call it the Fetzer flu—everyone ends up getting sick for about a week."

The grim reality of minor-league baseball at any level is the law of progression: If the parent organization doesn't think a player is headed in the right direction, or up the ladder of levels, he won't last long in its plans unless it can find another organization that wants to make a trade. During spring training, that reality can be especially harsh. Each day, players are released. Some hang around to say goodbye to friends. Others slink away to try to catch on with another organization as a free agent. Dreams die hard in a crowded, cutthroat place like Fetzer Hall. The only security is on the baseball diamond.

Gradually, Runnells' band of ballplayers began to assume a shape, a character, with clearly defined strengths and weaknesses. From day one, the manager felt that his pitching staff would be one of the Thunder's biggest assets and the middle infield a trouble spot against the Eastern League's talented opposition. Following his release as Montreal manager early in the '92 season, he had signed with Detroit to manage the Tigers' 1993 Double-A club in London. That team finished with a 63-75 record, sixth place in the eight-team Eastern League, or 33 games behind Baseball America's Minor League Team of the Year, the Harrisburg Senators. Some of those London players (particularly the veteran infielders) would be carryovers to the 1994 Thunder. Among the veteran Double-A players who took the field for the Thunder's first-ever exhibition game against Chattanooga at Plant City on March 17, 1994, were 26-year-old third baseman Dean Decillis, 22-year-old right fielder Darren Milne, 24-year-old catcher Pete Gonzalez, and 23-year-old first baseman Mike Rendina. Ironically, Runnells had talked Decillis out of retirement during the '93 season, and the Florida native had played well down the stretch. "I know what kind of effort I'll get from Dean; he's a veteran hitter," Runnells said.

EXHIBITION GAMES

A wave of scorching March heat accompanied the Thunder on their 15-mile journey to the Reds' minor-league complex on March 17, 1994, and several

Mercer County fans showed up to tan and watch the action from a small set of bleachers behind the fenced-in backstop. Among them was Executive Director of Mercer County Park Frank Ragazzo, Prunetti's right-hand man.

On this day, Ragazzo looked more like a tourist than a deadline-conscious administrator. Camcorder in hand, he chronicled the Thunder's nascent exploits. He filmed a contingent of five New Jersey college students who drove across the state from Daytona Beach to see their new minor-league team. They said they had read about the Thunder's first exhibition game in a Trenton-area newspaper before departing for spring break in a Chevrolet Caprice. As the students cheered, Ragazzo videotaped the first official lineup in franchise history, a list of nine names written beneath the word TRENTON for the first time.

"It was historic," Ragazzo said. "It gave me a chill to see the [gray, orange and blue Tigers'] uniforms in action. It gave me a feeling of satisfaction knowing what we had to go through, especially Bob Prunetti, to get everything approved. It didn't really matter whether they won or lost that day, just the fact that they were there. . ."

The Thunder won the game 6-2. DuBose scored the first run. Decillis blooped a stand-up double to right field ("Make sure you get that in the paper because you won't see many of those from Dean," one player bellowed from the dugout), and second baseman Kelley O'Neal smacked a three-run triple in the ninth inning. The winning pitcher was left-hander Rich Kelley, who would become known during the season for his outstanding pick-off move to first base.

While the Thunder players continued to prepare for their first-ever season in the New Jersey capital, they inquired daily about Waterfront Park's construction status. Rumors circulated through Tigertown indicated that it wouldn't be ready in time for the scheduled April 16 home opener against Reading. The inclement weather of the previous winter had delayed much of the structural work and placed completion of the playing surface far behind schedule.

In late March, as construction workers continued to struggle against time back in Trenton's South Ward, Prunetti visited Tigertown to meet some of the Double-A players and watch their practices. He wore a green Thunder home hat as he schmoozed with Runnells in the coaches' observation tower overlooking the minor-league fields. He also wore a proud, almost parental look as he strolled the complex. If all went according to plan, he would take the mound at Waterfront Park in less than a month to throw out the ceremonial first pitch.

"I've thought about what I will say, and how I will feel," Prunetti said as warm gusts of wind wafted through the tower. "It's such a sense of accomplishment, and it's hard to really describe. One of the reasons why I love what I do is that I'm able to, I guess, accomplish things that other people don't have an opportunity to do."

As Prunetti ensured that the Thunder's arrival would become a reality, public opinion gradually swayed into his corner. The prospect of having something good that Trenton could call its own was enough to convince some. For others, more tangible evidence, such as the physical completion of the stadium, was adequate proof. The county executive summed up the effort to sway public opinion, saying, "If you end up without a stadium, without a team, then you've lost. So you go after it and deal with how you got there later."

By March 30, news reached Tigertown that Waterfront Park would not be completed in time for the scheduled gala against Reading. Hodes and Mahoney conferred with county officials and team owners Caruso and Plumeri, Sr., to make contingency plans. Those alternate plans included three games, April 17-19, at Legends Park (home of the Single-A Carolina League Blue Rocks), in Wilmington, Delaware, and two games, April 20-21, at Veterans Stadium, home of the National League Philadelphia Phillies. Fortunately for the Thunder, the alternate sites were available because both teams were on the road at the time Trenton wanted to borrow their facilities.

Word of the rearranged schedule reached Runnells before his team traveled to Winter Haven to face Canton-Akron (the Indians' Double-A affiliate) for an afternoon exhibition game. "We might have to develop a slogan, 'Have Team Will Travel,'" Runnells said. "It is something that is out of our control, so we're not going to lose any sleep. I think everybody was real excited for the season-opener up there and hopeful that the stadium would have been done when it was scheduled to be, but I've been through similar situations." The new proposed home-opening date at Waterfront Park was April 27 against the Albany-Colonie Yankees.

Back in Florida, the scores of the Thunder's 20 exhibition games were largely irrelevant. Clark began showing signs that he could carry the team on his broad shoulders at the plate. Mashore dazzled with his outfield throwing arm and some of the outrageous things he said. The pitching staff weeded itself into a five-man rotation that included right-handers Brian Edmondson, Ken Carlyle, Shannon Withem, Dave Mysel, and 20-year-old lefty Trever Miller. All was prelude to the season-opener April 8 at Harrisburg's RiverSide Stadium against the defending Eastern League champion Senators.

From the outset of spring training, Runnells knew his team had too many question marks to be considered an Eastern League contender. He also knew that the Tigers didn't have enough free-agent talent to bolster his chances at the Double-A level, no matter how many season tickets had been sold in New Jersey. Detroit wasn't going to spend a lot of money to sign anyone to help the Thunder, either. (The manager would later say that was one of his greatest laments about the season.) The talent situation presented a major quandary for Runnells. Instead of prospects (Clark and DuBose were the two names most prominently mentioned as potential big-league players), he would be given a major helping of frustrated veterans and career farmhands on their last legs as professional athletes. Unlike the 1940s, when minor leaguers last roamed Dunn Field in Trenton and many played well into their thirties, the name of the game in the 1990s was player development, producing big-league talent to help the major-league club at all costs. In 1994, Detroit was widely recognized as one of the weakest farm systems in Major League Baseball.

To say that lack of baseball skill was the biggest of the Thunder's worries as the '94 season began, however, would be to misjudge the situation entirely. The rain and melting ice that covered the county-owned plot of land in Trenton's South Ward proved to be the franchise's most significant hurdle from the outset.

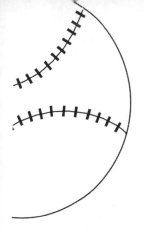

CHAPTER 5

From Anticipation to Reality

> "I really don't believe that this team has developed the character that it needs to—or is going to—yet. The seed is planted. The seed is there. I think it's a matter of them playing a few games together, going through some of this traveling."
>
> —1994 THUNDER MANAGER TOM RUNNELLS

By the first week of April 1994, the Tigers' Double-A roster had been finalized. All of the Thunder players had grown tired of Fetzer Hall, and they were ready to head north to Trenton in preparation for the franchise's first-ever game at Harrisburg. Opening-night pitcher Brian Edmondson, a right-handed, 21-year-old native of Riverside, California, loaded all his belongings into the bed of his black 1992 Toyota pick-up truck and drove Interstate 95 through Georgia, North Carolina, and Virginia to the Garden State. (At the time, the truck had less than 60,000 miles on the odometer. By August 1996, when he pitched for Binghamton, the truck had more than 120,000 miles on it.) During this 1994 trip north, Edmondson's new wife, Plant City, Florida, native Melanie (whom he met while pitching for Single-A Lakeland), occupied the seat beside him. Clark and Mashore drove to Trenton in Mashore's white 1993 Ford Probe; Mashore's wife Melissa and Clark's girlfriend Fran filled the other two seats. Gradually, the Thunder players who had their cars with them during spring training arrived at the Palmer Inn on U.S. Route 1 in West Windsor, New Jersey. "I hope it doesn't rain, or all of our stuff is going to get wet," Edmondson said after analyzing the overcast skies and covering the bed of his truck with a plastic liner.

Runnells and a small group that included Perona and Mendenhall touched down at the Newark Airport on Wednesday morning, April 6. They were greeted by Thunder officials for the first time and shuttled to the Palmer Inn, where Runnells coordinated the night's accommodations for his players. Part travel secretary and part field skipper, Runnells always carried a thick, notebook-sized leather organizer when his team was on the road. It was the only way to keep track of 23 young men, their wives, and their varied lifestyles.

Welcoming the players as they entered the lobby of the Palmer Inn was former London Tigers owner Dick Stanley, a middle-aged Staten Island resident who would help smooth the transition from Ontario to New Jersey for the Tigers' farmhands. Stanley would serve as the Thunder's official contact with Eastern League President John Levenda, a conduit through which information would be channeled during the field delays that plagued the early part of the season. On April 6, he worked with the front-desk personnel at the Palmer Inn to make sure that each and every team member's accommodations were agreeable. The Thunder franchise would pay for three nights at $42 per night while the players looked for permanent lodging in the Trenton area.

Outside the Palmer Inn's red brick facade, in the shadow of Route 1, hung a large white sign trumpeting the location as the "Official host hotel of the Trenton Thunder." Thousands of motorists passed the sign during their daily commutes. Situated approximately nine miles north of Waterfront Park, the Palmer was the closest Mercer County hotel with the necessary amenities to host visiting Double-A teams. Within walking distance of a mall and several restaurants, the hotel was tucked neatly into one of the busiest commuter corridors in the country. Trenton itself, however, was an urban shell, a slowly decaying metropolitan center that did not have a hotel within its city limits at the time of the Thunder's arrival.

Trenton was still very new to Runnells. After checking into the hotel, he shared many of his players' questions as he stepped into Charlie Brown's restaurant for a cup of coffee and order of chicken fingers. Wearing a pair of jeans, a dress shirt, and loafers, the manager discussed his hopes and fears for the 1994 campaign.

"I'm excited about the season," he said, his deep Florida spring training tan accentuating the lines around his eyes. "But we didn't really have the team we were going to break camp with until the last day or two, so there are still a lot of unanswered questions for me. It's warmer than the last time I was here, and it's wet.

"But hey, the people here have been absolutely tremendous. The reception to this team coming in has been tremendous. People are bending over backwards to help us out. I'm very, very happy, very pleased. The rest, I think, remains to be seen until we go out on the field and see what happens."

The postponement of the originally scheduled grand opening Thunder Waterfront Park gala from April 16 to April 27 didn't seem to faze the manager, at least outwardly. "Well, whether I like it or not, it's something we have to deal with; the players have to deal with," he said. "We're not going to hold that as any type of crutch or any excuse for what happens. We still have to go out and play the game on the field.

"I think it's going to be fun because I think we're going to see some parks that we normally wouldn't get to see. We're going to get an opportunity to play in Veterans Stadium. A lot of the kids may never again get that opportunity."

At 8:30 AM on April 7, with driver Alfred Reed behind the wheel of Starr Tours Bus No. 108, the Thunder rolled west along the Pennsylvania Turnpike to Exit 19 and Harrisburg's RiverSide Stadium. They conducted a brief, 11 AM workout on the Senators' soggy home field. Afterward, the players and coaches settled into their two-to-a-room suites at the Harrisburg Hilton.

On the eve of the Thunder's long-awaited debut, veteran outfielder Brian

Saltzgaber assessed the team's prospects. The 26-year-old Saltzgaber was one of Runnells' favorites, a utility player who could man any position on a baseball diamond. "Salty" had been a member of Runnells' 1993 London squad. In fact, he was the only member of that team to be named Eastern League Player of the Week during the season, a distinction he earned while filling in for an injured teammate, outfielder Danny Bautista.

"We look pretty good so far," Saltzgaber said in his hotel room as Decillis lounged on the twin bed across from him with an amused look on his face. "I'm excited about this team. I didn't know at first—there were a lot of question marks. But I think the chemistry of guys is a lot better this year than it was last year. Last year . . . we had some bad apples. When things were tough, they would start talking about things, trying to bring other guys down. I don't see that happening this year."

Later that evening, in the dimly lit hotel bar aptly named "The Bar," Saltzgaber, Decillis, and Guilfoyle—the London veterans—gathered for a few libations. They talked about beginning another season at the Double-A level. They laughed and relived stories from their years on the road together, meeting young women and playing ball. They wondered openly if Trenton could ever live up to the memories they shared from London. To a man, they trumpeted the friendly Canadian town as a great place to be a minor-league baseball player. Decillis had met his wife there; as such, his love for Ontario would forever be intertwined with that relationship. By midnight, the gathering began to break up. One by one, the players trekked back to the elevator and their rooms. Late-night cable television and in-room movies would entertain them for the next few hours.

OPENING NIGHT

Friday, April 8, 1994, began with a rising curtain of cold sunlight in the Pennsylvania capital. The Thunder players and coaches spent the morning hours either sleeping or milling around Strawberry Square, an indoor mall/food court attached to the Hilton by an elevated walkway. Also on hand was the Thunder radio broadcasting team of McCarthy and Simonetta. The 25-year-old McCarthy and 34-year-old Simonetta had spent the last few months helping the team's small front-office staff plan everything from billboard sales to single-game ticket plans. For this radio pair, opening night represented a first glimpse at the young men they would chronicle on the air for the next 5 months. Together, the broadcasters formed a unique pair. On opening night, they would begin a 140-game synthesis of style and approach. McCarthy could hardly contain his enthusiasm—or his desire to create a strong impression on the new audience back in the Garden State. As the Thunder completed batting practice, he interviewed Runnells for the first segment of the nightly manager's report.

As the hours counted down to the first pitch of the inaugural Thunder season, 80-year-old team partner and Trenton native Sam Plumeri, Sr., leaned back on a couch in the Hilton lobby. His father had owned one of the top semi-pro teams that played at Dunn Field during the 1930s. Pride and anticipation decorated his face as he pondered the significance of the Thunder's arrival. The culmination of his efforts to return minor-league baseball to his hometown for the first time in 44 years would take place later that evening. "Isn't this great?" he mused. "Best thing to happen in Trenton in decades." For the next 3 years, Plumeri would be a constant in the Thunder clubhouse. Win or lose, he was always on hand to offer a kind word to the players.

The first group of Thunder players to board the team bus for the 5-minute ride halfway across the swollen Susquehanna River included the 6-foot-8 Clark, who carried with him an equipment bag full of expectations and a playing résumé of unfulfilled promise. He—and everyone associated with Detroit— hoped that 1994 would be his breakthrough season, but that prospect depended largely on his health.

By 4:30 PM, as the sun began its descent behind the outfield wall of River-Side Stadium, a second Trenton bus made the short trek to City Island Park. The temperature hovered in the fifties. The Thunder players donned their generic, dark-green-mesh batting-practice jerseys, but because the jerseys had arrived so late at the Thunder offices, they had no numbers on the back. The only distinguishing mark was the blue, two-headed Thunderbird logo on the left breast of the shirt. The jerseys became an immediate source of humor in the Thunder clubhouse, starting with DuBose, whose chatter would form a back-drop for the season. "Hey, I look like the Green Lantern," he shouted, referring to the cartoon character. "We look like Leprechauns," Runnells told McCarthy tongue-in-cheek.

DuBose's light-hearted banter wasn't the only comic relief on display in this first-ever Thunder pregame clubhouse. On the inside of the exit door was a fax from the Detroit Tigers front office, posted and signed by big-league manager Sparky Anderson and General Manager Joe Klein. "To Tom Runnells, Trenton Thunder. Good luck in your 1994 season opener. Go get 'em, Thunder." The missive was self-explanatory, except for one additional signature in black ink. That signature belonged to Saltzgaber. The veteran player had pulled off his first prank of the season, and the first pitch had yet to be thrown.

The first-ever Thunder batting practice ended without incident, and an opening-night crowd of 5253 filed into 6300-seat RiverSide Stadium. Among those passing through the turnstiles were Mercer County Executive Prunetti and Plumeri. Trenton Mayor Douglas H. Palmer was unable to attend the game due to an untimely row-house fire that raged out of control back in the New Jersey capital earlier in the day. The blaze, which gutted a portion of a block on Locust Street, occupied the mayor's undivided attention. In Palmer's stead, Prunetti would throw out the symbolic first pitch with Harrisburg Mayor Steve Reed.

Inside the Thunder clubhouse, pitcher Brian Edmondson sat on a padded training table near the back of the room. His long black sleeves framed a lanky, 165-pound frame. He would wear No. 16 in the Thunder's gray road garb. He stared at the curious black hat with blue brim that he would wear to the mound. His thoughts ran the gamut from pitching to family—and his unsa-tiated desire to win a Double-A baseball game. A fourth-round pick in the June 1991 draft out of Norte Vista High School, he had received a $90,000 signing bonus. "I would have signed for five bucks," he admitted. He had been called up to London from Single-A Lakeland during the last month of the '93 season, losing four of his five starts and finishing with an 0-4 record and a 6.26 ERA after going 8-5 with a 2.99 ERA in 19 Single-A appearances. During his second season at the Double-A level, he was making $1600 a month. "I'm proud to be the first Trenton starter," he said. The second-youngest member of the Thunder rotation, Edmondson had relied on a slider, a change-up, and a sneaky fastball to get him to the Double-A level. His determination to start the year on a positive note was obvious as he walked toward the visitor's bullpen to begin his warm-up tosses.

At 6:52 PM, Harrisburg public address announcer Bob Morgan introduced the 1994 Thunder lineup for the first time. Before the starters were announced, the reserves and pitchers trotted out of the dugout to the third-base line.

Inside each of the odd-looking baseball suits was a unique tale waiting to be shared with Thunder fans. There was relief pitcher Pat Ahearne, a star of Pepperdine University's 1992 College World Series Championship. There was relief pitcher Matt Bauer, a 24-year-old lefty who had jumped two levels from Fayetteville to Trenton. There was 27-year-old utility infielder Joe Delli Carri, a member of the Binghamton Mets' 1992 Eastern League championship team who had been traded from New York to Detroit. Delli Carri was one of two New Jersey residents on the initial Thunder roster (Guilfoyle was the other). There was 22-year-old right-handed pitcher Dave Mysel, who was celebrating a homecoming of sorts because he grew up in nearby Hummelstown. None of them earned more than $2000 a month. And there was trainer Lon Pinhey, the quick-witted medic who would spend the entire '94 season without the benefit of modern training facilities at Waterfront Park because they weren't finished in time.

After the pitchers and reserves took their places, the first-ever Thunder batting order made its way from the dugout. One-by-one, the players doffed their new caps for the crowd. Batting leadoff—and accepting the first pitch in a minor-league game involving Trenton since 1950—was second baseman Kelley O'Neal, a 23-year-old from Belleville, Michigan.

Batting second was Kirk Mendenhall, the 26-year-old journeyman shortstop who had spent time both in the Triple-A and the Double-A level over the last three seasons. Mendenhall hit .204 for Runnells in '93, so the manager wasn't expecting any offensive heroics from the Illinois native, just solid defense. Batting third was DuBose, the ebullient Detroit native who grew up on the mean streets of one of the nation's most troubled urban landscapes, became a three-sport high-school star, and was signed by his hometown Tigers. Much was expected of "Doobie" in '94. Batting clean-up was Clark, who would establish himself not only as the best player on the inaugural Thunder roster but one of the true class acts of the Eastern League. The challenge of succeeding at the next level, of putting the ghosts of enormous potential behind him, was his only motivation.

Hitting fifth was another London veteran, 23-year-old first baseman Mike Rendina. For the El Cajon, California native, '94 was a make-or-break season. It also was his sixth season in the minors, meaning that if Detroit elected not to place him on the 40-man major-league roster at the conclusion of the year, he would become a six-year free agent, and he would be free to sign with any organization. If he improved on his 77 RBI performance of the '93 season, he might get to the next level. He was an above-average fielder, but like Clark, he possessed minimal speed on the basepaths. Runnells knew that for the Thunder to be competitive at all in an Eastern League stacked with prospects, Clark and Rendina would have to be the big one-two offensive punch—"Murderer's Row," he dubbed them.

Batting sixth was Dean Decillis, the Florida native who left baseball at the beginning of the '93 season only to return later in the summer at Runnells' behest and wind up with a .293 average. Next in the order was Darren Milne, the Brigham Young University product who rarely spoke voluntarily but always had something insightful to say when questioned about the game. Milne came to the Double-A level with plenty of expectations and a brand-new wife, Jill. Batting eighth was 24-year-old catcher Pete Gonzalez, a journeyman Latin player who was considered a better defensive catcher than Perona. During his ascent up the minor-league ladder, Gonzalez had played with Los Angeles catcher Mike Piazza.

Finally, opening the season in the No. 9 hole was the player Runnells eventually hoped to groom for the leadoff, 22-year-old Justin Mashore. Through spring training, Mashore had Runnells banging his head against a wall trying to get through to the young player, who had been voted the best defensive outfielder in the Florida State League in 1993. Mashore was a center fielder, but he also was California relocated to the Eastern seaboard—in a nutshell, he was laid back.

"I think it was just a feeling of excitement," Mashore said about his emotions before his first game at the Double-A level. "You're ready to get the season started. You feel like you're on top of the world. Nobody feels any pressure."

At 7:03 PM, the National Anthem wafted through City Island Park, signaling the start of the Thunder's first Eastern League season. Prunetti was escorted to the mound by Reed for his long-awaited ceremonial first pitch. Outfitted in a black satin jacket with green trim and Thunder logo, the county executive fired a strike to Harrisburg catcher Rob Fitzpatrick. After the ball was returned as a souvenir, he retreated to his seat to enjoy the game as several Thunder fans stopped by to exchange pleasantries and even thank him for his tireless efforts to return minor-league baseball to Trenton.

PLAY BALL

At 7:11 PM, the first pitch in Thunder history was delivered from right-hander Rod Henderson to O'Neal. It was a ball high that landed firmly in Fitzpatrick's glove with an authoritative pop. Inside the crowded press box, Skip Hutter barked out the game's starting time. The season was underway. With one off-target delivery—one fleeting instant—the Thunder crossed the threshold from anticipation to reality. O'Neal proceeded to smack a Henderson offering to center fielder Yamil Benitez for the first out in franchise annals. He was followed in short order by strikeouts from Mendenhall (swinging) and DuBose (looking).

Unfazed by Henderson's impressive start, Edmondson approached the mound in attack mode. His first delivery was a called strike that Gonzalez coaxed over the heart of the plate. Third baseman Matt Rundels struck out looking, as did Benitez for the third out. Sandwiched in between was a swinging strikeout by second baseman Mike Hardge. In the first inning of the first

Thunder game, Edmondson had struck out the side—with authority. It was quite an auspicious start. In the radio booth, McCarthy and Simonetta chronicled the first inning with a strange sense of novelty. History was theirs to relay back to the Delaware Valley.

"I was somewhat intimidated," McCarthy recalled, describing his opening-night mood as "timid." "I didn't know much about them. I wanted them to like Trenton, but we were still matching names with faces."

They chronicled Clark's first Double-A at-bat to begin the second inning. Big Tony struck out looking at one of Henderson's best pitches. Rendina walked to become the Thunder's first base runner but was stranded at first as Decillis popped out to second and Milne lined out to left field.

Feeding off the emotion of his perfect first inning, Edmondson forced the Senators' clean-up hitter, Jeff Kipila, to ground out to third base to begin the Harrisburg second. That's when the young righty ran into trouble. As a pitcher who relied heavily on control, Edmondson knew he had to paint the corners of the plate to be effective. He wasn't going to blow Double-A hitters away with his mid-80-mph fastball. With right fielder Kevin Northrup at the plate and left fielder Tyrone Horne at first after touching the Thunder for the first single in Trenton franchise annals, Edmondson worked the count to 2-1. Gonzalez put the signal down: slider. Edmondson left the ball high over the plate. With a loud pop, Northrup sent the pitch sailing over the left-field fence for a 2-0 lead. Just like that, the defending league champs had an early cushion, and Edmondson had barely settled into a groove as Morgan exhorted the crowd over the loudspeaker. Runnells signaled his pitcher to calm down and regain focus.

"It was just one of those mistakes that never should have happened, had I been thinking," Edmondson said after throwing 89 pitches over five complete innings. "It cost us, and I take full responsibility."

"He left it up, and it came back over the plate," Runnells added. "Brian's a sinker-ball pitcher, and that was one of the few bad pitches he made all evening."

When Harrisburg added an unearned run on three Thunder errors in the third inning, it became clear this would not be the night for Edmondson to break his Double-A funk. With one out in the top of the fourth, DuBose finally ended Henderson's stranglehold with the first base hit in Thunder history, a single to right. "Doobie," however, was stranded when the power guys—Clark and Rendina—grounded out and struck out, respectively.

Edmondson gave way to Bauer in the sixth, and the lefty allowed one earned run that gave the Senators a 4-0 cushion. Northrup scored his second run of the night after hitting a leadoff double. In the top of the seventh, DuBose added a pair of distinctions to his line, stroking a leadoff double to left off reliever Carlos Perez and crossing the plate on Clark's sacrifice fly to become the first Thunder player to have an extra base hit and score a run. The RBI was the first that Big Tony would plate in 4 eventful months with the Thunder.

Even so, Runnells' club went quietly—1-2-3—in the top of the ninth as Mendenhall and DuBose hit lazy fly balls to the outfield and Clark struck out for the second time to end the game. Harrisburg had a 4-1 win, and Runnells had plenty to complain to his players about in a brief postgame address. Three errors in one inning was the most pressing topic. From day one, the manager insisted that this team had no margin for such miscues. The look on his face during the first postgame press conference in Thunder history told the story of a man in distress.

"I think everybody was fairly relaxed," Runnells said. "We just didn't hit the ball." "You can't give them a three-run lead and expect to win," Edmondson added. "I was trying to take advantage of the adrenaline, and I burned myself by trying to use it too much." Edmondson's final line was five hits allowed, three runs, three walks, and seven strike-outs. Henderson allowed two hits in six full innings, walking one and striking out seven, then gave way to Perez, who earned his first save of the season. One year later, Perez was in the big leagues as an eccentric but effective Montreal starter.

In any sport, there is an unwritten rule that nobody should look happy in the losing locker room or clubhouse. The Thunder's first-ever postgame session was no different. DuBose was 2-for-4 with a double and his team's only run, but the Green Lantern wasn't in the mood for frivolity. The players dressed quietly and headed to the bus for the short ride back to the Hilton. Some went directly to their rooms for late-night pizza and private time with wives and girlfriends. Others, like Guilfoyle and Perona, headed for a Second Street watering hole named Zembie's. Home of the best buffalo wings on the 10-team Eastern League circuit, Zembie's is a living, breathing memorial to the Harrisburg Senators. On the walls are souvenirs from previous teams, including a list of Harrisburg alumni who have gone on to the big leagues. Following Harrisburg's opening-night victory, Zembie's was so crowded that the establishment had to stop admitting patrons not to violate the fire code.

BACK TO WORK

The second game of the opening series was a 2:05 afternoon matinee pitting Trever Miller against the Expos' highly regarded prospect Scott Gentile. The pitcher's duel never materialized, however, because Gentile couldn't throw the ball over home plate from the outset. The right-hander from Berlin, Connecticut, walked six Thunder batters in the first inning, allowing four runs in the process. O'Neal led off with a free pass. In order, Gentile also walked Decillis, DuBose, and Clark. Four men up, four men on. Unable to right the ship, he unleashed two wild pitches to help the Thunder cause before Perona smacked a two-run double to right field. As a result, Gentile didn't last the inning. He was pulled by Senators' manager Dave Jauss in favor of lefty Mike Mimbs after recording just two outs. "He had a big case of the jitters," Perona said during the postgame celebration as teammates cautioned him not to say anything he might regret later.

Miller cruised through five strong innings, allowing only two hits, walking two, and striking out one. He yielded a double to left fielder Horne in the second inning and a single to second baseman Hardge in the third before giving way to left-handed reliever Brian Maxcy. Maxcy was extremely effective over three innings, allowing only one hit and striking out three. Pitching coach Rich Bombard liked what he saw from Maxcy. He was equally impressed by right-handed closer Phil Stidham, who slammed the door on the Senators in the ninth inning to preserve the first-ever Thunder victory, a 4-0 shutout. The book on Stidham was that he reported to spring training overweight and out of shape. That probably cost him a shot at Triple-A Toledo to begin the season.

In the clubhouse, the Thunder players seemed very appreciative of Gentile's gift, also knowing they hadn't given their best effort during the season's first 2 days. "I didn't have my best stuff," Miller admitted. "I had a good sinker on my fastball, but my curve was a little short. But when you get a big lead early, you can go out there and relax."

Runnells dismissed notions his club felt pressure to win. "It's only the second game of the season," he replied.

Back in the radio booth, McCarthy and Simonetta took care of details first and gradually began to decipher personalities. It would be a slow but gratifying process. "I wanted to relish that first series," McCarthy said, "but we really didn't get to sit down and talk to the players until the second day. There was still a lot to do." On the contrary, Runnells and his players seemed to accept McCarthy as a member of their circle almost immediately. He would serve as a valuable conduit between the Thunder front office, the Mercer County government, the fans, and the team. Simonetta, on the other hand, quickly earned the nickname "Greg Brady" for his facial resemblance to the 1970s television character. He took the ribbing in stride, though. After all, it was a long way from law school and the stodgy corporate banking world of Manhattan.

In game three, the Thunder received another fine pitching performance, this time from right-hander Ken Carlyle. A blond Memphis, Tennessee, native who possessed a very business-like approach to the art of pitching, Carlyle spread three hits over six full innings to outduel the Senators' Miguel Batista on a very soggy RiverSide Stadium field. The start of the game was delayed 13 minutes as Harrisburg groundskeepers tried to groom the surface. Rain intensified early in the game, but the action continued at the discretion of umpires Mark Erramouspe and Larry Musolino. "It's ridiculous," Runnells said afterward. "I truly can't believe that we continued to play in that." During the fifth inning, Clark tripped over the first-base bag and dirtied the front of his gray size-50 uniform. Several deep breaths were taken in the Thunder dugout, but Big Tony rose from the spill without any noticeable side effects.

The Thunder scored two runs in the second inning on a two-run single by Gonzalez and went ahead 3-0 in the fourth when Gonzalez singled to left. The Senators countered with one run off Carlyle in the bottom of the fourth, but once again, the Thunder bullpen (regarded as the team's biggest asset) did the job. Ahearne, Guilfoyle, and righty Rick Greene pitched the final three innings, with the 6-foot-5 Greene earning the first save in Thunder history. "I've been feeling good since spring training, and I just swung the bat well tonight," Gonzalez said. "He looked like a different person, both offensively and defensively," Runnells added. "He called a good game, caught a good game, and made some good throws to second base."

In three games, the Thunder had outscored the defending Eastern League champions 8-5, a very promising start. Clark left the Pennsylvania capital with two RBIs, while Miller and Carlyle served notice they had the stuff to compete favorably on the Double-A level. "Taking this series is good, definitely," Guilfoyle said as he dressed for the short ride back to Trenton.

As for the field his team left behind in Harrisburg, Runnells said, "Those conditions were the worst I've ever played in." Back in Trenton, the rush to complete the Waterfront Park playing surface would cast that statement in a whole new light.

CHAPTER 6

Road Warriors

"I'll say it again. This is truly more like a big-league atmosphere than it is a minor-league atmosphere. I think the kids need to really enjoy this and learn from it."

—1994 THUNDER MANAGER TOM RUNNELLS

On the evening of Monday, April 11, 1994, six-hundred expectant fans packed Angeloni's Cedar Gardens banquet hall in Hamilton, New Jersey, to officially welcome the Thunder players and coaches to the Trenton area. While Perona, Guilfoyle, Mysel, Saltzgaber, and O'Neal signed autographs by the bar area to one side of the room, DuBose and Clark also were besieged by admirers. With his outgoing personality, DuBose was a natural with the crowds. He quickly blended into the Trenton scene as effortlessly as if he had lived in the neighborhood for all of his 22 years. At 6-foot-8, Clark also was an immediate target of attention. He obliged as many of the team's new fans as he could with a smile and a greeting while McCarthy and Thunder officials began settling the players into their places at the head table, which was two-tiered to accommodate all of the players and dignitaries.

At first, the Double-A players seemed somewhat overwhelmed, some not believing that all the hoopla could be for them. "This is shocking, really," said Clark. "They must really love their baseball here."

Also seated at the head table were Prunetti, McCarthy, Simonetta, and Hodes. Following dinner—pencil point pasta with marinara sauce and salad—and player introductions, Runnells stepped to the microphone. He put up a bold front about his team's level of talent. Excerpting a Harrisburg newspaper account of the Thunder's opening-night loss that had been written by *Patriot-News* beat writer Andrew Linker, he claimed that the '94 Thunder were more than just a recycled version of the '93 London Tigers. Deep down, however, Runnells knew the speech was a bluff, that he really had the "worst Double-A team" he had ever managed. Lost in the promising reality that the Thunder had taken two of three games from Harrisburg was the grim fact that they had only hit .151 during the series and committed six errors in the first two games.

"I can't tell you how pleased we are to be in this city," the manager told the Angeloni's crowd. "It's really a nice gesture to have this dinner for us, and though I came up here with a team full of surprises, I can guarantee you we'll give 100 percent on the field."

Playing to the enthusiastic gathering, Runnells introduced Prunetti as "the next governor of New Jersey." The county executive quickly delivered an update on the stadium's construction status.

"We still have the 27th as our opening date, and we're going to make it," he said forcefully. "I thought we could control everything, but there was one man I couldn't control . . . and that was God. So everyone just say a little prayer so we can have Waterfront Park ready for you to enjoy very soon."

During early April 1994, after the Waterfront opener had been postponed from April 16 to April 27, the Thunder's first individual-game tickets went on sale at their temporary offices, which had been relocated from the 400 to the 200 Building of the Riverview Executive Plaza. According to McCarthy, that morning represented a turning point for the franchise. "That's when the full effect of what we were doing took its toll. You could see, from the questions we received, that people didn't know much about the Thunder. I remember it was a cold day, and there was a line of over 500 people. We were giving out donuts. I guess that's when we really knew it would work in Trenton. It's like they say, 'Seeing is believing.'" The Welcome North Dinner was a continuation of that visual proof.

As the Thunder boarded their Starr bus to Harry Grove Stadium in Frederick, Maryland, temporary home of the Bowie Baysox, for a four-game series April 12–15, many of the players had yet to find living quarters in the Trenton area. Frustrated by the steep cost of housing, DuBose spoke out about the lack of suitable arrangements that had been made through Mercer County contacts. "I thought it was going to be much easier [to find accommodations]," he said. "Nobody really wants to rent for less than a 6-month lease, so it's hard. I thought something was going to be available for us already." Mashore and Clark signed a 3-month lease for a two-bedroom, one-bathroom apartment at the Korman Suites in Bensalem, Pennsylvania, about 20 minutes from Waterfront Park. Edmondson and Miller also decided to live together at the Korman Suites, which cost $900 a month for a two-bedroom unit. Said Mashore, "I don't know if signing a lease takes a burden off my mind, because now I don't have any money."

Mercer County officials weren't happy about this development. The whole point of bringing the team to Trenton was to help enhance the city's image. The matter of securing low-cost residences for the players before they arrived in town would be one of the major lessons of the inaugural Thunder season. "The most difficult thing [about the transition from London to Trenton] is a lot of the turmoil in dealing with the front office and not having a lot of the things preset," Runnells noted. "I don't think everything is written out yet with this club. The housing situation is extremely difficult to this point for the players."

TRAVELING SHOW

On April 12 in Frederick, Shannon Withem made his Double-A debut before an announced crowd of 423. The Thunder took a 1-0 lead against Bowie starter

Scott Klingenbeck in the top of the fifth on Milne's double and a Baysox error. In the bottom of the inning, Bowie rallied for three runs on five hits, chasing Withem from the game. His final line read: six innings, eight hits, two walks, and three strike-outs. The Baysox added a pair of runs against Guilfoyle in the eighth for a 5-2 victory that dropped the Thunder record to 2-2. After an 0-for-6 start in Harrisburg, Milne was 2-for-2 with a pair of walks. Ironically, he left his prescription contact lenses at the team hotel and played without them. "Maybe I won't wear them again," he deadpanned, but Runnells and Bradshaw weren't buying into Milne's theory. "He was working the counts into his favor and he was able to be aggressive," Bradshaw explained.

As the Thunder boarded the bus, Guilfoyle comically summed up the team's extended travel plans: "We're like the cloud that carries the Thunder, just floating from one place to another." Saddled with a similar predicament as they awaited the completion of their new 10,000-seat home, Prince George's Stadium, the Bowie players were determined to make the most of their Frederick experience. After all, many of them (including Klingenbeck) had played at Grove Stadium during their Single-A days. "But it gets rough, just living out of a hotel," the pitcher said. "That's the toughest part about spring training. By the time it's over, we're already tired of living out of a suitcase."

The second day of the transplanted series brought a late-afternoon thunderstorm that inundated the Frederick playing surface and postponed Mysel's Double-A debut. The 6-foot-5 righty had been placed in the starting rotation to get as many innings as possible. With the hardest fastball of the five starters, Mysel's future was in the bullpen; however, the rain-out meant that the teams would play a doubleheader (all minor-league twin-bill games are seven innings apiece, as opposed to the big-league standard nine) the following day at 6 PM. Mysel, who was celebrating his 23rd birthday on April 13, had not faced live batters since April 5 during an intrasquad spring training game back in Lakeland. Instead of pitching that day, he enjoyed dinner with his father, Gary. "One thing I dislike about being a starter is rain-outs, because I spent all morning going through my routines and got over to the stadium around four for the game," Mysel said.

Back in his hotel room, Runnells admitted, "With all the days off we've had, a four-man pitching rotation might have been better for us at the outset of this season. A lot of this was unforeseeable as far as the rain-outs and rescheduling, but we have to get a look at these kids. They are the future."

Turning to the ongoing effort to complete Waterfront by the new April 27 deadline, the manager added, "I know everyone back in Trenton is anxious to get things underway, but the field may not be there as expected on the date expected. At some point there is going to be some good baseball there, and I would tend to say, 'Let's don't rush it and do it improperly. Let's take the time needed and get things done the way they should be done.' I think people will appreciate it and enjoy it more when it's completely finished."

Because doubleheader games are shortened to seven innings in the minors, an early lead is a big advantage. As Mysel finally walked to the mound for his elusive first start of the season, he was hoping for a little offensive support. Through four games, the Thunder had just 18 hits.

After recording the first out, Mysel twisted his right ankle following through on a pitch. Shortly after the injury, he yielded a three-run homer to Bowie second baseman Edgar Alfonzo. The home-run pitch was a slider that hung long enough for Alfonzo to deposit it over the left-field fence. Later, Mysel admitted that he probably should have come out of the game but that "I hadn't pitched in 9 days, so I wanted to stay out there." In spite of the ice packed tightly around his ankle, Mysel insisted, "I'm not going to miss any time because of this. I'm not going to let it bother me." Ahearne relieved the injured Mysel after the first inning and allowed just one run over four innings, but the Thunder were overmatched by Baysox lefty Vaughn Eshelman. Clark and Perona had RBI singles in the 4-2 loss, which was witnessed by an announced crowd of 546. While wife Melissa videotaped the action, Mashore enjoyed his first multi-hit game at the Double-A level, finishing 2-for-3 with a run scored.

In the nightcap, Edmondson allowed just three hits over five innings but nonetheless fell to a 0-2 record with a 3-2 loss. "What do I have to do to get a win in this league?" he wondered afterward. Bowie starter Rick Forney scattered three hits to earn the victory, but one of them was the first homer in Thunder history—a two-run shot to left-center by DuBose. Through 4 2/3 innings, Forney had a perfect game. He was relieved by closer Armando Benitez in the seventh, and the hard-throwing (98-mph fastball) righty recorded the final two outs for his third save in the Baysox's first five games. With the win, Bowie improved to a 5-0 record. DuBose's seventh-inning homer did little to improve the mood in the Trenton clubhouse. In fact, Doobie didn't really want to talk about his historic hit. "It's always nice to get a homer," Runnells said. "We'll have to see if he can keep doing it."

Following the Bowie sweep, the Thunder's focus returned to the travel itinerary, which included the first "home away from home" game against Reading on April 17 at Wilmington's Daniel S. Frawley Stadium. "A lot of things are up in the air, and we're trying to win games in the meantime," Perona explained. "Runnells tries to tell us that you can't use life on the road as an excuse. You've got to go out and play ball and forget about that."

"It's beating us up right now," added Bauer. "You spend a lot of money on the road out of your own pocket. You'd like to get home and play in front of the home crowd and get their support."

Before the final game in Frederick, word had arrived that Reading would start major-leaguer Larry Andersen in the April 17 game. During spring training, Andersen had undergone arthroscopic surgery on his left knee. As a reliever for the '93 National League Champion Philadelphia Phillies, he led the club in strikeouts-to-innings-pitched ratio. Andersen would drive to Wilmington from Veterans Stadium, make a rehabilitation appearance, and drive back to the big-league park to ice his knee. With improved minor-league facilities in the mid-1990s, most big-league clubs did not hesitate to send stars down to the farm to hone their skills. These "rehab" appearances also helped the minor leaguers feel a little bit closer to their ultimate destination. At the very least, they enjoyed the chance to test their skills against major-league competition.

HOME AWAY FROM HOME

On April 15, another off-day for the Thunder, Prunetti announced that the April 27 Waterfront opener was still an attainable goal. "At this point, there is no plan to push back the date," the county executive insisted, adding that an additional $400,000 had been appropriated by the county freeholders to cover the cost of construction-related overtime. By the time the Thunder began play in Wilmington, workers prepared to hoist the stadium's six lightstands into position around the park. The outfield fence was a red-steel skeleton where the billboards would be placed. Privately, several construction officials said that the April 27 deadline was "a pipe dream." Some said the county would be lucky to finish the stadium by May 11.

In the meantime, Hodes planned to use the Wilmington game as a test run for his front office and staff. The entire group was on hand as a crowd of 2608 filed into Daniel S. Frawley Stadium. While the Blue Rocks' game-day staff worked the game, Hodes asked his people to observe and learn. "We have four people on our staff with previous baseball experience," he said. "Those aren't the people I'm concerned with. I told the others, 'You better look at the baseball game with very different eyes than you have before as a fan.' When I sit down at any park, I notice all the advertising. I notice how hospitable the usher is. I notice the hot-dog guy, whether he's throwing stuff or whether he's handing it to the customers and saying, 'Thank you.' I can tell my staff all of that, but until they actually do it themselves . . . That's one of the positives that came out of this process even though we're not actually in Waterfront Park yet."

As the 40-year-old Andersen made his warm-up pitches in the visitors' bullpen, Prunetti, Plumeri, Maloney, and Caruso took their seats behind home plate. The transplanted game, which officially was considered a "home date" for the Thunder, was being played on Runnells' 39th birthday. His wife, Kathy, was in attendance, as were many curious Trenton backers who made the 70-mile drive south. The Thunder's players donned their white home uniforms with kelly green pinstripes for the first time. They looked somewhat more appealing than the dull gray road suits, although the strange numbers were the same.

Unfortunately for Runnells and the expectant crowd, Andersen's rehabilitation appearance was a dominant one. His off-speed deliveries baffled the Thunder hitters, who had not swung the bat well from the outset of the season. The 6-foot-3, 205-pound Andersen threw 35 pitches, 22 of them strikes, in two innings of work. He struck out five batters: Mashore, DuBose, Clark, Perona, and Milne. "He's not overpowering, but he picks his spots with the off-speed pitches well," Clark observed. "That creates a balance that helps his fastball."

Before departing the stadium, Andersen entertained a small group of media members at his locker. Known as one of the biggest pranksters in baseball, he laughed and declared his outing a success. "That's probably one of the better

Double-A games I've ever pitched in my life," he said with a smirk. "I don't want to get in trouble by saying what I should and shouldn't do, but right now I don't see any reason to continue going through simulations like this. My arm strength is there, and my velocity was there." Andersen was activated by the Phillies shortly after his appearance against the Thunder.

The major-league reliever was replaced by Craig Holman, who surrendered a solo homer to Milne but little else as Reading defeated the Thunder and pitcher Trever Miller 3-1. An RBI double by Phillies' designated hitter Mike Gomez and an RBI triple by third baseman Rob Grable in the fifth dropped the Thunder lefty to a 1-1 record. Gomez's hit was particularly painful because it came on an 0-2 count. "He was mine, but the ball floated over the plate," Miller lamented. Offensively, the Thunder struck out a season-high 13 times. The loss was the team's fourth in a row.

"It was a bad day from the get-go," Runnells said forlornly in the Wilmington manager's office. "We got a few more hits [eight], but we just couldn't get timely ones. That was the difference."

If there was a silver lining, it had to be Milne's fifth-inning homer, which cleared the right-field fence and earned a standing ovation from the partisan crowd. "It was a fastball on the outside part of the plate," he said. "The ball was really traveling to right, and T.R. told me to get the ball up and let it carry." In the radio booth, McCarthy pondered a signature home-run call that would soon make its debut. Looking for something unique, McCarthy eventually decided on, "Goodbye, John Levenda," in reference to the Eastern League President whose signature adorned the league's Rawlings ROM-EL baseballs. When McCarthy informed Levenda of the call, the president smiled and said, "I like that." McCarthy's enthusiastic refrain soon became familiar to the entire WTTM listening audience.

The following afternoon, the Thunder arrived early at Frawley Stadium to take extended batting practice. After 10 days on the road, the Thunder offensive chemistry was anything but potent. Their team batting average was .168, with only 15 runs in seven games. Facing Double-A pitching for the first time, the badly overmatched O'Neal was 0-for-20 and searching for answers. "I believe I'll start hitting; that's what you have to believe," he said. Gonzalez was hitting .267 with four RBIs, while Clark and Perona had three apiece. The pitching staff had a 3.11 ERA, a number which had kept the Thunder close in every game. "We've got to get in a rhythm and have some games back-to-back. We're all frustrated," Runnells said.

Facing Canton-Akron for the first time (before another small crowd of 406), the Thunder produced a season-high 10 hits but still lost 8-6 as Carlyle yielded six earned runs in 5 1/3 innings to even his record at 1-1. The evening featured the first Double-A homer of Clark's career, however, a two-run, fifth-inning smash off the Indians' Carlos Crawford that cleared the second tier of billboards in right-center field approximately 380 feet from the plate.

Watching the Thunder's fifth straight defeat with beer in hand was Waterfront Park contractor Donald Burris. "We'll make the April 27 date if it doesn't rain in the next three days," he claimed.

In the final game of the Wilmington series, Withem authored the finest pitching performance of the Thunder's brief nine-game existence. For seven overpowering innings, the 6-foot-3, 210-pound righty mixed his deliveries with impressive command. In fact, the Michigan native didn't allow a hit until the sixth inning, when Canton-Akron catcher Ryan Martindale lined a single to right. Ultimately, he allowed just one run—which was unearned—in the top of the first as Indians' shortstop Damian Jackson led off with a walk and scored on a pair of errors. Otherwise, Withem was nearly perfect, striking out nine batters.

"He had everything going," said Gonzalez. "His fastball was sinking hard, he had a good breaking ball, and his change-up was nasty."

Withem didn't figure into the decision, however, because the Thunder couldn't solve Canton-Akron starter Paul Byrd until the bottom of the eighth. With two outs in that frame, DuBose stroked a two-out single and tied the game on Clark's double. Rendina broke the game open with a two-run homer—his first of the year. As the ball caromed off the outfield fence, every member of the Thunder squad jumped out of the dugout, waving his arms in celebration. "I finally got one out," Rendina said with relief, "but Tony's double was the key hit." Ahearne pitched a scoreless ninth for his first save, and the Thunder had a 3-1 victory. The losing streak was over. "Now we can laugh on the bus again," DuBose shouted. In the background, Greene rolled up his towel and whipped anyone he could find. In the manager's office, Runnells praised Withem. "It would have been a real shame for us to lose that ballgame 1-0 after Shannon's effort," he said.

As the Thunder boarded the bus again, they couldn't help but bask in the moment. With a much-needed victory in hand, they were headed to Veterans Stadium for a rare glimpse of life in the majors. For most, the next two games against Canton-Akron at "the Vet" would be the thrill of their professional baseball career.

THE VET

For a pricetag of $25,000, Thunder officials decided to relocate two of the franchise's home-away-from-home games to the AstroTurf playing surface of 62,382-seat Veterans Stadium. It was a move that invigorated the team and prompted it to play some of its best offensive baseball of the '94 season. Furthermore, simply by dressing in the visitors' clubhouse at the Vet, home of the 1993 National League Champion Philadelphia Phillies, the Thunder players enjoyed a rare insight into a world of professional baseball that certainly was alien to Double-A players.

"It was available, the price was good, and we thought it would be a good chance for the players to see a marquee facility," McCarthy said of the decision to play a pair of games against Canton-Akron in the major-league ballpark.

When Runnells' Detroit farmhands arrived at the Vet during the morning hours of Wednesday, April 20, the dressing quarters must have seemed immense by Eastern League standards. Elongated rows of dressing cubicles ran the length of both clubhouse walls. An automatic soda fountain at the back of the room invited anyone who was thirsty for a free drink. A large rectangular table in the middle of the players' dressing area offered cold cuts and a variety of party trays with cheese and crackers. A big-screen television adjacent to the soda machine was tuned to cable sports network ESPN as several Trenton players congregated their locker stools in front of its large wooden cabinet. "I could get used to this," said Greene.

"When we heard we were going to play Trenton twice here, to a man we were excited," said Canton-Akron outfielder Marc Marini. "Obviously, everyone's goal is to play in a stadium like this every day, but one also has to be realistic. Not all of us are going to make it."

While the experience was a novel one for the Thunder's major-league prospects like Clark, Mashore, DuBose, Withem, Edmondson, Stidham, Maxcy, and Bauer, it was a bittersweet time for Runnells. Just 3 years before, as the 36-year-old skipper of the Montreal Expos, he had managed within these same confines.

Before the game, batting practice was lively on the Vet's sleek AstroTurf playing surface. Each group of hitters took turns trying to "jack one out of the yard." The players marveled at a bright yellow star located above one of the portals on the 500 level (upper deck), a mark that was placed to commemorate a home run hit by Pittsburgh Pirates' slugger Willie Stargell during the 1970s. Clark hit several balls over the tall green outfield fence, including one that landed in the second deck of left-field stands. In the process, Big Tony gained the attention of several Philadelphia television crews on hand to chronicle the minor-league invasion of their municipal stadium.

A curious crowd of 483, some of them just stopping by on their lunch break, littered the seats behind home plate by the start of the 1:05 PM game. Because all of the Eastern League stadiums had natural-grass playing surfaces, there was no way to gauge what kind of effect the hard—and extremely quick—AstroTurf would have on the Double-A players' ability to field balls. As the game progressed, the surface disrupted the Indians' defense several times.

The Thunder opened with three runs in the bottom of the first inning as Saltzgaber worked Canton-Akron starter Alan Embree (one of the Cleveland organization's top young pitching prospects) for a walk, stole second, and crossed the plate on an RBI single by Clark. Rendina plated Clark and Perona with a two-run single to right field. As Runnells applauded the offensive breakthrough (the Thunder had scored just 22 runs in their first nine games), Mysel struggled with his control. To his father Gary's dismay, he walked loaded bases in the first before striking out a pair of Indians—Marini and Clyde "Pork Chop" Pough—both looking. Mysel departed after four innings that yielded six hits and six walks.

From the outset, however, it was clear that the Thunder's unique big-league matinee wasn't going to evolve into a pitcher's duel. Trenton added four runs in the third to lead 7-0. During the rally, Clark smashed an RBI double and Decillis turned on an Embree fastball to accomplish the thrill of a lifetime—a two-run homer over the left-field wall of Veterans Stadium. He flashed a major-league grin as he rounded the bases and accepted congratulations from Runnells at the third-base corner.

"I was looking for the fastball, and I was able to put a good swing on it,"

Decillis said without trying to attach too much significance to the crowd-pleasing blast. "The ball was carrying well to left, that's all."

Despite trailing by seven runs, the Indians also wanted to capitalize on the big-league atmosphere. Sparked by Martindale's solo homer to lead off the fourth, Canton-Akron scored seven runs in the next three innings to trim the Thunder advantage to 9-7. Only a two-run homer by Perona in the fifth kept the game from being tied. It also was the Trenton catcher's second homer in a big-league park in as many seasons. (During the '93 campaign, he hit one out of Baltimore's Memorial Stadium, the former home of the Orioles where Bowie played its temporary games.)

With the Thunder clinging to a one-run advantage in the top of the ninth, Stidham came in from the plexiglass-enclosed left-field bullpen and slammed the door on another Canton-Akron rally to preserve a 10-9 win for Trenton. In two-thirds of an inning, the red-headed fireballer struck out one batter with the bases loaded and ended the game with a ground-out to second baseman Delli Carri. In all, the game featured 27 hits (16 by the Indians) and required 3 hours and 10 minutes to complete. Clark was 3-for-4 and Perona 2-for-4 with three RBIs and three runs scored. The victory went to Guilfoyle, who set up Stidham's heroics. Not since opening weekend in Harrisburg had the Thunder authored back-to-back victories. "The Vet is a great hitters park," Runnells observed. "Always has been, always will be."

Meanwhile, up in the broadcast booth, McCarthy and Simonetta also enjoyed their 2-day stint in the majors. "Just the set-up itself was incredible," McCarthy said. "We had four different places we could put our radio equipment." From a vantage point behind home plate, the Thunder radio tandem had a perspective on the action that wouldn't be duplicated during the '94 season. To begin with, they were approximately 50 feet above the field and set back much further from the action than in any Eastern League venue. "It's definitely different," McCarthy observed.

The feverish offensive pace of the 27-hit April 20 game kept the broadcasters busy. Adding to the challenge was the rare temptation to entertain a little fantasy in the booth and actually pretend they were calling a Phillies game. It was a time to savor. "It's so easy to see the ball here," Simonetta said. "The green-and-black background is outstanding. In the other parks, picking up the ball against a background of white billboards is something we're just getting used to." Unlike all Eastern League stadiums, which feature outfield-fence advertisements for everything from convenience stores to hospitals, major-league outfield walls were uncluttered with the details of the commercial world.

"There's a special feeling about this," McCarthy added during a brief respite from his dual role of media relations director and broadcaster. "One of McCarthy's adolescent role models was veteran New York Mets broadcaster Bob Murphy. In fact, McCarthy even named his Yellow Labrador Retriever "Murphy" in honor of his radio icon. Suddenly, if only for 2 days, he was sharing the seat where Murphy spent part of every National League season plying his trade. Like the players on the green carpet below, who had to pinch themselves on occasion as a reminder that this was just a temporary situation, McCarthy and Simonetta were afforded a few hours of electronic whimsy. It was heady stuff for a radio team that had been together just nine games when they hauled their equipment to the press level of the Vet.

On Thursday, April 21, after scoring 19 runs in their last three games, the Thunder hitters were exhibiting a new-found confidence. Perhaps it was the Vet's aforementioned outfield backdrop, which offered a very clear view of a pitched ball from the batter's box. There was a looseness in the Trenton clubhouse as the players dressed amidst the trappings of baseball luxury for a second consecutive day. Before batting practice, pitching coach Rich Bombard allowed the pitchers to conduct a rare relievers versus starters game, during which they took turns hitting. Nobody hit one out of the park, but Guilfoyle hiked up his pants and did his best Babe Ruth imitation.

Sideshows notwithstanding, the 1:05 game against the Indians belonged to Edmondson, who will always remember where he won his first Double-A game—because the crowd came disguised as 62,000 empty yellow-and-red seats. For the lanky Californian, it was the beginning of a season-long streak of success that would earn him a place on Detroit's 40-man major-league roster. While Edmondson spun a seven-inning, three-hit gem, the Thunder lineup produced a season-high 13 hits, including Clark's second homer of the season, a towering shot that astonished McCarthy, Simonetta, and 508 onlookers.

"We hadn't seen a ball hit that hard or get out of the yard that fast before," McCarthy said following the Thunder's 9-3 triumph. "You can separate the special guys from the ones who just aren't going to cut it by the way they hit the ball. That home run bounced off the black tarp behind the home-run fence. I think he was trying to hit the Willie Stargell star."

The Thunder's offensive surge even included a 2-for-3, two-RBI performance from O'Neal, who had extended his season-opening drought to 0-for-22 before finally breaking through. A reserved Midwesterner, O'Neal didn't appear too concerned about his slow start, but deep down, he began to question his ability—and to wonder what kind of faith Runnells had in his ability. In minor-league baseball, as in life, prolonged self-doubt is a formula for disaster.

FINAL PREPARATIONS

After scoring 19 runs in two games at the Vet, the Thunder exchanged the whimsical big-league environment for the bucolic scenery of Berks County, Pennsylvania. O'Neal continued his attempt to dig out of his early hole the next evening at Reading's Municipal Stadium. With the Blue Mountains in the background, the second baseman stroked a three-run double, and the 20-year-old Miller notched his second victory in three tries as the Thunder won No. 4 in a row by an 8-4 margin. More significantly, the victory lifted Runnells' club back to the .500 plateau at 6-6.

During a spirited three-game weekend set in which Trenton scored at least eight runs each time, the Thunder extended their winning streak to six games with a sweep of the shell-shocked Reading Phillies. Without question, the highlight of the series was Clark's solo homer on Saturday evening. Falling behind in the count against Reading closer Bob Wells, he fought off several pitches before connecting for a game-tying blast in the top of the ninth.

"It was exciting," Clark admitted. "It got to the point where I heard the crowd. I fouled off three pitches, and then it got to the point where I had to step back and calm myself down and actually focus. Lord willing, I got ahold of one. I wasn't smiling when I rounded the bases because it only tied the game, but it was something I smiled about in the locker room later."

Miraculously, the Thunder had rallied from an early 7-0 deficit against Reading starter Ryan Karp, scoring four runs in the fourth and two in the sixth to set up Clark's gutsy round-tripper. Capitalizing on the dramatic momentum swing, the Thunder won the game 8-7 in extra innings. Also homering for Trenton as a regional SportsChannel Philadelphia television audience looked on were Milne and Mashore.

Meanwhile, as workers cut and framed the final pieces of grass around the Waterfront Park basepaths with wooden splints, Hodes and the Thunder staff surveyed their new field. Despite the feverish last-minute efforts of stadium contractors, opening night would have to be conducted in what amounted to a bare-bones facility. For starters, the ground-level clubhouses weren't anywhere close to being ready; in fact, they wouldn't be available until early May. Outside, construction personnel who worked around the clock had unfurled the playing surface spool by spool. In 30-foot segments, the sod (which had been purchased and delivered from Jade Run Turf Farm in nearby Burlington County) was placed in strips atop a muddy base. Starting in left field, workers moved in a clockwise direction around the diamond, slowly filling out a giant natural jigsaw puzzle. The smell of fresh grass and dirt permeated the air, framing some serious questions. Would the grass knit properly to the hastily prepared dirt base? Would the shallow seams left between the rolls of sod hold up to the wear and tear of daily batting practices, defensive drills, and games, or would the surface be ripped apart by the constant digging of spikes? Laying the sod at the last minute left no margin for error.

"The field is a mix of Kentucky bluegrass, which is the best for this kind of use because it repairs itself quickly," explained Jade Run President Sam Alloway III. "Bluegrass has roots that run horizontally, so it fills in when the blades are torn out." The original 108,000-square-foot Waterfront Park field cost approximately 14 cents per square foot, or a total of $15,120. The spools were approximately 18 months old when they were delivered to the stadium—"the prime age for transplanting grass," according to Alloway.

Alloway added that transplanted sod must be allowed to sit for at least a week to allow the roots to take hold, but he also insisted, "There are some cases where a newly sodded field has been used 2 days later without any trouble. You don't like to do that, but it can be done." At Waterfront Park, the Thunder and Mercer County officials would attempt to push that envelope of natural limits.

On Sunday afternoon, April 24, as the Phillies tried to salvage a win back in Reading, Mendenhall hit a pair of homers, DuBose went 4-for-6 with four RBIs, and Trenton drubbed the hapless Reading pitching staff for 14 hits. The resulting 14-3 Trenton victory gave Runnells' club an 8-6 record and a rare six-game winning streak. The realization that their road odyssey was nearing its conclusion was further inspiration for the Thunder players.

"You've got to take the ups with the downs," Bombard said. "You're going to have them, and we already have. We've had a losing streak, and we've had a winning streak. What you try to do is stay on a consistent basis as a team. Sure, it's a lot of fun when you're winning, and anybody who tries to tell you different is lying, but game one counts as much as game 142."

As the Thunder bus headed toward Canton's Thurman Munson Memorial Stadium for a pair of games that would set up the April 27 Waterfront Park grand-opening, Runnells continued to have reservations about the facility's readiness—or lack thereof. He knew that some serious pitfalls lay in his immediate path. He was girding himself for a battle.

"I hope that if we do rush into the stadium and get there that it will still be a very effective experience, a lasting experience, not just a 'let's-rush-in-there-to-say-we-got-in-there' type of thing," the manager said. "I know that it is going to be a tremendous facility once it's completed. I'd almost rather wait until we were very comfortable with the field conditions and the surroundings and the settings. It would also be nice to practice there first, but I don't know that we'll get an opportunity to do that."

On Monday, April 25, with a six-game winning streak on the line, Trenton ran into a 6-foot-3, 240-pound buzzsaw named Tony Mitchell. The previous day, during Canton-Akron's 18-3 triumph over New Haven, Mitchell had smashed a pair of homers. Facing Mysel in the third inning, he turned on an inside fastball. The ball literally exploded off the bat and caromed off the left-field light tower—some 110 feet up—before landing at the stunned DuBose's feet. "That's probably the furthest I've ever seen a right-hander hit the ball," Runnells said, comparing the prodigious blast to a homer by New York Met Darryl Strawberry at Montreal's Olympic Stadium in the early 1990s. Said the wide-eyed Mitchell afterwards, "I've never hit a ball that far before." And added one Thunder pitcher, "If I had given up a home run like that, I would have been the first guy to congratulate him at home plate."

Mashore homered for the third time in 15 games, matching his 1993 *season* total, but Mitchell's unforgettable homer had been too much to overcome. Embree picked up the win as Canton-Akron prevailed 10-6, dropping the Thunder to an 8-7 record. As his teammates showered, Mysel stood in the seating area behind home plate, staring into the distance where Mitchell's homer had landed. One game remained until Trenton returned to the Delaware Valley to open its new stadium.

In the final Waterfront tune-up, Perona enjoyed a magnificent outing, homering twice to provide enough support for Edmondson to improve to 2-2 with a 6-5 win over the Indians. Greene notched his third save, and Clark added his fourth homer in 16 games. Big Tony's round-tripper actually bounced off the front of the right-field wall, however, and was erroneously deemed a homer by field umpire Brad Geaslin. Clark illustrated the mistake by throwing a bag of potato chips at the base of a wall, but the solo shot turned out to be the winning margin.

Said Runnells of the imminent Waterfront opener, "I don't know what to expect. I didn't feel there was any possible way they were going to have it ready to go, but apparently they do."

CHAPTER 7

Waterlogged

"Ladies and Gentlemen, I have some disappointing news. We were not successful in our appeal to the manager of the Albany-Colonie Yankees to play this game, but the Thunder was ready to play."

—ROBERT D. PRUNETTI, APRIL 27, 1994

"This should be a big story. If you spend [$17.3 million] on a stadium, it should be ready to be played in. You shouldn't open it until it's ready."

—1994 ALBANY-COLONIE MANAGER BILL EVERS

For the bewildered gathering of expectant fans who filled Waterfront Park on the warm spring evening of Wednesday, April 27, 1994, opening night at Trenton's brand new municipal stadium was equal parts outdoor festival, autograph show, and political convention. It was not, however, a Double-A baseball game between the Thunder and the Albany-Colonie Yankees. Nothing that Prunetti, Hodes, or Runnells could do altered the irrefutable fact that the park's hastily laid sod wasn't safe for anybody to play on—let alone professional athletes, some of whom were destined to toil in the major leagues for million-dollar annual salaries.

Everyone in the Delaware Valley was anxious to welcome the team, to gather in the new playground that had risen in South Trenton. The originally scheduled April 16 opening date was one thing, but losing another grand opening was unthinkable to Prunetti and the Thunder ownership.

As the Thunder wrapped up action in Canton, the uncertain condition of their home field was on everybody's mind. All they could do was trust the assurances repeatedly given over the last 2 months. "I just hope it's safe for us," said Pete Gonzalez, echoing the prevailing sentiment in the Trenton clubhouse.

"It's not my job to think about what condition the field is in," Runnells said abruptly in the Canton dugout on the eve of the scheduled Waterfront opener. "I anticipate it looking like a baseball field. If it's anything short of that, then you can ask my reaction."

"I know how Jersey people work—and that it might not be done on time," Guilfoyle added. "But I'd still like to get that feeling of going into a new stadium."

On the morning of April 27, Thunder employees Geoff Brown, Curtis Nelson, and Rick Brenner spent a few hours hanging brown construction paper over the windows of a back room in the 200 Building of the Riverview Executive Plaza (behind the Thunder's temporary office) to create makeshift dressing quarters for both teams. The luxury boxes on the stadium's second level were hollow concrete shells. The public bathrooms on the stadium's main concourse had temporary plywood partitions between the toilet stalls. A large, white painter's tarp covered the press box because the windows had not been installed. Makeshift concession stands (operated by Harry M. Stevens Corporation in 1994) serving a limited menu of items were set up on the first- and third-base sides of the concourse. Construction debris littered the main entrance to the stadium, and mud covered the area that eventually would become a brick and concrete welcoming plaza. Everywhere you looked, unfinished details caught your eye. Only the handsome red-brick building facade with the inspiring silver block lettering "MERCER COUNTY WATERFRONT PARK" was complete. The name stood out like a beacon in a fog, a monument to yet-unfulfilled potential.

Was this the optimum backdrop for minor-league baseball's long-anticipated return to Trenton? Despite public assurances from Prunetti and others that the historic event would proceed as scheduled, Hodes maintained private doubts. An early morning visit from Runnells (just hours after the Thunder bus arrived from Canton) confirmed those trepidations. The manager took one look at the loosely packed grass and cringed. He read the daunting headline in *The Trentonian* newspaper: "FIELD OF SEAMS." He wouldn't stand for having his ballplayers exploited.

"I knew it was going to be a long day about a week prior [to April 27]," Hodes said. "Then T.R. came and basically told me what I already knew. The field wasn't playable. We talked about it as we walked on the new sod. I just really wanted to end it there, so I called up [Albany-Colonie manager] Bill [Evers] around 10 AM at the team hotel to see if he wanted to come down and walk the field with us. Obviously, we had enormous problems." Much to his dismay, Evers declined the morning invitation, opting to wait until later in the day to tour the field.

As the point man for the Thunder management and ownership, Hodes was in a very awkward position. Throughout the franchise's early days, Prunetti had been the Thunder's most visible representative. In a very real sense, he had staked his political reputation on Waterfront Park, but while workers frantically completed the field, the county executive was golfing in Florida, making frequent calls to Frank Ragazzo to monitor the stadium's progress. He returned to Trenton on the morning of April 27, eager to bask in the limelight of the opening gala. On several occasions, however, Hodes had warned Prunetti of the variables that might upset that plan.

"About a week to 10 days prior to the fact, I knew what was going to happen," Hodes said. "Bob gave me a call and asked, 'Is there any possibility that we're not going to play?'" Of course, Hodes wasn't new to the logistics of stadium construction. In 1993, when he was the assistant general manager at Rancho Cucamonga, the playing surface had been in immaculate condition long before the first game, nurtured to health by the warm Southern California climate.

"I told Bob there was always the possibility that we wouldn't be able to play," Hodes explained. "What did we have, 3 or 4 days to get the soil to knit to the ground? I knew that if we were lucky we could play in 10 days to 2 weeks after it was put down. For whatever reason, the growing season and the humidity, people said we could do it in less than that. At that point, we assumed it was just a matter of growing the grass in, that the soil underneath had been done correctly. Little did we know . . ."

Shortly after noon, seven hours before the scheduled first pitch between the Thunder and the Yankees' Double-A affiliate, Runnells was back on the choppy field, inspecting its patchwork surface with Detroit Director of Minor League Operations Dave Miller and Detroit Minor League Pitching Coordinator Ralph Treuel. Stepping gingerly through the soggy outfield, his hand gestures told the entire story. He was exasperated. He didn't want to look like the bad guy, the one who spoiled Trenton's party. Treuel, who later would become the 1996 Thunder pitching coach under much different circumstances, advised the manager that his counterpart, Evers, was probably going to make the decision not to play, thus saving Runnells from having to make the call. Treuel was right. There was no way Evers was willing to put his prospects at risk just to bail Prunetti and the Thunder out of their predicament.

Prunetti arrived at the stadium shortly afterward to discuss the situation with Miller and Runnells. He consulted with head groundskeeper Jeff Migliaccio. In a few short hours, 7000 eager fans would file through the unfinished stadium portals, and while Prunetti tried to reason with Runnells, the county executive admitted that conditions "weren't optimum." Meanwhile, Eastern League President John Levenda decided to leave the final decision to the respective managers—Runnells and Evers.

For Ragazzo, Prunetti's right-hand man, the days leading up to April 27 were tense. The county executive wanted every detail completed. Obviously, that wasn't possible in light of the deadline. Work crews were forced to prioritize. Despite good intentions, several shortcuts were taken during the construction process, including some very significant physical omissions in the field's underlying drainage system. "I don't think there was a person in the county office who slept the night before for fear something might go wrong," Ragazzo said. On personal inspection of the playing surface, his heart sank. "The field was like a trampoline," he added, using his hands to simulate the sensation of walking on the surface.

Throughout the afternoon, scores of curious onlookers filtered through the stadium gates to catch their first glimpse of Waterfront Park. Those who didn't have tickets gradually were shooed away. By 4 PM, some of the Thunder players gave the playing surface a cursory inspection. They were shocked. "It's just not playable," Rendina observed. "It's a fact. The field's in bad shape. It's no one's fault, and we blame no one. But you've got to look out for your players. Someone could get seriously hurt."

At 4:30 PM, Evers finally made the 20-minute drive from the Palmer Inn to the stadium. After a brief walk of the field, he concluded on behalf of the Yankees, "No, we're not going to play." He quickly departed Waterfront Park without bothering to summon his players from the hotel (one of whom was scheduled starting pitcher Tim Rumer, a Princeton native). Neither did he advise Prunetti of his decision.

"Quite frankly, I couldn't blame him," Hodes said of Evers' blunt refusal to accommodate the Thunder, "but at that point, people had already left from work to come to the stadium." For that very reason, Hodes had wanted to postpone the game early in the afternoon. With early arriving fans in danger of having their tickets torn in anticipation of the historic evening, his dilemma was compounded. Fortunately for the Thunder, there was a suitable alternative to turning people away empty-handed, with half a ticket stub in their possession. By 5 PM, when it was obvious the game would not be played, the decision was made not to tear tickets, thereby ensuring their use for a future date. A cash-refund policy was quickly implemented for those who couldn't attend the make-up date. "My staff had already held meetings and made contingency plans for something like this," Hodes said. "We sort of knew this was going to happen, but there was nothing we could do about it because other outside forces wanted us to attempt to get the game in that day. So we felt that the best possible option was to create some type of a festival atmosphere out of it."

NO RUNS, NO HITS, NO GAME

Slowly, the unfinished stadium began to fill. Of course, the nostalgia of the evening had created a huge demand for tickets. Some of the opening-night patrons had camped out overnight back in March to be first in line for the best seats. Along the right-field concourse, dignitaries and corporate sponsors sipped beer and munched on crab legs and jumbo shrimp beneath a hospitality tent. (The final bill for the seafood was $7000.) On the field, players and reporters milled around the Thunder dugout. Nearby, head contractor Burris grumbled about the "120 hours" he had spent over the previous week in a last-ditch attempt to prepare the facility for the grand opening. White numbers had finally been placed on the back of the Thunder's green-mesh batting-practice tops. Commemorative scorecards and yearbooks were on sale at the stadium entrance, and on the yearbook cover was a typographical error that made it a collector's item, "**Merer** County Waterfront Park." Hot dogs (which sold for $1.25) and a special microbrewed beer named Thunderbrau ($3) were available from the temporary concession stands. Most of the anxious arrivals already had invested in one of the Thunder's three baseball caps. Everywhere, there was a pervading aura of novelty and an abundance of smiling patrons. Minor-league baseball had returned to the New Jersey capital.

Or had it?

Inside the makeshift Thunder clubhouse, behind the hastily papered windows, Runnells met with his players to discuss the awkward situation. Stidham and Maxcy did not participate in the gathering—they had been promoted to Triple-A Toledo, making them the first-ever former Thunder players. They wouldn't have to worry about the Waterfront Park quagmire. Both pitchers departed for Lackawanna County Stadium in Scranton, Pennsylvania, where they would join the Mud Hens moments before the remaining Thunder players trekked through the muddy, construction debris-littered bowels of the Trenton stadium for ceremonial introductions. The name of the game in modern minor-league baseball is development, and both Stidham and Maxcy had inched within one level of playing in the majors. It was a proud moment for both. "I'm tickled for them, and at the same time I'm sad," Runnells said, taking a welcome moment to discuss baseball on what had already become a bizarre day. "There goes a strong part of our ballclub."

At 5:10 PM, shortly after Evers had toured the field, deemed it unfit for his players, and returned to the Palmer Inn, a brief but intense rain shower clarified the uncertain situation for the growing number of folks milling about the stadium. Inside the tarp-sheltered press box, drops of water seeped through the roof that would double as the floor of the 88-seat stadium restaurant later in the inaugural season. Employees scrambled to cover the electronic equipment that controlled the scoreboard and the sound system. Beneath the hospitality tent, executives in suits and ties huddled for shelter against the quickly passing storm. The players sought refuge in their new dugout along the first-base line. The poorly knit sod, further moistened, puddled up in several areas. It would be slow to drain—not a good omen. Within moments the rain subsided, leaving behind an unseasonably humid late-April evening, but the damage was done.

Inside the Thunder office, Hodes, the team owners and Detroit officials scrambled to make last-minute contingency plans. Prunetti continued to bargain with the Yankees, at one point even telephoning the big-league office in the Bronx and urging them to overrule Evers' decision. The effort failed. What was supposed to be a crowning night of achievement—the grand opening of his biggest municipal project—was becoming a logistical disaster. Within the hour, two skydivers were scheduled to land in center field to deliver the ceremonial baseball that Prunetti would use for his long-awaited first pitch. The county executive screamed at Eastern League President Levenda, who stood with a bewildered look as sweat beaded his face.

Meanwhile, Hodes had a much broader concern. Hundreds of fans had already entered the stadium. He needed a concrete back-up plan, a way to get them back in the park for a rescheduled opener. Perusing the Thunder schedule, he realized the team had an off day on Monday, May 9. Fortunately, so did Binghamton. He phoned Mets' General Manager R.C. Reuteman, a former Tidewater colleague and one of his best friends in minor-league baseball, to ask if Binghamton would be willing to play on May 9. Realizing the gravity of Hodes' dilemma, Reuteman agreed. The Thunder management and ownership breathed a deep sigh of relief, but the contingency plan wouldn't be made public until a press conference the following morning. "Through some friendships in the game and a couple favors, I was able to get Binghamton to commit to playing here," Hodes said later. "If it wasn't R.C. sitting in that chair, I don't think they would have done it."

As the Thunder General Manager finalized the agreement with Binghamton, the Thunder players were besieged by young autograph seekers along the first-base seating area. At times, the groups were four and five deep along the railing. It was a continuation of the affection that had first surfaced at the April 11 "Welcome North Dinner." In the background, the official team song "Thunder

Power" made its high-decibel debut. "COME ON EVERYBODY, DON'T YOU HEAR THAT SOUND. IT'S THUNDER BASEBALL IN TRENTON TOWN. IT'S A NEW TRADITION OF WINNING WAYS. . . . COME ON, FEEL THAT THUNDER POWER," echoed the chorus. By the end of the season, every diehard Trenton fan would know the musical refrain by heart.

At 6:00 PM, a frustrated Prunetti decided to take matters into his own hands. Parking his Cadillac in a handicapped space in front of the stadium, he left the motor running as he sprinted up the stairs of the main entrance to the press box. If the game wasn't going to happen, he didn't want to look like the bad guy, not on this night. As the nearly filled stadium turned to look toward the open announcer's booth where Prunetti was standing in a white dress shirt, the county executive seized the microphone and uttered three unforgettable sentences: "Ladies and Gentlemen, I have some disappointing news. We were not successful in our appeal to the manager of the Albany-Colonie Yankees to play this game, but the Thunder was ready to play."

Amidst a smattering of boos and groans from the several thousand fans scattered throughout the facility, there were looks of disbelief from Runnells and his players as they momentarily stopped signing autographs to hear Prunetti's announcement. Some called the brief disclaimer "a bush league" thing to do. Others used much sharper language. What exactly was he trying to do? they wondered aloud. As Prunetti spoke his piece, Hodes cringed.

"I was surprised Bob took the microphone," the Thunder General Manager confessed. "He was obviously very emotional and very upset. In fact, when he came in my office, he was livid. His county advisors told him to go on the loudspeaker because Waterfront Park was his baby from way back when. I think that was a mistake, but he was just in such a state that the game wasn't going to happen. He was just pissed off, and that's what came out."

"It was like a domino effect," McCarthy added. "I remember Wayne telling me to tell everybody the game was postponed. Then later somebody said the game was still on. I was very nervous."

Following Prunetti's address, some folks began to filter out of the stadium, past Trenton police who had been summoned to work overtime to handle the anticipated volume of pedestrian traffic. Shuttle buses ran back and forth from the stadium to one of the state government parking lots; however, most of those on hand at the time the game was officially postponed decided to stay and enjoy the outdoor carnival unfolding before them. After all, it had been 44 years since Trenton residents had enjoyed the opportunity to gaze out at their own minor-league team. The white hospitality tent was filled with people—some of them uninvited.

McCarthy took over the proceedings and introduced the Thunder players one by one. The young prospects clowned for photographers as they formed a line between home plate and first base. There was a huge ovation for Ahearne, the first player out of the dugout. DuBose played to the crowd as he joined the group. Finally, Clark took his place as the last player introduced. For a proud moment, the gathering stood and cheered their new team. Moments later, the parachuters appeared, ball in hand. A successful outfield landing was made, and Prunetti was introduced for his ceremonial first pitch. The delivery was a strike to Gonzalez, who returned the ball to the county executive with a hand-shake and a smile. It was an awkward moment, with no one who was involved quite sure how to react.

Back inside the press box, Trenton Mayor Doug Palmer tried to put a positive spin on the delay. "The excitement is great and the people are disappointed, but understandably so. I swear this is the greatest thing since Washington crossed the Delaware. We haven't had baseball here for more than 40 years, so we can wait another few days."

For many of the fans enjoying their first glimpse of Waterfront Park, the promise of what lay ahead was enough to make the night worthwhile. It was obvious that the stadium would be a magnificent place to watch a game when all of the details were complete. Following the introductions, the Thunder players continued to sign autographs, basking in the spotlight of their new, unexpected fame.

As he spoke to the many media representatives present, Runnells was happy to be off the hook. Thanks to Evers and Prunetti, he was not the scapegoat after all. He didn't want to put his players in jeopardy, either. "I have to agree with Bill Evers. As far as the safety of both teams involved and the substandard condition of the field, I think he did the right thing."

By 9 PM, Evers was seated at the bar inside Charlie Brown's Restaurant at West Windsor's Palmer Inn. He was enjoying a cold beer and trying to forget the Waterfront Park predicament. Advised of Prunetti's public announcement, he snapped, "What do I care what he thinks? He probably never wore a jockstrap in his life." The sarcastic comment was a final bizarre twist in an unforgettable day.

After calming down a bit, Evers defended his decision not to take the field. "You shouldn't open that stadium until it's ready. I can't send guys who are going to make $2 million a year in the majors out to play on that. The field was too soft, and it had too many undulations. Three days ago, they asked if I would be willing to play there with no clubhouse facilities. I told them we can dress at the hotel, but they also told me the field was playable. I had no idea the sod was just laid—it just wasn't playable."

The next morning, Trenton's competing newspapers ran the following headlines: "DAMN YANKEES" and "NO RUNS, NO HITS, NO GAME." Perhaps Ragazzo, the point man for Waterfront Park's construction and later for its maintenance, best summed up the feeling of those most closely involved with the aborted April 27 opener. "It was like moving into a new house. You get all your stuff to the door, and somebody says you can't come in; you have to sleep out in the street. For the night anyway."

Hearing Ragazzo's analogy, Prunetti added, "Worse than that, you wondered who invited all these friends over."

CONTINGENCY PLANS

At 10 AM the next morning, Thursday, April 28, inside the Mercer County Improvement Authority Offices in the 400 Building of the Riverview Executive

Plaza, the Thunder unveiled their contingency plans for the postponed home opener. Hodes' nimble scheduling with Reuteman and Reading General Manager Chuck Domino meant that everybody who held tickets to the original game would be accommodated. The entire four-game homestand slated for the weekend of April 28 to May 1 was rearranged and relocated as a result of the Trenton facility's unplayable field. The remaining Thursday night game against Albany-Colonie would be played as part of a May 18 doubleheader when the Yankees returned to Waterfront. The three weekend games against New Britain were moved to Reading's Municipal Stadium, where the Thunder would borrow the ballpark and only pay to operate the concession stands and the ticket booths. The pivotal Waterfront grand opening was etched onto the schedule for 7:05 PM, Monday, May 9. All tickets for the aborted April 27 game—which fortuitously had not been torn—would be honored on the new date. All in all, it seemed like a workable solution to both Thunder management and the Mercer County officials, who had taken the brunt of the criticism for the construction delays.

"First and foremost in our minds are the fans and their loyalty," Hodes said after stepping to the microphone. "We want to try to do something for them. If they are not happy with this weekend's arrangements, they can come in and exchange their tickets for a cash refund."

While the Thunder General Manager explained the logistics, Prunetti was preparing a public apology for the television cameras and reporters assembled at the hastily scheduled press conference. Looking back to the previous evening's events, he realized that he had overreacted. After making a wisecrack about Evers' jockstrap comment and mentioning his All-Mercer County selection as a Trenton High linebacker in 1970, he began the task of making amends.

"I want to apologize to the Albany-Colonie Yankees and their manager, Bill Evers," Prunetti said. "My concern was for the Thunder fans who camped out for tickets, who waited for hours. We felt like we did everything we could to have Waterfront Park ready."

In retrospect, the county executive was extremely disappointed that the visiting manager had left the stadium without informing him personally of his decision not to play. "If he had told me earlier, I could have gotten on the radio," Prunetti explained. "Instead, I was forced to take the lead. I felt it was my responsibility that the game wasn't going to be played. Things didn't go exactly as we wanted. The stadium was good enough for the fans, but based on the decision of professional managers, I guess it wasn't ready. But I hope the Thunder players understand that we have done all we could to have the finest facility for them and to make their entrance to Trenton very special."

The revised Waterfront Park opening plan called for the same gala celebration that had been precluded by the previous night's bizarre events. The extra 12 days also would give contractors an opportunity to prepare the clubhouses and tend to other major construction details. For that reason, Runnells and his players fully expected to find the stadium in working condition on May 9. During the press conference, the Thunder worked out for 3 hours on a recreational field at nearby Mercer County Park. "We have to take our time and wait until the field is ready," said reliever Cecil Pettiford. "What else can we do?" By that point, however, many of the young men felt very much like pawns in a three-way chess game between Prunetti, the Thunder front office, and the Detroit officials. None felt in control of his own destiny, at least for the moment.

Thankful for another opportunity to lift the curtain on his controversial new municipal showpiece, Prunetti announced, "The plan works. Thank God, it works. I don't think any of us have any doubt the field will be ready by then." Asked what kind of care the field needed in the interim, Prunetti replied, "Just water." Despite the setback, he recognized the delay wasn't a total public relations disaster. Thousands of people had seen how beautiful the ballpark would be when all of the details were complete. "For me, the most gratifying thing about Wednesday night was the fans who stayed and said it was a great facility and that they'll be back," Prunetti said, "but you've got to take the good with the bad. The worst thing for us is to tell fans that we're going to do something and we don't do it. I wanted every last brick in place by April 27."

THE LONG AND WINDING ROAD

On Friday morning, April 29, the Thunder bus traveled 78 miles west to Reading's Municipal Stadium, where Trenton played before a few curious onlookers during an afternoon doubleheader against New Britain. Among those in attendance were Ragazzo and Prunetti. Both stopped by the radio booth to chat with McCarthy and Simonetta. The unscheduled twinbill was played under dreary weather conditions, and the Thunder's performance mirrored the weather. Runnells' offense mustered just eight hits in 14 innings against a trio of Red Sox pitchers, losing the first game 6-0 and dropping the second 4-2. In the opener, all that stood between New Britain righty Joel Bennett and a no-hitter was a second-inning single by Decillis. In the second game, Red Sox outfielder Pat Lennon's three-run homer was enough to defeat Carlyle, who nonetheless pitched a five-hit, complete game. Faced with the prospect of a total of 26 road games before the revised Waterfront opener, the Thunder players appeared listless as they fell back to .500 (9-9) on the season.

"Sometimes you're going to come out ready, and sometimes you're going to come out flat," Carlyle said as his teammates dressed in the silence of the Reading home clubhouse. "We looked flat today. Maybe it's because we don't have a home stadium. We just didn't have any enthusiasm today."

As the Thunder boarded the team bus for the hour-and-a-half ride back to New Jersey, they were a team in need of a spark. The following afternoon, April 30, Withem provided it with the first complete-game shut-out in franchise annals during a 4-0 victory over the Red Sox. Another small crowd watched him throw 106 pitches; command his fastball, change-up and slider at will; and allow just three hits. He struck out four batters and did not walk a single New Britain batter to improve his record to 2-1. He received a standing ovation from a small contingent of Trenton fans as he walked off the field. In the clubhouse, the mood was festive as Withem discussed his effort. "The only thing that would have been better was if I had thrown a shut-out for the Tigers today," he said with a tone of self-assurance.

"Unbelievable," Runnells added. "He was on a roll, and you could see it. During the seventh inning, we talked in the dugout about whether he could finish it, but there's not a whole lot of decision-making going on there when a guy is throwing as well as he is."

The game also featured DuBose's second homer—a 375-foot solo shot to left field—and a magnificent lunging catch by Mashore that was made just before he slammed into the center-field wall. During the season's first month, Mashore had demonstrated many of the defensive skills that had made him a highly touted outfield prospect. His throwing arm was particularly impressive, and he recorded several superb outfield assists in the early going.

Following Withem's stalwart performance, the Thunder enjoyed a day off on Sunday, May 1. The completion of the month-long, season-opening road trip called for a four-game series at New Haven and three weekend games at Binghamton.

Trenton's first-ever game at Yale Field was a clunker for Runnells and his prospects, as the Ravens' righty Lloyd Peever struck out 10 batters to earn a 7-0 shut-out victory and drop the Thunder back to .500. "Their hitters looked weak on the outside part of the plate," Peever observed. The next night, Edmondson absorbed a 6-2 defeat as New Haven scored six runs on six hits. "Nothing is clicking right now," he said. "It's just a little bit off." The Thunder pitcher also had some choice words for the Yale Field pitching mound, which he called "the worst I've ever thrown on."

The New Haven trip grew even bleaker during a Wednesday afternoon game the Thunder lost 6-1, marking the club's fifth defeat in its last six games. Miller was roughed up for 12 hits over six innings, and DuBose's 2-for-4 performance wasn't nearly enough to keep Trenton in the game. "All the flaws are hidden when you're swinging the bats well and scoring runs," Runnells said in the dressing trailer. "When you're not, those flaws are magnified. Right now, our at-bats aren't consistent enough to make a quality threat."

Nonetheless, in the final game of the New Haven series, Decillis became an unlikely—but thankful—hero. Trailing 4-0 after seven innings against Ravens' ace and 1994 Eastern League Pitcher of the Year Juan Acevedo, Trenton rallied in the top of the ninth with three runs off reliever Mike Kotarski, a lefty. With DuBose and Clark on base and nobody out, Decillis smashed a low fastball from Kotarski over the left-center fence for the improbable late-inning tie. "That was probably one of the most gratifying homers of my career," Decillis admitted after DuBose singled Mashore home in the tenth inning and Greene recorded the final three outs to nail down a 5-4 victory. "I'm happy we got out of here with one win," Runnells said, adding that Decillis' homer was a "lucky hit" and that the real credit belonged to Carlyle, who struck out six batters and was charged with a pair of unearned runs on Decillis' sixth-inning error.

As the Thunder opened their three-game series in Binghamton on Friday, May 6, Hodes, Prunetti, Ragazzo, and Burris conducted another walkthrough tour of Waterfront Park. The playing surface had been approved—once and for all—for the next Monday's home opener. As the quartet of officials suspiciously analyzed each clump of grass, work continued on the clubhouses. Beige carpeting would be placed on the day of the game. The toilet stalls in the Thunder players' bathroom remained without partitions, later prompting relief pitcher Rick Greene's hilarious plea, "My kingdom for a shitter separator."

With two victories in Binghamton—both by a one-run margin—the Thunder returned home with a respectable 13-13 record. The fatigue of 26 days on the road, constantly living out of a suitcase, and sleeping in hotel beds had not buried the team in the Eastern League standings. "For them to come here 13-13 after what they've been through is really an accomplishment," Hodes praised, and Runnells added, "I think playing at home is going to give everybody a lift. It will be nice to finally play in front of a partisan crowd."

Following the Thunder's 8-7 victory at Binghamton on Saturday, May 7, Gonzalez decided to stay out late. By the time he returned to the team hotel (with a pair of dates in tow), it was 5 AM. After the game, however, Runnells had decided to check curfew to make sure his players were behaving. When his catcher sauntered through the lobby to the elevator, the manager was watching from across the room. Figuring he would have Sunday off because he caught the Saturday game, Gonzalez had used the night of revelry to become seriously inebriated. "They checked curfew tonight," his roommate, pitcher Blas Cedeno, said when he returned to the room. "I don't give a shit," the catcher replied. After a few hours of sleep, Gonzalez reported to the stadium wearing mirrored sunglasses—and Runnells was waiting. "The guys who missed curfew last night, you know who you are," he said in the clubhouse. "I expect $25 on my desk." He summoned Gonzalez—who admitted he was still drunk—for an on-field conversation. After cursing at him for several moments, the manager said, "Pack your bags." Thinking he was being released, Gonzalez replied, "I don't need this game anyway." Finally, Runnells told the bewildered catcher, "No, you're going to Triple-A." According to several sources, however, the move was more an excuse to get the player out of the manager's sight than a promotion.

Curfew violations aside, a final inspection of the Waterfront field on the day before the first game revealed several wet spots in left and right-center field, but there was no way such minor irritants could postpone history another time. "We're going to try to do some fun on-field type things, but since it's the inaugural game, we just want to play baseball," Hodes proclaimed. "If I had to put a percentage on how close the stadium is to being complete, I would say 70 percent."

While anticipating New Jersey Governor Christine Todd Whitman's ceremonial first pitch, Hodes was taking nothing for granted. He wanted minor-league baseball's return to his home state to be a critical and, more significantly, economic success. "I think this will be a very satisfying experience," he said on the eve of the May 9 festivities. "I just hope everything goes off without a hitch. The basic rule of thumb in this business is, 'If you're 50 percent happy, you're doing a hell of a job.' I'll try to smile as much as I can, but I think if you're satisfied with something, you become complacent."

As the Thunder bus rolled down the Northeast Extension of the Pennsylvania Turnpike on the evening of May 8, the stage was set for Waterfront Park's belated debut, when Mets' staff ace and future major leaguer, 21-year-old lefty Bill Pulsipher, would match his 4-1 record and 3.12 ERA against 20-year-old lefty Miller, who was 2-3 and 5.53 ERA. The Louisville, Kentucky, native would try to etch his name in Trenton baseball lore as the first winning pitcher in Waterfront annals, hoping to build on his distinction as the franchise's first winning pitcher back on April 9 in Harrisburg. Monday's forecast called for partly sunny skies and temperatures in the mid-seventies. Everyone associated with Trenton's new baseball venture was ready to watch Runnells and his Detroit farmhands take the field and play ball in their new stadium.

Finally.

CHAPTER 8

Home at Last

> "This team is not a sideshow. It's not a recreational softball team, and it's not a Single-A team. This is a Double-A baseball team, and they can't do things half-assed for these guys. To rush this just to get 7000 fans in here is a joke."
>
> —THUNDER MANAGER TOM RUNNELLS FOLLOWING THE FIRST-EVER GAME AT WATERFRONT PARK
>
> "I loved the crowd. I gave a little tip of my hat when I came out. That was more people than I've ever played in front of in my life."
>
> —THUNDER STARTING PITCHER TREVER MILLER

At 6:55 PM on Monday, May 9, 1994, Republican Christine Todd Whitman, New Jersey's first female governor, threw out the ceremonial first pitch at Mercer County Waterfront Park as the long-anticipated preface to the Thunder's first home game against Binghamton. The symbolism of the moment was unmistakable: a trend-setting politician was paving the way for a trend-setting minor-league baseball venture. The gubernatorial delivery was a ball low and outside to O'Neal. Accompanying Whitman to the mound for the historic moment were Prunetti and Palmer. As 6941 opening-night patrons filed into the "70 percent complete" facility past scaffolding and makeshift concession stands, there was a sense of novelty that carried over from the aborted April 27 opening. Opening night T-shirts bearing the new date were a popular item along the concourse. Vendors hawked souvenir inaugural season yearbooks, which had been corrected to read "**Mercer** County Waterfront Park" over the last 12 days. From the $5-an-hour parking-lot attendants to Hodes and his full-time staff, there was considerable anxiety about the evening's carefully scripted activities. In the press box, Hardison prepared for his debut at the microphone. His game script included detailed announcements for each half inning, everything from promotional giveaways to the "Guess the Attendance" quiz. With clear skies and warm evening temperatures, it was a perfect night for minor-league baseball's return to Trenton.

The soft playing field that had been watered and nurtured for almost 2 weeks since Evers had deemed it unfit would have to suffice. As the Thunder took afternoon batting practice for the first time on the loosely knit surface (using a batting cage borrowed from Mercer County Community College), the players offered various observations about the condition of the field. "I could see somebody getting hurt, but I'm not here to get hurt; I'm here to play baseball," Mashore explained in his unique manner before adding, "I could care less what the field is like as long as we don't have to get on a bus for 3 hours."

Clark, who had 24 RBIs in the Thunder's first 26 games, tying him for third in the league in that category, was more diplomatic in his assessment of the nappy grass carpet. "We're playing tonight, aren't we?" Big Tony wondered rhetorically. Added Edmondson, "I can't believe how much they did since April 27. They've done a lot. The last time we were here, the only thing I can remember was pulling up handfuls of sod. Realistically, now it's playable."

As a last-minute preparation for the game, groundskeeper Jeff Migliaccio installed "between 500 and 700" sod staples at various points throughout the field. "I put one wherever I thought it needed it," he said, adding that he was working round-the-clock attending to the myriad details involved with the opening of the new stadium. The staples were designed to aid the knitting process of sod to the moist dirt underneath. Regardless, after taking infield practice on the fresh surface, shortstop Kirk Mendenhall cautioned, "Ten home games in a row is going to tear this field up."

"It looks a lot better than it did the last time I was here," Dave Miller said after inspecting the field for 45 minutes. "And I really like that scoreboard. That's real nice." Meanwhile, Runnells was underwhelmed by the progress that had been made on his team's new field. Unlike April 27, when the visiting team simply decided not to show up, he didn't have a clear alibi. His vociferous complaints could be heard from the dugout hours before the game. The veins in his forehead underscored his frustration. "People tell me one thing, and when I come to the stadium, I see another," Runnells said loudly. "I'm very disappointed with the work that's been done since April 27."

Once it became clear that baseball would be played, the focus shifted from the poor condition of the field to the players. It was a refreshing deflection of energy. The Binghamton Mets arrived as the Eastern League Northern Division leader with an 18-9 record and were led by center fielder Ricky Otero, designated hitter Frank Jacobs (a former Notre Dame University football player), third baseman Chris Saunders, and a strong pitching staff. Manager John Tamargo ("J.T.") penned Otero into the lead-off spot on his line-up card, meaning that the 5-foot-5 outfielder would accept the historic first pitch from Miller. As a result, Otero would always be the answer to the trivia question, "Who was the first batter at Waterfront Park?"

"Everybody thinks I'm too small to make it to the big leagues, but [screw] them. I'm going to show them. You wait and see," Otero had told one of his American Legion teammates several years before.

Down the hall from Tamargo's office, some 2 1/2 hours before Miller's first pitch, Runnells drew up the first-ever home Thunder batting order, which he delivered to McCarthy to distribute to the large opening-night press contingent. Amidst all of the chaos, McCarthy copied the lineup that included two third basemen: Decillis and Delli Carri. Decillis actually was the designated hitter. In order, Runnells' historic lineup posted on the clubhouse wall read:

13   Mendenhall 6 (ss)
31   DuBose 7 (lf)
9   Decillis DH
33   Clark 3 (1b)
22   Perona 2 (c)
25   Delli Carri 5 (3b)
24   Mashore 8 (cf)
15   Saltzgaber 9 (rf)
2   O'Neal 4 (2b)

On the field before the game, Decillis was honored as the Thunder's first-ever Eastern League Batter of the Week for his 10-for-21 (.476) performance against New Haven and Binghamton. Those 10 hits included two homers, a double, a triple, and seven RBIs.

Conspicuously absent from the line-up was Rendina, whose left-handed power stroke did not match up with lefty Pulsipher. Furthermore, the brooding Californian was batting just .188, with one homer, in his first 22 games. He would watch the action from the dugout.

Inside the hastily prepared Thunder clubhouse, the players joked about their unpainted plywood locker stalls, which didn't even have hooks for their clothes. Workers scurried around the room as the players dressed. Clark and DuBose took up residence in the far right corner of the room, an area that was playfully dubbed "The Ghetto." On the left side, relief pitchers Greene and Ahearne named their row "The Suburbs." An hour-and-a-half before the first pitch, the players donned their white uniforms with green pinstripes. Most elected to wear black sleeves underneath. Clark added a pair of green wristbands that were distinctively marked with his No. 33.

As the grandstand filled, the hospitality tent on the right-field concourse was once again packed with dignitaries, many of whom had been on hand for round one of the stadium-opening saga. Down below, inside the Thunder dugout, McCarthy and Runnells taped the nightly manager's report for the pregame radio show.

Just as they had been in Harrisburg on April 8 and again in Wilmington on April 17, both teams were introduced and asked to take their places along the first- and third-base lines. The 6-foot-8 Clark received an especially boisterous ovation. Runnells and Tamargo exchanged lineups with home-plate umpire Eric Cooper. McCarthy and Simonetta manned their unfinished radio booth, preparing for their first-ever Waterfront broadcast. "By that time, it was so late in the season that it wasn't really a novelty any more," Simonetta explained. "The nervousness was gone."

The game also represented the Thunder franchise's home television debut. One of Hodes' first goals as general manager was to secure a television package for the Trenton franchise. With a presence in millions of Garden State homes, the New Jersey Network (NJN) was the perfect outlet. Throughout the inaugural season, NJN broadcast Thunder games on Friday and Saturday nights with announcers Randy Stevens and Rick Cerone.

As the television cameras prepared to relay the historic evening to viewers across New Jersey, Miller made his final warm-up tosses to Perona in the home bullpen along the right-field line. Across the field, Pulsipher delivered his preparatory strikes to catcher Alberto Castillo. The bullpen mounds had been lowered since April 27. At that time, the irrepressible Guilfoyle had commented on their steepness, claiming, "I'm going to become the first man to motorcycle jump from a bullpen mound into Pennsylvania."

After singer Terry Cashman completed the National Anthem, the premonitory excitement was raised to a fever pitch. Near the picnic area down the left-field concourse, smoke from the temporary grill drifted toward the outfield. By 7:02 PM, Miller was on the mound, adjusting to its fresh contours and throwing a few more warm-up pitches. In the on-deck circle, which had been cut from the fresh sod, Otero shook a weight from his bat and headed to the plate. At 7:06, with the overflow crowd cheering in final realization that Trenton's minor-league dream had come true, Miller reared back and made his initial delivery. The pitch was a ball high. As the baseball settled into Perona's glove, Waterfront Park had crossed the threshold. Looking on with a sigh of relief, Prunetti smiled. In the dugout, Runnells simply wanted his young starter to throw the ball over the plate.

Perhaps a bit overwhelmed by all the attention, Miller walked the speedy Otero on four pitches, eliciting another Waterfront first—the first boos. It was a half-hearted, sarcastic salvo, and Miller wiggled out of the early jam thanks to Perona, who caught Otero trying to steal second with a strong throw across the infield to O'Neal. "I had to adjust to that pitching mound," Miller explained. "It was a little different than the bullpen, but I think with all those eyes on him, Cooper was a little more nervous than we were. Once he settled down, I did, too." As the pitcher strolled off the field following the first half inning, the fans behind the home dugout stood and applauded.

At 7:14, Mendenhall settled into the batter's box for Pulsipher's first delivery, which Cooper authoritatively called a strike. Waiting for a pitch he could drive, the willowy shortstop almost sent the crowd into first-inning euphoria as he lifted the second pitch to left-center field. Getting a quick jump on the play, Otero guided the ball into his glove at the warning track. The crowd, uncertain how to judge the distance of fly balls in the new facility, gasped at the near miss. Mendenhall dropped his head as he rounded first base, and Pulsipher quickly settled down.

With one out in the top of the second, Chris Saunders doubled, marking the first-ever Waterfront base hit. In spite of that opportunity, Miller kept the Mets off the scoreboard through the first four innings. Capitalizing on some sloppy defense, the Thunder plated an unearned run in the bottom of the second as Delli Carri and Saltzgaber etched their names in Waterfront's list of firsts. Delli Carri reached second on a fielding error by Saunders and scored the first run—the first minor-league run in Trenton since September 1950—on a single by Saltzgaber. The 26-year-old Saltzgaber would be released by the Tigers on June 6 (with a .169 batting average) and offered a Single-A coaching position—which he accepted. Nonetheless, one of his 12 hits during the '94 season would always be that first Waterfront single, which tailed away from Otero for an RBI and a 1-0 Thunder lead.

That cushion lasted until the fifth, when Binghamton right fielder Ed Fully doubled to right-center and scored on an RBI single by Otero. The Thunder rallied in the bottom of the inning to score a pair of runs on a one-out single by DuBose, a Decillis walk, an RBI single by Clark, and an RBI double by Perona. The damage could have been greater, but Pulsipher buckled down to strike out Delli Carri and Mashore to end the inning.

By the seventh, Miller was beginning to tire. Almost immediately, he allowed a pair of Mets to reach base. Quickly, Runnells made the call to the bullpen, summoning Venezuelan righty Blas Cedeno. One of the most good-natured young men to wear a Thunder uniform during the first three seasons (Guilfoyle became responsible for teaching him a new English word every day), Cedeno had been promoted from Lakeland on April 27 to replace Maxcy. As Miller sauntered off the field, he tipped his hat and smiled, grateful for the opportunity to pitch on the historic evening.

Meanwhile, Cedeno attempted to bail the Thunder out of the mess. First baseman Omar Garcia stroked a two-run double to the left-center gap to tie the game. "I made a mistake," Cedeno said in broken English. "Sometimes one pitch can turn things around. I know if I get that guy out, we win. The pitch was too high." Both runs were charged to Miller, who departed to ice his elbow in the clubhouse with a line that read: 6 1/3 innings, five hits, three runs (all earned), five walks, and three strike-outs. Afterward, Runnells lauded his pitcher's ability to keep the Thunder close.

While Miller looked on helplessly from the dugout, Pulsipher worked through the eighth inning without allowing any further damage. Garcia made him a winner with an RBI single off Cedeno in the top of the ninth. Left fielder Jeff Berry drove in another run as much of the overflow crowd began filtering through the exits. Mets closer Andy Beckerman pitched a scoreless ninth for his seventh save of the season, nailing down the 5-3 victory for Binghamton.

"That's the biggest crowd I've ever played in front of," said Virginia native Pulsipher, who would complete the '94 season with a 14-9 record, a 3.22 ERA, and 171 strike-outs to earn Eastern League Pitcher of the Year honors. "But I really didn't feel much pressure. We might have thought about ruining their opener a little bit, but you have to play 142 games in this league. So this was really no different than the others."

While Pulsipher spoke for the Mets, the reaction to Waterfront's opening was much different down the hall in Runnells' dark, unfinished office. As reporters and television cameramen filed into the cramped room for postgame interviews, he decided to unload more than a month's worth of frustration for the media. The loss was bad enough, but he had other things on his mind as he began shouting in front of his tiny shower stall. "Let's do the interview here, because this is where I feel most comfortable," he implored with a sarcastic, look-what-I-have-to-go-through-to-get-dressed tone.

Picking up steam as the cameras rolled, the manager added forcefully, "It was nice finally playing in front of a partisan crowd. There was a great deal of enthusiasm, electricity. I just wish the field was a little better. It has a tendency to pull down the quality of players we have. I think the conditions are awful.

"There are some things that are rectifiable, and there are other things that we are going to have trouble with all year. We have to represent Trenton and the Detroit Tigers, and it's going to be difficult to do that when we can't even hang our clothes in our lockers or leave things in here because there are workers coming through. It will be a tremendous place someday, but I don't know if it will happen this year."

As Runnells completed his tirade, Bombard and Bradshaw sipped beer from a can and nodded their heads in agreement. "We might as well be on a road trip, except that we played in front of a big partisan crowd," the manager bellowed, his face turning flush. "They don't even have water to wet down the infield. The outfield is saturated and the infield is like a pavement." Problems notwithstanding, the homestand would continue the next night.

HOME SWEET HOME

The first Waterfront Park homestand, which included 10 games between the May 9 stadium opening and a May 18 day-night doubleheader, drew a total of 52,297 fans (an average of more than 5200 per stadium opening). Several chilly, overcast days held the attendance down a bit, but overall, the park's reception was nothing short of incredible. The parking lots surrounding the stadium were well-patrolled, well-lighted, and most significantly, safe. Hodes' Thunder staff was friendly and accommodating. Ushers were stationed throughout the park to help patrons find their seats quickly. The right-center field scoreboard was a lime-green entertainment showpiece, just as Hodes had predicted. The beer at the temporary concession stands was cold and the hamburger smoke from the grill enticing. Word quickly spread that the ballpark was sensational, offering affordable food and beverages and spectacular sight lines. "There's not a bad seat in the house," said many who passed through the turnstiles during the first week-and-a-half.

On May 10, before a second-night crowd of 4024, DuBose smashed the first homer in Waterfront history, a 440-foot shot off Binghamton starter Robert Person that cleared all three tiers of center-field billboards. McCarthy and Simonetta chronicled the moment for the radio audience as DuBose, the Thunder's No. 3 hitter, circled the bases to a standing ovation. Also during the 9-5 loss to Binghamton, Perona hit the first triple in stadium history. DuBose finished the evening with a 2-for-4 line that included four RBIs. Through 28 games, he was hitting .281 with four homers and 17 RBIs (trailing only Clark's 25 among Thunder batters). From all indications, he was an emerging star, certainly capable of hitting .300 at the Double-A level. Over the next 11 days, however, his average fell 25 points as he homered once, drove in two runs, and struck out nine times. For DuBose, sudden celebrity in Trenton held a dangerous attraction. Unlike most of his teammates, who found living accommodations outside the city, he and reliever Cecil Pettiford lived in the heart of the city, on Liberty Street. Almost immediately, DuBose befriended scores of young black children. He was their Pied Piper, and they showed up at Waterfront Park before games to play catch. "Brian, Brian," they shrieked as he clowned with them.

"I figured it was going to be like this," said DuBose, who turned 23 during the first homestand (on May 17). "I meet a lot of kids . . . a lot of kids." During spring training, he had talked openly about his desire to be a role model for urban children. Trenton, with a minority population of more than 51,000 in 1994, was a perfect forum for that desire. He gave away countless tickets to his new friends. He took many of them into the clubhouse to meet his teammates. "Not many city kids play baseball anymore; I'd like to show them that it's cool," he explained. "These days, all of their heroes are basketball players. So I like to sit around and talk to them for a little while." As a result, all of the young admirers loved "Doobie."

For DuBose, the greatest danger of Thunder notoriety involved the Trenton nightlife, which held a magnetic attraction for him. Many of the new players were lured into local taverns by owners who wanted to attract patrons to "hang out with the Thunder." As a result, free drinks were available at any number of stops. "I never had to pay for a drink while I was in Trenton," said one '94 player. One of those establishments was the Soho on Mott Street, located several minutes from the stadium. Owner Bill Rednor relished the Thunder business. To keep the players happy and ensure that other patrons knew they were in the establishment, he instituted a house policy that they could drink free as long as they paid for their food. The Soho gradually became the unofficial Thunder bar. At the end of the inaugural season, the players presented Rednor with an autographed Thunder batting practice jersey, which he proudly sheathed in plastic and hung behind the bar.

Each night, following the game, DuBose made the rounds of Trenton nightspots. While Clark and Mashore shuffled home to their Bensalem apartment for a night's rest, Doobie often drank himself into oblivion. His final 1994 numbers would reflect that penchant for mischief. In spite of his promising start, a careless lifestyle and a suspicious back injury limited him to 378 at-bats and a .225 batting average, almost 100 points lower than his '93 Single-A average. He drove in just 41 runs and hit nine homers (only four of them coming after June 1). Runnells expressed great disappointment with his work ethic and commitment. By the end of the season, he was removed from Detroit's 40-man roster. Some said the back injury was the reason, but others admitted the truth. DuBose had developed a substance-abuse problem. He missed the entire '95 season before trying to sign with the Seattle Mariners before the '96 spring training. When the team discovered that he had a drug record, he was finished. Clark, who by 1996 was firmly entrenched as Detroit's everyday first baseman, kept in touch with his old friend, but their career paths had taken very different directions.

GROWING PAINS

On Friday, May 13, 1994, Trenton fans who came dressed in Halloween costumes received $1 off admission for terrace seats. On Saturday night, May 14, an overflow gathering of 6614 watched Runnells' club lose to Eshelman and Bowie 4-2. The following afternoon, a crowd of 6419 saw Miller beat the Baysox 10-4, as Clark hit a two-run homer in the seventh. Big Tony's blast sent the fans home with free pizza as a result of a promotion that was valid "each time the Thunder score nine runs in a home victory." When he came to the plate in the eighth inning, Clark was introduced by Hardison as "the pizza man."

Throughout the first 9 days of the Thunder's Waterfront Park tenure, construction workers continued scrambling to provide the stadium's necessary amenities. In the midst of the Eastern League season, the facility was truly a work-in-progress. Everywhere there were details to complete, from painting the dugout rails to carpeting the luxury boxes. Other projects, like the Thunder's indoor batting cage and the team's permanent stadium offices, remained months from being finished. "I'm tired of complaining about everything," said Withem, echoing his teammates' sentiments. Gradually, electricity was provided for Runnells' office, and toilet partitions were installed in the Thunder clubhouse. "You couldn't even sit down in there without looking at somebody else," Greene observed about the temporary inconvenience. Without the use of a permanent training room, Lon Pinhey was forced to improvise with his treatment of the players' bumps and bruises. Throughout the first 9 days, the Thunder uniforms were sent to a local dry cleaner because the stadium didn't yet have washing room facilities. On the field, several left-handed batters insisted that the white tooth billboard in left-center field prevented them from seeing the ball properly as it left the opposing pitcher's hand. "I can't believe they put that tooth in that position; that's a big concern," Runnells said. For the entire franchise, moving into Waterfront Park required a great deal of improvisation and adaptation.

On May 17, Albany-Colonie's Tim Rumer finally took the mound at Waterfront. For the quiet left-hander, the wait was well worth it. Before a gathering of 3888 that included actor James Earl Jones (who read the National Anthem), he defeated Withem and the Thunder 7-1. Rumer scattered six hits, walking two and striking out five. Mendenhall and Delli Carri had two hits apiece, but Withem was shelled for six earned runs on 11 hits. On the first pitch of the game—a fastball—he served up a solo homer to Yankees' third baseman Andy Fox. The ball cleared the right-field fence and bounded into the river.

"People started calling me the ace of the staff," the superstitious Withem said in disgust. "Since then, I've gone straight downhill." At one point during the season, he would lose nine decisions in a row.

Before the May 17 loss, Lipsman gathered Runnells and his players in the home clubhouse to relay a bit of unexpected news. As a goodwill gesture and a way of helping the team after a rare day-night doubleheader on May 18 (both games would be nine innings, the first one starting at 12:35 PM and the second at the regular 7:05 PM), the Thunder ownership had decided to fly the team to Portland, Maine, for its four-game weekend series. Several days earlier, Runnells had halfheartedly inquired about the possibility of airplane (rather than the normal bus) travel, but he was sure the request would be denied. Airplane travel simply wasn't part of a Double-A team's budget. As Lipsman told the team they would depart from Newark Airport at 10:00 AM on Thursday morning, the players stood and applauded. Full-time Thunder driver Curley Pleasant would drive the bus to Portland and meet the team there.

" The owners and I realized that all of the rescheduling was quite a strain on the players," Hodes explained. "We decided as an organization to alleviate some of the pressure that has been put on the team over the last month."

"It's unheard of at the Double-A level to fly," Runnells explained. "This is an absolute first for me. I'm fired up, and I think the players are very happy. I don't think people understand how big this is. My jaw dropped when I heard the news. This helps smooth things over. Most of the things that were going on early in the season were just unavoidable because we were trying to get the new stadium ready in a new city."

Buoyed by the flight plans, the Thunder swept the day-night doubleheader against Albany-Colonie, winning the day game 4-3 and the nightcap 6-5 to improve their record to 18-18. (They had finished the first homestand with a 5-5 mark.) The day game—a "Businessperson's Special"—drew 6329, and they watched in awe as Clark slammed a homer off the green hitting backdrop in straightaway center. The nightcap featured the first rehab appearance in Waterfront history. New York Yankees' left-handed reliever Steve Howe threw 22 pitches (18 of them strikes), allowing two hits and two unearned runs. He also threw his hat into the crowd as he left the field. The 36-year-old Howe (the 1982 National League Rookie of the Year when he pitched for the Los Angeles Dodgers) was long gone by the time Perona hit a two-run homer off Keith Seiler for the game-winning margin. Guilfoyle, who pitched extremely well during the first homestand, picked up the victory to improve to 3-0. Clearly, the outgoing lefty enjoyed his maiden New Jersey professional baseball journey, lowering his ERA by almost a full run, from 4.82 to 3.86, over the 10-game span.

A TEAM IN FLUX

In spite of the revised travel accommodations to Portland, the Thunder struggled miserably in southern Maine, losing all four games by a combined 25-7 margin. What was a .500 record when the team arrived at the Newark Airport became an 18-22 mark when Starr Bus No. 108 left Portland's Hadlock Field in the rearview mirror. Edmondson, Miller, and Withem each suffered losses in the Sea Dogs' first-year facility, as did Guilfoyle. Incredibly, three of the Thunder's seven runs were scored on solo homers by Clark. Following each Portland loss, as the visitors trudged across the field to the clubhouse, they were forced to watch the hydraulic lighthouse behind center field celebrate the Sea Dogs' accomplishment. "I don't care if I never see another lighthouse as long as I live," Runnells told McCarthy.

During Trenton's fourth straight loss at Portland, a 10-2 Sunday afternoon drubbing, Withem deliberately threw a pitch at catcher Charles Johnson's head. It was not a good idea. "I just blew up," the young righty said. "I was frustrated. My last three games have been terrible." Runnells talked to Withem about the incident, which wound up costing him $300 and a five-game suspension after he was ejected. It was the first suspension in Thunder history. The fine and suspension were handed down by Levenda from the league office in Plainville, Connecticut.

Returning to their normal mode of bus travel, the Thunder arrived in Albany,

New York, on May 23 for a four-game series with the Yankees at Heritage Park. Clark had played in all 40 of the Thunder's games—a career high. He had driven in 36 runs, second in the Eastern League behind Canton-Akron's Marc Marini. He was hitting .264 and doing a much better job handling breaking pitches. Three of his Portland hits came off curveballs. Most importantly, though, he was staying away from the training table and the slew of injuries that had limited his professional career.

"I didn't set any goals this year because, as I said from day one, my biggest concern was just to stay healthy and get as many at-bats as possible," he said as he relaxed in the Albany dugout. "I can't really say I'm on pace right where I want to be. I'm just happy that I've been able to play every game this year." With that, he rapped on the wood bench below him.

Projected over a full 142-game Double-A season, Clark's late May numbers indicated that he could hit 35 homers and 128 RBIs—certainly major-league-type production. Through May 22, his 36 RBIs were almost twice as many as DuBose and more than twice as many as every other Thunder player. Trenton was hitting .234 as a team—the worst in the league—providing little protection for the switch-hitting Clark in the clean-up spot. "Can you imagine how many runs he would have driven in if he had better players around him?" wondered one major-league veteran after analyzing Clark's 1994 numbers.

Before crowds of less than 1000, the Thunder split the series with Albany-Colonie, winning the first two games before dropping a pair. In the opener, a 3-2 Trenton triumph, Mysel allowed just two runs on five hits to outduel the Yankees' Brian Boehringer, who threw a complete game but nonetheless took the loss. Mendenhall was 3-for-3 with an RBI and run scored, and Mashore was 2-for-3. The Thunder took the second game 5-4 despite walking 10 batters. A two-run single by O'Neal (who was hitting .163 through 34 games) provided the winning margin for Edmondson (who improved to 4-5). Later that night in the hotel bar, Miller celebrated his 21st birthday (actually, he was a couple days early because he was born on May 29, 1973) with a few rounds of drinks. In a place far from his Louisville, Kentucky, home, he had officially reached adulthood. It was just another by-product of life on the road in the minors. The bartender bought him a free drink to commemorate the occasion.

Through the first 40 games, injuries hadn't presented a problem for Runnells and his players. That changed on May 26 during a 2-1 loss to the Yankees when the Thunder lost Decillis to a strained rib-cage muscle. Hitting .291 with 15 RBIs at the time of his injury, Decillis had settled into the No. 3 spot in the lineup, in front of Clark. His absence spelled major trouble for Runnells and the Thunder. It also meant that Delli Carri had to start playing on an everyday basis. Figuring that Decillis would miss at least a week to 10 days, Detroit signed free-agent infielder Bobby Perna, a Philadelphia native who had been released by Cincinnati on May 15. The 25-year-old Perna arrived at Waterfront in time for a three-game weekend series against Portland on May 27. Unfortunately, Perna wasn't the cure for the Thunder's offensive woes. He hit .103 in 18 games before his late June release, earning distinction as perhaps the worst hitter of the first three Thunder seasons.

The crowds during the three-game set against the Sea Dogs confirmed what those who had visited Waterfront already knew—Delaware Valley fans were starved for minor-league baseball and its attendant pageantry. The Thunder won a 7-6 game on Friday, May 27, before 6271 paying customers. On Saturday night, a standing-room-only throng of 7169—the first 7000-plus crowd to witness a Trenton minor-league game since 1947—showed up to see Mysel drop a 6-1 decision. The following day, 6522 more enjoyed one of the longest homers of Waterfront's first three seasons—a 450-foot shot by Charles Johnson that sailed over the left-field fence and bounced across Route 29 as a pair of gleeful children chased the souvenir. Fourteen-year-old Keith Tolbert of Willingboro and 13-year-old Dustin Overton of West Trenton haggled over the ball after dodging traffic to claim it. "He got every bit of it," Edmondson replied when reporters inquired about Johnson's pulverization of the fastball delivery. "He hit the crap out of it."

Ironically, Johnson had just returned from a brief, five-game stint with the major-league Florida club, where he hit his first big-league homer off Philadelphia ace Curt Schilling. Johnson handled his first glimpse of the majors with mature perspective, but he "couldn't find a good comfortable point to get into a groove at the plate" against Double-A pitchers until Edmondson served up his gopher ball. Despite the 220-pound catcher's towering homer, the Thunder won the game 8-6 to improve to a 22-25 record. Clark was 2-for-5 with three RBIs, and Bauer secured his third save by striking out four batters in two innings. "The last week or so, I haven't been getting the key hits, so this feels pretty good," Clark said at his locker while celebrating the two-run, seventh-inning double that won the game.

By the first week of June, Mysel was beginning to get the hang of the Eastern League. Following 8 2/3 strong innings at Albany on May 23, he authored his best Double-A performance on Friday, June 3, at New Britain's Beehive Field. Before the game, Clark set up a minishrine inside his locker. Atop two black bats, the big slugger placed a plastic-encased baseball card of Hank Aaron from his days with the Milwaukee Braves. The karma seemed to rub off on Mysel. The result was a complete game that would have been a shut-out if not for a solo homer by New Britain shortstop Randy Brown in the bottom of the fourth inning. Instead, Mysel spun a six-hitter and tied the Thunder single-game best with nine strikeouts. "I feel a lot more confident," he admitted. Milne was 2-for-4 with a pair of RBIs. The game also featured the first managerial ejection in Thunder annals, as New Britain skipper Jim Pankovits was tossed by home-plate umpire Brian Gilbert for arguing one of Mysel's strikeouts. The victory improved Trenton to a 23-28 record, but the team's roster was about to be shuffled by parent club Detroit. Already, hitting coach Kevin Bradshaw had been replaced by Dan Raley. The quiet, hard-working Bradshaw was named manager of the Tigers' rookie-league team in Bristol, Virginia.

On Saturday, June 4, Runnells learned that relief pitcher Phil Stidham had been promoted from Toledo to Detroit, making him the first former Thunder player to earn a ticket to the major leagues. As the manager relaxed in his fourth-floor room at the Ramada Inn, he discussed the 25-year-old righty's accomplishment with pride. "I'm really fired up about it," Runnells admitted. "He deserves it. He pitched very well for us [three saves and a 0.00 ERA in six April appearances]."

The manager also announced that relief pitcher Matt Bauer had been summoned to Toledo, taking with him a 2-0 record, a 1.07 ERA, and three saves in 14 Thunder games. He would be replaced by left-hander Sean Whiteside, a 23-year-old Georgian who was promoted from Lakeland. During his brief, 2-month Double-A stint, Bauer had established himself as one of the team's most popular players. He had posed for a team poster with Perona as a promotion for "Arm and Hammer Night." With him, a key part of Runnells' bullpen was departing. "You get into that emotional twist of being a manager when you have a good player, a vital cog in your team and your success, leave," the manager said. "When you lose him, it hurts a little bit."

Later that afternoon, Stidham made his major-league debut. It was a rocky beginning, to say the least. During Detroit's 21-7 loss to Minnesota, he allowed six earned runs on six hits over 1 2/3 innings. He also struck out two batters. He would appear in five games before being returned to Toledo. Over that five-game span, he compiled a 0-0 record with an unsightly 24.92 ERA.

Following Bauer's promotion, Detroit made several more adjustments to the Thunder roster in the first wholesale round of promotions and demotions in Trenton franchise history. The inevitable part of minor-league baseball is that some Single-A players cannot make the grade at the next level. It is a big jump. On Monday, June 6, a rare off-day, O'Neal and Greene (1-1, 7.91 ERA, three saves) were sent back to Lakeland. Taking their places on Runnells' roster were second baseman Evan Pratte and left-hander Rich Kelley. During the New Britain series—his last as a professional player—Runnells threw some extra batting practice and implored Saltzgaber to hit one out of the park (the attempt was unsuccessful). Salty's place was taken by outfielder Roberto Rojas. In 43 Thunder games, O'Neal hit .194, with five doubles and 13 RBIs. He also committed seven errors. In 20 appearances out of the bullpen, Greene was 1-1 with a 7.91 ERA. He walked 21 batters while striking out just five. He also recorded three saves. "Right now, I'm a thrower, not a pitcher," Greene admitted. "I'm struggling."

Despite the personnel changes, each day the 6-foot-8 Clark's stature grew among the new Trenton fans. Perhaps it was a product of his prodigious power at the plate. Perhaps it was his giant stretch off the first-base bag as he fielded an infield throw. Most of all, though, Tony Clark became a symbol of the inaugural Thunder season because of his infectious, gentle personality. After each home game, as another sell-out crowd filed out of Waterfront Park, Clark waded through the throngs, signing scores of autographs along the way. On the road, he often delayed the Thunder's bus departure as he patiently accommodated Eastern League signature seekers. Everything about him was genuine—including his major-league potential.

CHAPTER 9

Tony Clark Emerges

> "The great thing about baseball is that you've got 7 days in a week, and chances are, you're playing on all seven of them."
>
> —1994 THUNDER ALL-STAR TONY CLARK

More than anything else, baseball is a game of moments and images. A towering homer. A spectacular defensive play. A dramatic collision at the plate. The final pitch of a no-hitter. A pennant-clinching fleshpile. All have a way of becoming embellished and assuming a life of their own as they are passed along for succeeding generations to enjoy. For the Trenton Thunder franchise, the '94 season was filled with historic firsts, moments that brought the team's cartoonish, two-headed logo to life. None, however, was more dramatic than what occurred on June 7 in the sixth inning of game two during a Waterfront Park doubleheader against Bowie.

From the September 1993 day when ground was broken for the stadium, Trenton-area baseball fans pondered the inviting possibility of home-run balls traveling over the fence and into the Delaware River. Through the first month of the inaugural season, no one had accomplished this feat with any real authority. Several balls may have trickled down the bank and into the muck, but none landed in the brown water with a plunk—on the fly. Who would be the first? The most obvious answer to that question was the switch-hitting Clark, who conducted daily exhibitions of raw batting-practice power. Occasionally, Runnells stood behind the batting cage, rating Big Tony's hacks. "That's 1 million dollars. That's 500,000 dollars. That's 200,000 dollars." It was all in good fun.

On June 7, the Thunder looked uninspired during a 4-0, game one loss to the Baysox and talented left-handed strike-out specialist Jimmy Haynes. Game two was a different story. By the time clean-up hitter Clark came to the plate to face right-handed reliever Steve Chitren, Trenton had the game well in hand. Batting from the right side of the plate, Clark unloaded on a fastball with a concussive thud. The result was the first grand-slam homer in Waterfront history. As if on cue, the ball cleared an 80-foot light tower in right field before sailing into the Delaware River—with a splash. A nearby fishing boat meandered in the direction of the landing place, its occupant thankful not to have taken a direct hit. The computer-generated, World War II vintage air-raid siren that accompanies all Thunder homers wailed into the South Trenton night.

A crowd of 4924 stood and applauded en masse as Clark lumbered around the bases. In the radio booth, McCarthy and Simonetta were stunned. "That was a prime-time at-bat for a prime-time player," McCarthy observed. Estimates of the homer's distance ranged from 475 to 500 feet, but the ever-humble Clark wasn't buying into the hyperbole. "It went further than the fence, and that's all I'm concerned about," he said of his eleventh homer in 55 games. Others in the Trenton clubhouse expressed awe. Guilfoyle, who had watched the ball sail over the Thunder bullpen, preferred a humorous analogy. Pointing to the nearby Route 1 toll bridge connecting Trenton and Morrisville, Pennsylvania, he quipped, "The red light is flashing and the bells are going off at the toll booth. I think Tony owes Pennsylvania 50 cents because he hit that ball into another state."

Make no mistake, Clark arrived in Trenton with the burden of great expectations saddled to his 250-pound frame. During Runnells' introductory press conference, he described the infielder as "one of the most powerful players in professional baseball. You're not going to believe some of the balls he hits."

Nonetheless, as Clark ascended to the top of the Eastern League power statistics, even the manager was impressed with his gradual improvement. McCarthy had a theory about their relationship. "I don't think [Runnells] knew what to expect from Tony. There were questions about whether he was tough enough to succeed in Double-A, but I think T.R. was proud that he kept after him every day and that Tony was able to maintain an even keel. When you look back 20 years from now and ask, 'Who was the catalyst for Thunder baseball?'—it was Tony. He's the guy everybody heard about during that first season."

The key to Clark's sudden emergence was his work ethic. The field problems that interrupted the season had little effect on him. Following one rainout, he took batting practice from Runnells in the Thunder clubhouse using taped-up socks. Once, after a day game, he begged the manager to stay afterward and give him some extra hitting work. As Runnells threw pitches, the manager's family waited patiently in the stands. They were headed to the Jersey Shore for a rare bit of relaxation—but not until Clark was satisfied with his swing.

When the Thunder were on the road, Clark kept largely to himself, preferring quiet time with his pregnant fiancée, Fran. He often lifted small, portable weights in his hotel room. He carried stockpiles of fresh fruit in his suitcase. He liked to read stories to his unborn child. Occasionally, he stopped by a restaurant for a postgame dinner, but he never stayed around to partake in late-night revelry like many of his Trenton teammates. There was always another at-bat, another chance to move closer to the big leagues, where all the experts had predicted he would ultimately wind up.

HARRISBURG HEARTACHE

By the time he took the mound to face Harrisburg at RiverSide Stadium on June 10, 1994, Shannon Withem was a frustrated pitcher. He had served a 5-day suspension and paid the league office $300 for his Portland antics. He had not won a game since April 30—dropping five consecutive decisions in the process. Facing the league's best team on their home field, he was intent on reversing the tide. And for eight innings, that's exactly what he did. Before a crowd of 3524, the Michigan native took a 1-1 tie into the bottom of the ninth. Along the way he had scattered seven hits while striking out six batters and walking none. He didn't allow a Harrisburg runner past second base until the seventh inning. His control had been impressive, but the Thunder had left nine runners on base, eight of them in scoring position. Senators' shortstop Mark Grudzielanek led off the ninth with a single, and second baseman Mike Hardge sacrificed him into scoring position with a bunt. What happened next summarized Withem's rapidly mounting aggravation. Harrisburg center fielder Yamil Benitez stroked a clean single to center, which Mashore fielded and relayed perfectly to Perona at the plate. By all appearances, Perona tagged Grudzielanek for the second out, but home-plate umpire Greg Gibson didn't see it that way. He called "Grudz" safe. The Senators improved to a 35-23 record with the controversial 2-1 win. Withem went ballistic, bumping Gibson in protest as the umpire tried to leave the field. Bombard sprinted from the Trenton dugout to restrain his irate pitcher. As Gibson turned away, he shot Withem a look that said, "That'll cost you, buddy."

"I knew it wasn't going to help," Withem said of his argument. "I just wanted to get a few words in. No, I didn't make contact. I just told him I didn't agree with the call. . .with a few expletives."

The irony of the situation for the Thunder was that Runnells wasn't around to witness the dramatic conclusion. Gibson had thrown him out in the eighth inning for arguing a strikeout by Mashore. As he headed for the showers, Runnells gestured toward the umpire by extending his right thumb as if flipping a coin. "He changed his call, and he gave me a very unsatisfactory reason," Runnells said about his first ejection of the season. "He told me he forgot what the count was. I mean, here's the home-plate umpire forgetting the count with the game on the line. . ."

While he didn't see Withem's tirade, Runnells stuck up for his hard-luck starter. "He [Grudzielanek] must have been out," the manager told the press. "I think the umpire stuck it to us. I think he just shoved it right up our ass. And when that happens, I'll tell you what—I have no respect for that."

Witnessing Withem's ill-advised protest, however, was league president Levenda. Even so, Levenda promised to wait until he read Gibson's game report to decide on another fine or a suspension for the Thunder pitcher.

Unfortunately for Trenton, the heartbreaking, one-run loss was followed by another devastating turn of events. The following night, Harrisburg player/coach Lance Rice's tenth-inning RBI single off Guilfoyle lifted the Senators to a 5-4 victory that dropped the Thunder to a 25-33 record (eight games under .500 for the first time all season). DuBose homered for the first time in 28 days, but Rice— who entered the game only because regular catcher Gary Hymel had lost a contact lens—was thrilled to provide the coup de grace. "Harrisburg has my number," Guilfoyle (4-3) said. "I'm not even a challenge for them."

Following the June 11 setback, the Thunder had dropped eight of their last 11 games. The next day, on a clear Sunday afternoon in Harrisburg, they showed some rare signs of resilience and character. With Miller on the mound, Trenton fell behind, 3-1, after two innings. In the third, however, Clark ripped a 420-foot homer to right-center off Senators' starter J.J. Thobe. The shot was just one of eight extra-base hits the Thunder would author on the day. Mendenhall enjoyed a rare show of power with a three-run, fourth-inning homer that put Trenton on top to stay, 6-3. "It's been a while," the shortstop admitted. "We felt like we deserved this one." Clark also doubled, giving him 28 extra-base hits and 46 RBIs in 59 games. "Statistics aren't really too big of a concern for me," he said after Trenton completed its 10-6 win (one of only four triumphs in 18 season meetings against Harrisburg).

Runnells took the victory in stride, although he realized his team—at 26-33—was waging an uphill battle to maintain contact with Eastern League Southern Division leaders Bowie (37-23) and Harrisburg (37-24). "We had chances to win both of those last two games, and I feel that any time we have a chance to win, we should," the manager observed matter-of-factly. "I've been a little upset because I don't like to lose the way we have been, but I was real happy with the way the guys came back and battled. Hopefully, it will be the start of a good thing."

Toward the end of the game, Mysel's father, Gary, stuck his head in the River-Side Stadium press box. "Tell those guys to save some runs for Dave," he pleaded.

Nearly halfway through the season, the fourth-place Thunder led Eastern League Southern Division cellar-dweller Reading (18-41) by eight games. Trenton picked up two more games over the next 2 days with back-to-back wins over the Phillies at Municipal Stadium. Carlyle improved to 3-4 and lowered his ERA to 3.05 with his fourth complete game of the season, a 6-0 shutout, and Mysel followed with a 7-3 victory that lifted his record to 4-5. The Thunder returned to Waterfront for a four-game series against New Haven with a 3.84 team ERA, third in the league behind the Ravens and Binghamton.

DOWNWARD SPIRAL

On June 16, the Thunder welcomed the franchise's hundred-thousandth customer, a Trenton elementary school student named Joe Cermele. Cermele showed up with a kelly green cast bearing the Thunder logo on his left arm. Due to the injury, he couldn't throw out a ceremonial first pitch, but he did collect a $100 prize for his fortuitous entrance, or approximately $33 for every hit the Trenton lineup produced against New Haven pitcher Juan Acevedo that evening. Acevedo, who ultimately led the Eastern League in victories during the '94 season with 17, was brilliant, striking out 11 batters and walking three. Edmondson had no chance. He allowed 12 hits over six innings and fell to 4-7 with the 7-0 loss.

On Friday, June 17, a crowd of 6358 watched Miller and the Thunder trail New Haven righty Ivan Arteaga 2-0 in the bottom of the eighth inning. With DuBose on first and one out, Tony Clark came to the plate with an opportunity to tie the game through one mighty swing. The anxious crowd was on its feet. Runnells, frustrated at his team's flagging offensive output, took himself out of the third-base coaching box and sent assistant coach Dan Raley out on the field. He was hoping for some good luck. Many of the new Thunder fans were looking for a dramatic conclusion. They got one—but not the one they were looking for. Clark struck out for the seventy-first time in 240 at-bats. His trend of feast-or-famine continued. He couldn't win every game by himself. No baseball player can. New Haven hung on for a 2-0 shut-out that extended Trenton's scoreless streak to 24 innings. Runnells was entirely frustrated. "I was trying to shake things up," he said of his unorthodox decision to remain in the dugout rather than the third-base coaching box. "As you can see, my influence was tremendous as we pounded out three hits [for the second consecutive day]."

In spite of this defeat, the Thunder players and coaches spent a portion of Saturday, June 18, making autograph appearances at local shopping malls in Burlington and Lawrence, New Jersey, as well as in Middletown Township, Pennsylvania. The franchise's effort to reach out to the community and draw in new patrons was intensifying. That evening, as a weekend crowd of 6823 settled in, the Thunder inducted the first two members of the Trenton Baseball Hall of Fame—late Trenton Senator and Washington Senator George Case, Jr., and former Trenton journalist/broadcaster Bus Saidt. Accepting Saidt's plaque was his widow, Helen Martin Saidt, enjoying her first glimpse of Waterfront Park.

"I like it—it's very intimate," she said. "I like the fact that it's so close to the river, which makes it unique." Following the induction, she changed into a Trenton Thunder T-shirt and toured the facility.

Meanwhile, back on the field, the Thunder struggled against a New Haven pitcher for the third consecutive evening. Without Decillis—who was "getting close" to coming off the disabled list as his rib injury improved—the Thunder lineup was anemic. Carlyle tried to keep his team in the game, but three runs by the Ravens in the top of the fourth opened the gates for a 5-1 New Haven victory. The run that Trenton scored against New Haven lefty and former Rutgers University star Phil Schneider was unearned. "No matter who's out there, we're just playing great baseball," Schneider said. "Everything is clicking for us right now."

The final game of the New Haven series was played on Father's Day, Sunday, June 19, with scorching temperatures and an intense midday sun baking 6809 Waterfront patrons. The high that day was 100 degrees, and several customers were treated for heat prostration. Because of Waterfront's open design, which is slanted toward the southwest, there is very little shelter from direct sunlight during day games. Furthermore, the forest green seats reflect little of the sun's rays. Hardison came over the loudspeaker several times to admonish everyone in attendance to drink plenty of fluids. One of the most interested spectators was Gary Mysel, who celebrated Father's Day by watching his son, Dave, wage a dual battle against the conditions and the red-hot Ravens. Gary woke up early that morning to drive 142 miles east to Trenton from his Hummelstown, Pennsylvania, residence. Before the game, he watched as a Thunder staffer searched for a fan to keep Dave cool between innings. The young pitcher popped his head over the dugout. Recognizing his dad, he smiled and said, "Happy Father's Day."

"It's pretty hot out here," Gary said. "You better try to stay cool. And challenge the hitters today. I want you to go after them."

Dave flashed a big grin and asked his father, "Is it OK if I pitch in my shorts?" Knowing that a victory would be the best Father's Day present he could bestow, Dave pitched well, throwing more than 100 pitches over eight innings. Gary sat and sipped lemonade, analyzing his son's performance. New Haven was simply too tough, however, and the Thunder dropped a 3-1 decision, their fifth loss in a row. Afterward, Dave treated Gary to a hamburger at Fuddrucker's in Langhorne, Pennsylvania.

"It's a father's dream to sit there and watch him pitch," Gary added. "To think about what he's going through out there, it's a thrill to know I had a little part in it. "

Trenton's losing skid reached six games the following night against Canton-Akron as Withem absorbed a 4-2 loss—his eighth in a row. The Thunder finally broke the drought in the sixth game of the homestand with a 10-5 triumph over the Indians. Edmondson was the winning pitcher, improving to 5-7 (although his ERA was a bloated 5.29). In the six home games, the Thunder had drawn more than 36,000 fans. They also lost five times, falling to a 29-39 record, 13 1/2 games behind first-place Bowie, their next opponent.

CURLEY

When the Thunder traveled, they were chauffered by veteran Starr Tours bus operator Curley Pleasant. A likable, outgoing man in his early fifties with a distinctive way of talking that often was hard to understand (some players could do an impressive "Curley" imitation), Pleasant quickly became one of the most valuable members of the Thunder entourage. From the outset, he laid down one simple law for the Trenton players—"Clean up after yourselves on the bus. I'm not a janitor. If you want to ride in a dirty bus, that's fine with me." Inevitably, the bus driver plays a huge role in the team's daily operations. He loads the players' heavy equipment bags in the bus' cargo hold. He shuttles players and coaches from the team hotel to the stadium and to late-night dining spots. He helps the team trainer with his equipment. He is on call 24 hours a day for travel emergencies and trips to the airport or train station.

Curley handled his responsibilities with a style and panache that was unique to his personality. One '94 player was particularly grateful when he returned to the bus after certain games only to find a six-pack of his favorite beer waiting in his seat. Curley also took care of the harder liquor needs of some of the coaches. He was a frequent late-night diner with Clark and DuBose, whom he treated almost like members of his own family. He once took Clark to a soul food restaurant in Binghamton and watched the first baseman consume $30 worth of ribs and collards. For dessert, he wolfed down a whole sweet potato pie. "And to top it off, he ate my piece of banana cake," Curley added incredulously.

Once during the '94 season, Curley realized that a Thunder player had a female guest in his hotel room. The problem? The player's wife had just showed up in the hotel lobby for a surprise visit. Scampering to the elevator, Curley evacuated the young lady just in time to bail the player out of a major jam. The player later thanked the bus driver profusely.

Another member of the '94 team owned a rather sizable collection of pornographic videotapes. During a trip down I-95, the player placed one in the bus VCR, and the four monitors on the 47-seat coach filled with the sights and sounds of carnal activity. Quickly taking note of the new and unauthorized film, Pleasant flew into a rage. "You guys trying to get me in trouble," he mumbled before insisting that the tape be removed. "I can get arrested for that." Within seconds, the video was restored to the player's equipment bag.

"I could tell you some stories about Curley that you wouldn't believe," Edmondson said, but he always got us where we were going quick. And he'd B.S. you and make you laugh. You've gotta love a guy like that."

Among Curley's other job perks was an occasional opportunity to suit up in a Thunder uniform and play catch during batting practice. He particularly enjoyed catching balls behind the backstop. At those times, he was fair game for a little good-natured ribbing from his full-time passengers. "He looks like something out of the movie *Brewster's Millions*," remarked one Thunder player, referring to Curley's facial resemblance to the film's star, Richard Pryor.

As Curley and the Thunder rolled into Bowie's Prince George's Stadium for the first time on June 22, 1994, they were eager to see the Baysox's new, 10,000-seat facility. Then again, the schedule called for six games in 5 days. The season was reaching the make-or-break point. Runnells knew that if his team was ever going to make a move in the standings, it would have to be soon.

MARYLAND MAYHEM

Like life, minor-league baseball is extremely unpredictable. As the Thunder drove through the dusty parking lot of Prince George's Stadium to the temporary dressing trailer that would serve as their clubhouse, Miller sensed something positive was about to happen. Decillis had been activated, and everyone felt that his offensive ability should help down the stretch. "After we lost six in a row, we said, 'Hey, wake up, we're not that bad,' " Miller pointed out.

The wake-up call came inside a brand-new facility that, like Waterfront Park, still had many unfinished construction details. In fact, a large banner over the entrance implored fans to "Please pardon our progress." Despite the structural improvements that remained to be done, Bowie's Bermuda grass field was in immaculate shape. Unlike Waterfront, it had been completed with plenty of time to spare before the first game, which had been played on June 16, six days before the Thunder arrived. "This is so much better than Waterfront," said one Trenton player. "It's a nice field," muttered Runnells over and over as the Thunder took batting practice before the June 22 doubleheader.

In the first game, Miller outdueled Jimmy Haynes, who struck out six batters but was unable to extricate himself from a seventh-inning jam. Trenton scored twice in the final frame for a 3-1 victory. The game also featured a third-inning defensive gem that was almost the first triple play in Thunder annals; the effort fell just short when second baseman Evan Pratte's relay throw to Clark at first was an instant late. "It was real close," Clark explained, holding his index finger and thumb together for emphasis.

In the nightcap, Decillis homered on the first pitch he had seen in almost a month, and Rendina was 3-for-4 with a homer as the Thunder scored five runs in the fifth and held on for an 8-7 triumph that had everyone in the dressing trailer feeling pretty good about the situation. Spot starter Ahearne improved to 3-0 with five innings of solid pitching, and Guilfoyle notched his fifth save. Said Runnells, "It got sloppy, but we got some good hitting tonight, which I think is a real key for us."

Following a rain-out on June 23, the Thunder and the Baysox played another doubleheader on June 24. The Thunder lost the first game 7-2 as Bowie's Brian Sackinsky struck out nine of the 21 batters he faced. Clark was 0-for-3, as were Decillis and Pratte. In the second game, however, Clark enjoyed one of his trademark offensive explosions. Facing Scott Klingenbeck with one out in the first, he smashed a three-run homer to right, his fourteenth round-tripper of the season. With the Thunder leading 3-0 in the third, he hit an RBI double, his nineteenth two-base hit of the year. One inning later, a two-run single scored Delli Carri and DuBose to give Clark a franchise-record six RBIs in the game. The result was a 9-4 Trenton victory. Afterward, Clark joked about narrowly missing a rare baseball achievement—hitting for "the cycle." All he had needed for the cycle was a triple. "For me to hit a triple," he said with a chuckle, "whoever catches it has to fall down and I have to run faster than I ever have before in my life."

On Saturday, June 25, a Prince George's crowd of 7264—including Detroit General Manager Joe Klein, Detroit Minor League Pitching Coordinator Ralph Treuel, and Ragazzo—saw Withem attempt to reverse his string of personal misfortune. During his eight-game losing streak, he had cut off all contact with the media, saying only that he'd talk when he won another game. For five complete innings, it appeared that his self-imposed silence might be over. Entering the bottom of the sixth, Withem had dueled Vaughn Eshelman to a scoreless tie. After yielding two runs in the sixth on a double by left fielder Bo Ortiz, however, Withem was feeling the heat again. In the bottom of the seventh, the Thunder pitcher made what looked like a successful tag along the first base line—and for the second time in 15 days, an outraged Runnells sprinted from the visitor's dugout to argue with umpire Greg Gibson. Face-to-face, the pair had at it for several moments. Finally, Gibson tossed the Thunder manager from the game. Runnells did a chicken scratch—digging his cleats into the dirt—before departing. Withem soon followed—with another loss. In less than 1 year, he had gone from a 10-2 record in Single-A to a 2-10 record in Double-A. "I felt the wrong call was made, and it doesn't matter what umpire was out there," Runnells said of his continuing feud with Gibson.

After showering, Withem boarded the bus without speaking to the press. His downcast look did his talking for him. "The main thing is that he goes out and gets quality performances," Bombard said. "Sure it's frustrating, but it's not the end of the world. It's not a panic situation or anything like that."

While the Thunder completed their Bowie trip, speculation began about the July 11 Double-A All-Star Game, which would be played at Binghamton's Municipal Stadium. Each of the 28 Double-A teams was guaranteed at least one player. Since Trenton was a first-year franchise, most observers thought the

Thunder would have at least two representatives. Clark, who led the Eastern League on June 24 with 59 RBIs in 71 games, was the most logical choice. "It would be great to play in that game, but it's not my biggest concern right now. I just need to keep playing every day and stay healthy. I'd love to go to the All-Star Game because that means somebody else would have noticed the work I've been putting in. That's a sign of achievement I would love to accept."

AN ALL-STAR SNUB

On June 28, before the Thunder's home game against Portland, the rosters for the 1994 Double-A All-Star Game were announced. Everybody in the Trenton clubhouse and front office was shocked. Tony Clark's name was nowhere to be found on the American League squad (the game's format matched representatives of the 14 American League affiliates against players from the 14 National League affiliates). (Ironically, the Eastern League first-base representatives on the American League All-Star Roster were Canton-Akron's Pough and Albany-Colonie's Tate Seefried.) Pitchers Carlyle (3-6, 3.04 ERA, five complete games) and Guilfoyle (4-3, 3.15 ERA, five saves) had been chosen to wear the Thunder colors in Binghamton. Publicly, Clark didn't admit that the omission bothered him. In the off-the-record privacy of "the Ghetto" portion of the Thunder clubhouse, however, he wondered aloud, "What more do I have to do? I guess I haven't paid my dues yet." As of June 30, he was hitting .283, with 19 doubles, 14 homers, and 60 RBIs. Quite simply, he was carrying the Thunder offense, which had received little contribution from DuBose since mid-May. Through 74 games, Doobie was hitting .234, with eight homers and 33 RBIs.

"It's a shame Tony's not going, because he's proven himself in this league," Guilfoyle said in the Waterfront bullpen after accepting sincere congratulations on his All-Star selection from Clark.

"Well, Tony is the All-Star of this team," Carlyle added. "His numbers pretty much say what he's done for us the whole way. As Tony goes, our team goes. I just hope that this doesn't affect him, that he just keeps doing what he's doing."

Runnells didn't say much about Clark's All-Star omission. He had more significant concerns—namely, his team's anemic offense and the ongoing Waterfront Park field drainage problems.

CHAPTER 10

Hope and Sorrow

"They're giving it everything they've got, but there's nothing you can do. They put in all these man-hours, and it's still not safe."

—THUNDER MANAGER TOM RUNNELLS ON THE WATERFRONT GROUNDS CREW'S MID-SUMMER EFFORTS TO UPGRADE THE PLAYING SURFACE

On the morning of Thursday, June 30, 1994, a hot summer sun rose above Waterfront Park before a scheduled 12:35 PM Thunder Businessperson's Special against Portland. A near-sellout crowd was expected for the matinee, but following mid-week thunderstorms that dumped large amounts of rain on the field, it was in no shape for a baseball game. The 2-inch puddles of standing water throughout the outfield's thin, scraggly grass told part of the story. The signs at the stadium entrance—"Today's Game Rained Out"—told the rest. An advertising plane that had been hired by a local Buick dealership flew circles over the park, unaware that the game had been postponed.

Ultimately, Waterfront's poor field drainage forced nine separate postponements—June 7, June 27, June 29, June 30, July 14, July 24, July 26, July 28, and August 17. The July 24 and August 17 dates weren't rescheduled. In addition, on several occasions, games were played under extremely questionable conditions. The resulting logistical problems for the Thunder players were considerable. With no indoor batting cages at Waterfront, they had no options for extra hitting work. "With these rainouts, you don't get any swings at all," Perona explained. "An indoor batting cage is a very necessary thing in minor-league baseball. At this point, there's nothing we can do. Whenever T.R. voiced his frustration, he was looked at as a complainer."

"The field just wasn't playable," Hodes said after inspecting the surface. "Of course we want to get the games in for the fans. They're the reason the facility is here, but by no means are we going to let anyone get hurt." By late June, Hodes had a theory about Waterfront's massively inadequate underground drainage system. "Several months ago, I contacted some people and they recommended we use a certain base for the sod, and I believe it wasn't used," he said. "That's where this all stemmed from."

On July 1, one week after Ragazzo visited Bowie and talked to Baysox personnel about their field, the Thunder and Mercer County officials called in consultant Ray Cipperly, whose high-school baseball field at East Brunswick's Vocational Technical School was considered one of the finest in the Garden State. After one walkthrough of the Waterfront surface, he told Prunetti, Ragazzo, and Hodes without hesitation, "You're going to have to rip the whole thing out after the season."

The trio cringed at the recommendation. "Are you sure?" they repeated.

"Absolutely." According to Cipperly, who subsequently was hired on a full-time basis to help salvage the Thunder season by keeping the grass alive through the end of August, the '94 sod never established roots of any kind. Furthermore, the drainage system that had been set up on a grid of three giant "V's" throughout the field was useless because water couldn't filter through the dirt base to the drains.

On June 30, as disgruntled fans and Thunder players surveyed the beautiful summer sky and realized there would be no game, there was an overriding feeling of helplessness. Upstairs in the 88-seat restaurant, Caruso and Stanley met with concession officials, who estimated that the postponement meant a loss of more than $20,000 in revenue (based on a crowd of 5000 spending $4 each). The previous night, Thunder officials had waited until 8:11 PM—or 1 hour and 6 minutes after the scheduled 7:05 start—to postpone the game against Portland. During the extended delay, the players signed autographs and made small talk while a crowd of about 4500 grew restless. "I'm never coming back," some of them promised after Hardison announced that there would be no game. Cipperly suggested several stopgap options, which included drilling several giant drainage holes in the outfield and a huge roller to flatten the grass into the dirt below. Neither method helped much. He also painted the grass a dark shade of green to enhance its appearance.

"I guess maybe I've come to the realization that there's not a whole lot more that I can do about the condition of the field," Runnells said after one of the nine postponements. "It doesn't do me any good to get upset or to argue with anybody. Maybe over the rest of the year, some things can be rectified. We'll see."

In spite of the continuing field saga, home games against Reading on July 4 and 5 proved one thing for the Thunder management: nothing brings fans to the park like a good fireworks show. On July 4, as the United States celebrated its 218th birthday, a Waterfront Park gathering of 7036 stayed around for some pyrotechnics following Trenton's 5-3 loss to the Phillies. As the casings exploded over the Delaware, the Thunder (33-44) trailed first-place Harrisburg (51-31) by 15 1/2 games. Less than half the season remained. The team's .236 batting average was 14 points worse than any other club in the Eastern League. Decillis was hitting .294 following his 3 1/2-week stint on the disabled list, but Mashore (.244), Perona (.232), Mendenhall (.212), and Rendina (.187) were floundering against some of the best pitching prospects in all of the minor leagues. Rendina's .187 slugging percentage was particularly pitiful for a guy who was expected to thrive during his second Double-A season.

"We're scrapping right now," Mashore admitted. "Tony is the only guy driving in runs with any consistency. Until somebody else starts driving in runs. . ."

"We can't rely on one guy," Runnells added in disgust following Clark's 0-for-4 effort during a 7-3 loss to Reading on July 5 in front of a record Waterfront crowd of 7241 who enjoyed a post-July 4 fireworks display. The July 5 defeat also was another in a season-long litany of shoddy defensive efforts by Mendenhall, who committed two errors on one play to raise his team-leading total to 24. He ended the season with 35 fielding miscues, a dubious record that remained intact through the first three Thunder campaigns.

THE FIRST THUNDER ALL-STARS

On July 11, before a record Binghamton Municipal Stadium crowd of 6542 and a national-television audience, Carlyle and Guilfoyle pitched in the fourth-annual Double-A All-Star Game against their National League counterparts. The Thunder pair rented a car and drove up the Northeast Extension of the Pennsylvania Turnpike. Amidst false rumors that Birmingham Barons outfielder Michael Jordan might show up to announce his minor-league retirement (someone posted his baseball number—45—on a piece of masking tape in a corner of the American League clubhouse), Carlyle threw 10 pitches and allowed one hit during a scoreless sixth inning. Guilfoyle made 11 deliveries and recorded two outs—a pop-up and a strikeout—in the eighth. "I wanted to finish the inning," he said later. As both Thunder pitchers departed, they were saluted by a small group of Trenton fans who had made the 3-hour journey to witness the event.

"It's been an unbelievable year for me so far," Guilfoyle said. "I'm hoping the All-Star Game will get me over the hump again."

New Britain outfielder Matt Stairs was 2-for-5 with a home run to earn the Howe Sports Data Eastern League "Star of Stars" award. Ironically, on July 7 at Waterfront, Stairs had ended one of the worst slumps in his professional career with a game-winning, three-run homer off Guilfoyle. During the postgame All-Star party at the Holiday Inn-Arena, Stairs and Guilfoyle discussed the season. When he left the bar, Stairs looked at the Thunder pitcher and laughed, saying, "And by the way, don't hang me any more curveballs." Guilfoyle rolled his eyes and admitted, "He got me." (Stairs spent the rest of his evening looking for a go-go bar. When he finally found one, he was told by the bouncer, "Sorry, we're closed." In the background, Stairs heard music. He implored, "Please let me in; I'm the MVP of the Double-A All-Star Game." The bouncer replied, "Sure you are, pal.")

Most baseball players have some superstitions, and those who say they don't are probably lying. During the weeks before the game, Guilfoyle had resorted to all types of strange actions in an attempt to dig out of his brief slump. He threw his old baseball glove in the toilet. He wore an extra sock on one foot. A Thunder fan gave him a good luck hat. Guilfoyle was no stranger to adversity, however. In October 1989, he was mugged by a group of strangers in northern New Jersey. "I took a straight beatin'," he recalled. (The scars on his cheek were a result of the ensuing plastic surgery.)

While Guilfoyle searched for a rhythm, Runnells' patience was being tested by all facets of the Thunder situation. Three days before the All-Star Game, the manager conducted a closed-door team meeting "to discuss team goals for the rest of the season." The Thunder reached the 2-day All-Star break with a 37-48 record, fourth place in the Eastern League Southern Division. The team had won three consecutive games against New Britain following Stairs' homer. During the meeting, Runnells advised his team "not to put any pressure on each other." For one weekend, at least, it worked. Immediately following the meeting, the Thunder outscored the Red Sox 21-7 over three weekend games. Withem was particularly impressive in an 8-2 Saturday win, notching his first victory since April 30 and improving to a 3-10 record. "I feel relief, definitely relief," Withem said after snapping his nine-game personal losing streak and allowing the media to share his feelings for the first time in weeks. He allowed nine hits, walked none and struck out eight batters. Clark hit his fifteenth homer, and Decillis—who was forced to play left field when starter Roberto Rojas was ejected for arguing a called third strike—was 3-for-4 with two RBIs on his twenty-seventh birthday.

The star of the closed-door meeting was Mashore. According to Carlyle, the flamboyant center fielder "put in some good words, and I'll leave it at that." Two years later, Edmondson revealed those words during an interview.

"We were talking, just brainstorming as a team," Edmondson recalled. "We all agreed that we knew what we had to do, and then Justin stood up and shouted, 'Things can't get any worse.' Everybody just laughed for a few minutes. It was just the way he put it, but I think Justin had very good intentions. He just didn't know how to express them most of the time."

Reminded of Mashore's outburst, Runnells admitted, "I couldn't believe he said that. After that meeting, things only got worse."

THE DOG DAYS

How bad did the situation become for the '94 Thunder during the dog days of summer? One of the team's veteran players spent most of his afternoons lounging by his apartment pool sipping Bloody Mary's. Others spent their evenings drinking free beer at the Soho. "Given the circumstances, why bother?" seemed to be the prevailing sentiment among the older members of the club, particularly the ones whose minor-league careers were coming to an inevitable conclusion.

In spite of the ongoing field problems, crowds continued to pack Waterfront on days when baseball was actually played. The Thunder's average home attendance during May was 5393 for 15 games. In June, it improved to 5665 (for 10 dates). By July, the average increased to 6383 (for 11 dates).

When Albany-Colonie returned to town on July 13, a record gathering of 7292 was treated to a rehab appearance by Yankees' left-hander Sterling Hitchcock and the first Double-A homer by shortstop Derek Jeter. During a 6-4 Albany-Colonie victory, Hitchcock threw 62 pitches, allowing one run on four hits, walking none and striking out seven batters. The 20-year-old Jeter, later named the Baseball America's Minor League Player of the Year, was 3-for-4 with a pair of RBIs. Yankees' General Manager Gene Michael watched the action from a box seat behind home plate. "He's legitimate," Runnells said of Jeter, who hit

.377 in 34 Eastern League games before being promoted to Triple-A Columbus. "I'm not really a home-run hitter," added Jeter in the visitor's clubhouse.

Mashore's prediction—"Things can't get any worse"— proved to be wishful thinking. In their first 10 games following the All-Star break, Trenton lost nine times. There were five consecutive losses at Portland—and five straight postgame celebrations featuring that interminable Hadlock Field lighthouse. There was desperation in the Thunder clubhouse. At times, even Clark's spirits seemed to flag following another defeat. One late July night in New Britain, he was besieged by autograph seekers following a particularly bitter loss. He hung his head and trudged to the bus—but not before accommodating everyone who asked for his signature.

While his team slid inexorably down the Eastern League standings, Clark stayed healthy and continued to plug away toward a promotion. On Sunday, July 24, during the first game of a scheduled doubleheader at New Britain's Beehive Field, he shattered his single-game RBI record by driving in seven to spark a 13-3 win over the Red Sox. In a facility known as a notorious pitcher's park, he homered twice (No. 18 and 19) and singled. Several observers commented that he looked like he was playing on a Little League field.

"He was in a zone," McCarthy recalled. "You look back to the youth leagues when you just want to bat and bat. That's how he was that day. He was a kid again, dominating grown men."

In the Beehive dugout, Clark expressed wonder at his effort. "Wow!" he said, raising his eyebrows and smiling. He had 77 RBIs in 98 games.

With the win, the Thunder "improved" to 40-58. A mid-afternoon storm canceled the second game of the doubleheader, however, leaving the unanswered question, "How many runs might Clark have driven in on the day?" New Britain groundskeepers tried in vain to prepare the field for the nightcap. Several Thunder players placed a row of metal folding chairs in front of the dugout and pretended they were rowing a boat. A handful of patient fans cheered the effort. "We should have known better than to name this team after the weather," Simonetta quipped during the long wait until the game was officially called off.

PERFECTION AT WATERFRONT

On July 30, a crowd of 6808 pushed Waterfront Park attendance over the 200,000 plateau (in just 34 openings). The game was memorable not only for the attendance milestone but also for the virtuoso pitching effort of Bowie right-hander Rick Forney. During an 8-0 win, the 22-year-old Forney pitched the fourth perfect game in the Eastern League's 72-year history. Twenty-one Thunder hitters came to the plate, and 21 were retired. "I had horrible stuff in the bullpen, but I was able to throw my forkball a lot early in the count for strikes, which kept them guessing," Forney explained. Of the 21 outs, 12 were groundballs, four were fly balls, and five were strikeouts. The standing-room-only crowd was somewhat oblivious to the accomplishment, many of the patrons figuring the Thunder simply were having another poor offensive game.

"There's no skill to a perfect game," Forney said during his postgame celebration in the visitor's clubhouse. "You just have to be really lucky. . .and I was one really lucky S.O.B. tonight.

"What can you say?" added Clark. "When a guy has his pitches working the way he did, it's going to be a rough night. You have to give the guy a whole lot of credit. He didn't make any mistakes."

"You see something like that happen, and it's just really, really fun to be a part of," Bowie manager Pete Mackanin said in the visiting manager's office. "It's easy for a pitcher to go through the order once. The real test comes when they keep digging in the rest of the game. Rick just kept them guessing for seven innings."

On July 31, Carlyle received a long-awaited promotion to Triple-A. He took with him a 3-9 record and a 4.10 ERA in 19 starts, but he also departed secure in the knowledge that he had pitched much better than his numbers indicated. At Toledo, he appeared in 12 games during the month of August (mostly as a long reliever), compiling a 1-0 record and a 4.07 ERA.

THE END OF AN ERA

The Thunder opened August by losing three consecutive games to Harrisburg at RiverSide. In the series, Clark was 1-for-10. "There's a lot of accumulation of frustration on this team right now," Runnells said after his club was outscored 14-4 in the series. Decillis was thrown out of the third game by umpire Mark Facto for arguing a questionable call on the basepaths during the sixth inning. He dressed hurriedly and watched the rest of a 4-1 Trenton defeat from the stands, silently stewing about the ejection.

The following day, as the Thunder bus rolled into Binghamton to begin a four-game series, Clark was determined to reverse his fortunes. On a chilly midsummer evening, he deposited a third-inning Bill Pulsipher delivery over the 30-foot center-field hitting backdrop, 400 feet from home plate. During batting practice, Mysel had challenged Clark to try to drive a ball over the bright blue wall. As the Thunder clean-up hitter trotted back to the dugout following his twentieth Double-A homer, Mysel was the first to congratulate him. "He showed me," the pitcher said. Clark's heroics and Withem's eight-hit pitching paced a 5-3 Trenton victory. Withem improved to a 5-11 record, and closer Blas Cedeno recorded his second Double-A save by escaping a bases-loaded, one-out jam in the bottom of the ninth. (The happy-go-lucky Cedeno would receive his first U.S. driver's license several days later.)

On August 6, during a 6-3 loss to the Mets, Clark hit his twenty-first—and final—homer in a Thunder uniform. The solo shot off Binghamton right-hander Robert Person gave him 83 RBIs, the most of anybody in the three Double-A leagues. He was wearing out his welcome in the Eastern League, proving that he could remain healthy and produce huge offensive numbers.

"I think Tony's stayed fairly focused," Runnells said. "I think he's done a great job out there." Knowing that his slugger was about to be promoted, the Binghamton series was a bittersweet time for Runnells. Losing Clark would be a kiss of death for his light-hitting team. Following a 5-4, 13-inning loss to the Mets on August 7, Clark's Thunder career was ended by a phone call from Dave Miller, who delivered orders to report to Toledo. Clark returned to Trenton on the bus to pack his belongings. Although he did not play on August 8 against Reading, a Waterfront crowd of 6678 bid him a nostalgic farewell before the Thunder's 8-6 win over the Phillies.

Clark also became the first Thunder player to win a free suit for homering off the Byer's Men's Shop billboard in left field. The black-and-white billboard enticed hitters with the promise, "Hit the Sign. Win a Suit!" On the morning of August 8, Clark was fitted for his size 50. In September 1995, when he was called to Detroit for the first time, he telephoned Byer's to order three more suits, but this time, he gladly paid for the custom-tailored trio. "They had my measurements," he said. "In the big leagues, you're not going to wear sweats to the ballpark. You just don't do that, so I thought the best and most convenient way for me to get some suits and Byer's came to mind. Now I have a little wardrobe."

Looking back on his Trenton experience, Clark later said, "That was the best year I've ever had. Not just for playing, baseball-wise, but being in that town and playing in front of those people. It was great."

"From where he was at the beginning of the year to where he wound up, it was impressive," McCarthy said. "You simply have to look at his work ethic and his enthusiasm."

Before the '95 season, Thunder officials decided that no franchise player would ever again wear Clark's No. 33. For thousands of fans who flocked to South Trenton's brand-new ballyard to enjoy the city's minor-league baseball revival, the jersey would always belong to the gracious, 6-foot-8 slugger from California.

On August 12, four days after Clark was promoted to Toledo, Major League Baseball went on strike. The walkout focused even more attention on the Thunder. In 11 Waterfront games after the strike began, the smallest crowd was 6869. During August, the Thunder averaged 7038 patrons per game. Ironically, on the night of the strike deadline, Philadelphia Phillies right-hander Tommy Greene made a rehab start for Reading at Waterfront. (During late May, he had undergone shoulder surgery.) He threw 95 pitches in a 4-2 win over the Thunder as 6805 enjoyed the performance. Afterward, he pondered the labor impasse which would end his comeback prematurely. "These guys in the minor leagues have asked me a few basic questions about the strike like, 'What's going on?' " Greene said. "But it's like I told them, 'We're fighting for y'all.' The major leaguers fought for me when I was down on the farm." Down the hall, Mashore added his perspective about the imminent strike, which meant no September call-ups for rising stars like Tony Clark.

"Sure, the salaries in the majors are outrageous, but look how much Prunetti and politicians like him get paid for doing nothing," Mashore said candidly—and the county executive laughed heartily when he read that quote.

"We've got to realize as players what the [Major League Baseball] Players Association has gotten us," Runnells added. "It's gotten us the best pension plan in all of America; it's gotten us some of the best insurance, and it's gotten us one of the nicest average salaries and minimum wages of any profession in the world. But I know the players are poised for a long sit-out, and it sounds like the owners are more serious about it this time than they have ever been."

UNFORESEEN TRAGEDY

On Tuesday, August 16, a crowd of 6871 packed Waterfront to watch Miller drop his fifteenth game of the season (and eighth in a row), a 7-2 loss to Binghamton. The overflow gathering included a pair of stepbrothers, 15-year-old Michael Rogers and 8-year-old Harold Bottchenbaugh of Jersey Avenue in Trenton. They were dropped off at the stadium by their mother, who promised to pick them up later. During the game, they decided to do some exploring along the Delaware River, like any number of Trenton youngsters before them. Spotting an open well behind the Riverview Executive Plaza buildings, they crawled through a stand of trees to get a closer look. At approximately 8:30 PM, Harold fell 22 feet into the well before landing in 10 feet of water. According to Trenton Police Captain Joseph Golden, Rogers immediately realized what had happened. Sadly, just moments before the accident, he had warned his brother to stay away from the well.

"It was so dark that he couldn't see," Golden said of Rogers' effort to summon help. "He heard the splash, called for his brother and got no response." By the time Thunder Director of Security Joe Wroblewski arrived, Bottchenbaugh had been under water for almost 20 minutes. "It was like the opening scene of *Tales from the Crypt*," Wroblewski recalled of his arrival at the well, which was located at the bottom of a spiral staircase.

"I just happened to see two shoes in the water, about 4 feet under the surface," Wroblewski added. Bottchenbaugh was airlifted by helicopter to Cooper University Medical Center in Camden, where he was pronounced dead. Instantaneously, a pall was cast over the Thunder front office, which had worked so hard to make its product appealing to children. "Just when we thought we'd seen everything, along came this tragedy," said Lipsman.

The following day, Prunetti and Pae conducted a somber press conference to address the uncapped well. Prunetti revealed that it was part of an abandoned, county-owned pump house that sat on a 5.3-acre plot that extended up and down the river. "I am personally deeply saddened, but I'm not ready to say that we're liable for anything," he said. "In this setting, it's going to be impossible to be sure that someone isn't where they shouldn't be or doing something that presents danger to them."

Also attending the press conference was Mayor Palmer, who had been at the game when the accident occurred. "I saw the fire engines, but I didn't think anything of it—until I saw the helicopter," he said. "This is a real tragedy. My sympathies go out to the family and to the brother, who is taking it very hard."

On August 19, moments before the Thunder dropped a 3-1 decision against New Haven, a crowd of 6869 stood and observed a moment of silence for

Harold Bottchenbaugh. The incident occupied the front page of both Trenton newspapers for several days. It also made Waterfront's field problems seem trivial. "It was awful . . . awful," said Thunder Assistant General Manager Mahoney. "I personally didn't put it into the scope of the entire season. It was a terrible event unto itself. It was so much bigger and more significant than anything that happened here. I still get a sick feeling in the pit of my stomach just thinking about it."

CHAPTER 11

Changes Along the Delaware

"Our ultimate concern is producing a winner in Trenton. We're not here just to sell hot dogs."

—1994 THUNDER PARTNER AND LEGAL COUNSEL JAMES F. MALONEY

On Friday, August 19, 1994, several hours before young Harold Bottchenbaugh was remembered silently, Bob Prunetti conducted a press conference in the Waterfront Restaurant to discuss the county's plans for replacing the Thunder's shoddy playing surface. "I never want to have a baseball season like the one in '94 again," he said, his words carrying a bristly edge. "It's very difficult to pinpoint one particular reason for the problems because it was a combination of factors. We were on a very, very tight timeframe to get the stadium operating. We had to live up to certain agreements and commitments. The criticisms we have received throughout the season are legitimate, but we have to keep in perspective all the factors involved." The county's detailed new plan, which was approved by Woodbury, New Jersey, turf consultant Turfcon, involved ripping out all of the old sod and transporting it to a nearby public park. It would be replaced with a 10-inch base of topsoil and sandy subsoil and a 6-inch level of rock drainage that would be installed before the new sod was unfurled. Furthermore, beginning September 1 (the day after the inaugural Thunder home schedule concluded), the 108,000-square foot field would be fitted with an extensive network of underground pipes connecting 300 field drains. The existing underground sprinkler system also would be expanded to include the infield.

"We have a plan that we feel is economically viable based upon a shared responsibility," Prunetti said. Breaking down the project's $300,000 cost, the county planned to chip in $100,000, while the original contractor would finance the other $200,000. "We decided to get the Cadillac of drainage systems," the county executive added.

Apprised of Prunetti's comments, Runnells responded, "Let's hope it's not a '54 Cadillac."

Following Clark's August 8 promotion, the Thunder was clearly the worst team in the Eastern League. Runnells spent an increasing amount of time on the golf course, whittling away at his handicap—which already was zero. There

were a few highlights of the season's final month, however, including a franchise-record, 14-strike-out pitching performance by Withem during a 7-2 win
at New Haven. Throughout the year, the 21-year-old righty had been the Thunder's best starter. His final '94 numbers showed a 7-12 record and a 3.44 ERA,
tops among the Trenton rotation. That win-loss total also included several cases
of extremely bad luck, but during his record strikeout New Haven outing,
Withem used his change-up to keep the Ravens off-balance throughout the
complete-game gem. The off-speed pitch was his bread and butter. "I can say it
again, 'He's pitched a lot better than his record,' " Runnells said in the cramped
Yale Field dressing trailer. "He's got big legs and a strong frame, so he utilizes
his whole body when he pitches. He's a bulldog, and he goes out there and bat-
tles every time."

On Sunday, August 21, at Waterfront, the Thunder defeated New Haven 8-7
in the bottom of the ninth on back-up catcher Tim McConnell's RBI double.
Among the 6976 in attendance during the day game was 47-year-old Tom
Krenchicki. Nicknamed the "Chicken Man" by his friends on the Trenton police force, the 6-foot-3 Mercer County native was suffering from a rare form of
soft-tissue cancer. As a minor-league shortstop during the late 1960s, he had
played in the Dodgers' organization with Bobby Valentine, Steve Garvey, and
Bill Buckner under manager Tommy Lasorda. Although he was confined to a
wheelchair by his illness, one of Krenchicki's greatest wishes during the summer of '94 was to visit Waterfront. Before the game, he spent a few moments
with Runnells in the Thunder clubhouse. As he watched the action from the
balcony outside the stadium restaurant with his wife Doreen and his 5-year-old
daughter Corinne, he marveled at the new ballpark. During the middle innings,
the scoreboard flashed his name, welcoming him to the stadium. He smiled
appreciatively. "I anticipated it being beautiful," he said. "Obviously, everybody's been talking about the grass, but there are wrinkles in everything."

"Tom's cancer puts it all in perspective," Runnells added. "The game on the
field doesn't mean anything compared to something like that." For a few hours,
at least, Krenchicki's mind was taken off his medical problems. Waterfront Park
had that liberating effect on a lot of people.

During the '95 season, Krenchicki passed away. His funeral was attended by
hundreds of admirers.

NEGOTIATING A NEW PDC

As the inaugural Thunder season neared its conclusion, attention turned to the
franchise's Player Development Contract with Detroit. The agreement would
expire at the end of the '94 season, meaning that Hodes and the Thunder could
either renew their working relationship with Detroit or seek another affiliate.
Without question, the construction and field problems that had plagued Runnells' prospects over the course of the season had strained the relationship with
the Tigers. On August 29, Detroit General Manager Joe Klein met with Hodes,
Plumeri, Stanley, and Maloney. The facility that Klein visited was very different
than the one that had opened its doors back in late April. The permanent con-

cession stands were fully operational, and the luxury boxes were complete. The sprawling plaza outside the stadium also was finished, and much of the work beneath the stadium was taking shape as well. "Outstanding," Klein responded when asked his reaction to the park.

Klein's approach to renegotiating the Tigers' PDC with the Thunder, however, quickly offended the Trenton contingent. "He came into the meeting with guns blazing, telling us we had to do this and do that," said one Thunder representative. Afterward, Hodes and Maloney were determined to shop their product around. "We have a decision to make on behalf of the fans here in Trenton, and that's who we'll make the decision for. The Tigers know our ultimate concern is producing a winner here." During the '94 season, Detroit's minor-league winning percentage ranked twenty-fifth among the 28 major-league teams. Klein told Thunder officials that if he was running their franchise, he would budget for a .500 record every year. That wasn't what Caruso, Maloney, Hodes, and company wanted to hear. "Our feeling is that no matter who is here, we're going to be successful," Hodes added, "but we want to make sure that we have the best possible product on the field. We feel we owe it to ourselves, the fans, and the ownership."

FAN APPRECIATION

The final seven-game homestand of the '94 Thunder season certainly wasn't a winner anywhere but at the box office. Runnells' club dropped four of its last five Waterfront games, completing the 58-date home schedule with a 23-35 mark. On Thursday, August 31, a record Waterfront crowd of 7869 crammed the stadium's concourse on "Fan Appreciation Night" to salute the '94 team despite its woeful 54-79 record. Withem lost a 6-2 decision to Eastern League Southern Division champion Harrisburg. Following the home finale, the majority of the Thunder's 24-player roster headed to the area beside the Thunder dugout and heaved their sweat-stained green fitted caps to the applauding throng. DuBose. Second baseman Evan Pratte. Edmondson. Miller. Guilfoyle. Perona, who a few days earlier had been awarded a $1000 watch by Hamilton Jewelers for being voted the "Thunder fan favorite." The cap toss was Lipsman's idea. He wanted the players to do something to thank the crowd for its unfailing support. "Everything was preplanned," he said, "but I had to prod them to come out of the dugout after they lost." Gradually, the players flung their hats to the waiting masses, and Runnells played along, throwing his cap into the tenth row.

Beneath the grandstand, however, a different scene was playing itself out. Two players—Decillis and Rendina—had refused to part with their headwear. They walked off the field muttering, "Screw Trenton." They would not be bowed by the impulse of the moment. It was their silent form of protesting a nightmare season.

Lipsman took the snub very personally. "All of the players came back into the clubhouse, and we gave them all new fitted hats as a souvenir of the season," he recalled. "Mike and Dean said, 'No, we don't want them.' It was an embarrassment."

Insistent on taking one final shot at the Trenton situation, Decillis added,

"It's tough enough to play baseball with all the ups and downs that go along with it. With the condition of the stadium, the lack of living arrangements, and all the other distractions this year, it just added to the uncertainty. We're trained as ballplayers to deal with the on-field stuff, but when you add in everything else that's happened, it's been very difficult."

The outspoken Mashore was even more to the point. "The season itself has been a total mess. There were some days that were so bad that you just wish you could grab at some of those days and say, 'Hey, come back here; I want to try again.' But it doesn't work that way."

In spite of the Thunder's abysmal on-field performance, which included a league-worst .229 batting average and 173 errors, the fans had continued to flock to Waterfront. There was no let-up. Everyone wanted to be part of the scene. "The best thing about this whole year has been the fans," DuBose said without hesitation. "How can you as a player not love the support we've had?"

As the huge final home crowd filtered down the steps from the main concourse and out of the stadium, Hodes stood by the turnstiles and watched with a look of satisfaction. He knew he had weathered the storm. The franchise had survived in spite of all the obstacles thrust in its path. The last 11 games had been played without a weather-related postponement, and the Thunder could start anew in the '95 season with a more refined product and a new field. The construction phase of the team's development would be complete.

At one point, a father and his young son stopped to talk to Hodes. "I think what you've done here is fantastic," the man told the Thunder General Manager enthusiastically. "All I know is that my son came to a game and learned how to sing, 'Take me out to the ballgame.' I'll never forget that. Thank you."

The final attendance numbers from the inaugural season confirmed the Thunder's immediate impact on the Delaware Valley's entertainment scene. A total of 313,329 patrons had visited the park over 51 dates, an average of 6144 per opening. Projected over a full 71 game Eastern League home schedule, that average indicated the Thunder could become the first franchise in league history to eclipse the 400,000-fan mark for one season. Hodes knew that the key was building on the '94 debut—and avoiding rainouts at all costs.

THE OHIO FINALE

As workers began ripping the grass from the 108,000-square-foot Waterfront field, the '94 Thunder completed the regular season by dropping five of their last six games in Canton-Akron. The Detroit farmhands simply were playing out the string. Pratte donned Clark's No. 33 uniform, hoping to generate some offense for his team. Many of Runnells' players knew that this series could be the last of their professional careers. For some, the biggest concern was how they would get their cars to eastern Ohio so they wouldn't have to return to Trenton. Simonetta drove McConnell's car across the Pennsylvania Turnpike so the catcher could drive home to Michigan immediately following the September 5 finale. (On the way, the broadcaster was ticketed by a state trooper for traveling 72 mph in a 55-mph zone.)

During a 6-2 loss to the Indians on September 1, Edmondson fell to an 11-9 record. His 11 wins were a franchise record, but his final 4.56 ERA was a disappointment. Throughout the season, he had been alternately effective and overmatched. He usually kept the Thunder in the game, though, and that had been enough to earn him double-digit victories. He also had the best curveball on the inaugural Thunder staff.

While Edmondson reflected on his '94 roller-coaster ride, Perona discussed his Trenton experience, which had culminated with his fan favorite award. "There were so many problems with the stadium. It seemed like everyone was blaming everyone, but when I look back, I'm really going to remember the fact that we were treated almost like big leaguers in Trenton. I never really thought I'd feel that way, but for the first time after a bad game, I found myself wanting to sneak away without signing autographs."

After losing a doubleheader on Friday, September 2, the Thunder desperately wanted to play well for the 21-year-old Miller the following day. Since June 28, Miller had lost nine consecutive decisions, falling from a 6-7 to a 6-16 record. No other pitcher in the Eastern League had 16 losses. As a result, Miller was at a crossroads when he took the mound for his twenty-sixth— and final—start of the season. Before a Thurman Munson crowd of 4034, he broke his two-month streak of personal heartache, defeating the Indians 3-1. He stranded eight baserunners over 7 1/3 innings, and left-hander Sean Whiteside closed out the game to pick up his fifth save. Pratte was 2-for-4 with two stolen bases, and Decillis was 2-for-4, including the game-winning RBI single in the eighth. The win was the fifty-fifth—and last—of the Thunder season.

"Believe it or not, I kind of said a prayer during the game that we could get Trever a win; that was our No. 1 focal point tonight," Runnells said. "I can't tell you how happy I am for him."

Inside the tiny visitors clubhouse, Miller wore a look of relief as he iced his left arm. "I love winning, but it's been a long, long drought. I finally made the pitches I needed to get out of innings tonight. This season has been a big confidence-builder for me, a real learning experience. The biggest thing you have to remember is that this game is fun. You have to take responsibility for the losses, but I'm a 'glass-is-half-full-instead-of-half-empty' kind of guy."

Later that night, many of the Thunder players congregated at a Canton bar called The Pub. They drank to their season. They drank to togetherness. They drank to forget how bad their '94 performance had really been; after Clark had been promoted, Trenton lost 22 of its last 33 games.

In the Labor Day finale (a 6-3 loss—what else?), Rendina tied a career high with his eleventh homer. He was a 6-year free agent after the season, making him eligible to negotiate with any organization, but his final .227 batting average and 46 RBIs represented precipitous drop-offs from his '93 London numbers. Even more damning were his statistics in key situations. He hit .202 with runners on base, .184 with runners in scoring position, and .193 with runners in scoring position and two outs. He blamed much of his misfortune on the white-tooth billboard at Waterfront, but Runnells wasn't buying the excuse. "He didn't have a good year," the manager said bluntly. "After what he did in

'93, he should have come in here and been a dominating figure. He's not swinging the bat anywhere near the way he was."

Summarizing his team's 55-85 season record before boarding the bus back to Trenton to pack his belongings, Runnells said, "I'm very sad because there's a good possibility that I won't have an opportunity to see some of these young men again, but I'll always remember the number of fans that continued to show up for a last-place ballclub and relationships that were formed because of that. All you ever remember from a baseball season, even when you win, are the personal relationships. The record is irrelevant."

Nonetheless, Runnells admitted that the '94 Thunder "never ever, not once, got on a roll as a team and played really good baseball for 7, 8, 9 days in a row."

On the last bus trip home, the Thunder players presented Curley with a $500 tip as a token of their appreciation for his season-long efforts as their driver. Included in that total was $100 from Clark. "I'll never forget those guys," Curley said. "They were all good guys." (DuBose reportedly chipped in a 5-dollar bill when the funds were collected.)

In the Eastern League Southern Division, Harrisburg (88-51) and Bowie (84-58) advanced to the playoffs, while Binghamton (82-59) and New Haven (77-63) squared off in the Northern Division playoffs. After losing the first two games at RiverSide Stadium, the Senators rallied to defeat the Baysox in their best-of-five series, three games to two. The Mets eliminated the Ravens, three games to one. In the best-of-five championship series, Pulsipher threw a no-hitter as Binghamton defeated Harrisburg in four games to capture the Eastern League Championship. Grudzielanek was named the Eastern League MVP, and Pulsipher was awarded the league's Pitcher of the Year trophy. Other postseason Eastern League All-Stars who later made their major-league debuts during the '95 and '96 seasons included Bowie pitcher Haynes, Bowie outfielder Curtis Goodwin, New Britain outfielder Jose Malave, Portland catcher Johnson, and of course Tony Clark.

Despite the Thunder's last-place finish, the season hadn't been a total disaster, particularly for four of the starting pitchers. Edmondson (11-9, 4.56 ERA, 2 complete games), Miller (7-16, 4.39 ERA, 6 complete games), Withem (7-12, 3.44 ERA, 5 complete games),and Mysel (5-10, 4.58 ERA, 2 complete games), all were placed on Detroit's 40-man major-league roster during the fall.

ANOTHER DEVASTATING BLOW

During the early morning hours of Tuesday, September 6, the Thunder franchise was rocked by another totally unexpected tragedy when 49-year-old Thunder partner and legal counsel Jim Maloney passed away in his Haddonfield, New Jersey, home after suffering a heart attack. Less than 24 hours after Trenton had completed its trying but publicly acclaimed inaugural season, its guiding legal force and one of its true benefactors was gone. The timing of Maloney's death was catastrophic for the Thunder front office and ownership, which was carefully plotting a change of major-league affiliation for the '95 season. No one was more involved in that effort than Maloney.

One of the first to receive the bad news was Plumeri. Joe Caruso called to tell the 81-year-old co-owner that his friend and business associate was gone. "It was a real shock," Plumeri said sadly. Moments later, Plumeri called Hodes at the Thunder's new Waterfront office, which had just been completed. As his cellular phone rang, Hodes couldn't help but think it was odd to be receiving a call so early in the morning. On hearing Plumeri's news, he was stunned. "We've just been through a very trying season, albeit successful, and we were just about to take a little bit of a break and regroup, thinking nothing else could happen," Hodes explained. "And now this."

"I had a meeting with Jim last Thursday about things we wanted to do," Lipsman added. "In fact, I left a call on his office machine over the weekend to confirm a couple of things. This is unbelievable. We thought we'd seen it all this year."

Within hours, Detroit formally announced during the afternoon of September 6 that it had terminated its 1-year affiliation with Trenton. "We wish the Trenton club, the ownership, and management nothing but the best for the future, but the Tigers will be looking for another Double-A affiliate for next season," read the official statement from Klein. The news didn't come as a shock to Hodes and Caruso, who had already decided to shop their product to several other organizations, including the Kansas City Royals and the Boston Red Sox. Knowing that the National Association of Professional Baseball Leagues (NAPBL) guaranteed Trenton a Double-A franchise for 1995, the Thunder's plan was to forge a new affiliation with a team that had a stronger farm system. Runnells would remain with Detroit and be promoted to Triple-A Toledo to manage the Mud Hens for the '95 season, while the Tigers would sign a 2-year PDC with Jacksonville, Florida.

Meanwhile, Runnells made one last visit to the Waterfront clubhouse. Parking the gold Saturn automobile that had been loaned to him for the season by a local car dealership, he expressed great sorrow about Maloney's death. "It doesn't matter what we've been through as a team this year. This is life and death. This is very tragic. I feel for his friends and family. I know Sam's very shaken up about it." Behind Runnells, bulldozers continued to rip up the playing surface. "Best it's looked all year," the manager observed about the field.

Three days later, Maloney's public viewing was held at his Haddonfield parish, Christ the King. Placed inside the open casket was a green Thunder hat. It was a tribute to his love for minor-league baseball and his part in the successful effort to return the game to New Jersey. Among the dignitaries who filed past the coffin and Maloney's grieving family—wife Marilyn and teenage daughters Margaret and Anna Mae—were Gov. Jim Florio, U.S. Senator Bill Bradley, and many other influential New Jersey political figures. Jim Maloney had been a well-loved man—a minor-league baseball man.

TIME TO REGROUP

Following Maloney's death, Hodes and the Thunder ownership had until September 25 to forge a new affiliation. If they were unsuccessful, the NAPBL would assign one. On September 8, Kansas City Director of Minor League Operations Bob Hegman made plans to tour Waterfront Park. Rated by one national publication as "the best farm system in the American League," the Royals were a natural fit for Trenton because of their Single-A Carolina League affiliation with Wilmington, Delaware.

The other leading candidate was Boston. The Red Sox badly wanted out of New Britain's Beehive Field, and Trenton, with its promise of vastly improved 1995 playing conditions, was a very attractive option. On Monday, September 11, Boston General Manager Dan Duquette and Director of Minor League Operations Ed Kenney toured Waterfront. Over lunch at Chianti's Restaurant, the Boston representatives discussed a possible affiliation with Hodes. "It's a great privilege, as well as a necessity, to have a great facility," Duquette said later. Convinced that "the Boston Red Sox are just ticketed for Trenton," he signed a 2-year PDC with the Thunder on September 16, in the process ending a 21-year association with New Britain owner Joe Buzas. In turn, Buzas signed a 2-year PDC with the Minnesota Twins and made plans to build a new, 6200-seat stadium for the '96 season.

During Boston's introductory press conference at Waterfront, Duquette beamed. With the Red Sox logo in the background (where the Detroit symbol used to be), he claimed, "This is one of the best facilities in Double-A. To me, Double-A baseball is a direct reflection of how your organization is doing. It's a make-or-break time for those players, and we will not skip this level to move them along."

"I couldn't be happier to be associated with the Red Sox," Hodes said, adding that he had been elated that Boston was on the list of available affiliates at the conclusion of the '94 season. "I just think this is going to be a great relationship for the team, the ownership, and most importantly, the fans of the Thunder. The one thing that was truly out of our control was the product on the field, and our fans deserved better."

Deep down, Hodes knew that Maloney would have lauded the decision. "The fans stuck by us through some tough times," said Maloney's law partner, Joe Finley. "And if they liked '94, they're going to love '95."

At the end of the inaugural season, the Thunder donated more than $31,000 to Trenton's Young Scholars Institute through an innovative funds-matching program known as the Educational Winner's Circle. For each ticket sold to Trenton games, CoreStates Bank and the Thunder contributed a nickel apiece to a local charity jointly selected by both. Another Thunder-sponsored program was the TKO (Take Kids Out to the Ballgame), which treated a countless number of inner-city children to a free night at Waterfront Park. TKO was the brainchild of Princeton University tennis coach Louise Gengler. Interestingly, Gengler was a diehard Detroit Tigers fan, and although Boston was Waterfront Park's new tenant, her support for the Tigers would remain steadfast.

KEN MACHA TAKES THE REINS

At the time its 2-year PDC with Trenton was finalized, Boston was searching for a new major-league manager. Duquette eventually settled on former Texas

Rangers skipper Kevin Kennedy. By late November, a Boston source confirmed that the Red Sox would assign 44-year-old Ken Macha to Trenton as the new Thunder manager. A former major-league utility infielder and coach with Montreal and California, Macha lived in Export, Pennsylvania, a suburb of Pittsburgh. During the fall of '94, he managed the Tempe Rafters of the Arizona Fall League (AFL). Ironically, one of the players in the '94 AFL was Tony Clark. Another rising AFL star was Boston farmhand Nomar Garciaparra, a slick-fielding shortstop from California.

Back in Trenton, groundskeeper Migliaccio oversaw phase two of the field construction. "Yeah, I'm still here," he said as his crew once again placed wooden splints to frame the infield paths, "but as soon as this is over, I'm going to take a vacation." On November 29, after almost 3 months of intensive labor, the new field was pronounced fit for public inspection. "Is this freakin' good enough for you guys now?" Prunetti wondered during a press walkthrough.

Squinting into the dusk, the county executive definitively proclaimed the end of the Thunder's drainage saga. "Needless to say, we're very happy with the results. It doesn't appear we'll have so many rain-outs." Several days later, a heavy rainfall left no standing water on the revamped $300,000 playing surface.

On Saturday morning, December 17, Macha pulled into the Waterfront parking lot in a red pickup. He had driven 5 hours across the Pennsylvania Turnpike to attend his introductory press conference. For Macha, taking over for Runnells was an ironic professional twist. In 1991, he had lived with the former Montreal manager and served as one of his Expos coaches. Following the season, Runnells had fired him. Wearing Clark's old No. 33 jersey (size 50 was the only uniform large enough to fit over his 6-foot-2, 225-pound frame), Macha shook hands with Thunder fans as they shopped for Christmas gifts inside Waterfront's brand-new, concourse-level Dugout Shop. The '95 season would be his first as a minor-league manager after 9 years as a big-league bullpen and third base coach. He had decided that taking a Double-A job was the best route to his ultimate professional goal—becoming a major-league manager.

Ironically, New Jersey held a painful memory for the new Thunder manager. On May 22, 1992, with 38-year-old bus driver Carl Venetz at the wheel, the California Angels were en route from Yankee Stadium to Baltimore. Suddenly, without warning, the vehicle drifted off the New Jersey Turnpike in Deptford Township, severely injuring manager Buck Rodgers. Macha, who was seated behind the manager, suffered cuts and bruises and was released from the hospital later that night, but he remembers the immediate trauma of the crash as one of the low points of his professional baseball career. He even remembers the movie that was playing at the time of the 1:47 AM accident—*The Delta Force.*

"I was sitting in the third seat on the right, and the second seat was empty," Macha recalled. "It had the rest of the chicken that nobody wanted to eat. I was just leaning back watching the movie. At first, I could hear stones hitting the bottom of the bus, like gravel being kicked up. And then I could hear, 'Da-da-da, da-da-da, da' against the bottom of the bus.

"Then I realized that we were going off the road, so I got down in the airplane crash position. We went off the right-hand side of the road. Then it was like the bus was bouncing around but still going. I was curled up, and something hit me on my lower back." Police reports later indicated that the bus had traveled 350 feet on its side, stopping mere inches from a large oak tree and within feet of a steep embankment.

Macha's first reaction was to reach for his glasses, which had been knocked off by the impact of the crash. Then he quickly scurried to the first row to check on Rodgers, who said, "No, I'm not all right." The force of the collision had shattered the manager's elbow into many pieces and broken his leg. It took paramedics half an hour to extract him from the wreckage. Also injured in the crash was Angels' hitting instructor Rod Carew. Macha later removed pieces of glass from his wallet when he showed authorities his identification.

Macha believes that Venetz simply fell asleep at the wheel. "There was no swerving or anything. It felt like the bus went straight off the road." New Jersey State Trooper Denis White cited the driver "for careless driving due to the fact that [he] lost control of his vehicle."

"That could have really turned ugly," Macha observed after recounting the details in vivid imagery. "We were very fortunate to come out of it the way we did." In spite of his brush with catastrophe, Macha insisted he felt "safer on a bus than on an airplane."

Over the next two seasons, however, he would frequently lean over toward Curley and ask, "How you doing up there? You're not going to fall asleep, are you?" Back in the minors for the first time since he was a player in the mid-1970s, Macha would spend countless hours in the front row of Starr Tours Bus No. 108. In December 1994, he was eager to try his hand as a manager for the first time.

CHAPTER 12

A Second Spring

"If I go out there and enjoy the game, then I'm doing all right. I'm not a numbers person, but I love fans. When they're cheering, it's a great feeling. That's what it's all about. I hope they enjoy the game as much as I do."

—THUNDER SHORTSTOP NOMAR GARCIAPARRA DURING 1995 SPRING TRAINING

On a warm March evening along the Caloosahatchee River in Fort Myers, Florida, Nomar Garciaparra sat at an outdoor cafe table sipping a bottle of light beer. His dark features blended into the night as he discussed his new team—the Thunder. A large, white, multilevel yacht sailed by the dock behind him. Just 21 years old with the promise of a very successful—not to mention lucrative—Major League Baseball career ahead of him, Garciaparra motioned toward the vessel and predicted with a laugh that was part serious, part whimsy, "I'm going to own one of those someday."

During the summer of 1994, while the inaugural Thunder team played out the string, Garciaparra signed with the Red Sox for a franchise-record $895,000 bonus. Selected by Boston in the first round (with the twelfth pick overall) in the June 1994 amateur draft, he began raising eyebrows from the moment he donned a Single-A uniform for Sarasota. Before the '95 season, he was rated the No. 1 prospect in the Boston organization by *Baseball America*.

At Georgia Tech, he was a marketing major and a first-team All-America shortstop who compiled a gaudy .427 batting average during his junior season. During that campaign, he became only the fourth Yellow Jacket player to record 100 hits in a season. He helped lead Georgia Tech to the '94 College World Series Championship Game in Omaha, Nebraska, where the Yellow Jackets lost a 13-5 heartbreaker to national champion Oklahoma. Nomar homered in each of the final two World Series games before embarking on his professional career.

A 1991 graduate of St. John Bosco High School in Bellflower, California, where he also starred in football and soccer, he originally was drafted by the Milwaukee Brewers in the fifth round of the June 1991 amateur pool, but he elected not to sign at that time. The decision paid handsome rewards when he became the only true freshman selected to play on the 1992 U.S. Olympic team that competed in Barcelona ('94 Thunder reliever Rick Greene also was a member of that team). The Americans did not win the gold medal, losing instead in the bronze-medal game and settling for fourth place. Nomar frequently mentioned that setback as his greatest regret. "I wanted a medal, any medal," he said.

"Nomar didn't play like a freshman, and he didn't act like a freshman," Greene recalled.

The 6-foot, 172-pound Garciaparrra's unique first name was coined by his parents. Quite simply, it was his father's name—Ramon—spelled backward. During the '94 Arizona Fall League (AFL), Nomar blossomed on a circuit that included many Triple-A veterans. In 32 games for manager Terry Francona's Scottsdale Scorpions, he hit .328 to finish fourth in the league. As the Tempe manager, Macha watched his future shortstop with great interest throughout the AFL season.

Boston's minor-league spring training began amidst the continued uncertainty of the ongoing major-league strike. In Lakeland, Runnells had taken over for Sparky Anderson as the interim Detroit manager because Anderson refused to work with replacement players. Members of the Tigers replacement roster included Guilfoyle and Pete Gonzalez. Similar dilemmas existed for minor leaguers everywhere as long as the major-league 40-man rosters remained on hold. Nobody in the Red Sox front office, however, dreamed of asking Nomar to become a replacement player. He was simply too valuable a prospect to put in such an awkward position. He would be the cornerstone of Macha's '95 Thunder roster, a defensive stalwart who could solidify the middle infield and provide a maturity and work ethic that extended far beyond his 21 years.

Unlike their Detroit counterparts during spring training, the Boston minor leaguers lived in a motel—the Days Inn in North Fort Myers—rather than a crowded dorm like Fetzer Hall. They ate their meals at a Denny's adjacent to the motel, which had a pool and several restaurants within walking distance.

As Macha rehearsed signs and fundamentals with his team at the Boston minor-league complex throughout March, he gradually learned more about their personalities. Not only would the '95 season be his first as a minor-league manager, it also would be his first as a part of the Boston staff. All of the motivational lessons he had learned in the big leagues under managers like Chuck Tanner, Dick Williams, and Buck Rodgers would be put to the test during the Thunder's 142-game season. "I try to treat everyone the same—like a professional," Macha explained. During the first week of practice, Lipsman and Schofield arrived for round two of their preseason headshots. This time, there were fewer skeptical questions about the Waterfront Park playing surface.

In addition to Nomar, the core of Macha's offense would include first baseman Ryan McGuire (a 6-foot-2, 210-pound UCLA product who was Boston's third pick in the June 1993 draft), first baseman/designated hitter Doug Hecker (Boston's second pick in the June 1992 draft out of the University of Tennessee), second baseman Lou Merloni (Boston's tenth pick in the '93 draft out of Providence College), outfielder Aaron Fuller (a 31st-round pick in '93), catchers Jeff Martin and Walt McKeel (Boston's second pick in June 1990), and outfielder Andy Abad (a 16th-round pick in '93). During the '94 season at

Lynchburg of the Carolina League, McGuire hit .272, with 10 homers and 73 RBIs. The rest of Macha's position roster played with Nomar at Sarasota of the Florida State League. The Sarasota club had been eliminated by New York Yankees' affiliate Tampa in the first round of the league playoffs. Hecker hit .276, with 13 homers and 70 RBIs; Merloni hit .286, with 63 RBIs Martin hit .244; McKeel hit .277; Fuller hit .261, with a league-leading 89 runs scored and 45 stolen bases; and Abad hit .288, with 20 doubles. A likely Double-A candidate who was missing during spring training was infielder and Mississippi native Bill Selby, a left-hander who hit .310, with 19 homers and 69 RBIs to earn All-Carolina League honors for Lynchburg in 1994 before he was promoted to New Britain. Selby was a member of Boston's 40-man roster, but he wouldn't join the team until late April, 3 weeks after the major-league strike finally ended.

As he evaluated his club's strengths and weaknesses, Macha was concerned about a lack of right-handed power. That issue was resolved on April Fool's Day, when Boston Minor League Coordinator Bob Schaefer played a cruel trick by opting to send 25-year-old slugger Clyde "Pork Chop" Pough to Trenton. Pough, a 1994 Double-A All-Star who hit .298, with 20 homers, for Canton-Akron before he was promoted to Triple-A Charlotte, signed with the Red Sox as a 7-year free agent with the intention of beginning the season in Triple-A. During spring training, however, he looked awkward in the field, at one juncture misplaying a routine infield fly at third base. The dilemma for Boston was that he had no natural position. Thus, he became the perfect designated hitter for Macha's young roster.

"I thought I was going to Pawtucket," he said incredulously. As he packed up his equipment at the end of spring training, Pork Chop had two choices: he could pout about his situation; or he could show the Red Sox that they made a mistake. After a long conversation with Macha, he decided to accept his Double-A assignment.

Born on Christmas Day of 1969 in Sebring, Florida, Pork Chop earned his catchy nickname during Little League. As a child, his nickname was "Pokey." On his Little League team was another youngster nicknamed Pokey, however, and because the other kid was the coach's son, Pough's nickname was unceremoniously changed to Pork Chop. Not surprisingly, it stuck. After a stand-out high-school career in central Florida, he was drafted in the third round of the June 1988 amateur selection pool by Cleveland. For 7 long years, he made a slow climb up the Indians' organizational ladder, spending portions of 1991 and 1992 on the Indians' 40-man major league roster. In 1991, he hit .304, with 11 homers and 73 RBIs, for Columbus, Georgia, of the South Atlantic League. In 1993, he hit .270, with 13 homers, for Kinston of the Carolina League. Gradually, he inched toward his dream of playing in the major leagues, all the while buoyed by encouragement from his cousin, Tom "Flash" Gordon, a right-handed pitcher for the Kansas City Royals. Gordon also advised him that the road to the "bigs" was littered with potholes and setbacks.

By 1995, Pork Chop was a familiar face for many Eastern League observers. In fact, if one player knew first-hand the popularity surge of minor-league baseball during the mid-1990s along the Eastern Seaboard, he was the guy. Much to his dismay, he toured the region at the Single-A and Double-A levels with no apparent end in sight to his major-league quest. Somewhere along the way, he passed over the imaginary line that separates a prospect from a journeyman. The bottom line for most major-league scouts is age. When they see a 25-year-old stuck at Double-A, they have some serious questions. Pork Chop's Trenton experience, however, would prove that being a prospect and a minor-league entertainer are not mutually exclusive concepts.

THE '95 PITCHING STAFF

While his lineup was strengthened considerably by Pork Chop's addition, Macha figured that his starting pitching staff was in good hands. Under the guidance of 36-year-old former Boston right-hander Al Nipper (who pitched game four of the 1986 World Series against the New York Mets), the Thunder would begin the season with a five-man starting rotation that included righties Jeff Suppan, Wes Brooks, and Dean Peterson and lefties Rafael Orellano and Shawn Senior. The 20-year-old Suppan, rated the No. 4 prospect in the Red Sox farm system by *Baseball America*, was 13-7, with a 3.26 ERA, 50 walks, and 173 strike-outs in 27 starts for Sarasota during the '94 season. After losing his first five starts, he won 10 of his next 11 decisions. During an 8-0 playoff victory over Tampa, he walked two and struck out 10 over eight scoreless innings. In addition, he was named Boston Minor League Pitcher of the Week twice during the season. Brooks, at 22, was 12-12 with a 4.80 ERA and four complete games for Lynchburg (which won only 52 games in '94). Peterson, at 23, was 9-7 with a 3.64 ERA, six complete games, and three shutouts for Sarasota. Orellano, 21, Boston's No. 6 prospect according to *Baseball America*, had a benign tumor approximately the size of a tennis ball removed from the back of his leg in the '93 season and was slowed by elbow tendinitis early in 1994. He recovered to finish 11-3, however, with a 2.40 ERA in 16 Sarasota starts, displaying perhaps the best change-up in the Red Sox farm system. Finally, Senior, at 22, was a native of Cherry Hill, New Jersey, a 30-minute commute from Waterfront Park. A fourth-round pick in June 1993 out of North Carolina State, he was 4-4 with a 3.54 ERA at Lynchburg in 1994 before moving to Sarasota, where he finished the season 8-3 with a 3.02 ERA. In 43 professional appearances, Senior had compiled a 24-9 record, earning the reputation as a "guy who just knows how to win." He was looking forward to playing minor-league baseball in his home state, where he could have dinner in his mother's kitchen and drive to the South Trenton stadium in time for the game. Overall, the 1995 Thunder starting rotation appeared to be a vastly improved unit from the '94 starting group that had included Edmondson, Miller, Carlyle, Withem, and Mysel.

If there was a concern among the '95 starters, it was Suppan. Throughout spring training, he suffered a nagging groin injury that limited his work. In fact, he spent more time in jogging shoes than in baseball spikes. Nonetheless, one bullpen catcher insisted that he possessed incredible command of four pitches—fastball, curveball, slider, and "fosh" change-up, which was the name given to the off-speed delivery Nipper taught his top prospects. "Nip" spent the '94 season with Suppan, Orellano, Senior, and Peterson in Sarasota, so Macha basically let him make all of the pitching decisions during spring training. Nip wanted to start Suppan in the Thunder home opener against Canton-Akron on April 6, but a combination of the cold weather and "Soup's" sore groin made him change plans and opt for Brooks instead.

Originally selected by the Red Sox in the second round of the June 1993 draft (49th overall), Suppan used his leverage as one of UCLA's prized recruits to negotiate a $200,000 signing bonus. California agent Scott Boros helped to convince the Boston front office that the money was worth the risk. Then again, all of Soup's amateur pitching numbers suggested a rapid climb through the Red Sox minor-league system. As a 14-year-old at Crespi Carmelite High in West Hills, California, Soup became the first freshman in school history to be a starter on the varsity baseball team. Over four seasons, he compiled a 28-10 record with a 1.39 ERA, striking out 323 batters. On days when he was scheduled to pitch, his teammates liked to say, "Soup's on." His American Legion career was equally impressive: a 20-5 record with a 1.90 ERA and 283 strike-outs.

The youngest of five children, and by a considerable margin, Suppan was guided smoothly through adolescence by his parents, Larry—a retired air-traffic controller—and Kathy. "I tried to encourage him to sign out of high school, because I knew he wanted to be a professional baseball player," Larry said. Contract in hand, Jeff boarded a flight from Los Angeles to Fort Myers on June 30, 1993. While pitching for the Gulf Coast rookie-league Red Sox, he immediately established a bond with Nipper.

"Being with Al has been the greatest thing for me," Suppan said during spring training. "He's a very visual coach. I think with the work ethic that I have and his guidance, I should be able to challenge a lot of hitters this year."

Born on January 2, 1975, Soup was the youngest player ticketed for the '95 Thunder roster. While his decision to sign with Boston rather than attend UCLA was paying handsome dividends, the practical matter of being the baby in a clubhouse full of 23- and 24-year-olds was sometimes tricky. At one point during his rookie season, Soup had ballooned to 222 pounds, or more than 20 pounds above his high-school pitching weight. A personal trainer and extensive bicycle riding helped him return to form for the '94 season.

"That was my first year being away from my family, and it was hard," he admitted. "I was homesick, and I put on a lot of weight. It affected a lot of things, but I was serious about getting back to where I was."

As the major-league strike lingered into April, *Boston Globe* columnist and ESPN baseball analyst Peter Gammons spread the word through Florida spring training sites that Soup might not spend much time at the Double-A level before he was summoned to Boston. Macha enjoyed his first live glimpse of the young pitcher's considerable talents during a mid-March bullpen session. On March 29, Suppan threw 32 pitches over two innings against Pawtucket, striking out four batters—all on called third strikes.

While the Thunder's starting rotation was set, the bullpen was another matter entirely. Medford, New Jersey, product Joe Hudson, Macha's anticipated closer, also was on Boston's 40-man protected roster. As a teammate of outfielder Michael Jordan's on the '94 AFL Scottsdale Scorpions, he had recorded 10 saves in 22 appearances, but he spent March back in New Jersey, waiting for an opportunity to pitch. "I'm really disgusted at this point," he said from his Burlington County home. "Last fall they put me on the 40-man roster, but it was like they said, 'We're sorry, you can't play because you're on strike.'" In Hudson's absence, Boston filled the Thunder bullpen with 25-year-old righty Scott Bakkum (3-6 and 5.22 ERA at Sarasota in '94), 27-year-old righty Glenn Carter (8-7 and 4.79 ERA at Triple-A Pawtucket), 25-year-old righty Tim Cain (2-4 and 5.68 ERA at New Britain), 26-year-old righty Dominic Johnson (7-9 and 4.69 ERA in 31 games with Double-A Midland), and 25-year-old lefty Gregg Langbehn (3-3 and 5.44 ERA at Binghamton). It was this veteran core that gave Macha and Nipper a cushion for the young starters if they struggled.

FINAL PREPARATIONS

During the Thunder's 15-game spring exhibition schedule against Double-A and Triple-A opposition, it quickly became even more obvious to Macha that Nomar was special. He could plainly see that managing a player of his caliber was going to be an unforgettable experience. For example: the way his feet were always in motion when a pitch was delivered; the cuts he made to spear the ball once it was hit; his laser-like flips across the diamond to first base; the jokes he told Merloni while shielding his mouth from view with his glove. Occasionally, opposing hitters seemed startled when he made a difficult play look routine. His shortstop range was incredible, particularly flowing to his right. At the plate, he was a "gap-hitter," and he sent several balls into the alleys in right- and left-center field during spring training. When one of those hits fell in, he rarely broke stride on his way to second or third base.

With his Thunder roster finalized, Macha headed north to Trenton on Monday, April 3. The following night, a crowd of 600 greeted them at Angeloni's Cedar Gardens during the second-annual "Welcome North Dinner." Meanwhile, just as the big-league season was about to begin with replacement players, the major-league strike ended. Selby and Hudson reported to a belated spring training along with the rest of the true major leaguers, and many of the replacement players were left without jobs. Anderson returned to the helm in Detroit, relegating Runnells to Triple-A Toledo.

During the Welcome North Dinner, Pork Chop, Garciaparra, and Suppan were the star attractions. Brooks, the opening-night starter, also was besieged by autograph seekers. The banquet provided a valuable introduction for Soup, who met Jack and Nancy Ross of Feasterville, Pennsylvania. He would live with the couple in their suburban home throughout his Thunder stint, and they graciously mapped out directions so Soup could find his way around the new area.

On Wednesday, April 4, the Thunder conducted a public workout on Waterfront's new playing surface. As Puerto Rican native Orellano bundled up against the 40-degree temperatures ("I've never seen weather this cold," he insisted), a small crowd watched Brooks try to adjust to the Trenton mound. In addition, Suppan tested his groin injury in the chilly conditions. Afterward, he reported some soreness. In conjunction with Duquette and the Boston front office, Macha would monitor his prodigy's condition very closely. "I can only tell you my experience with a groin problem," the manager said. "I was playing in Japan [in the early 1980s], and I hit a ball and pulled the muscle all the way up into my stomach. Even a whole year later, I had problems. He isn't that severe, but he's got to take his time and feel comfortable with it."

With Suppan's status in doubt as the fifth starter, Brooks was eager to take the ball for the opener. "We'd like to catch fire early," the Illinois native said. "I'm pretty sure this team will be competitive."

"I think everybody is excited on opening day," Macha added. "I remember Willie Stargell saying, 'If you don't have butterflies on opening day, you're fooling yourself.'"

The Delaware Valley was certainly ready for the second Thunder season. During February, a crowd of 400 at the Hyatt Regency Princeton had heard Macha promise a competitive team during the franchise's first-annual "Winter Warm-up Dinner." By early March, almost all of the remaining Waterfront construction details had been completed. All that remained for groundskeeper Migliaccio and his crew were landscaping projects around the stadium's periphery.

On a frigid, early March Saturday morning, single-game tickets for the '95 season had gone on sale at the Waterfront ticket office. The previous night, a small group of diehard Thunder fans camped out on the concrete plaza in front of the stadium waiting to be the first in line for ducats to the April 6 opener against Canton-Akron. Snow flurries fluttered from the sky as they huddled around a kerosene heater. Before leaving for the evening, Mahoney distributed free merchandise to the group. Around midnight, the Corner Inn delivered a pizza courtesy of the Thunder, and the steaming cheese pie was devoured within moments. None of the overnight campers thought their actions were extreme. They did it for the love of minor-league baseball in Trenton.

"The Thunder was friendly fun, and we got hooked," said one. "This place is so much more intimate than the big-league parks. Last season was almost a reflection of everybody's life. They were under the gun to make deadlines, just like anyone. I think people could relate to that."

Brain Edmondson throws the first pitch in Thunder history at Harrisburg, PA, April 8, 1994.

1994–95 Thunder broadcasters Tom McCarthy and Nick Simonetta.

1994 Thunder
stars Tony Clark
and Brian DuBose.

April 27, 1994—the "home opener" that never was, at Mercer County
Waterfront Park.

1994 Thunder
manager Tom
Runnells wearing
Trenton Giants
replica uniform.

Mercer County Executive Robert D. Prunetti accompanies New Jersey
Governor Christine Todd Whitman to the mound at Waterfront Park
for the ceremonial first pitch, May 9, 1994.

Making history again: left-hander Trever Miller delivers the first pitch at Mercer County Waterfront Park, May 9, 1994.

Thunder first baseman/designated hitter Tony Clark signs autographs for young fans.

Thunder mascot "Boomer" gets up close and personal with an umpire.

1994 Thunder pitcher Rick Greene.

1995 Thunder manager Ken Macha and team owner Sam Plumeri, Sr.

1995 Thunder star Ryan McGuire poses with a young fan.

Sam Plumeri, Sr. with 1995 team members (from left) shortstop Nomar Garciaparra, first baseman Ryan McGuire, and coach Rico Petracelli.

1995–96 Thunder manager Ken Macha throwing batting practice to his players.

1995 Thunder
pitcher Jeff Suppan.

1995 players Lee
Tinsley (left) and
"Pork Chop" Pough.

A Waterfront Park mainstay: the "Dizzy Bat" Race.

Boomer chases a youngster around the bases.

The renowned Byer's Men's Shop billboard.

New Jersey native and 1995–96 Thunder pitcher Shawn Senior.

1995 Thunder shortstop Nomar Garciaparra (left) with Reading second baseman David Doster.

1996 Thunder pitchers and "Grumpy Old Men" Brent Knackert (far left) and Erik Schullstrom (second from left) take tickets on a rainy evening at Waterfront Park.

1996 Thunder shortstop
Donnie Sadler.

1996 Thunder sluggers
(from left) Tyrone Woods,
Todd Carey, and Adam
Hyzdu.

A fan roams Waterfront Park following a sweep of New Britain, April 28, 1996.

1996 Thunder pitcher Carl Pavano, the minor league pitcher of the year.

Boomer and (from left) Trenton Mayor Douglas Palmer, Governor
Christine Whitman, Ken Macha, and Mercer County Executive Robert
Prunetti smile with young fans at the 1996 Double-A All-Star Game at
Waterfront Park.

1995–96 Thunder
catcher Walt McKeel.

Trot Nixon takes a turn at bat during the 1996 season.

Infielder Lou Merloni prepares to make a catch during the 1996 season.

1996 Thunder outfielder Adam Hyzdu signs autographs.

1996 Thunder pitcher Carl Pavano takes a breather.

New and Improved

> "This is without question a more fan-friendly place than it was last year. It is slowly becoming what we'd all hoped it would be."
>
> —THUNDER GENERAL MANAGER WAYNE HODES BEFORE THE '95 HOME OPENER AGAINST CANTON-AKRON

The '95 Thunder season began with an eight-game homestand that lifted the curtain on Trenton's prosperous affiliation with Boston. Everything from the playing surface to the young prospects who would call it home had been upgraded. Gone were the everyday concerns about whether the field would hold water. The 300 drains placed throughout the 2.5-acre playground ensured that it would remain dry. Hodes' unspoken goal was to have the Thunder complete their 71-game home slate without a single rainout. Sixty of those dates would be accompanied by some sort of promotion, including Boomer's First Birthday Party, a batting-helmet giveaway, and a frisbee dog show. Most significantly, though, the franchise's focus turned to baseball and entertainment—without distractions.

The concession stands, which had been equipped with closed-circuit television monitors so fans wouldn't miss any of the action, had added everything from Taco Bell burritos to Kentucky Fried Chicken nuggets. The stadium's public address system was improved. A "Speed Pitch" booth was located on the right-field concourse, and beneath the first-base stands, Runnells' coveted indoor batting cages—which had never materialized during the inaugural season—were ready for Macha's charges. All three clubhouses had been refurbished, prompting the Thunder to move down the hall from the '94 team's dressing quarters. Groundskeeper Migliaccio had spent the last 3 months sprucing up the outside of the park, landscaping a riverside walk, planting flowers, and installing permanent picnic tables on the entrance plaza. The dark green hitting backdrop in straightaway center had been expanded from 40 to 56 feet, and the dreaded tooth billboard had been moved to the right side of the backdrop. Everything about the facility was new and improved, waiting for the steady stream of patrons who passed through the turnstiles during the inaugural season to return for an encore.

From the moment Macha came north with his players, it was clear that

Boston's approach to developing players was different from Detroit's. With rigidly based organization rules and a manual written by minor-league coordinator Bob Schaefer that outlined the Red Sox farm system, Boston was much more serious about its commitment to win at every level. "What we're trying to do is provide the best opportunity to develop skills through teaching, guidance, and providing a sound environment to play," Schaefer explained. "That's why we're so excited about Trenton. They have a great facility and great fans. But our big thing is teaching, and it's going to be like school for a lot of these guys."

Macha—who had been a substitute teacher during the off-season of his major-league playing days (he once even directed an art class)—suited Boston's approach. "There shouldn't be a day when you don't have some type of development, even if you have a rainout," the new Thunder skipper said. Breaking into a wry smile, he provided a glimpse into the dry humor that would consistently entertain those who had the opportunity to develop a professional relationship with him over the next two seasons. "But I heard we're not going to have any rainouts this year," he deadpanned.

On a more serious note, Macha evaluated his 1995 assignment. "I feel fortunate that I'm here in Trenton, and I know the Red Sox feel the same way," he said. "I have aspirations of managing in the major leagues, and this is also a vital step in my development. But this whole thing is going to be a learning process for everybody. We want to get the players involved in the community— that's something that's been missing from baseball. And here, they're going to have to answer to people, just like they're going to have to if they get to the big leagues."

For Macha, to whom handling players was a much less rigidly disciplinarian task than for his predecessor Runnells, the No. 1 team rule was "Conduct yourself like a professional at all times." That edict included dealing with the media and the community. "It's easy to go out and talk about yourself when you've done well," Macha said. "It's very difficult to talk about yourself when you haven't done well. The key is to learn how to handle yourself in both positive and negative situations. In the minor leagues, you're going to have both."

Inside their new clubhouse, Nomar and Merloni settled into lockers near the back corner of the new dressing room. Suppan, Orellano. and Brooks selected cubicles nearby. Pork Chop also chose a locker in the same row. Macha's office, which was located along the hall leading to the training room, included a desk, private shower, fax machine, and personal telephone he nicknamed "the bat phone." Over the next two seasons, news of promotions or demotions was always filtered through the bat phone.

Behind the manager's office, trainer Chris Correnti had a spacious, fully equipped treatment room that also was connected to pitching coach Al Nipper's office. Early in the season, Nipper asked the Thunder to bring him a rollaway bed for the back room so he could sleep over during long work nights. On the new clubhouse wall, Macha posted his opening-night lineup:

  5   Garciaparra 6 (ss)
  7   Merloni 4 (2b)
 17   Hecker 7 (lf)
 22   Pough DH

21   McGuire 3 (1b)
 8   McKeel 2 (c)
12   Abad 9 (rf)
13   Nava 5 (3b)
14   Graham 8 (cf)

An opening-night crowd of 6994 watched Brooks pitch extremely well for six innings against Canton-Akron. "Brooksie" allowed one run on three hits, but the Thunder offense was ineffective, evoking unpleasant memories of its '94 predecessor. Abad singled twice and McGuire once, and Canton-Akron reliever John Hrusovsky walked the bases loaded with two outs in the eighth. The Indians escaped, however, when Hecker popped out weakly to short. Garciaparra was 0-for-3 with a walk, a strikeout, and an error, and Pork Chop was 0-for-3 with a strikeout in the 3-0 shutout loss.

In game two of the opening series, Shawn Senior made the most of his long-anticipated New Jersey homecoming, spinning six innings of one-hit baseball for 4156 patrons. Reliever Tim Cain spelled Senior and thwarted the Indians for three complete innings to earn his first save as the Thunder held on for a 2-0 win. "As far as being home and throwing, I definitely had a little more adrenaline tonight," Senior confessed.

The offensive highlight was Doug Hecker's fourth-inning solo homer to left-center field, the first of the Thunder season. Nomar was 0-for-4, and Pork Chop was 0-for-2. Although he issued four walks on the night, Senior was able to battle out from each of his self-induced predicaments. Watching with pride was his mother, Bernadette. Before the game, she prepared Shawn a special pasta-and-bean soup. "He's always been a hard worker," she said. "That's what got him here. If he doesn't get to the major leagues, it won't be because of his work ethic. I'm so proud of him. You really can't believe."

"He used both sides of the plate well," Nipper said of his starter. "When it gets warmer, these six-inning games are going to be turning into complete games."

Macha, providing an early glimpse of his pragmatic approach, was asked how it felt to win his first game as a minor-league manager and replied, "It's better than two losses in a row or a sharp stick in the eye."

Following Saturday afternoon's 1:35 PM game (the start time for Thunder weekend games during the cold months of April and May), Macha announced that Suppan had been placed on the 7-day disabled list because of his groin injury. The young pitcher calmly packed his red-and-blue equipment bag and caught a flight back to Fort Myers, where he would heal in the Florida heat while the major leaguers conducted an abbreviated spring training. "I just want to get this taken care of, by whatever means they want me to," he said.

"I think he's down a little bit," Larry Suppan added. "He's never had an injury before, but I've said all along this is better than an elbow problem."

"We've got a guy here who's a highly regarded pitcher, and we're going to take our time with him," Macha said, adding that his orders came directly from Duquette. "It could be May before he returns."

Through the first two games, Nomar and Pork Chop were a combined 0-for-11. During the third game, a Saturday matinee, Orellano made his Eastern League debut, scattering four hits over six innings and striking out six batters.

Nomar produced his first hit of the season, a two-out RBI single in the fifth off Canton-Akron starter Steve Kline; however, the Thunder trailed 5-1 in the bottom of the eighth when Pork Chop finally made his veteran influence felt. Already, the Trenton fans had begun to enjoy shouting his one-of-a-kind nickname. "The name brought so much animation with it before he ever picked up a bat," McCarthy said. Facing Hrusovsky, Pough unloaded for a two-run homer that pulled his team within two runs. The early season tension melted from his shoulders as he shook Macha's hand in the third-base coaching box. No. 5 hitter Ryan McGuire followed with a solo homer, and the Thunder won the game 6-5 in the bottom of the ninth as McGuire drew a walk with the bases loaded to score center fielder Tim Graham. In three games, Macha's club hit three homers—the '94 Thunder didn't hit their first until the sixth game.

"The first couple of games, I was pressing, wanting to do so well against these guys," Pork Chop said about facing his former team. "Once I hit that one, the homers kinda come in bunches. I hope I'm not sticking my foot in my mouth by saying that."

Quite simply, the come-from-behind win had been an encouraging early season sign. "I think a lot of it is that we have some younger guys who are maybe too stupid to know that we aren't supposed to win in that situation," McGuire said. "We just lucked out today."

On Sunday, April 9—"Big Mac Day" at Waterfront (sponsored by the brand-new McDonald's located less than a mile from the stadium on Cass Street)—Peterson looked strong for eight innings (allowing one run on four hits with six strikeouts). The Thunder bullpen surrendered three runs to the Indians in the top of the eleventh inning, however, and Trenton lost its first extra-inning game of the season 6-3. Third baseman Todd Carey hit his first Double-A homer, continuing the Thunder's early season long-ball spree. In spite of the chilly temperatures, the four-game series drew 20,246 patrons, an average of more than 5000 per opening.

Next into town were the renamed Hardware City Rock Cats, the first-year affiliate of the Minnesota Twins, who had taken up residence in New Britain after Boston vacated Beehive Field and moved to Trenton. Taking Suppan's place in the starting rotation, Dominic Johnson was ineffective, allowing five earned runs on five hits over five innings to absorb a 5-0 loss. "Dom tried to muscle his fastball, and he got behind," Macha explained. "If you fall behind in this league, they're going to hit you hard." Rock Cats' righty Brett Roberts allowed just one hit in seven innings—a single by McGuire. Nomar helped the Thunder defense turn four double plays, however, an early sign of things to come.

After beginning the season with a 2-3 record, the Thunder took advantage of the remaining homestand to win three in a row from Hardware City. Wes Brooks was stellar during a 6-0 shut-out in the sixth game, played on April 11. Before the smallest crowd in Waterfront history (2883), the righty used the change-up he had learned from Nipper to great advantage. Pork Chop laced an RBI double, Walt McKeel was 2-for-2 with a triple and two RBIs, and third baseman Lipso Nava hit a two-run homer in the second. Nava was simply manning the position until Selby arrived from major-league spring training, but Macha appreciated his contribution.

The next night, Pork Chop homered for the second time during the home-stand, and Senior miraculously pitched out of a bases-loaded, nobody-out jam in the top of the first by striking out Hardware City's No. 4 and 5 hitters and inducing a fly out to end the threat. The result was a 1-0 win that made Senior 2-0. "They're going to have to replace the front edge of those seats because those fans must be wearing them out," Macha said after his pitcher allowed seven hits but no runs. "The bases loaded in the top of the first, nobody out. Getting out of that is almost impossible. The guys did a hell of a job." Pork Chop's solo homer came on a fourth-inning fastball from Rock Cats' starter Travis Miller.

Despite his early offensive slump, Nomar let his glovework do the talking. Among his first-week gems was a magnificent double-play throw during Senior's 1-0 shutout victory. With runners at first and third, the Thunder pitcher wheeled on the mound and threw out designated hitter Kenny Norman in a rundown between first and second. Pork Chop quickly relayed the ball to Nomar, who threw home to nail shortstop Ramon Valette at the plate. "Pork Chop was the key to that play because he got rid of the ball so fast; everything had to be perfect," Nomar said in an "Aw, shucks" manner.

Macha was more candid. "All the years I've been in the big leagues, I've never seen a double play like that. That's why they pay money to go to the ballpark, to see something they've never seen before." For many Thunder fans who had grown accustomed to watching Mendenhall butcher play after play during the inaugural season, Nomar was a genuine treat. Some of the season-ticket holders began calling him "the Vacuum."

The Thunder took the final game against Hardware City, which also was the first Businessperson's Special of the '95 season, by a 7-6 margin on Abad's two-run double in the eighth. With a crowd of 3526 chanting, "Loouuu," Merloni hit his only homer of the season, a two-run shot in the sixth. For the rest of the year, Merloni promised everyone who would listen that he was going to hit another one out of the yard.

Game eight also marked the Thunder debut of closer Glenn Carter, a red-headed fastball pitcher who patterned himself after '93 Philadelphia Phillies reliever Mitch Williams. Over a span of 14 games, before he asked for and was granted his unconditional release from the Red Sox, "Wild Thing" Carter would record eight saves, moving past Guilfoyle and Whiteside's Thunder record of five. He also added color to the clubhouse. "I'll have to learn how to be a closer because I've never done it before," he admitted. "The Red Sox think I'm a little on the lunatic side. They don't think I'm smart enough to be a starter, but I'm dumb enough to be a closer. They think I can put a little fear into hitters."

With a fastball that topped out in the low nineties, Carter was more than a bit of a lunatic. He talked to baseballs. He yelled at opponents after he struck them out. He flirted shamelessly with women throughout the game as he waited in the bullpen. During a mid-April trip to Binghamton, Macha spotted Carter drinking Jack Daniels at a downtown restaurant. "You getting ready for tomorrow's game?" the manager inquired, and Carter replied, before lifting his shot glass to his mouth, "Why do you think all my friends call me whiskey?" On that same trip, a waitress gave him a giant inflatable Jack Daniels bottle, which he proudly transported home on the bus.

PORK CHOP BREAKS OUT

The first road trip of the '95 season carried the Thunder to New Haven for a three-game series. Picking up where he left off at the end of the opening homestand, Pork Chop homered in the first Connecticut game. The three-run shot to left off Ravens' pitcher John Thomson sparked a 7-5 Thunder victory. Through nine games (and six wins), Pork Chop was 6-for-31, with one double, three homers, and nine of the Thunder's 31 RBIs.

"He's the bus driver," Macha said during batting practice at Yale Field. "He's the guy in the middle of the lineup, and those young guys around him don't have the experience he does. For that reason, we're going to get up on his back and ride him."

The first game of the New Haven series also was a breakthrough for Nomar, who was 4-for-31 (.129) during the opening eight-game homestand. Perhaps all he needed was to be a little closer to his ultimate professional destination—Boston. Playing in New Haven for the first time, he went 2-for-4 with a pair of doubles (his first Double-A extra-base hits). "That was a great job," Macha praised. Through the season's first week-and-a-half, the manager toyed with his lineup, inserting the speedy Fuller in the leadoff spot even though that job would eventually go to Nomar. From the outset, the switch-hitting Fuller seemed overmatched by Double-A pitching. Consequently, he couldn't use his speed if he couldn't get on base. In 58 games with the Thunder, he would hit .196, with 10 RBIs and 15 stolen bases.

The Thunder saw their four-game winning streak halted during the second game of the New Haven series as Johnson was buried during a 12-8 loss. In 3 1/3 innings, he allowed seven earned runs, hit a batter, threw a wild pitch, and walked four. Nipper was furious. Not only had Johnson taken Suppan's place in the rotation, he was blowing the team ERA apart. After two appearances apiece, Senior was 2-0, with a 0.00 ERA; Brooks was 1-1, 0.69; Peterson was 1-0, 1.98; and Orellano was 0-0, 3.86. On the other hand, Johnson, the oldest member of the rotation, was 0-2, with a gaudy 12.53 ERA. Privately, Nipper wanted him gone, but Macha would only say about the situation, "When you score eight runs and you're not in the game, that's a problem. The two games we've been out of, it's been when his spot in the rotation came up." McGuire homered, and Pork Chop was 2-for-4 with a double. Even so, the Thunder couldn't rebound from a 12-4 deficit after five innings. Reliever Joe Caruso gave Johnson little support, coughing up five earned runs in 1 2/3 innings.

On April 24, Nipper received his wish—Johnson was released.

Pork Chop continued his torrid April the next day during an Easter Sunday matinee before 2576 Yale Field patrons, doubling in the winning run in the top of the ninth inning for a 7-6 Thunder victory. Nomar had the day off, but shortstop Todd Carey didn't seem to notice, going 3-for-4 with a double. Scott Bakkum earned the victory in relief of Brooks (who allowed five earned runs in six innings), Carter picked up the save, and the Thunder headed to Binghamton with a 7-4 record, a game-and-a-half behind Reading in the Eastern League Southern Division.

BLASTING THROUGH BINGHAMTON

Buoyed by his fine series in New Haven, Pork Chop was on a high as he arrived in New York's Southern Tier for a three-game series against the Mets. The first game began with Macha's first look at the Mets' prized righty Paul Wilson (a Florida State product who received a $1.55 million signing bonus as the first pick in the June 1994 draft) and lasted a Thunder-record 15 innings before Trenton finally prevailed 5-4. Senior was long gone by the time Mets' reliever Todd Siegel walked in the winning run to give the Thunder their fifth one-run victory of the season. A crowd of 2578 watched as the electronic thermometer below the right-center field scoreboard dipped from 56 degrees at game time (7:05 PM) to the low forties when the matter was finally settled shortly after 11:00 PM. "Well, we finished up before closing time," Macha quipped. "This team is showing me it can win close games. I need a no-brainer."

While Pork Chop prospered as the hottest slugger in the league, Nomar was battling to adjust to the cold. Born July 23, 1973, in Whittier, California, he was raised in the warm shadow of the Pacific Ocean. The Binghamton series represented a reunion with his former Georgia Tech teammate, Mets' outfielder Jay Payton, but their paths crossed under very different circumstances. Through 10 games, Nomar was hitting .158, while Payton (the eventual league MVP) was burning up the circuit at a .382 clip. The pair enjoyed an afternoon together discussing their experiences in Nomar's hotel room.

"I know he doesn't like cold weather," Payton said. "When it warms up, everybody will see the real Nomar. He has great range. He's got a great arm, and he can go in the hole and throw runners out. He's a clutch hitter, too."

Before the April 18 night game, Macha held a rare team meeting. Deciding he wasn't in the mood to eat anything on the pregame spread table, Orellano picked up the clubhouse telephone and called Domino's. Moments later, in walked a red, white, and blue-clad delivery man.

"Who ordered the pizza?" he asked as the Thunder players looked on in amused silence.

"I did," the pitcher replied in a guilty tone.

"What the hell is going on here?" Macha bellowed.

The manager recalled with incredulity, "I'm trying to conduct a meeting and he's ordering pizza. And what's he doing eating pizza an hour before he's supposed to pitch, anyway?"

"It was pepperoni," Orellano said with a smile afterward.

Pizza controversies aside, the no-brainer that Macha had ordered was delivered right on time. A small Binghamton Municipal Stadium crowd of 1840 watched in amazement as Orellano, the Puerto Rican lefty, pitched no-hit baseball for 6 1/3 innings and Pork Chop authored a 4-for-5 performance that included six RBIs and a Thunder-record 12 total bases (breaking the mark of 10 established by Clark at New Britain on July 24, 1994). The result was a 14-3 victory that stunned broadcasters McCarthy and Simonetta. Never before had a Thunder team scored 14 runs in a game. Outfielder Aaron Fuller broke loose to set a franchise record with three doubles, and Trenton pounded a quartet of Binghamton pitchers for a team-record 16 hits. Orellano left the game with a no-hitter intact because his pitch count was over 100. Given his history of elbow problems, Macha and Nipper would not leave him in the game just for the sake of a no-hitter. Some of the Binghamton fans gasped when the pitcher left with zeros on the board, but five walks had pushed him over the top. Would Orellano have pitched a no-hitter if his control had been better? That question will forever remain unanswered. "They didn't have a clue how to hit him," McKeel said after catching the game.

"I thought he was favoring his elbow and coming under his pitches," Macha said. "I went out there and told him, 'I don't want you to get hurt.' He wouldn't have gone the distance anyway." Afterward, Macha said he felt Orellano was trying to overthrow his fastball.

"He thinks he's got to juice it to be successful at this level," the manager said, reiterating a conversation he had with his young pitcher. "He doesn't. And he's very demanding of himself. He gets frustrated and throws that much harder. It's all a maturing process."

Pork Chop's two-run triple in the first inning was followed by a three-run homer (his fourth) in the fourth. Leading off the seventh inning against Mets' reliever Tom Engle, he slammed a towering solo homer over the train tracks behind the left-field wall. The ball even cleared the slowly moving coal cars as they headed east. In the radio booth, McCarthy and Simonetta looked at each other in disbelief. "That's gotta be one of the longest homers I've ever seen hit here," Binghamton scorer Steve Kraly said, comparing it to Clark's blast the previous August.

"Once I hit it, I just dropped my head and went into my trot," Pork Chop said. "I'm not trying to make a statement. I'm just trying to do my job."

Also starring during the blowout was Nomar, who retired Payton on a miraculous force play at second base during the second inning. Following each game, Macha filled out a game report that was faxed to Boston officials Schaefer and Duquette. On the daily form was a special section reserved for observations and great plays. Following the April 18 win, Macha wrote, "Nomar—worth the price of admission."

On Wednesday, April 19, moments before the Thunder checked out of their hotel rooms to prepare for an afternoon game against the Mets, many of them sat transfixed before the television as scenes from the bombing of Oklahoma City's Alfred P. Murrah Federal Building unfolded. Peterson gave up back-to-back homers in the first inning and hit the next batter to earn an ejection from home-plate umpire Brian Gilbert. With his team trailing 3-0, Johnson was pressed into emergency duty. He worked 4 1/3 innings, allowing three runs on three hits, walking four, and striking out six batters. Five days before Boston released him, Johnson earned the 9-7 victory, largely because Abad finished the day 3-for-4, with three RBIs. Carter nailed down his fourth save in as many opportunities, but Macha admitted, "I'm nervous every time I hand him the ball."

"This is kinda like junior college when I woke up knowing we were going to win," Carter said following the three-game sweep. "Everybody's got a good attitude on this team, and it's awesome. And the amount of runs the offense is giving us as pitchers is a luxury." With an off-day scheduled for April 20, the Thunder headed home with a 10-4 record. A three-game weekend series at first-place Reading awaited.

MIXED RESULTS

Entering the '95 season, not much was expected of the Phillies, who had finished three games ahead of the '94 Thunder with a 58-82 record. The Philadelphia farm system was improving under the direction of head scout Mike Arbuckle, however, and Reading's early '95 performance reflected that trend. In the first game of the series, Carter suffered his first loss of the season, 3-2, after blowing a save in the bottom of the ninth inning. The Thunder rebounded for a 10-6 Saturday afternoon victory as Pork Chop smashed a triple and a homer to drive in three runs in his four at-bats. Senior was roughed up for all six runs in six innings of work, and Nomar was 2-for-5 with a pair of runs scored. During Sunday's 6-4 Reading win, Pork Chop homered for the second consecutive day and the fourth time in the last week, but Orellano was ineffective, allowing six runs in 5 2/3 innings. McGuire was 2-for-3, extending his hitting streak to eight games. Phillies' catcher Gary Bennett also was 2-for-3, with three RBIs, and Reading (11-4) led the Thunder (11-6) by a full game at the end of Trenton's 10-day, nine-game road trip (during which Trenton was 6-3). On Monday, April 24, Pork Chop was named Eastern League Batter of the Week.

"Great trip . . . tremendous trip," Macha summed up in the Reading visitor's clubhouse. "All the guys are together, and the atmosphere is great. They know they're going to be in every game. Chop's kind of carried us on this trip. I just told him I hope he's not around here too long. I'd be sorry to see him get promoted, but that's the idea around here."

Returning home to face Bowie on April 24, the Thunder received a magnificent pitching performance from Dean Peterson during a complete-game, 6-2 victory. The former Allegheny College star worked 7 2/3 innings before giving up a hit to Baysox right fielder Roy Hodge. At the time, a Waterfront crowd of 3925 couldn't have known that it was witnessing the only one-hitter of the first three Thunder seasons. After he was thrown out of the Binghamton game on April 19, Peterson had used the extra time to rest his arm. "It was like I had eight days off," he said. When he worked a 1-2-3 first inning, Macha greeted him in the dugout with, "Hey, you made it longer than last time." Everyone within earshot laughed.

During the eighth inning, Macha leaned over to Nipper and asked, "Ever had one of your guys throw a no-hitter?" The pitching coach thought for a moment and replied, "Tonight." Of course, in baseball etiquette, such a conversation is the kiss of death, and Peterson settled for the one-hitter.

"The cut fastball was the pitch I was throwing all night," he explained. "Their guys were aggressive hitters and just missing it."

The outing improved Peterson's record to 2-0. Ironically, it also was his apex as a Thunder pitcher. In 20 games (14 starts), he wound-up 4-8, with a 5.38 ERA. He couldn't sustain his early effectiveness. The second or third time opposing batters saw him, the cut fastball didn't have its same bite. After allowing four runs in 1 1/3 innings of relief on July 14, he was demoted to Sarasota. Before leaving Trenton, however, he was married in a Hamilton courthouse ceremony.

The first month of the '95 season concluded on an extremely positive note with the April 24 arrival of Selby and Hudson from major-league spring training and Suppan's April 28 return to Trenton from Ft. Myers. After a late-night meal at the Soho Restaurant with several teammates the night before, Soup prepared for his April 29 Double-A debut. An almost-capacity crowd of 6044 filled Waterfront for the 1:35 PM first pitch on a warm spring afternoon. A swirl of anticipation surrounded the 20-year-old right-hander as he took the mound wearing white No. 20. Over six complete innings, he allowed one earned run on three hits. He walked one and struck out five batters. His presence on the mound was impressive, his expression unchanged from batter to batter. His anxious parents, Kathy and Larry, watched the action from the family seats behind home plate.

Although Soup departed with a 4-2 lead, he did not pick up a decision. The Ravens scored a pair of unearned runs off Scott Bakkum before the Thunder rallied for a 7-4 victory with three runs in the eighth. Mahay scored pinch-runner Fuller with the winning margin. Answering questions about experiencing hard luck in his first Eastern League appearance, Soup replied, "That's baseball sometimes."

"He had some overpowering stuff," Macha added. "The first three innings, his ball was just exploding up there. And then he went into pitching mode."

With Soup back in the fold, the Thunder completed April with a 13-11 record, three-and-a-half games behind Reading. Their team batting average was a healthy .243. Winning fans daily, Pork Chop was named the Boston Organization Minor League Player of the Month for April. In 24 games, he hit .312, with six doubles, three triples, nine homers, and 25 RBIs. He led the Eastern League in homers, RBIs, slugging percentage (.731), extra-base hits (18), and runs scored (22). The offensive carnage left him scratching his head about the future.

"I was just asking myself what I have to do to get promoted," he admitted before an April 27 game at Bowie. "This is the best start I've ever had. I'm ready to move, but I guess I just have to sit tight and keep doing my thing. Now would be the best time for me, though."

"We hope to get him to Triple-A before the year's over, but there are some things going on up there," Schaefer explained. "We hope he stays sharp until we can get him there."

Macha certainly appreciated Pork Chop's professionalism. Quite frankly, he needed his big right-handed bat in the lineup. "His attitude has been great, but a promotion is something you have no control over," the manager said.

Contrary to his professional goal of moving up the ladder, the longer Pork Chop stayed in Trenton, the more popular he became. The adulation made his disappointment somewhat more tolerable. He was in great demand for public appearances, autograph shows, and clinics. During one session at a Hamilton supermarket, a group of Thunder fans asked him to hold up a pair of pork chops for a photo opportunity. He smiled graciously with a package of USDA-approved meat in each hand.

CHAPTER 14

Pork Chop and Soup: Trenton Entertainers

> "Personally, I'm enjoying myself. The guys are just an extreme joy to work with. Their attention has been great. Their work habits have been great. I don't have personality problems with anybody."
>
> —KEN MACHA AFTER HIS FIRST MONTH AS THUNDER MANAGER

During a May 3 Businessperson's Special at Waterfront Park, Pork Chop authored one of the most dramatic moments of his unforgettable Thunder career. A very vocal crowd of 5022, many of them in suits and ties, watched Trenton battle first-place Reading to a 4-4 tie through 8 1/2 innings. Phillies' reliever Ron Blazier dug in for the challenge of trying to send the game into extra innings as Pork Chop led off the bottom of the ninth. Amidst the waving arms that accompanied each of Pork Chop's at-bats were a plethora of green-foam hands. The hands—which had the index finger extended in a No. 1 gesture—became a best-seller in the Thunder Dugout Shop during the '95 season. At $4 each, Pork Chop should have received a commission on their sales.

As Pork Chop entered the batter's box, Blazier swallowed and looked to catcher Gary Bennett for the signs. Pork Chop quickly ran the count to two balls and no strikes as the big right-hander missed a pair of fastballs.

Still looking to throw his 90-mph heater, Blazier paid dearly for the indiscretion as Pork Chop tagged the third pitch over the left-field billboards and into the parking lot. Expecting to see another fastball, he had guessed right. The heroic homer, saluted by a boisterous standing ovation, prevented the Thunder (14-13) from falling below the .500 mark and dropped Reading to 17-7. It was a key early season swing game.

"He threw that ball right down the shooter," Pork Chop said of his league-leading tenth homer. "That felt great."

The dramatic May 3 victory also featured Nomar's second homer of the season and seven strikeouts from Orellano, who worked 8 1/3 innings but did not figure into the decision. "I told Pork Chop that was a good job," Orellano said. "I feel good, and the team won, so what can I say? Forget about me not getting the win."

Day by day, the Pork Chop phenomenon took greater hold of Waterfront Park visitors. How could he help but play to the crowds who came to watch him?

"Trenton is by far the best place I've ever played in the minor leagues," he said with a tone of genuine fondness. "The fans there are so good to me that I feel guilty when I make an out. I'm serious. It's incredible."

During the first 4 months of the '95 season, Pork Chop's Trenton love affair was reciprocal. Nobody in kelly green pinstripes was more popular than the veteran minor-league slugger. Someone joked that he should run for city council, or even mayor. Each time the 6-foot, 200-pounder came to the plate at Waterfront Park, Hardison bellowed into his microphone, "Now batting for the Thunder, No. 22, PORK . . . CHOP . . . POUGH." As the phenomenon caught on, arms began waving in the air, rhythmically, like the Tomahawk Chop craze first popularized by Atlanta Braves fans. "Yo-o-o-o-o-oooo, Yooooooo." By late May, it was a Trenton ballpark ritual, as indigenous as pork roll and tomato pie.

By the middle of the season, the scoreboard in Waterfront's right-center field fanned the frenzy with a giant lime-green graphic that simulated a hand chopping up and down before each of Pork Chop's at-bats. Occasionally, the Pork Chop phenomenon even surfaced during road games, like the May evening in Norwich when the Navigators' electronic scoreboard operator flashed the message, "BARBECUED PORK CHOP" after a Pough strikeout. Everyone, it seemed, had fun with the nickname. Pork Chop was routinely hounded for autographs, not only as a result of his unique moniker but also for his slugging talent, and he rarely refused a request.

Everything that Tony Clark represented to the inaugural '94 Thunder campaign through his incredible power and willingness to accommodate fans with a gracious smile and an autograph, Pork Chop perpetuated during the second season. His package of talent and personality was engaging. His gold tooth. His Popeye forearms and staccato-quick bat. His ability to produce in the clutch. His willingness to play every day. Thunder fans flocked to him relentlessly, most of them shouting his name in unison.

During Pork Chop's power surge, first baseman/outfielder Ryan McGuire enjoyed the opportunity to watch and learn. After suffering a bruised left hand at Bowie on April 27, he spent a week on the disabled list.

"Pork Chop strikes out some, but most of the time he's taking good swings," McGuire said appreciatively. "He doesn't get baffled or really get beat badly. Whenever I see him strike out, I feel like if you gave him another pitch or two, that he would get a hit. He's kinda like one of those leaders who's quiet and does his own thing."

Following the no-decision in his Trenton debut on April 29, Soup made his second Double-A appearance on a cold and blustery evening against Hardware City at New Britain's Beehive Field. A blanket-toting crowd of 1336 braved gusts that whipped the infield dirt across the first-base line and into the bleachers. In the first game of a doubleheader against the Rock Cats, Soup looked extremely uncomfortable on the mound. He struggled with his control, allowing three earned runs on six hits over 4 1/3 innings, walking three and striking out two. One of his major early season problems was keeping opposing baserunners honest. As he labored with his high leg kick, New Britain stole four bases. He simply wasn't getting the ball to catcher Jeff Martin in time to allow a successful relay throw to second. After Suppan's departure, the Rock Cats won the game 4-3 on a ninth-inning RBI single by left fielder Matt Lawton. It was Soup's second consecutive no-decision, but at least it was better than the five consecutive losses with which he began his '94 Sarasota campaign. The mood in the cramped Thunder clubhouse was particularly grim as Wes Brooks prepared to start the nightcap. Nipper, who pitched the first Beehive game in 1983, balled his facial muscles into a tight fist. Earlier in the week, he stated that he would gladly push the dynamite plunger on the 'Hive if and when they demolished it. The Thunder promptly lost the nightcap 3-2.

From New Britain, it was on to Norwich and the Thunder's first look at brand-new Thomas H. Dodd Stadium, where the Yankees' Double-A affiliate had relocated after a decade in Albany, New York. As the Trenton players surveyed the spacious facility, Suppan thought to himself that it would be an ideal setting for his first Double-A victory. After all, Norwich was Schaefer's hometown. It also was less than a 2-hour drive from Boston.

Behind superb pitching from Peterson and Orellano, the Thunder won the first two games of the series, 3-2 and 4-2, improving their record to 17-15. On Wednesday, May 10, an all-day rainstorm forced a postponement of that night's game, necessitating a Thursday doubleheader. Inside the bar at the Thunder hotel, the Radisson-New London, Nipper and Macha watched baseball on a wide-screen TV and sipped Budweiser. Suppan and Senior were seated at a table near the back wall, enjoying a rare early dinner. Soup swigged from a glass of Coca-Cola, privately thirsting for that elusive first victory. A repeat of his 0-5 Sarasota '94 start was not in his plans.

A CASINO FORAY

Meanwhile, as the rain continued, Nipper and trainer Chris Correnti decided to brave the weather for a 30-minute trip to Ledyard, Connecticut, and the Foxwoods Resort and Casino. Owned and operated by the Mashantucket Pequot Indians, Foxwoods is a 24-hour-a-day mecca for gamblers all over New England. During the short ride to the casino, Nipper told stories of the night he and Roger Clemens lost $11,000 playing roulette in Las Vegas.

After valet parking their vehicle and taking a quick walk around the game room, Nipper began studying the roulette wheels. Outfitted in a blue sweatsuit with deep pants pockets, he quickly decided that one particular wheel had a tendency to return black numbers. Cashing in a $100 bill for four $25 chips, he began to build a nest egg with which to fill his pockets. Hitting on approximately three of every four black numbers he bet, he built a pile of chips worth more than $500 in a little over 30 minutes. Studying the ricochet of the little white ball with an intent stroke of his jet-black mustache, he rarely varied his bets. Black. Even. As winnings accrued, he began betting $50 and $100 on each spin. Cocktail waitresses outfitted as Indian squaws traipsed by with free beer refills at various intervals.

During his winning streak, Nipper hit on black No. 20 several times. It was a very good omen that did not go unnoticed by the superstitious pitching coach. "That means Jeff is going to get his first win tomorrow. Give me another chip on black, even."

Just as quickly as he built his pile of winnings to almost $1000, however, the wheel turned on Nipper. In many ways, it was like the saga of a career minor leaguer who doesn't realize that his major-league dream is over. Someone—usually a manager or an administrator—has to do it for him. In a span of less than 30 minutes, Nipper lost all of his chips. With a proud, unbowed look of disgust, he turned his back to the wheel, having lost only his original $100. Hungry from his mental exertion, he summoned Correnti to a nearby restaurant that faced the illuminated water fountain in the center of the Foxwoods complex, and he ordered a beer and a lobster-tail dinner, as if to remind himself that Double-A isn't too far from the majors. At one point during his meal, he proclaimed, "I guarantee you this [Thunder] team will make the playoffs."

The next evening—with a lighter wallet—Nipper watched in amazement as Brooks took a no-hitter into the sixth inning of the scheduled seven-inning first game against the Navigators. Then, just as suddenly as Nipper's winnings had gone down the drain the previous night, Brooks self-destructed. A solo homer by designated hitter Kevin Riggs curled around the right-field foul pole to tie the game 1-1. Riggs' round-tripper was followed by a two-run homer by the Yankees' No. 1 prospect, Ruben Rivera. Not only had Brooks lost the no-hitter, he also suffered a 3-1 defeat. The gloom in the spacious visiting clubhouse was tangible as Soup steadied himself for Double-A appearance No. 3.

For a team in drastic need of a lift, Soup was the Thunder's answer. He quickly worked into first-inning trouble by allowing a pair of lead-off singles before rebounding nicely for a pair of groundouts and a strikeout. It was a classic case of bearing down on the hitters. The Navigators would muster only two more hits during the rest of the game.

The Thunder took a 2-0 lead in the top of the second on catcher Jeff Martin's two-run double. A third-inning single by Nomar set up an RBI for Pork Chop. The 3-0 cushion was all Soup needed to record his first Eastern League victory—a complete-game shutout. He wound up with two walks and eight strikeouts. It was the first complete-game shutout of Boston's affiliation with Trenton. His success didn't alter his composure, however, or his penchant for easy, self-assured answers. He iced his arm and showered before explaining his effort.

"It really wasn't about getting my first Double-A win," he said. "I had something to prove to myself. I needed a good start. If I did that, I felt we would win."

"He's got overpowering stuff, alright," Macha added. "His next big step is his first step in the big leagues."

Outside the entrance to the visitors clubhouse, Larry and Kathy Suppan waited in darkness to congratulate their boy. It was a scene that had been repeated countless times during his adolescence, only now the stakes were higher. Nobody felt more relieved that Jeff had broken his pattern of early season frustration. Larry didn't seem to notice the cold as he shook hands with several well-wishers. Inside the coaches' office, Nipper swigged a can of beer, wondering why he didn't bet No. 20 more often the previous night.

NOMAR COMES ALIVE

Between May 1 and May 15, Nomar Garciaparra parlayed a torrid hitting streak to lift his batting average from .226 to .282. As Payton had predicted, warmer temperatures meant a warmer Nomar. Over the 15-day span, he was 17-for-45, a .378 clip. More significantly, he did not commit an error during the first half of the month. "Mark my words, he's going to wind up leading the league in hitting," Schaefer predicted.

While Macha liked to refer to Pork Chop as "the bus driver," Nomar was his "quarterback." He looked to the shortstop for intangibles like solid defense and intelligent baserunning. The manager knew that if his team was going to make the playoffs, it would have to win more than its share of close games. "See all this gray hair," he said, pointing to his head. "This is what one-run games do to me."

On Saturday, May 13, during a three-game series at Portland, the entire Thunder squad was treated to an extravagant lobster dinner aboard DiMillo's Floating Restaurant in Maine's Casco Bay. DiMillo's, which is anchored to a municipal dock, is one of Portland's most popular dining establishments. Following a 5-0 Thunder loss, oil tycoon and diehard Red Sox fan H. Allen Mapes feted Macha and his players with an evening of crustaceans and libations. At a cost of "approximately $1500," Mapes dined with Nomar, Suppan, Pork Chop, Macha, and Nipper. "It was wonderful," Macha said. (During April, the manager and the pitching coach had bought the team dinner at a Reading-area all-you-can-eat establishment named Good & Plenty—at a cost of $13.50 per person.) Said Macha, "I saw one player's check and it was about $800 after taxes. That's tough."

"It's something I've always wanted to do for these young men," Mapes said of his dinner idea. "I remember a long time ago when Portland had a semi-pro team, the owner took them out for lobster. I thought it was a great idea."

During the dinner, which was filled with free drinks and revelry, Mapes promised the team another evening of celebration at DiMillo's if the Thunder played at least .500 baseball between May 13 and the next scheduled visit to Portland in late June. When the Thunder returned to Trenton on May 16, Nomar became the self-appointed keeper of the "Lobster Watch." He posted a sheet of white paper on the door to the Thunder clubhouse. Beneath two columns—"W" and "L"—the shortstop tracked the result of each game with a black marker. The ledger served as a visual reminder that a second trip to Maine could mean a repeat of the mid-May lobster feast. "We're going back, definitely," Nomar promised repeatedly. When the Thunder departed Portland on May 14, their record was 19-18. They would play 35 more games before they returned to Maine on June 23. Nomar was determined to make the most of them. His motivation was no secret—he liked lobster.

MAHAY MAKES THE SHOW

On April 26, outfielder Ron Mahay joined the Thunder roster after hitting .318 in 11 games for Triple-A Pawtucket. During spring training, he had been a replacement player. When the strike ended, he was shuffled off to Pawtucket, but not before he gained national recognition for an ESPN television segment about the trials and tribulations of being a replacement player. Blessed with matinee-idol looks and a streaky left-handed bat, the 23-year-old Chicago native quickly made an impact on Macha's team. During the Thunder's 8-7, 15-inning loss to Reading on May 1—a game that took 5 hours and 2 minutes to complete—Mahay established a Trenton record with five hits. Two days later, he was 3-for-3. In the three-game series against the Phillies, he was 9-for-13.

By May 19, Mahay had played 18 games in a Thunder uniform, hitting .298, with four doubles and six RBIs. Nothing could have prepared him for the news that arrived that day, however, just hours after a crowd of 6929 had watched Trenton edge Portland 5-4 behind Pork Chop's eleventh homer and Joe Hudson's second save. In a move that shocked many, Boston promoted the 6-foot-2, 190-pound Mahay directly from Trenton to the major-league roster to spell injured Red Sox outfielder Lee Tinsley. In the process, he joined Phil Stidham and 1994 reliever Sean Whiteside as the third Thunder player to be summoned to the majors, but he was the first non-pitcher. Macha relayed the news to his stunned player in his clubhouse office.

"I told him we need him to run to the store and get some Coke," Macha said. "And I told him while he was out to keep on going—right to Boston. You should have seen the look on his face." Mahay departed in a taxi to catch a flight from Philadelphia International Airport to Boston's Logan Airport.

"This tells you that every pitch, every at-bat is important," Macha added. "You never know when you might get the call. There are only two ways to impress somebody. You can either make a good impression or a bad impression."

Mahay's first journey to the majors was not without complications, however. Before his arrival, Boston captain Mike Greenwell conducted a team meeting to discuss how they would handle "a replacement player, a scab." After some heated debate in the Red Sox Fenway Park clubhouse, the Boston players decided, "We're a team, and we have to act like a team. We're professionals and grown men, and we have to handle it like that." Nonetheless, the quiet Mahay knew he was walking in a hornet's nest. He would be the first replacement player to earn a spot in a major-league lineup (Milwaukee's Ron Rightnowar was the first pitcher). "I had to prove myself to guys on the team," Mahay said.

The best way to do that was with his performance on the field. On May 21, in his first big-league at-bat—against Cleveland—he smacked an RBI double. Later in the game, he robbed Indians' All-Star outfielder Albert Belle of an extra base hit in right field. Boston lost the game 12-10, but Mahay had made it clear that he belonged. He made the highlight reels on the nightly sports reports, and he patiently answered questions from the Boston media. "It's a bother because they keep asking me the same stuff," he admitted.

For 1 week, Mahay enjoyed a whirlwind of exciting firsts. He became the first ex-Thunder player to: 1) make a major-league plate appearance; 2) score a major-league run; 3) record a major-league hit; 4) record a major-league extra-base hit; and 5) record a major-league defensive put-out. Mahay saved the best for last, however. On Friday, May 27, during a 12-1 Boston victory over California, he homered off Angels' right-hander Mike Butcher. After the game, Boston manager Kennedy called him into the office. "We're sending you back to Trenton," Kennedy said. In five major-league games, Mahay had hit .200 (4-for-20), with two doubles, a homer, and three RBIs. He also struck out six times.

After catching a red-eye flight from the West Coast, Mahay rejoined the Thunder on Saturday, May 28. Outfitted in a dark blue sweatsuit, he visited with his Double-A teammates. "It was the best experience of my life," he said. Back in the minors, he would struggle to maintain his edge. Once you've been in the show, parting is indeed sweet sorrow.

HARRISBURG REVISITED

On Friday, May 26, against Harrisburg before a Waterfront crowd of 6018, Nomar became the second Thunder player to win a free suit by hitting the black-and-white Byer's Men's Shop sign in left field. On a 3-1 delivery from Senators' reliever Ralph Diaz, he joined Clark as a member of the exclusive free-menswear club. To this day, though, Nomar and most of his teammates insist the ball didn't really hit the sign. Mahoney—who wears glasses—made the call from the press box. "I didn't think I hit it," Nomar confessed, "but I've gotta get a free suit now."

It was somehow appropriate that Nomar and Clark became linked in such a manner. Both were first-round draft picks who signed for a significant amount of money. Both were native Californians, and both spearheaded the Thunder's drive to gain an identity in the Trenton community.

"I know Tony, and he's a great individual," Nomar said. "Not only is he a great player, but he's super off the field and I really respect people like that. It would be a great compliment if Thunder fans were to compare me to Tony, but I really don't try to compare myself to anybody. I just like to be myself, just be different."

Nomar was certainly unique. On a '95 Thunder team that endured 91 roster moves and three coaching changes, he was a constant. From his locker stall in the back right corner of the room, he provided stability and competitive fire.

Always one of the first players to arrive at the stadium, Nomar quickly discovered the Ballpark Deli, which is located one block from Waterfront on Cass Street. Owned by Dave Conrad, the Ballpark opened during the final month of the inaugural campaign and capitalized on the Thunder's success. Players frequently called in sandwich orders, which were delivered to the clubhouse. Befitting of a burgeoning local celebrity, Nomar had a sandwich named in his honor. "The Nomar Special" can be ordered by name—a tasty combination of hot roast beef, provolone cheese, and bacon on a torpedo roll. "Nomar liked his with lettuce, tomatoes, and onions," Conrad recalled.

"Delicious," Nomar added. "It's a key to my pregame preparation."

Lou Merloni, Nomar's personable double-play mate, also had a sandwich named for him during the '95 season—the "Gooey Louie." The Massachusetts native's creation consisted of corned beef, turkey, and cole slaw.

The '94 Thunder season had begun to unravel on Harrisburg's City Island during the early June series, when Withem lost his cool in a one-run loss. The

'95 Thunder arrived in the Pennsylvania capital on May 27 having dropped four consecutive games. With a 23-24 record, they were alone in second place of the Eastern League Southern Division, six games behind Reading.

Desperately looking for someone to stop his team's downward spiral, Macha sent Soup to the hill at Harrisburg against the Senators'.Everett Stull, one of Montreal's top pitching prospects. What followed on a pleasant, 69-degree evening was Soup's Double-A signature game. It also was one of the best birthday presents of Kathy Suppan's life.

From the moment he made his first delivery to Harrisburg lead-off Matt Rundels before 4146 RiverSide Stadium patrons, it was obvious Soup had his best stuff. He entered the game with a 1-0 record and a 3.54 ERA. As the crowd settled into its aluminum bleacher seats during the first inning, he struck out the side—all swinging. Larry Suppan peeked his head into the press box and shrugged a proud smile. "Looks like he's got it tonight," Dad said.

For eight innings, the domination continued. Soup struck out the side again in the third and seventh frames. Pitching with a 5-0 lead after the Thunder scored five runs in the first three innings, he let it all hang out. The change-up. The sneaky-quick fastball. Even the nasty curveball. He allowed one run and left the game after eight innings with 13 strike-outs, one short of Withem's Thunder record of 14 from the previous August 14 game at New Haven. Quite simply, the effort was a masterpiece that pointed Soup even closer to Boston. During a postgame radio interview with McCarthy, Soup seemed oblivious to all the fuss. He was just doing his job.

"I've been going out and second-guessing myself," observed Soup, who was nicknamed "the brilliant one" by Simonetta. "I wasn't going after batters 100 percent. Tonight, I took a different frame of mind. Each batter was a different challenge. I really went after the inside part of the plate."

Inside the coaches' office, Macha and Nipper pored over the game charts. Of the 116 pitches Soup had made, 70 were strikes.

"He threw the ball extremely well," the skipper said. "It was nice giving him a five-run lead, but if I had known the [Thunder] strikeout record was 14, I might have left him in there." Macha laughed at the last part of his statement.

"He's hard-pressed to have better stuff than that," said catcher Jeff Martin. "He had command of all four of his pitches."

As Nipper leaned back in his chair, beer in hand, he said, "He was dominating. Tonight, he had good location and he was trusting his stuff. Before, he was nitpicking." The outing lowered Soup's ERA to an even 3.00 and sent him hurtling toward that anticipated promotion. There would be nine more Thunder starts for him, most of them effective if not overpowering. Meanwhile, Boston was firmly lodged in first place of the American League East. Duquette was waiting for the right time to thrust Soup into major-league duty.

On May 28, Senior was activated from the disabled list after spending 11 days out of action with a slight groin pull. As his parents watched eagerly in the stands, the left-hander worked five innings of two-hit ball, improving to a 4-1 record with a rain-shortened, 4-2 win over the Senators. "I didn't want to think about my injury," he said. "I was struggling with my mechanics a little bit, but I was able to keep the ball down." Mahay also was back in the lineup, going hitless in three at-bats. The offensive hero for the Thunder was catcher Martin, who was 2-for-3, with a double and a pair of RBIs. In fact, over a four-game span, he raised his batting average from .262 to .289. His offensive surge meant that fellow catcher Walt McKeel was demoted to Sarasota on May 31. Martin had won the everyday job, and Boston officials wanted McKeel to play on a regular basis. Clearly, he wasn't going to do that in Trenton.

While the Thunder struggled to a 13-15 overall record in 28 May games, Nomar slowly rounded out into one of the best all-around players in the league. He was a notorious first-pitch hitter, and opposing pitchers usually paid for it if they threw a fastball down the middle on the first delivery. For the month of May, he hit .301, with two doubles, two triples and two homers. On May 28, he had a remarkable 28-game errorless streak end. When the Thunder arrived at RiverSide Stadium that day for the two-game weekend series, Senators' official scorer Skip Hutter was apprised of Nomar's streak, which dated back to April 25. "I'll fix that," Hutter said with a laugh. Sure enough, during the rain-shortened Sunday afternoon matinee, Nomar went to field a slow infield roller by Harrisburg center fielder Phil Dauphin and booted the ball. It was a tough way to lose such an impressive string of defensive wizardry. Clearly, the play could have been scored a hit. In the press box, Hutter gave a loud "Harumph," as if to say no Double-A shortstop prospect was good enough to go a full month without committing an error.

In the Thunder clubhouse and Macha's office, there was amused reaction to Hutter's scoring. "What kind of horseshit is that?" wondered one player. Macha had no intention of protesting the call (although minor-league managers have been known to take umbrage with official scorers on occasion). He didn't necessarily agree with it, either. "There are probably seven other shortstops in the league who wouldn't be able to make that play," Macha said, refusing to criticize Hutter directly for his discretion.

Meanwhile, Nomar wandered around the L-shaped room taking a poll.

"Hit or error?" he asked. Not surprisingly, he was greeted with unanimous cries that he had been robbed.

CHAPTER 15

Macha's Magnetic North Pole

"There's no reason with the ability that this team has, the aggressiveness and determination, that we shouldn't be playing better than .500 baseball."

—1995 THUNDER INFIELDER BILL SELBY ON JUNE 4, 1995

After losing two of three games at Bowie and falling to a 26-26 record, the Thunder returned to Waterfront for a three-game series against Binghamton. On June 2, 1995, Pork Chop delighted an overflow crowd of 7065 with his thirteenth homer. After his torrid April, his bat had cooled. In May, he hit just three round-trippers. Vowing to make June another month to remember, he hit a two-run shot of Binghamton's Paul Wilson. In addition to the long-ball theatrics, the game was a superb pitcher's duel between Wilson and Soup. Wilson scattered three runs on eight hits over eight innings, and Soup struck out five batters and allowed four hits in 6 1/3 innings. "That matched its billing," Macha said. "You had Wilson and Suppan, and both of them pitched tremendous." The action was interrupted briefly when the infield sprinklers were activated for the second time in a month. Soon afterward, Thunder officials placed a lock over the sprinkler controls.

Both Wilson and Suppan were out of the game by the time Fuller's one-out bloop single scored Mahay in the twelfth inning for a 4-3 Thunder victory. The win went to Trenton reliever Tim Cain, who improved to 4-2 out of the bullpen.

On June 3, Boston officials announced that outfielder Lee Tinsley would rehab his right quadriceps injury in Trenton, making him the first major leaguer to serve a rehab stint with the Thunder. Later that evening, before a Waterfront gathering of 7187, the Thunder battled back from a 5-0 deficit after three innings to send the game into extra innings knotted at eight. A 1-hour, 16-minute rain delay sent much of the crowd scurrying for cover, but the outcome wasn't decided until the thirteenth, when Binghamton shortstop Kevin Morgan won it 9-8 with an RBI groundout. Merloni was 3-for-7 with three RBIs, and Abad was 3-for-5 with a double. In spite of the impressive rally, Macha was in a rare state of vocal disappointment when the press arrived in his office.

"We played like horseshit," he said. "It was a hell of an effort, but we should have won the game. We have some guys here with a lot of fight, but a couple are worried about how many hits they have and what the umpire is calling, and that's not the way to play the game."

Over 4 1/3 innings, Senior had been ineffective, allowing six runs on six hits and walking three. Wild Thing (Carter) struck out four batters in four innings, but he also served up a ninth-inning run that prevented the Thunder from winning the game with four runs in the bottom of the ninth. With a 27-27 record, Trenton was back at .500. Nipper spent the night on a cot inside his office, brooding over the defeat.

Concerned about his team's approach, Macha conducted a rare, closed-door team meeting before a June 4 Businessperson's Special against the Mets. There was no Runnells-esque yelling and screaming, just a clearing of the air and a defining of team goals. The meeting produced immediate results. Facing Binghamton starter Hector Ramirez in the 12:35 PM game, the Thunder took a 5-1 first-inning lead on Mahay's grand-slam homer. Batting leadoff, Tinsley had an immediate impact with a pair of singles and a run scored. Right-hander Brent Hansen, who joined Trenton on May 17, scattered three earned runs over 6 2/3 innings. Hudson picked up his fourth save. The resulting 9-7 victory prompted Selby to quip, "Sometimes, you've gotta step back, kick yourself in the butt, and say, 'Let's go.' " That self-administered butt-kicking was witnessed by 7073, bringing the three-game total for the Binghamton series to 21,325. "I was impressed with the crowd," Tinsley said.

With Tinsley in the lineup, the Thunder lost a pair of games to Norwich, 2-1 and 4-1. For some reason, Trenton just didn't seem to match up with the Yankees' affiliate, which boasted top-prospect Ruben Rivera, 6-foot-5 Harvard product Nick DelVecchio, and a powerful lineup. In spite of the defeats, Tinsley conducted his rehab with class and dignity. Following the second Norwich game, he stopped in the Thunder office to personally thank several members of the Trenton staff for their assistance. It was a rare occurrence. Most major leaguers' only rehab concern is when they will report back to the big-league club.

On June 7, however, Tinsley contributed directly to a dramatic Thunder win at Reading. With the score knotted 3-3 in the top of the eleventh, he doubled to spark a 5-3 victory. Before the game-wining hit, Tinsley had played cheerleader in the dugout. "It felt real good," Tinsley said after Trenton (29-29) moved within one game of first-place Reading (30-28). "I guess I'm part of the [Eastern League] pennant race now." Added Macha, "I might have to lie on the game report so we can keep him a little longer." Suppan started and worked seven innings, but he threw 41 pitches in the first two innings alone. Nonetheless, the Thunder improved with the win to 7-1 in games that he had started. Afterward, Macha received orders that Tinsley was ready to return to Boston, and the next morning, the first rehab in Thunder history was over.

ON TO THE SHOW

On the morning of June 9, 1995, Thunder closer Joe Hudson was promoted directly from Double-A to Boston for his major-league debut. As Macha and Correnti scrambled to make travel plans for the elated pitcher—who needed to go approximately 100 miles from the Thunder team hotel in New London, Connecticut, to Fenway Park—the Holy Cross High graduate savored his first big-league call-up. "Your first trip to the majors; it's something you never forget," said a nostalgic Nipper later that afternoon.

After exhausting all other travel options, Correnti decided to send Hudson to Boston in a taxi. The ride cost about $200, but Hudson's presence in the Boston bullpen was an urgent matter. Sensing the importance of his cargo, the cab driver put his foot on the accelerator without regard for the posted 55-mph speed limit. Heading east on the I-95 in Rhode Island at more than 80, he noticed flashing lights in his rearview mirror. "Oh, no," Hudson thought to himself. "This isn't exactly what I had in mind."

A Rhode Island state trooper approached the vehicle with caution, asking both the driver and Hudson to step out slowly. He eyed both occupants suspiciously. If they were going to wiggle out of the predicament in time to get to Fenway, the pitcher knew he had to exert some influence.

"What's your hurry?" the trooper inquired gruffly.

"We're on our way to Fenway so he can pitch for the Red Sox," the driver replied earnestly.

"Sure you are," came the response.

After frisking the pair and procuring some Red Sox player identification from the distraught Hudson, the situation was diffused. The pitcher, a naturally laid-back person who largely kept to himself, autographed a few items for the trooper and hopped back into the cab for the rest of his unforgettable maiden journey to the majors. The story was one of those typically amusing behind-the-scenes baseball anecdotes that grow in stature over the years—by the time Hudson relates it to his grandchildren, the cab driver will probably be driving 120 instead of 80.

On June 10, Hudson made his major-league debut against Oakland, working two-thirds of an inning, allowing one hit, and striking out one. It was heady stuff for a 26th round draft pick out of West Virginia University in June 1992.

Furthermore, the Double-A-to-the-bigs promotions of Mahay and Hudson brought home a reality for many of the Thunder players—specifically, that Boston wasn't afraid to promote a player two levels. It was a valuable motivational incentive for Macha and his staff. It also was a powerful carrot for Schaefer to dangle before his minor leaguers. The message: It doesn't matter where you play. If the big-league club has a need and the Red Sox feel that you can fill it, you could be on your way at any time. Hudson and Mahay were living proof that the dream could come true at a moment's notice.

Back in Norwich, the Thunder trudged onward without their closer. On June 10, Rivera smashed the first grand slam in Dodd Stadium history to hand Thunder pitcher Brett Hansen a 7-2 defeat. On the Navigators' giant electronic message board, Rivera's home-run trot was framed by the words "FEEL THE THUNDER." As Trenton fell three games below .500 for the first time in 1995 (29-32), Macha proclaimed that a crowd of 5994 had witnessed "our worst game of the year." Nomar broke out of an 0-for-17 slump with an RBI single, but that was the extent of the silver linings for Trenton. "Tomorrow is a big game for us," Macha admitted.

Backed into a self-imposed corner, the Thunder began their June 11 tussle against the Navigators on a positive note—with a lead-off double by Nomar. After four innings, however, Trenton trailed Norwich lefty Tom Carter by 2-0. "It was not encouraging," Macha said, but in the bottom of the fifth, the Thunder sent 11 men to the plate, taking a 7-2 lead they wouldn't relinquish on their way to a 13-2 blowout. McGuire was 3-for-5 with a pair of doubles. Merloni was 3-for-4. Hecker was 3-for-4 with a pair of RBIs. On back-to-back Sundays, Trenton had produced 33 hits. "They must be going to church," said assistant coach Rico Petrocelli, who joined Macha's staff on a part-time basis June 2. "We're playing the percentages, so let's skip the weekday games," said Nipper, ever the gambler.

THE MID-SEASON SURGE

On Thursday, June 15, during another Businessperson's Special (against Binghamton), Macha inserted Pork Chop at third base, giving Bill Selby a day off in the field. Ironically, the opposing pitcher was an old Thunder friend—Brian Edmondson—who had been waived from Detroit's major-league roster during the strike-delayed big-league spring training. He was quickly signed by Mets' General Manager Joe McIlvaine, and he entered his Waterfront homecoming with a 3-1 record and 3.50 ERA.

Pork Chop, playing to an overflow crowd of 6923, cared little about Edmondson's nostalgic appearance. He greeted the righty with a two-run, first-inning double that skittered just inside the third-base line. Edmondson later insisted that it was about a three-foot foul. While the former Thunder ace lasted 6 1/3 innings and threw a season-high 115 pitches, the day belonged to Pork Chop. He finished with two doubles, two runs scored, two RBIs, and two walks as the Thunder triumphed 7-2. At third base, he was flawless, robbing three Mets of certain base hits with some standout defensive work. Back-to-back acrobatic stops in the eighth prompted Mets' manager John Tamargo to look at Pork Chop and inquire sarcastically, "What do we have to do to get a hit off you?" The veteran infielder smiled, his gold tooth glimmering in the afternoon sun. The pair of doubles raised his league-leading extra-base hit total to 33, and the Thunder evened their record at 33-33.

"It's been a while since I had a game like that," Pork Chop said at his locker. "I was very pleased."

Added Macha, "That one inning, he put on a clinic. That was nice to see."

In many ways, the performance epitomized Pork Chop's brief Thunder career. Not known as a particularly good third baseman, his showmanship surfaced at the most inexplicable times. The effort seemed quite removed from the infield pop-up that dropped in front of him during spring training. He seemed to be gaining confidence on a daily basis. You got the feeling that Macha was lobbying Boston officials for that promotion that Pork Chop so desperately wanted. It would be his way of saying thanks for carrying the load.

On June 17, Suppan was roughed up for five runs on nine hits during a 7-0 Saturday night loss to Norwich. It was Soup's first Double-A defeat. During the

'95 season, manager Jimmy Johnson's Navigators won all seven games they played at Waterfront, intensifying some of the rumors circulating that the Yankees might be interested in relocating their Double-A affiliate to Trenton. A crowd of 7356—the third-largest in Waterfront history to that point—watched Norwich left-fielder Kevin Turner chase Suppan from the game with a two-run, eighth-inning homer. "It's going to happen," the pitcher said with a bit of an amused tone outside the home clubhouse. "I just thought tonight I didn't make the right pitch selection. I was really surprised that I didn't pitch better than I did."

"You can't ask Soup to go out there and throw a shutout every time," added McGuire, who was 3-for-4 in the game to improve his team-leading average to .349. "Even if he did, we'd still be playing because we couldn't get him any runs."

Before the June 17 game, Al Downing and Jim Maloney became the third and fourth members of the Trenton Baseball Hall of Fame, joining George Case and Bus Saidt. Downing, a Trenton native whose 17-year major-league career included stints with the Yankees, Athletics, Brewers, and Dodgers, is best remembered for delivering the pitch that resulted in Hank Aaron's record 715th homer. As a youngster, he led the 1955 Trenton Babe Ruth squad to the World Championship. Maloney was represented by his daughters, Anna Mae and Margaret. Inscribed on his plaque was one of his favorite sayings: "The greatest thing the fans could give us is their time."

On June 19—about the time the Nomar Special was becoming a Waterfront clubhouse tradition—27-year-old outfielder Patrick Lennon joined Macha's roster. A muscularly chiseled, 235-pound athlete with 91 days of major-league service in the Seattle organization, Lennon arrived at Waterfront after a long, brooding drive from Pawtucket. Following the demotion, he took out his considerable frustrations on several items in the Triple-A clubhouse. A born-again Christian, Lennon had served prison time during the early 1990s on a manslaughter charge. He was an imposing figure who had been a high-school football teammate of Oakland Raiders' defensive lineman Chester McGlockton. After consulting with his agent, Scott Boros—who also represented Soup—Lennon decided to join the Thunder. Nine years of searching for steady major-league work had left him with no other choice. As a member of the New Britain Red Sox during the '94 Eastern League season, he had lost the batting title on the last day by a slim margin when a controversial infield hit was ruled an error. Instead, he wound up with a .326 average. Not surprisingly, his addition to the Thunder roster prompted Macha's club to play some of its best baseball of the '95 season.

"I'm here not to represent the Boston Red Sox but to represent Pat Lennon," the newcomer said frankly. When he joined the Thunder, they were 33-36, having just been swept at Waterfront by Norwich. Macha called the new arrival into his office and asked him if he was ready to play. "Put me in the lineup tonight," Lennon insisted. Possessed of perhaps the biggest arms in organized baseball (Lennon claimed they were as big as 23 inches in circumference at times during his career), he added valuable hitting support for clean-up hitter Pork Chop when Macha inserted him in the No. 5 position. In his first game, he singled three times to spark a 13-7 win over Harrisburg. "Pat really picked us up there," Macha admitted.

"When I see him standing in the on-deck circle, he looks like he's just getting ready to crush something," Pork Chop added. "I mean, he's a one-man wrecking crew."

While the June 19 victory was merely one small step along Trenton's 142-game regular-season journey, it was an especially significant win for the Thunder. Lennon's hulking presence seemed to harness the potential this team had displayed through their first 69 dates. He walked around the clubhouse shirtless, scowling at everyone, but no matter how he felt about his new assignment—after all, he was Seattle's first-round draft pick way back in June 1986—he was determined to grit his teeth and get on base. What followed was 10 wins in 13 games, which thrust the Thunder into sole possession of first place in the Southern Division from June 23 through July 7. Macha later pointed out that he thought the team—at that particular time—was the best team in the league. "I would have put us up against anybody and liked our chances," the manager said.

The 13-7 victory was quickly followed by 7-6 (11 innings) and 6-0 (a complete-game, five-hitter by Hansen) wins over Harrisburg that moved the Thunder back to .500 and set up a daunting 8-day, eight-game road trip to Portland and New Haven. On June 21, Trenton moved into a tie for first place with slumping Reading. Both teams had 36-36 records, but it marked the first time in the Thunder's 2-year history that the franchise could wake up the next morning to see its name atop the Eastern League Southern Division standings. Helping move Macha's club to the top was Boston right-hander Aaron Sele, who worked 2 1/3 innings during a rehab appearance during the June 21 victory. Sele was recovering from tendinitis in his right shoulder but he took Orellano's place in the Trenton rotation because the Puerto Rican lefty had contracted chicken pox. While Orellano stayed home not to infect anybody else, Sele wore Soup's No. 20 uniform. He threw 37 pitches—25 strikes and 12 balls. "I think all the guys enjoyed seeing a bona fide big-league pitcher work," Macha said.

On Friday, June 23, the Red Sox optioned Hudson back to Trenton, giving Macha a reliable closer once again. In addition, middle reliever Scott Bakkum was emerging as one of the top stories in the Red Sox organization. Through 24 Thunder appearances, Bakkum had a 6-4 record and a 0.86 ERA. Opponents were hitting .154 against him.

Also on June 23 at Portland's Hadlock Field, Suppan defeated the Sea Dogs by twirling an eight-inning gem. Hudson came on to record his fifth save, nailing down a 2-0 victory. The following day, a windy Saturday afternoon, Pork Chop enjoyed another one of his patented power explosions, crushing two homers against Portland during an 11-8 win—the Thunder's fifth straight. Macha's lineup set a franchise record with 20 hits. Pork Chop became the third player in Hadlock history to hit a ball over the left-center scoreboard, joining Charles Johnson and '94 New Britain outfielder Jose Malave.

When they arrived in Portland, the Thunder were 17-18 on Nomar's lobster watch, but Suppan's shutout victory earned the team a second dinner for reaching the .500 plateau just in the nick of time for another feast at DiMillo's. Along for the trip was Sele, who had been unable to pitch his rehabilitation start because of arm stiffness. No fool, Sele stuck around long enough to enjoy dinner with Mapes and his temporary Trenton teammates.

The next morning, Nomar approached Macha and asked for a rare day off. Too much late-night revelry had left him in no condition to play. The manager laughed a bit and granted his star's hangover-induced request. He penned minor-league veteran Mike Hardge into the leadoff spot, leaving Nomar to nurse his headache in the dugout.

As Lennon worked on a hitting streak that eventually would reach a Thunder-record 18 games, his new team made it six wins in a row on Sunday afternoon, June 25, behind a nine-strikeout effort by righty Brent Hansen. Hansen had missed much of the '94 season with arm troubles, but he was extremely effective in 11 Thunder appearances, compiling a 4-5 record, a 3.26 ERA, and three complete games. After Portland loaded the bases on two Trenton errors with nobody out in the bottom of the first, the 24-year-old Hansen wowed a Hadlock Field record crowd of 6860 with one of his best performances of the season. He worked out of the early jam with a pop-up and a pair of strikeouts, prompting Macha to say his starter "gave us a mulligan; that was gigantic." Relievers Bakkum and Hudson finished off Portland with swift effectiveness. "If they keep pitching like they have, we're going to lose them," Macha said of his relief duo. Afterward, in the clubhouse, Macha addressed his team. "Well, at least I know you guys can play with a hangover." Everyone laughed, most with an accompanying glance in Nomar's direction.

The six consecutive victories tied the Thunder mark established by Runnells' 1994 squad between April 19 and 24. More significantly, the Thunder (39-36) had won six in a row against the Northern Division leader Sea Dogs (47-25), a remarkable feat considering the '94 team had lost all nine of its Hadlock dates.

On getaway day in Portland, a 5-4 Thunder loss, word arrived that Macha was about to receive another first-round draft pick. Outfielder Greg Blosser, Boston's first choice in the June 1989 draft, would join the team in New Haven. Like Lennon, he had been demoted from Pawtucket. To make room for Blosser and activate Orellano (who had spent a week on the disabled list), the Red Sox assigned outfielders Doug Hecker and Aaron Fuller to Single-A Visalia of the California League. The news was swift and painful for both players, who had struggled mightily against Eastern League pitching. While Fuller elected to accept the reassignment, Hecker returned to Wantaugh, New York, to mull over his future and discuss options with his agent. In 61 games, he hit .204, with 16 doubles, five homers and 32 RBIs. Eventually, he reported to Visalia and was converted to pitching. As a former stand-out pitcher at the University of Tennessee, he certainly had the potential to resurface in Double-A.

The Thunder split four games in New Haven to complete their pivotal trip with a 5-3 record. Macha was pleased. In his first 11 games, Lennon was 19-for-45 (.422), but he wasn't hitting for power. In fact, of his 39 hits in 98 Trenton at-bats before his July 20 release, 31 were singles. Nonetheless, when Lennon asked to be let go (he later latched on with Minnesota Triple-A affiliate Salt Lake City), Macha had mixed emotions. During a mid-July batting practice, the powerful outfielder showed incredible pop, smashing ball after ball into the Waterfront parking lot.

AN ALL-STAR TRIO

When the time came for Eastern League officials to vote for the '95 Double-A All-Stars in late June, Pork Chop was a no-brainer on most of the ballots. Three late June homers pushed his total to a league-leading 17 (including one that hit the Byer's Men's Shop billboard to win a free suit) when the American League Double-A All-Star team was announced to the Thunder players on June 28. Inside a cramped dressing trailer at Yale Field, Macha summoned a trio of players—Pork Chop, Nomar, and Orellano—to his small office to inform them that they had been selected to play in the fifth-annual Double-A All-Star Game in Shreveport, Louisiana, on Monday, July 10. They would join '94 pitchers Mike Guilfoyle and Ken Carlyle as Thunder All-Stars. Pork Chop was less than elated at the honor, however. A second consecutive trip to the Double-A game wasn't his idea of progress. He wasn't trying to be an ingrate, but it was familiar territory, like repeating a grade.

"I'm not sure if I'm going to go," he said with conviction. "It depends how much the flight ticket for my girl costs. The goal I set for myself was to make the Triple-A game, but I was sent here. Oh, well." Trying to force Pork Chop to smile, infielder Mike Hardge yelled in a deep voice, "Hey, you and Nomar can wear matching suits [from Byer's, of course]."

Pork Chop was not amused.

Meanwhile, Orellano, who was 6-4 with a 2.95 ERA on June 28, was thrilled about the honor. "This is my first All-Star game at any level," he said proudly. "I've been thinking about it a lot. I think it will be a fun time." Like many Latin players, "Raffy" came from a large family, and he sent a portion of his $1500 a month paycheck home to them. When they heard his good news, they were thrilled.

Over the next few days, Pork Chop worked out a deal with Hodes that allowed his girlfriend, Racquel, to accompany the Trenton delegation to Shreveport. "I was looking at my numbers, and it's still an honor to be selected," he said after pondering the situation. He also wanted to enter the annual home-run competition—and bring home the trophy to his loyal Thunder followers. "That's a pretty good reason to go, right?" he asked before an unforgettable two-home run performance against Bowie on July 5. A Prince George's Stadium crowd of 4419 watched him smash a pair of balls out of the yard during a 6-3 Bowie victory. The first homer—off Baysox righty Garrett Stephenson—cleared all three billboard levels. With a season total of 19, he inched within two of Clark's Thunder record of 21. Comparisons between the sluggers were unavoidable except for one undeniable fact—Clark was fast-tracked to the majors, and Pork Chop was having trouble getting out of Double-A. "I'm not playing to break records," he insisted. "But records are made to be broken, and who better to break T.C.'s records than Chop? I'm sure he wouldn't mind." It was a rare baseball sight—a player whose team had just lost a heartbreaking, one-run game enjoying a moment of personal achievement. Then again, Pork Chop had a way of making things fun.

BAMBOOZLED IN BOWIE

The Thunder completed the month of June with a 15-13 record (41-39 overall), which put them two-and-a-half games ahead of second-place Reading (38-41) and four games ahead of Bowie (36-42). Soup was 5-1 with a 2.53 ERA. Hansen was 4-3 with a 3.32 ERA. Pork Chop was hitting .288 and leading the league in homers and RBIs. In 12 games, Lennon was hitting .426, but Mahay had come back to earth, hitting .268 through 46 games. On the other hand, McGuire was feasting on Eastern League pitching, with a .347 average and .443 on-base percentage. Every time you looked up, he seemed to be on base. Meanwhile, Nomar was hitting .259 with 22 stolen bases. On July 2, following a 3-2 win over Canton-Akron, Hudson was recalled to Boston—this time for keeps. In 39 games for the American League East champion Red Sox, he would compile an 0-1 record and a 4.11 ERA with one save.

With or without Hudson in his bullpen, Prince George's Stadium was a chamber of horrors for Macha during the '95 season. For some reason, the Thunder didn't match up well with manager Bob Miscik's Baysox. In athletics, some rivalries are like that—one team finds a way to win in the most incomprehensible ways. The Thunder arrived in Maryland playing perhaps the finest baseball in franchise history, but it didn't matter. They lost a pair of games by a combined 18-10 margin. Pork Chop's slugging antics aside, Trenton seemed to be in a pre-All Star break rut. By sweeping the short series, Bowie (41-42) moved within one game of the Thunder (43-42).

During Trenton's 6-3 loss on July 5, Macha was incensed that Bowie pitcher Garrett Stephenson hit Lennon with a pitch moments after Pork Chop smashed his second homer. The pitcher was immediately thrown out of the game, but the Trenton manager wasn't willing to let the incident die. "That guy Stephenson is a gutless pussy," Macha said. "You can write that in the fucking paper. The Bowie paper, too. We've got a lot of games left against them." The threat was Macha's way of challenging his players.

The Bowie series also was notable because the Thunder players received a visit from Boston psychological consultant Doug Stewart. Stewart's role was to address alcohol and drug problems and help the minor leaguers adjust to the ever-changing environment surrounding their vocation. As he flew east from Albuquerque, New Mexico to join the Thunder in Bowie, seated on the plane next to him was an 8-year-old boy named Joe. Asking Stewart who he was and what he did, Stewart patiently explained his role in the Red Sox organization. At the time, most baseball fans were still somewhat bitter about the '94-'95 strike and the '94 World Series cancellation. Joe, wanting to somehow let the Boston players know that he was thinking about them, offered to send some of his $11 in spending money with Stewart as a precocious gesture of appreciation. Considering Joe's limited budget, the pair settled on a one-dollar bill as the appropriate gift. "But who will I give it to, the major leaguers or the minor leaguers?" Stewart asked the youngster.

"Give it to the minor leaguers, they need it more," was Joe's measured response. Knowing how much the story would mean to Macha and his Double-A players, Stewart took a pair of scissors and divided the bill into 30, tiny rectangular pieces. After relaying the story of "Joe's Dollar," he distributed the pieces to the players and coaching staff. According to Macha, it was a humbling moment. "That was very special," the manager said later as his piece of the dollar bill sat on his desk.

LIMPING INTO THE BREAK

The two-game sweep at Bowie was followed by a four-game homestand that produced four consecutive Waterfront sellouts. The overflow gatherings saw Macha's club continue to struggle, however. On July 6, a gathering of 7408 watched Trenton fall back to .500 as Peterson was ineffective during a 7-3 loss to Reading. After throwing his early season one-hitter, it was all downhill for him. He had won only one game between May 8 and July 1. Nomar was 3-for-5 with a double and a triple, but consecutive loss No. 4 prompted Macha to quip, "We're back at the magnetic North Pole, .500. We've been sucked down the abyss. It's the little things that win ballgames, and we're not doing them right now."

On July 8, Trenton placed Merloni on the 7-day disabled list with a sore right thumb. A 6-2 loss to Binghamton later that night tied the '94 Thunder's record losing streak of six. Orellano, who dined with *Boston Globe* columnist Bob Ryan and Plumeri before the game, allowed five runs (three earned), walking one, and striking out six batters in his final appearance before the All-Star Game. "We have to go out and score some runs to take the pressure off our pitchers," Macha noted, and McGuire added, "We've been getting good pitching, but our hitting has been atrocious and our defense has been even worse than that."

The final game before the All-Star break was a 1:35 PM Sunday afternoon contest against Binghamton. For five innings, Mets' righty Robert Person was unhittable. Person, a converted reliever, threw 83 pitches and faced the minimum 15 Thunder batters before he was removed. "I guess if I'm going to leave, I might as well leave with a no-hitter," he joked afterward. Trenton aided Person's cause with four errors—giving the Thunder 11 defensive miscues in their last four games. A crowd of 6886 booed the Boston prospects and cheered sarcastically when catcher Jeff Martin hit a sixth-inning single off Binghamton reliever Darren Paxton. "It's been getting worse every day as we go along, and today we just had nothing," said Thunder second baseman Todd Carey. The final score was 7-2. Trenton had lost seven in a row, and Senior took the defeat to fall to 6-4. Pork Chop, Nomar and Orellano departed during the middle innings to catch a flight to New Orleans, where they would connect to Shreveport for the All-Star Game. During his postgame comments, Macha didn't raise his voice, preferring only to say, "Let's try to win a fucking game this week."

"The fans don't want to come to the ballpark and watch that kind of performance," the manager later told the press. "To me, if you're getting booed, you're doing something that's worth booing. That was not a pretty sight. But there's only one place to lay the blame, and that's with me. If I don't have those guys playing up to their potential, it's my fault."

At 43-46, Trenton trailed first-place Bowie (43-44) by one game and second-place Reading (43-45) by half a game. The playoff race was shaping up as a three-team dogfight, and despite their early July collapse, the Thunder figured to be a part of it. As his players enjoyed a couple of days off, Macha headed to Atlantic City to spend some time with his family.

CHAPTER 16

All-Stars and Basebrawls

> "I think the people in Trenton love baseball, so they deserve the All-Star Game."
>
> —RAFAEL ORELLANO IN SHREVEPORT, LOUISIANA, ON JULY 10, 1995

On Monday, July 10, Pork Chop, Nomar and Orellano sat inside the air-conditioned Expo Hall in Schreveport, Louisiana, listening to the droll Cajun humor of guest speaker and renowned television chef Justin Wilson. Outside the spacious convention facility, the mercury poked its head toward the 100-degree mark. "My kind of weather," Orellano mused.

The annual Double-A All-Star pregame luncheon is an opportunity for local politicians and corporate sponsors to dine with the players. This day was different for Hodes and Thunder legal counsel Joe Finley, however. A unique opportunity to enhance the Thunder's already considerable sphere of minor-league influence lay on the immediate horizon. After carefully plotting the groundwork for a 1996 Double-A All-Star Game bid, the Trenton pair fully expected the game to be awarded to the Delaware Valley. Inside Double-A circles, the Trenton game was a done deal. The Thunder had put together an impressive package for the event that included a possible appearance by the U.S. Olympic team during "All-Star Week," but for Hodes, Finley, and Prunetti, there was still the matter of an official vote. That would take place following the prime-rib luncheon during a 2 PM gathering of all 28 Double-A front-office and ownership officials.

After the three-player Thunder contingent was forced to spend July 9 in a New Orleans hotel because of travel delays, they arrived at Shreveport in time for Captains public address announcer Dave Nitz to call their names to the 40-table crowd. With three representatives, the Thunder had more than any of the other nine Eastern League teams. Orellano received a 10 AM visit from American League manager Mario Mendoza, who asked the lefty if he wanted to start the game. Orellano, who was 7-5 with a 2.99 ERA and 96 strikeouts at the break, said he would be honored.

Following the 2-hour luncheon, Prunetti conversed with Dick Stanley in the lobby of the Holiday Inn-Downtown, where the Double-A Association meeting would decide Trenton's All-Star fate. Once the meeting convened, Prunetti waited in the hallway. He spoke candidly to a reporter about the Thunder phenomenon that had sprouted from his vision for Mercer County and, more specifically, Waterfront Park. He expressed everlasting gratitude for the franchise's warm public reception, adding that fans frequently approached him with a word of thanks for returning minor-league baseball to Trenton. He also admitted that he had maintained a lower profile at the stadium during the '95 season because "it's an election year." (In November 1995, he would win re-election in a surprisingly close vote over Ewing Democrat Jim McManimon.)

"I foresaw this as being a very successful endeavor, I really did," he said of the Thunder's impact. "Did I think it was going to be this successful? I never could have foreseen this."

As Prunetti prepared to enter the meeting room for a few official remarks about Trenton and the Mercer County region, he looked tired but satisfied—as if he knew he was about to witness another sizable chunk of Delaware Valley history. The Double-A committee, chaired by Con Maloney of Jackson, Mississippi, awarded its 1996 All-Star Game to Trenton by a unanimous 27-0 vote (the Thunder did not have a vote). Prunetti enjoyed a brief opportunity to say, "Thank you." The sixth-annual Double-A All Star Game would be played at Waterfront Park on Monday, July 8, 1996, less than 3 years after ground had been broken for the stadium. The Major League Baseball All-Star Game would be played the following night at Veterans Stadium. Handshakes and backslaps filled the room as the Thunder contingent accepted congratulations. Moments after the vote, Prunetti exited the room and caught a shuttle to the airport for a flight to Dallas. The trip had been well worth his time.

"It's all about baseball, but it's also a chance for the whole region to shine, so I think that's why Bob came down here and did a real nice job," Finley said. Back in Trenton, word that the All-Star Game was coming to town spread rapidly. One of the first to hear the news was Plumeri. "This is a great tribute not only to our organization and our fans, but to our city and our area as well," the 81-year-old owner said proudly. "This is going to be a tremendous event for us to host. It will certainly put the spotlight on Trenton."

The first Thunder player to hear about the Trenton All-Star award was Orellano. As he rode a shuttle bus to 6200-seat Fair Grounds Field, he smiled at the news. "The fans there are great people, and this is great for the Thunder organization," he said in broken English. "They've been great friends to me."

On the sweltering Shreveport field, ESPN2 television personnel readied the facility for the live broadcast. All of the workers soaked in the blistering heat. The production crew prepared an introduction comparing Nomar to Cincinnati Reds' shortstop Barry Larkin. Outfitted in royal-blue tops, the National League affiliates took batting practice first. Nomar and Pork Chop donned their black Thunder batting-practice tops when the American League entered the cage. Orellano played cards in the American League clubhouse, and Pork Chop was asked for several interviews, having already been profiled in the Shreveport paper that morning.

With 19 homers and 64 RBIs at the All-Star break, Pork Chop fully expected to be a part of the Shreveport home-run contest. In the dead heat of western Louisiana, however, less than an hour before the contest, he learned that he would not be participating after all. Hardware City second baseman Todd Walker, a native of nearby Bossier City with 10 homers at the break, would take his place. "You're kidding right?" Pork Chop said after hearing the news.

The Thunder slugger watched disconsolately as Walker hit just one of 10 gopher pitches over the fence. The contest was won by Midland catcher Todd Greene, who hit three homers through the sweltering summer air. "I wanted to be in it at least," Pork Chop said, silently vowing to make up for the oversight.

The players and coaches were introduced to the sell-out crowd of 6247 before the 7:40 PM Central Standard Time first pitch. Hodes, Finley, and Stanley arrived moments before the game started, sweat beading from their foreheads after spending a couple of hours in the right-field hospitality tent. Savoring the heat, which reminded him of his native Puerto Rico, Orellano warmed up in the bullpen.

Baseball All-Star games are a unique experience for pitchers; nobody expects them to work more than an inning or two. Orellano knew when he took the mound that he would pitch the first inning and head for the showers. With the sun beginning its slow descent into the western sky, he allowed a leadoff single to Eastern League nemesis Payton on a 1-2 count. He struck out Portland second baseman Ralph Milliard, and he retired the next two batters on groundouts. It was a neat, tidy performance: one inning, one hit, one strikeout, 13 pitches. He walked back to the dugout, tipping his cap to polite applause.

Meanwhile, Pork Chop was due up in the second inning. Hitting in the No. 6 position for the American League squad, he would face Binghamton star Paul Wilson, who was well on his way to Eastern League Pitcher of the Year honors. In 120 innings of Double-A work, Wilson had struck out 127 batters. As Pork Chop dug into the batter's box, thoughts of the home-run derby slight steeled his focus. Wilson worked the count to 2-1, missing with a pair of change-ups after delivering his 97-mph fastball with authority. On the fourth delivery, however, Pork Chop was waiting. Looking for high heat all the way, he slammed a solo homer to left field that parted the still air with the thrust of a meteorite. With one swing, he had tied Walker's effort—against perhaps the best pitcher in all of minor-league baseball—and he circled the bases with a sly grin of satisfaction.

"I think Pork Chop was a little mad he wasn't in the home-run contest," Wilson observed later. "And he took it out on me. I thought this was all fun and games, but he's a good hitter."

"I was just hoping to hit one against Wilson," Pork Chop said modestly. "I mean, he throws 100 miles per hour."

In a game that required only 2 hours and 15 minutes to play, Pork Chop's homer provided the impetus for a 3-1 American League victory. Orellano was the winning pitcher, and Nomar played in the late innings, finishing 0-for-2. Pork Chop also singled in the fifth and scored another run. Moments after the game's completion, the Thunder slugger received the Howe Sportsdata "Star of Stars" Award during an on-field presentation. He would return to Trenton with a trophy after all.

"I had a great time," he said. "I hope the guys back home saw it. I know they're pumped for us."

"Best nickname in the minors," said one national newspaper columnist about Pork Chop's wide-reaching impact on the All-Star festivities. "People really have a ball every time they announce his name," added Mendoza.

During the game, Hodes was interviewed live on ESPN2. All in all, it was the perfect capper for a red-letter day in Thunder history.

Following a postgame stop at the Holiday Inn, the Trenton contingent—players and executives—headed to a gala party at Harrah's Riverboat Casino. On one side of the banquet room was a giant buffet that included cold cuts, jalapeno poppers, and fried shrimp. Cocktail waitresses circulated the room with free beverages. Hodes, Finley, and Stanley stood proudly near the spread table, making small talk with Levenda. "Trenton is going to reset the standard for this game with a whole lot more people," the league president predicted. "Their potential is unlimited—the only limit is the Thunder's imagination."

The party began to shut down shortly after 1 AM, but the casino remained open. Nomar headed for the gaming tables with a group that included Wilson. A resident of Las Vegas during the off-season, Nomar gravitates to a roulette wheel with a level of comfort exceeded only by his skill on a baseball diamond. As a small crowd looked on, he won several hundred dollars by playing his uniform number—red 5. The scene was eerily reminiscent of the night Nipper won big with Suppan's No. 20. By 4 AM, most of the players had shuffled back to the hotel, thankful for the break from the daily grind of the minor-league season. Payton and Wilson were headed to Triple-A Norfolk later that morning, but their late-night revelry caused them to miss their original flight. Without Payton and Wilson, Binghamton lost 35 of its final 57 games. For the Thunder franchise, however, July 10, 1995, was not just another date on the schedule. It was a crowning day of legitimation, far removed from the headaches of the '94 campaign. In just 364 days, Waterfront Park would be the focus of the Double-A baseball world.

SOUP'S GONE

While in Atlantic City, Macha visited a palm reader along the boardwalk. She charged him $5 for the following prediction: "You are going to undergo 6 weeks of intense stress, but eventually everything is going to turn out O.K." Seven weeks remained in the Eastern League regular season. The manager paid with a $10 bill and put the change in his wallet for his next visit to the Jersey Shore.

Informed of Macha's psychic reading, Soup replied, "To each his own."

Meanwhile, on July 12, Soup pitched a gem in the first game of the second half, defeating Binghamton 9-6 to improve his record to 6-2. Macha and Nipper limited his pitch count to 100, however, fully aware that Boston was monitoring his every delivery. A Municipal Stadium crowd of 3455 also watched Pork Chop belt his twentieth homer. Selby added his sixth homer, and reliever Ken Ryan—who had been shipped to Double-A after a rough stretch in Boston's bullpen—worked the ninth. "Tonight was a chance to get off to a good start, not just me but the whole team," Pork Chop explained.

Before the win, Macha held a team meeting that consisted of "me asking some questions and the players doing most of the talking. I wanted to hear what they had to say." Later that night, he lost relief pitcher Scott Bakkum, who had been an extraordinary set-up man throughout the season. The veteran righty was headed to Pawtucket, taking with him a 6-4 record and a stellar 1.34 ERA in 28 Thunder games. Considering that he had been 4-12 as a Single-A starter in 1994, the move to the bullpen had salvaged his major league dream.

On July 13, hard-luck starter Wes Brooks (2-9) spun a complete-game performance to defeat Edmondson and the Mets 5-2. Selby was 3-for-4 with another homer. Lennon was 3-for-4, and Nomar erased Mashore from the Thunder record books with his sixth triple. "Brooksie had tremendous control of his slider," Macha said. "I think he threw 26 of them, and only one was a ball. That's outstanding." One of the genuine good guys on the '95 Thunder roster, Brooks handled his accomplishment with typical class. "When you have tough luck like I've had, you start to doubt yourself," he said. "When I was going bad, it was really tough coming to the ballpark. If you're doing well, everybody wants to be around, but when you're not, I found out that you should want to be at the park more than ever." The Thunder (45-46) left Binghamton tied with Bowie (44-45) in the consistently mediocre Southern Division, but on Friday, July 14, the Baysox beat Dean Peterson 10-6, moving one game ahead in the standings.

More significantly, it was the Thunder's sixth consecutive home loss. Not since July 2 had the home nine sent the fans away with a victory. The franchise was well on its way to Hodes' goal of 450,000 patrons for a 71-date season, however. In addition, Prunetti's "Cadillac of Fields" was holding up quite nicely.

Following the July 14 defeat, Soup arrived at Leeston's Pub in Trenton's Chambersburg section for a postgame radio talk show with WTTM hosts Ron Berkowitz and Bill Tortorella. If he knew he was headed to Boston in 2 days, he didn't offer any clues. At the end of the interview, he shook hands with several fans and climbed into his black Nissan Pathfinder bearing California vanity license plates "SOUPS ON." (The plates were a gift from his sister.)

Game two of the mid-July series against Bowie featured a major-league rehab start by lefty Vaughn Eshelman, who had been acquired by Boston in the Rule V free-agent draft of December 1994 after a successful season in the Eastern League. Nursing a tender left shoulder, Eshelman was scheduled to throw 45 pitches before giving way to knuckleballer Jared Fernandez, who would be making his Double-A debut after being promoted from Single-A, short-season Utica of the New York–Penn League. Eshelman gave Fernandez a head start by working three hitless innings. A crowd of 7141 arrived in sweltering 95-degree heat to see the Thunder score two runs in the second and three more in the fourth for a 5-0 advantage. Fernandez took the combined no-hitter into the seventh, but Bowie third baseman Scott McClain lined his first delivery of the inning into left field for a single. "I was mostly concerned about the no-hitter," Fernandez confessed. "Baseball's a superstitious game and you're not supposed to say anything about that in the dugout, but they sure were. They were giving me a hard time."

The 5-2 Thunder win not only snapped the home losing streak and tied the Baysox for first place, it featured an unbelievable play by Nomar that robbed the visitors of a certain base hit in the third. The defensive theft was vintage Garciaparra. "Wow!" Eshelman exclaimed. "He can just flat out do it."

Despite the win, there was terseness in Macha's postgame address. He wasn't his usual dry, sarcastic self. As he wrapped a white towel around his waist, he said in a resigned tone, "Stay tuned, there's a big move coming."

The July 15 game also was noteworthy because it featured the first triple play in Thunder history—unfortunately, *against* the Thunder. On an eighth-inning bunt attempt with Greg Blosser on second and Selby on first, catcher Dana Levangie popped out meekly to Bowie catcher B.J. Waszgis. The Baysox backstop subsequently relayed the ball to first base, where Selby was doubled off the bag. Bowie first baseman Billy Owens then had time to retire Blosser at second for the rare single-inning trifecta. In attendance that humid evening was Boston roving instructor Dick Berardino, who was responsible for all of the baserunning drills in the Red Sox farm system. Following the 5-2 Thunder victory, Berardino was driving his rental car north on Route 1 to the Palmer Inn. Losing track of his speed as he analyzed the game, he was stopped by a Lawrence Township police cruiser.

"I'm sorry, officer, but I'm the Boston baserunning instructor, and the Thunder hit into a triple play tonight," he offered as an excuse.

"O.K., I'm going to let you off with a warning, but be more careful in the future," the officer replied.

At 10 AM on Sunday, July 16, 1995, Soup and Nipper climbed into a limousine in front of Mercer County Waterfront Park. Hastily packed but overjoyed, they headed to Philadelphia International Airport for the short flight to Boston to join the Red Sox. The limo had been hired by the Thunder front office as a gesture of appreciation to the pair.

The previous night, when Soup first learned that he had been promoted, he called his mother, Kathy, at the family's California home. "Mom, are you sitting down?" he asked. "I'm going to the Show."

When the Thunder began arriving at the stadium for the 1:35 PM game against Bowie (a 2-0 loss), Soup and Nip were long gone. The pitching coach left behind the back-room office where he tutored his pitchers and the cot that that had been procured from the Palmer Inn so that he could sleep at the stadium when his workload became too large. There were several nights during the '95 season when Nip also had asked the clubhouse guy to bring him a six pack of beer for some late night company.

During his 3 1/2 months on Macha's staff, Nip's approach was exhaustive. He demanded the same from his pitchers, particularly Suppan. At times, the pair spent hours together, discussing everything from mental approach to fundamentals. Soup was Nip's protégé, and their relationship blossomed to the point that a few of the other starters felt excluded. Both Brooks and Senior seemed distracted by the pitching coach's preferential treatment of the young right-hander. Following each start, Nip made his pitchers fill out a five-page, self-analysis questionnaire. He kept a library of baseballs with each prospect's finger tracings. "How were you holding the ball when the pitch was working for you?" he demanded. Much of the attention was dedicated to Soup's four-pitch arsenal.

The father of one '95 Thunder player recalled, "Nip always felt that Soup was going to get him to the big leagues." In tandem, the pair departed under a veil of uncertainty. Would they return to Trenton? Nobody—including Macha—really knew.

"I think they just want him to be comfortable," the manager said. "There are going to be a lot of things going on. Nip may add to his comfort level."

"In that situation, you just hope you can start off well, but it's going to be tough for a guy who's only 20," added Senior. "But who knows? He might never come back. They're looking at who's doing the best. And he's proven he can pitch at every level."

Meanwhile, the feelings that went through Soup's mind at the news he would start Monday's game against Kansas City formed a collage of anxiety, pride and anticipation. At 20 years, 6 months, and 15 days of age, he was about to become the youngest pitcher to make his Red Sox debut in almost 26 years. On September 22, 1969, Mike Garman won his first major-league start at 20 years and 6 days. Soup would wear No. 55, trading his Thunder No. 20 for Boston's home white uniform. In another lifetime, he would have been entering his junior year at UCLA; in this one, his occupational training had resulted in an almost-immediate jackpot.

"I don't know how I'm going to feel out on the mound at Fenway," Suppan said before climbing into the getaway limo. "This is something I have been preparing for all my life. Last year, when I was in Single-A, it seemed so far away, but Nip told me to always be ready. Making it to Fenway this season was a goal of mine. Whether it was September or sometime during the season, I thought it was a realistic goal."

While some minor leaguers wait until their late twenties or early thirties—or never get the call to the bigs—Soup's three-season ascent through the Boston farm system had been a thing of meteoric promise. "Get him here as soon as he's ready," was the mandate delivered to Nip and Macha from the Boston front office. Gammons had been right. Soup's stay in Trenton was a brief one, Waterfront Park a mere way station on his journey to the majors.

"The fans in Trenton have been great, but I hope they appreciate the talent we have here," Macha explained.

In 15 starts for the Thunder, Suppan was 6-2 with a 2.36 ERA. After struggling a bit at first, he turned into perhaps the Eastern League's best pitcher during late June and early July. He left behind a marvelous ratio of 26 walks and 88 strike-outs. He allowed just 86 hits in 99 innings, and opponents hit .205 against him with runners in scoring position.

On Monday, July 17, at Boston's Fenway Park, Suppan lost his major-league debut 4-3. Larry and Kathy watched in agony as he worked a full count to the first batter he faced, the Royals' Keith Lockhart, before allowing a leadoff homer. In 5 2/3 innings, he allowed three runs on nine hits, walking two and striking out four. Despite the loss, he was the talk of Beantown. He was the first pitcher in the Red Sox organization to make the jump from Double-A to the majors since Jeff Sellers in September 1985. He also was the first Thunder starter to make such a jump. In eight major-league appearances for the '95 Red Sox, he compiled a 1-2 record and a 5.96 ERA, walking five and striking out 19. His only win came on September 17 at Cleveland, when he entered a 6-6 contest and forced Albert Belle to ground into a double play. After Soup secured the victory, Boston reliever Rick Aguilera presented him with the game ball.

Meanwhile, on July 18, hours before the Thunder lost a 7-0 decision at Reading, news arrived that Nipper had replaced John Cumberland as Boston's pitching coach. He would not be returning to Trenton after all. Macha was mystified and would operate for the next week without a pitching coach. Furthermore, he had not spoken to Nipper since his Sunday-morning departure.

"It looks like he's big-leaguing me," Macha said. "When I played in Japan during the 1980s, I had this interpreter who was around during World War II. He was in Tokyo when they dropped the atom bomb on Hiroshima. He said they knew something had happened, but they didn't know what. That's kinda how I feel right now."

It was a classic Macha analogy—witty, insightful, and dry as a bone in terms of delivery. The bottom line, however, was that Nipper was back in the big leagues and Macha wasn't.

PORK CHOP MOVES ON

On July 19, Pork Chop finally received his reward for leading the Thunder through two-thirds of the '95 season. At last, the Red Sox felt the time was right to ship him north to Pawtucket. When the call came, nobody was happier than Macha. Also promoted on the 19th were Tim Cain and Brent Hansen, a valuable pair of pitchers. "Just a few words about those three guys that are going up," Macha said after an overflow Waterfront crowd of 7383 feted Pork Chop with his farewell salvo during the Thunder's 7-6 win over Reading. "Not only did they all put up good numbers, but they were all good people. They earned their way out of here. All three."

Added Boston Minor League Field Coordinator Bob Schaefer, "Chop deserves a shot. He has some holes in his swing, but we know he'll keep working hard. If anyone deserved a shot, it's him."

In 50 games at Waterfront Park, Pork Chop hit .255, with 13 doubles, three triples, eight homers, and 30 RBIs. On the road, he hit .302, with 10 doubles, two triples, 13 homers, and 39 RBIs. Overall, he hit .278, with 21 homers (tying Clark's franchise record) and 69 RBIs. He was later named to the postseason Rawlings Eastern League All-Star team.

Fittingly, after singling in his last Thunder at-bat, he was removed from the game to a standing ovation featuring thousands of flailing arms and green-foam fingers. "The ovation was indicative of the way people in Trenton felt about him," McCarthy recalled. "Of the first three Thunder seasons, that's one of my favorite memories of Waterfront Park."

After the game, McCarthy conducted his final radio interview with Pork Chop. "I'm always going to have memories of this place, just the fans," the excited player said. "I'll never forget the guy in the stands with the pork chop on his hat. This has been the greatest experience of my life. All the other teams I've played for, I've forgotten about them. This place is definitely No. 1 in my heart. There's no more I can say."

Playing to the crowd was never one of Pork Chop's shortcomings, either. After his final game, he stayed until every last autograph request had been fulfilled.

Despite his fondness for Trenton, however, he didn't plan to look back, but for the Thunder franchise, Pork Chop would always be a favorite son. That giant green hand on the scoreboard, encouraging 7000 fans to wave in unison, told half the story. Pork Chop's mighty home-run stroke told the rest.

"Who is Tony Clark, anyway?" he asked McCarthy in jest, and with that, the Pork Chop era of Trenton Thunder baseball came to an end.

Two days later, following an 8-3 victory at Harrisburg, Macha sat in his office and discussed the personnel loss. "We took Pork Chop off the menu," Schaefer said from across the tiny room. "Yeah, we're a rice-and-beans team now," Macha countered.

In 30 games with Pawtucket after his promotion, Pork Chop hit .232, with eight doubles, five homers, and 23 RBIs.

BAD BOYS

During the '95 season, many Thunder players continued to enjoy free drinks at the Soho Bar and Grill. The relationship between the establishment and the team finally—some might say inevitably—came to a head on July 20, following a 4-0 Businessperson's Special loss to Reading when outfielder Andy Abad and infielder Mike Hardge tangled with a pair of Hamilton Township siblings. According to eyewitnesses, the Thunder pair made suggestive comments to the women accompanying the locals, and one thing led to another. Some blows were exchanged. Some glass was broken. No arrests were made, but word of the incident, which also involved four Thunder players who were outside the bar at the time the skirmish erupted, gradually spread through the community. When it made the front page of a daily newspaper, Macha and his players took an unwanted place in the spotlight. Contacted in his Harrisburg hotel room several days later, Abad was asked if he threw a punch. "I might of," he foolishly replied to *The Trentonian*, and the story stayed in the headlines for the next 3 days.

Abad was later fined $150 by Macha for lying. "I have very few team rules, and he violated one of them," the manager explained. "By the time these guys reach Double-A, they should know how to conduct themselves." Gradually, the uproar died down, replaced by the intensity of the '95 Eastern League pennant race, but Abad's relationship with the manager had been severely damaged. On August 7, the 22-year-old outfielder was shipped back to Sarasota. At the time, Macha insisted it was a total coincidence, but he later changed his story and admitted that he asked Red Sox brass "to get him out of my sight."

"I've gotta pay the consequences of what happened, but this isn't going to be the easiest time for me," Abad said. "I never really had any comment on the situation because I wanted to avoid the worst possible scenario, but the worst possible scenario happened . . . it was in all the papers . . . and I guess that's what people are going to think of me."

"This is sort of the focal point of the revitalization of Trenton," Hodes said after expressing his disappointment about the incident, "and we expect the players to get out in the community."

"I don't think anybody wants this thing to be run down because a couple of guys got in a scuffle," Macha added. "There have been scuffles in bars all over the place. What I say is, 'For the most part, I've got a good bunch of guys'. They're being portrayed as hoodlums, and they're really not that way."

Soon after the incident, Soho owner Bill Rednor called a press conference to explain his side of the story. Sufficiently alienated, most of the Thunder players stopped frequenting the establishment.

BLOSSER AND BASEBRAWL

The Thunder arrived in New Britain for a four-game series with the Hardware City Rock Cats on July 25 with a 50-51 record. Twenty-five-year-old lefty Joe Ciccarella had been asked to fill the starting void created by Suppan's promotion. During any baseball season, frustrations become a major factor 100 games into the journey. Old, dilapidated Beehive Field seemed to bring out the fight in the Thunder players, particularly the veterans like Ciccarella, reliever Mike Sullivan, first baseman Ben Shelton (who had been signed as a free agent to replace Pork Chop on July 22) and Greg Blosser. All of them had played in the weather-beaten facility before, and the 4-day Connecticut showdown against the Rock Cats began on a positive note for the Thunder as Shelton, Selby, and Blosser each homered in an 8-4 victory.

The following day, Orellano made the most of his twentieth Double-A start, scattering five hits over eight innings and improving to 9-5. The crafty pitcher had added a new pitch—a cut fastball—that "acted like a slider." The offense supported him with a six-run eighth inning that polished off an 8-1 victory. The pivotal hit in that outburst was Blosser's second homer in as many days, a three-run shot to right field. In 2 days, the 6-foot-2, 225-pound left-hander had demonstrated the power that made him the sixteenth overall pick in the June 1989 draft out of Sarasota High School. In 1994, he had made Boston's major-league roster, hitting .353 with 15 RBIs during spring training. At that point, he was a solid bet never to return to Double-A, but he struggled in the big leagues and wound up back in Pawtucket. Playing at Beehive Field in July 1995 was a major insult to his already fragile professional psyche. "It's depressing," he admitted. "I'm not going to lie. It feels kinda like a setback, which it really is. I just want to get out of the Boston organization."

Ever the teacher and the fatherly professional, Macha was working hard to improve Blosser's mechanics at the plate. He conducted several extra batting practices for him on off-days. "He has to learn he doesn't have to swing so hard every time," Macha said. Added Blosser, "I've been trying to keep my hands in a certain position, and I feel a lot more comfortable." After his second homer in as many days, he headed to a nearby family's house for a home-cooked meal; he had lived with them during his New Britain playing days.

The third game of the series featured a noon first pitch and pitted Ciccarella (2-0, 1.93 ERA) against Hardware City's Todd Ritchie (2-6, 6.82 ERA). As Ritchie warmed up, scores of recreation groups milled about the grandstand looking for unoccupied general admission seats. The promotion was billed as "Parks and Rec Day," but Hardware City officials joked that is was more like "Wreck the Park Day."

At 12:01 PM, Macha jogged to the third-base coaching box and began flashing signs to his lead-off hitter—veteran Double-A infielder Mike Hardge. Hardge was in the same boat as Ciccarella, Blosser, Sullivan, and Ryan. As a member of the '93 Eastern League Champion Harrisburg club, he had enjoyed all the circuit had to offer. He had fully expected to earn a shot at Triple-A during the '95 season, but a falling out with Montreal minor-league officials led him to sign with Boston as a free agent. He played 29 games for Pawtucket before he was shipped to Trenton on June 20. One of the loudest, most-entertaining members of the Thunder roster, he was a dead ringer for rap singer Tone Loc. Not surprisingly, he could perform a flawless imitation of the artist's hit song, "Wild Thing."

Hardge singled Ritchie's first pitch into left field. Selby quickly followed with a first-pitch double to put runners on second and third with nobody out. Clearly shaken by his rude greeting, Ritchie walked Ryan McGuire on five pitches to load the bases. That set the table for the clean-up hitter—Blosser. Having homered in two of his last six plate appearances, the odds were extremely long that he would clear the sacks with one swing. Then again, this wasn't shaping up as an ordinary series for him. On Ritchie's first pitch, he smashed a towering grand-slam homer that sailed over the right-field fence and into the grass beyond. The children applauded loudly—apparently not caring that the guy circling the bases was wearing the visitor's uniform. As he received a handshake from Macha, Blosser pumped his fist. In the stands, a sarcastic New Britain fan yelled, "Hey, Blosser, why couldn't you do that when you were here?"

Staked to a 4-0 lead, Ciccarella cruised through the first three innings. In the fourth, he yielded a lead-off homer to outfielder Matt Lawton. Outfielder Anthony Byrd followed with a drag bunt single that the hard-throwing Ciccarella did not appreciate. He let Byrd know just that, laying the groundwork for the ensuing bench-clearing brawl. "You pussy," the pitcher muttered on his way back to the mound. All-Star second baseman Walker Todd followed with a patient at-bat that resulted in a double, but Thunder outfielder Jose Zambrano cut the ball off in time to prevent Byrd from scoring. Next up, 5-foot-9, 225-pound clean-up hitter Tim Moore fell behind in the count 0-2 before sending a long fly ball to right field. What happened next seemed to occur in suspended motion. Byrd tagged third and sprinted home with the Rock Cats' second run, scoring on the sacrifice fly. Ciccarella took his appropriate defensive position behind home plate, backing up catcher Alex Delgado. The pitcher still had his glove on when Byrd intentionally bumped him. The contact escalated into further face-to-face name calling, and Byrd's helmet grazed Ciccarella's left eye. By that point, both dugouts had begun emptying—even the relief pitchers in the bullpens began sprinting toward the plate. In the tiny third-base press box, McCarthy and Simonetta strained to call the blow-by-blow action. The fight was a first for both broadcasters.

"I remember being very surprised because nothing like that had ever happened before," McCarthy recalled. "Out of the corner of my eye, I could see fists starting to fly. I was so shocked. I think the first thing I said was, 'Get a load of this.' When you don't see something for more than 250 games, you don't think you're ever going to see it."

Explained Ciccarella, "He pushed me. I pushed him. He started swinging. I started swinging . . . You see it all the time, the game getting the best of two people. I guess I would have done the same thing he did."

Countered Byrd, "When I crossed home plate, he was right in front of me. I had nowhere to go. So I stopped right there at his chest. He bumped me. I pushed him, and we went from there."

As umpires Mitch Schwark and Jim Reynolds tried to separate 50 feuding players, Macha bull-rushed his way from the first-base dugout to the center of the altercation, throwing Hardware City manager Sal Butera out of the way. The Thunder skipper put Byrd in a bear hug and walked him out of harm's way. For an instant, he looked like Moses parting the Red Sea as his long arms cradled the incensed outfielder from behind. In the meantime, Moore and Sullivan were staging a side confrontation. Sullivan, a martial arts specialist, swayed from side-to-side, imitating a gorilla for the stocky designated hitter. "I was trying to get closer to him [Sullivan]," Moore said. At least 5 minutes passed before order was restored. Gloves littered the area around homeplate, and the scene looked a bit like a fire alarm on an elementary school playground.

Basically, the brawl was a result of mutual frustration, stoked to a boil on an 85-degree afternoon. Ciccarella later admitted that bunting for a base hit hadn't been a bad idea on Byrd's part. "He was probably ticked off he gave up a homer run to Lawton," Butera surmised. "It was obvious he said something on the bunt. That to me just shows his mentality."

Added Macha, "Things get said everywhere. I don't condone either side's point. Byrd went up to Joe and smoked him behind the plate. That's not right, either. We're not in this business to promote professional wrestling, but when games are played, emotions are high. We're here to get guys to the big leagues, not promote organized mayhem."

As the umpires conferred about ejections, Ciccarella picked up his glove and strolled back to the mound, a welt forming in the outside corner of his left eye. Macha walked to the field to inform him that he and Sullivan had been ejected (along with Byrd and Moore). Ciccarella returned to the dugout and started jawing at Macha. Quickly taking control of the situation, the manager told his pitcher to get the hell off the field. Ciccarella continued his protest, prompting Macha to turn up the expletives a notch and make an example of the player. In seconds, Ciccarella was headed to the clubhouse, where he pondered the incident for the rest of the game. "I'm not going to have anybody on my team yelling at me," Macha said authoritatively, an unusual edge framing his words. "I'm in charge here, and when I tell you to get off the field, you get off."

Ciccarella was replaced by Australian righty Brett Cederblad, who was making his Double-A debut in the aftermath of the brawl. He picked up a 4-2 victory, and Ryan recorded his second save. Macha held a closed-door meeting afterward. Nonetheless, Ciccarella did not offer an apology until the next day, further exacerbating the tension between pitcher and manager. "One of the things I've been preaching all season is not to lose control of your emotions," Macha said. "In that case, Joe lost control. But the whole team was out there defending our guys, so that was good."

The Hardware City office received plenty of feedback about the melee, which was chronicled in a full-color picture on the front page of the July 28 *New Britain Herald*. "We got so many calls from parents whose children were at the game," said General Manager Gerry Berthiaume. "They wondered, 'How can you let them fight on Parks and Recreation Day?' "

The final game of the series pitted Senior against Rock Cats' lefty Dan Serafini. Macha was particularly high on Serafini, who had pitched in the '94 Arizona Fall League and entered the night with a 10-6 record and a 2.74 ERA, third in the league. The Thunder were on a Blosser-led roll that would not be thwarted, however. Serafini lasted just 4 2/3 innings, allowing seven earned runs on eight hits as Trenton swept the four-game series with a 9-5 victory. The crowning blow was a one-out, seventh-inning solo homer by Blosser off reliever Scott Moten, which made him the first player in the Beehive's 13-year history to hit one out of the park in four consecutive games. During the entire '92 season as a New Britain player, he had hit just four there! It was an incredible outburst considering almost 1000 Double-A games had been played at the facility by future major-league sluggers like Jeff Bagwell, Mo Vaughn, Cliff Floyd, Albert Belle, and Manny Ramirez. Blosser would add another round-tripper at Waterfront the following night during an 8-1 triumph over Bowie, making the homer streak five games in a row.

"To be honest, I was trying to juice one tonight," he admitted after the New Britain finale. In the series, he was 6-for-18 with 11 RBIs. Furthermore, he had hit for the "home-run cycle," which included a solo shot, a two-run shot, a three-run shot, and a grand slam. "I don't think you can get much better than that," Macha said. The Thunder headed home with a 54-51 record, having lost just once on a 7-day road trip. Blosser bid goodbye to his old friends, swung his equipment bag over his broad shoulders, and headed to the bus—nostalgia be damned. He wanted to get as far away from Beehive Field as possible.

The same was true for Joe Ciccarella.

CHAPTER 17

Chasing a Pennant

"Everybody here is very concerned about the playoff race. Everybody here wants to get there. We want a ring at the end of the season."

—1995 THUNDER DESIGNATED HITTER BEN SHELTON

On Wednesday, August 2, 1995, before a Waterfront crowd of 7259, Nomar hit the fifth grand-slam homer in Thunder history. The dramatic round-tripper was served up by Reading 6-foot-6 righty Carlton Loewer, Philadelphia's first pick in the 1994 draft. At the time, Nomar hadn't seen his family in 8 months. They had traveled to Trenton from Whittier, California, just to watch the series against Reading, and Nomar didn't disappoint. "This was a big night for him," Macha explained after Nomar's homer sparked a 7-2 Trenton victory. "He was pumped coming around third base after that homer. That's the first time I've seen his eyeballs wide open like that."

"I was smiling and laughing because my family was here," Nomar admitted. "I had to show them something." The homer came on a 2-2 fastball after Loewer had walked the bases loaded. It also made a winner of Senior, who improved to 9-5 despite working behind the Reading hitters for most of his six innings. Nomar punctuated his memorable effort with several outstanding defensive plays.

By early August, it was obvious the Thunder would battle Reading and Bowie for the Eastern League Southern Division's two playoff spots. Trenton entered the month with a 56-52 record, a half game ahead of Reading and Bowie (both 55-53). On August 1 at Harrisburg, pitcher Brett Cederblad yielded a one-out, ninth-inning grand slam to Harrisburg right fielder Antonio Grissom, and the Senators prevailed, 8-4. Grissom, the younger brother of Atlanta Braves outfielder Marquis Grissom, basked in his achievement inside the Senators' clubhouse while Macha pondered his team's sloppy performance, which included four errors and four Harrisburg double plays. "We gave them too many chances," the manager lamented.

Poor defense aside, Macha had another pressing concern. Before the game, Levenda had distributed 23 suspensions and $4700 in fines to the Thunder as a result of the July 27 brawl at Hardware City. The Trenton players joked that they were going to conduct a benefit car wash to raise the money. Both Ciccarella and Sullivan were docked $250 and suspended for three games. The other 21 players were fined $200 each and suspended for two games for leaving their positions. Senior and Orellano, who had been charting pitches in the stands, were not fined.

In light of the blanket disciplinary action—which was standard procedure mandated by the National Association rules—Macha was forced to juggle his lineup on a daily basis for the next 3 weeks. Levenda's written orders insisted that "there are to be no more than two position players and one pitcher suspended on any given day."

"This whole thing is a huge pain," Macha countered. "If there's a fight on the pitcher's mound and you're a shortstop just standing there watching, you're going to look like a complete jerk. These mandatory suspensions do nothing for the development of a player."

Without Suppan or Pork Chop—the marquee attractions for the first 4 months of the '95 season—Trenton was forced to rely on Nomar, Orellano, Senior, Brooks, Blosser, Selby, Merloni (who spent most of July on the disabled list with his sore right thumb), and McGuire. After hitting 5 homers in five days in late July, Blosser cooled off considerably. In spite of the embittered Blosser's brief Connecticut slugging outburst, McGuire and Selby had really carried the team offensively during July. For the month, McGuire hit .343 (37-for-108), with two homers, eight doubles and 17 RBIs to earn the Topps Eastern League Player of the Month in a balloting of league managers. The UCLA product wasn't even named Thunder player of the month, however, because Selby hit .333 (35-for-105), with seven doubles, seven homers, and 26 RBIs. His notorious temper had been calmed somewhat by his success, but he still had moments of frustration, when he smashed his bat or his helmet in the dugout. "I'd hate to be Selby's batting helmet this year," Boston Minor League Hitting Coordinator Steve Braun observed in a memorable burst of understatement. In spite of Selby's offensive awakening, the numbers show that the '95 Thunder were never a consistently winning outfit. In fact, they were the epitome of a .500 club, compiling a 13-11 record in April and finishing 13-15 in May before recording back-to-back 15-13 efforts in June and July. Furthermore, despite the nightly standing-room-only Waterfront crowds, the '95 Thunder were considerably better on the road than at home. At Waterfront, they compiled a 34-37 record; in the league's other nine ballparks, they were 39-32. Macha attributed the discrepancy to his club's lack of right-handed power, which was a prerequisite for success at Waterfront. With strong winds usually blowing in from the river and over right field, it was difficult for the Thunder's lefty-dominated lineup—McGuire, Selby, Blosser, and Carey—to generate a lot of homers. Nonetheless, the '95 club didn't win regularly at home because it hit just .244 with 39 homers (eight by Pork Chop and five by Nomar). On the road, it fared much better offensively, batting .267 with 64 round-trippers (including 10 by Selby and eight by Blosser).

In late July, Nipper was replaced as pitching coach by 40-year-old Rick Peterson. An avid student of East Asian philosophy, Peterson had been fired as the Chicago White Sox's bullpen coach on June 2 along with manager Gene Lamont. Almost immediately, Macha was impressed with Peterson's knowledge of baseball. The pair spent many nights together discussing the game over the next month-and-a-half. Following the season, Macha strongly recommended Peterson to the Boston front office as a candidate for the '96 Thunder pitching coach position that eventually went to Ralph Treuel. Soon afterward, Peterson took a position with the Toronto Blue Jays as their minor-league pitching coordinator. "We just couldn't offer him as much money as they did," Schaefer explained. Added Macha, "I hated to see him go."

The staff that Peterson inherited included a worn-down Orellano, a shell-shocked Brooks, a steady Senior, and an eager Cederblad. Peterson's impact was most obvious in Brooks' August performance. Brooks finished the regular season with a 5-11 record and a respectable 4.12 ERA despite his 2-10 start. He also allowed just 149 hits in 161 2/3 innings. His ledger was a classic case of "not getting the breaks."

"Same old, same old," Brooks grumbled after yielding five unearned runs during a 10-0 loss at Reading on August 9. Added Macha, "It seems like when Brooksie's out there and we give the other team a little crack, they kick the crap out of us."

The Reading series also marked the Double-A debuts of outfielder Trot Nixon and Australian reliever Shayne Bennett, a righty who recorded 24 saves at Sarasota before his August 7 promotion. The 6-foot-1, 190-pound Nixon arrived in Trenton with the burden of great expectations. He was the seventh pick overall in the June 1993 draft after a storied career at Wilmington's New Hanover High School. During his first full season—at Single-A Lynchburg of the Carolina League in 1994—he hit .246, with 12 homers and 43 RBIs. Everywhere he played, great things were expected. Baseball America had named him Boston's No. 1 prospect before the '94 campaign, but he was sidelined by a lower back injury midway through the season. In 73 games with Sarasota before his '95 promotion, he hit .301, with 10 doubles, four triples, five homers, and 39 RBIs. He also reached base safely in his first 37 games, a remarkable accomplishment at any level.

"It's almost ridiculous the amount of attention he gets," said McGuire, a '94 teammate of Nixon's, " but he's a great competitor. He truly wants to win. I hope he doesn't feel he has to come up here and personally help us win the pennant—because that's a lot of pressure to put on someone—but if he comes here and plays like he can play, he'll help." In his first Double-A at-bat, Nixon almost hit a solo homer to right field off Reading righty Larry Mitchell. Instead, he finished 1-for-4 in the lead-off spot. "I was impressed with Trot," Macha observed.

The following night, a Municipal Stadium crowd of 5911 watched in awe as Bennett was asked to convert an almost-impossible save in his first Double-A appearance. With the bases loaded, nobody out, and Trenton clinging to a 4-3 lead in the bottom of the ninth, Macha strolled to the mound to remove Sullivan. Handing the 6-foot-5 Bennett the ball, he said, "I know this is not a very good situation. We might need some divine intervention here, but give it your best shot." At the time, the Thunder had lost four in a row. With the Reading crowd on its feet clapping in unison, it was up to Bennett to stem the tide. He began by striking out right-fielder Steve Solomon. Next, he induced catcher Gary Bennett to pop out to Nomar for the key second out. Finally, he struck out center-fielder Rick Holifield—swinging—on a 3-2 pitch that ended the game and prompted a wild celebration that continued in the tiny visitor's clubhouse. Bennett pumped his fist and hugged Martin. "That situation is virtually impossible to get out of," he said. "But I'm new here, and they hadn't seen me before. That helps." Instead of falling two-and-a-half games behind first-place Reading (59-57), Trenton (59-58) was only a half game back. The shadow boxing in the standings would continue until the season's final day. More significantly, the teams had completed their 18 regular-season meetings, with the Phillies winning 11. If the season ended in a tie, Reading would have home-field advantage for the playoffs based on that head-to-head mark.

The two-game Reading trip had been a time of great personal introspection for Macha. In the August 7 editions of the *Philadelphia Daily News*, copy editor Doug Darroch had taken a very public shot at him for the July 20 Soho incident involving Abad and Hardge. Macha had thought the uproar over the unfortunate altercation was over. He was dead wrong. In a column labeled "Dingers and Zingers," Darroch erroneously wrote, "The parent Boston Red Sox have fined Thunder manager Ken Macha and six players for their part in a barroom brawl that left a Trenton restaurant in shambles." The column concluded with the kicker, "And since when do managers drink with their players, anyway?" After McCarthy showed him the article, Macha was livid. "Do you know any good lawyers?" he inquired brusquely, knowing that he had been nowhere near the Soho on the night of the trouble. "What if [Phillies manager] Jim Fregosi reads that?" Macha wondered. "What's he going to think?" The next day, the *Daily News* printed a retraction, which calmed the Thunder manager somewhat. Gradually, his anger subsided, and no legal action was taken.

WATERFRONT MILESTONES

During an August 17 Businessperson's Special against New Haven at Waterfront, the Thunder became the first Eastern League franchise in 73 years to eclipse the 400,000-fan mark. A crowd of 7156 brought the 64-date '95 total to 402,650. The 400,000th patron was Catherine Jenkins, who was presented with an official Thunder jacket during a seventh-inning, on-field ceremony. During the game, Boomer fired a Super Soaker water gun into the crowd. Hodes proclaimed that the 450,000-fan plateau was well within the Thunder's reach, and designated hitter Ben Shelton won the game with a ninth-inning single off the Ravens' Jacob Viano. Before the game, Migliaccio was honored as the 1995 Eastern League Groundskeeper of the Year. It was a triumphant moment for the man who just 1 year earlier had been responsible for overseeing two field constructions within an 8-month period. "I think this award is a huge accomplishment considering what we went through last year," Migliaccio said, "but we're just doing our job."

The Thunder's bizarre '95 home saga continued on August 24 during a 13-10 loss to Bowie. A crowd of 7325 watched the Baysox torch Brooks for nine earned runs in the first five innings only to see the Thunder rally from a 9-2 deficit to send the game into extra innings tied at 10. The comeback included a

3-for-6 outing by Nomar, who scored the tying run in the ninth. McGuire was 4-for-6 with three RBIs, and Nixon was 2-for-5. Although Bowie scored three runs in the top of the tenth to make a loser of relief pitcher Shayne Bennett, nobody in the Thunder clubhouse was devastated. Trenton (67-65) still trailed first-place Reading (67-64) by a half game, while the Baysox (64-67) lurked two-and-a-half games back.

"It was a great game," McGuire said cheerfully after his two-run double in the ninth knotted the affair. "To me, that was one of the best efforts of the year as far as two teams answering each other back."

"We battled," added Garciaparra. "That's definitely a positive. When you're playing good offensive baseball like we did tonight, you can't hang your head."

DOWN THE STRETCH

The following night, before a Prince George's Stadium crowd of 11,157, the Australian Cederblad—who had been nicknamed "The Thunder from Down Under"—pitched a complete-game three-hitter, and Trenton pounded 15 hits to defeat Bowie 14-0. McGuire was 5-for-6—matching Mahay's single-game Thunder record of five hits—with five RBIs, lifting his average to .346, the best in the league. "What can you say?" Macha wondered wistfully about McGuire's performance. Cederblad threw 104 pitches, walked one, struck out eight, and retired the final 13 batters he faced. Afterward, he credited Peterson for helping set up his fastball as a perfect complement to his superb curveball. "I was in the most aggressive mood of my life tonight," he added.

Trenton's brief two-game journey to Maryland ended, however, with a dramatic 6-2 loss before a Prince George's record crowd of 13,994—which also was the largest gathering to watch the Thunder during their first three seasons. Orellano squandered a 2-0 lead in the sixth inning by allowing a pair of runs, but the decisive blow came on a two-out slider from Sullivan to third baseman Scott McClain with the bases loaded and two out in the bottom of the ninth. As outfielders Nixon and Eddie Zambrano gave chase, McClain smashed a grand slam over the left-field billboards. Nixon stopped at the wall, pounding it with his fist. "I couldn't believe he threw me that," the Bowie infielder said of Sullivan's fateful delivery. The loss dropped Trenton a game-and-a-half behind Reading with eight games left to play, while Bowie remained two-and-a-half games behind the Thunder. Bowie had won the 18-game season series against Macha's club by a 13-5 margin. During the 3-hour bus ride back to Trenton, the Thunder players watched the movie *Hoosiers*. A four-game homestand against Harrisburg awaited.

On Sunday, August 27, before a crowd of 7251, Senior outdueled the Senators' Jose Paniagua for a 6-3 victory—his eleventh of the season, tying Edmondson and Orellano for the franchise record. Before the game, he was named the Eastern League Pitcher of the Week. In addition, McGuire was named Eastern League Batter of the Week for his 14-for-27 effort in the midst of the pennant race. Senior's triumph was followed by a 5-1 Thunder loss. After a 4-3 Thunder win in the third game, a Waterfront record crowd of 7886 packed the ballpark to see Cederblad punctuate the season with a 3-2, complete-game victory. Mc-Carthy recalled the final out of that August 30 game as one of the highlights of the first three Thunder seasons, the lanky Australian pitcher peeling a curveball past Harrisburg catcher Lou Hymel for a called third strike. "I'll never forget the excitement of that moment," the broadcaster said. Afterward, the Thunder players tossed their caps into the stands with considerably greater enthusiasm than their '94 predecessors. Nomar received a standing ovation after going 2-for-3, recording two put-outs and six infield assists and stealing his franchise-record thirty-fifth base. All night, he resembled Pac-Man in kelly green pinstripes. One of the assists was a ranging play behind third base that shocked Senators' first baseman Tony Marabella. "I just couldn't believe he made that play," Merloni said. "I was laughing hysterically as we came off the field." Added Macha, "That was so unbelievable it was funny."

Catcher Alex Delgado's three-run, first-inning homer had been the game winner. Before the first pitch, Nomar was presented with a framed print of Fenway Park—his ultimate baseball destination. The artwork was a gift from the Thunder management and ownership. That evening, the franchise's thirtieth consecutive sell-out pushed attendance over the 450,000 plateau—the final total was 453,915. Remarkably, the season had included 71 games without a rain-out—an incredible achievement in any league. The "Cadillac of Fields" had purred through the season without interruption. Not since August 17, 1994, had a Thunder home game been postponed by Mother Nature.

Meanwhile, four games in Canton were all that remained of the regular season. At 71-67, Trenton trailed Reading (72-66) by one game. Bowie (67-71) had fallen four games behind. The Thunder's first-ever playoff appearance was all but ensured. Any combination of one Trenton victory or one Bowie loss would put Macha's battle-weary club in the postseason.

The Thunder would have to do it without Senior, however, who was unexpectedly promoted to Pawtucket on August 30. "I was looking forward to pitching for Trenton in the playoffs," he admitted. Like the Thunder, the PawSox were in the midst of a tight pennant race. Senior made his first Triple-A start against eventual International League champion Ottawa on September 1, allowing four runs on nine hits in his only Triple-A appearance. Pawtucket lost the game and was eliminated from playoff contention. At a time when he appeared to be turning his season around, Senior was out of Macha and Peterson's playoff pitching equation.

Following an off day, the Thunder bus pulled into Canton on Friday, September 1. For the Trenton franchise, Stark County, Ohio, was a traditional finishing point. The '94 team had arrived with a woeful last-place record, playing out the string. The '95 club arrived at the tail end of a prolonged—and ultimately trying—pennant race. Two different sets of personalities. Two entirely different sets of circumstances. Said Selby before the opening game of the final '95 regular-season series against the Indians, "I know we only need one game to get in the playoffs, but it'd be nice to hit a winning streak, to get hot and stay hot."

Despite those intentions, the Thunder did not come out swinging their bats well in the first game, a 4-2 loss. Orellano scattered three runs on seven hits, but one of them was a two-run, fifth-inning homer by veteran minor league infielder Ed Smith. "I wanted to win the game to clinch a playoff spot," the Thunder pitcher lamented. Ironically, Smith grew up in Pemberton, New Jersey, a small town on the outskirts of Fort Dix that is only a short ride from Waterfront. "Maybe he should send a limo to our hotel to make sure our pitching staff gets to the park on time," Macha quipped about the 240-pound Smith.

Of more urgent concern for the Thunder was a freak injury to Merloni. During the sixth inning, he was hit in the middle of his back—near his spine—by an 0-2 fastball from Indians' starter Rod Steph. Afterward, the area was extremely tender. X-rays were negative, but the Thunder could ill afford to lose their emotional catalyst. During the final homestand, he had received the second annual Fan Favorite award, joining first-season winner Joe Perona. He proudly wore the $1000 watch that was presented to him by Hamilton Jewelers. Throughout the season, Merloni—the 1993 Big East Conference Co-Player of the Year at Providence College—had accommodated Thunder fans with his congenial personality and his hustle on the field. During a mid-season pizza-eating competition sponsored by Domino's, he had wolfed down a large cheese pie while Hardge, his personal "trainer," egged him on from behind. Quite simply, Merloni was the epitome of a minor-league prospect making the most of his ascent up the developmental ladder.

As Merloni iced his back, however, and the Thunder trudged off the field on Friday night, September 1, they didn't know that Bowie had lost to Harrisburg by an identical 4-2 margin. The pressure was off. Trenton had backed into the postseason, but there was no champagne and little celebration. "Now that we're in, maybe the guys will start loosening up," Macha said.

Playoff status assured, the manager's next immediate concern was setting up his playoff pitching rotation. With Fernandez on the staff, he had some flexibility. The knuckleballer could pitch on very little rest. Orellano, on the other hand, was another matter. In 27 starts, he had worked a league-high 186 2/3 innings. Macha was worried that he was running out of gas. Furthermore, he had a history of elbow problems. Did he have one or two more quality starts to give? The Thunder's playoff prospects hinged on that answer. "It's been a long season," Orellano admitted.

On September 2, a cool Saturday afternoon, Blosser smashed a three-run homer to spark a come-from-behind, 9-5 Trenton victory. Nixon enjoyed perhaps his finest game of the '95 season, going 2-for-4 with a double, a triple, and an eighth-inning sacrifice fly. The victory—No. 72—secured the first winning season for a Boston Double-A affiliate since 1990. "This is quite an accomplishment for these guys," Macha said, adding that his "official" playoff rotation would be Fernandez in Game 1, Orellano in Game 2, and Cederblad in Game 3. Reading also had won on Saturday, leaving the Thunder one game behind with two remaining. Clearly, the season was coming down to the final day. "We'll see how good the Thunder front office is at making contingency plans," the manager joked.

Later that evening, Macha and Peterson dined at an Italian restaurant, East Side Mario's. They discussed their team, which seemed to be winning with mirrors at times. "We're not that good," Peterson insisted. The 59 players who had been shuffled through the Trenton clubhouse had a lot to do with that statement. While the coaches ate pasta, Nomar took most of the players to Damons, a local rib establishment. They paid for the meal with kangaroo-court fine money that had been accumulated over the season. During kangaroo court—which often was conducted on the bus—one player (Merloni in '95) served as the judge and doled out minimal fines for offenses "that embarrassed the team." Once, Simonetta was fined a couple of dollars for wearing a tank top into a shopping mall. "His arms were just too pale," commented the judge. Another time, Abad was cited for having his cellular phone ring during a game. As fate would have it, just as Abad's fine was being levied, his phone rang on the bus. Everyone witnessing the scene roared with laughter. Abad simply shrugged and paid an increased fine.

As the final series wound down, McGuire was still very much in the hunt for the league batting crown. Entering the Canton series, he was hitting .343, two points behind Binghamton's Jay Payton, who had been in Triple-A since July 11 but had accrued enough plate appearances to qualify for the batting title. In the first game, the strawberry-blond "Mac" went 1-for-4, dropping his average one point to .342. His dream was still alive. An 0-for-4 effort on Saturday afternoon lowered his average to .338. With each at-bat, it appeared he was losing ground. Macha left him in the lineup, but he was pressing, trying to make things happen. McGuire was well-known for his trademark hustle. When he drew a walk, he always sprinted to first base. At the end of an inning, he sprinted in from his left-field position, often beating the infielders to the dugout. Hodes loved his style of play. "He's my favorite Thunder player of the first three seasons," the General Manager said in late August 1996. On Sunday, September 3—NFL Opening Day, 1995—McGuire went 0-for-5, dropping his average to .333. His quest was over. Macha called him off the field and gave him an appreciative pat on the behind.

Ironically, as McGuire struggled on Sunday afternoon, the Thunder set a franchise single-inning scoring record with a 13-run outburst in the eighth frame of a 16-2 victory. Coupled with Reading's 15-2 loss at Portland, the win meant the clubs were tied with identical 73-68 records and one game remaining. Macha had worn Merloni's No. 7 as a tribute to the injured player, who watched the action from the dugout. The deadlock in the standings was unlikely but exhilarating. Through 141 games, there was nothing to separate the front-runners Reading and Trenton. Trenton and Reading.

Trenton's unprecedented September 3 inning featured two homers by Blosser, who was inserted as a pinch hitter. In the frame, the Thunder sent 16 runners to the plate. McCarthy missed the barrage—he was back in Trenton attending a wedding. Simonetta called the onslaught by himself. The Thunder fireworks began against Canton-Akron reliever John Hrusovsky, who had been nicknamed "The Sad Hungarian" because of his ineffectiveness during the season. By the time Hrusovsky recorded an out, he had been charged with seven earned runs. Blosser and Delgado hit grand slams in the frame. Only two other minor-league teams had exceeded the Thunder's 13-run outburst in one inning during the '95 season—Single-A Kane County (April 18) of the Midwest League and Double-A Wichita (July 30) of the Texas League had both enjoyed 14-run innings.

It all came down to one Labor Day game to decide where the Eastern League

Southern Division playoffs would begin. A Reading win, and the best-of-five series would start at Municipal Stadium. A Thunder win and a Reading loss and it would open at Waterfront. If both clubs lost, it would begin at Municipal because the Phillies owned the head-to-head tiebreaker. The Thunder players, knowing that their road record was superior to their home mark, said it really made no difference. The Portland-Reading game began at noon, meaning it would be over before the Thunder's 3:05 PM start in Canton. Early reports out of Maine confirmed that the Phillies were way behind. They rallied in the late innings before losing 12-10. The Thunder heard the score before fill-in starter and Philadelphia native Chuck Malloy took the mound to face the Indians. The 6-foot-4, 230-pound Malloy—whom one Thunder player dubbed the possessor of "the worst body in professional baseball"—had been promoted from Sarasota just to pitch the regular-season finale. He was taking Senior's place in the rotation. Macha couldn't help but wonder what Senior would have done in the same situation. The Thunder quickly took a 2-0 first-inning lead on solo homers by Selby and Carey, who was giving Nomar one more day off at shortstop. Canton-Akron countered with three runs in the second, two of them unearned, as a Hardge error was critical in the rally. The jockeying continued as the short-handed Thunder tried to claim home-field playoff advantage, but a solo homer by Indians' first baseman Rod McCall off reliever Kurt Bogott in the seventh gave Canton-Akron a 6-5 victory. As a result, the Eastern League Southern Division crown belonged to Reading—and Trenton. Manager Bill Dancy's Phillies found out that they would be heading home for Game 1 at a rest stop on the Maine Turnpike. "We knew we were going in that direction," Dancy said later. "We just didn't know where we were going to end up." The Thunder loss meant that Game 1 would be played on Tuesday, September 5, in scenic Berks County (where the Thunder compiled a 4-5 mark during the regular season). For the Trenton franchise, the postseason was uncharted territory. As his dejected players walked off the field in Canton, Macha said simply, "You guys have had a great season. Don't let this change the way you feel about it. We've still got the playoffs."

In his office, the manager laid the blame for the loss squarely at Hardge's feet (and glove). "That was the division right there," Macha said in summation. Hardge, who had spent the last month begging for playing time ("I'm a winner," he insisted), had blown his opportunity. He would spend Game 1 of the playoffs on the bench, grumbling about his plight.

While Hardge dressed, Merloni expressed confidence that his bruised upper back wouldn't prevent him from taking the field in Reading. "I'm ready to go, but it's up to 'Mock,' " Merloni said.

"We need him," countered the manager. "He's a stabilizing force out there. He's going to play."

CHAPTER 18

On to the Playoffs

"I'm extremely pleased with the development of this team. We sent a ton of guys out of here up to Pawtucket and Boston. Hopefully, these guys have learned a little something."

—THUNDER MANAGER KEN MACHA DURING HIS FINAL PRESS CONFERENCE OF THE '95 SEASON

Starr Bus No. 108 pulled up to Reading's Municipal Stadium just after 4 PM on Tuesday, September 5. Macha held a team meeting in the clubhouse to discuss the events of the weekend, which included several comments from disgruntled Thunder players about the absence of champagne following the playoff-clinching. Instead, the Thunder front office had sent a few cases of beer for the ride from Canton to Reading. After covering that matter, Macha spoke with a rare twinge of parental emotion. Despite all the changes in his roster—64 personnel moves during the regular season alone—he genuinely liked the '95 team. During the September 5 meeting, the rookie skipper "told them I didn't want them to put any extra pressure on themselves. I knew they wanted to be considered winners, and I appreciated all the effort they had given."

Afterward, the Thunder took batting practice beneath a crystalline blue sky in their black mesh batting-practice tops. The Reading players were outfitted in red practice shorts and blue T-shirts rather than their regular batting-practice uniforms. "They look like fags," said Macha. In the background, Philadelphia owner Bill Giles settled into his box seat. Plumeri strolled into the stadium, eager to spread his best wishes. Wearing a dapper brown suit in spite of the sunny, 80-degree temperatures, he stopped to have a photo taken with Giles. "We'd like to honor you in Trenton," Plumeri said. "Maybe in Trenton, but not in Allentown," countered Giles in reference to the Phillies' decision to block that Eastern Pennsylvania municipality's effort to acquire a minor-league franchise. According to National Association rules, major-league clubs had the right to block any minor-league club that wished to move within 75 miles of their home stadium. In 1993, the Phillies allowed Kansas City to move its Single-A club to Wilmington. The next year, Trenton (and Detroit) received the Phils' blessing. As a result, many Wilmington and Trenton fans spent their evenings at Frawley Stadium and Waterfront Park rather than Veterans Stadium. Although Plumeri laughed at Giles' Allentown reference, he understood that he owed a sincere debt of gratitude to the Phils' owner.

Moments before the National Anthem, both teams were introduced, the Thunder along the third-base line and the Phillies along the first-base stripe. A small but enthusiastic crowd of 3038 greeted the first Reading team to qualify for the playoffs since 1989. Moments later, the driver of a fan bus carrying Thunder supporters called to ask for directions to the stadium. He was lost in nearby Morgantown. In the visitors' radio booth, McCarthy and Simonetta prepared to call their first-ever playoff game. It was game No. 283 of their broadcast career together.

Following Monday afternoon's loss at Canton, Macha had solicited lineup suggestions from his staff and the reporters who covered the team. In Game 1, the Thunder would face Phillies' righty Larry Mitchell, who was 4-0 with a 0.80 ERA in five 1995 appearances against Trenton. Mysteriously, Mitchell had a gaudy 7.23 ERA against the other nine Eastern League teams not wearing the insignia "THUNDER" on their jerseys. "His number is going to be up sooner or later," Merloni predicted, and after considerable deliberation, Macha decided on an offense that included:

Garciaparra (ss)
Selby (2b)
McGuire LF (lf)
Delgado (c)
Blosser (rf)
Merloni (3b)
Carey (1b)
Dana Levangie (c)
Nixon (cf)

Delgado was the biggest surprise—but a strong right-handed batter—and Merloni would play with sore back and all.

For 4 2/3 innings—until Merloni singled to center—it appeared that Mitchell might equal Bill Pulsipher's 1994 feat and throw a rare postseason no-hitter. In the first four frames, the Thunder batters were unable to work the count more than four pitches into any at-bat. "No patience," Macha grumbled from the third-base coaching box. After Fernandez struck out three of the first six Phillies, Reading edged ahead 2-0 in the bottom of the third on an RBI fielder's choice by right-fielder Wendell Magee and a sacrifice fly by shortstop Kevin Sefcik. The Phillies also added two runs in the bottom of the sixth. Selby led off the seventh with a display of long-awaited discipline, drawing a walk. McGuire followed with a single that spelled the end for Mitchell. Dancy removed him after just 76 pitches, opting for lefty Robert Dodd, who had spent most of the '95 season at Single-A Clearwater. As Giles looked on from the third row, Dodd served up an RBI single to Delgado that scored Selby and allowed Trenton to charge a run to Mitchell's line for the first time since August 3. The Reading reliever buckled down to strike out Blosser and retire Merloni on a fly ball to center for the second out, but a walk to pinch hitter Shelton scored McGuire.

With the deficit pared in half at 4-2—and the bases loaded—Nixon came to the plate with a major opportunity to draw his team even. A single likely would have tied the game. Dodd quickly worked the count to 1-2 before retiring the Thunder outfielder on a called strike three. There were loud groans from the small but vocal Thunder contingent, which had finally arrived at the stadium during the early innings. "That was a poor at-bat," Macha observed later, "but you can't fault him entirely. Here's a kid fresh out of A-ball."

"I lost the game right there," Nixon said in a burst of self-flagellation. "I should have hit that ball. I faced that guy before in A-ball and hit him. I guess it's a quick trip from the penthouse to the outhouse."

The Phillies padded the lead in the top of the eighth as second baseman David Doster led off with a double and scored on a wild pitch by Thunder reliever Mike Blais. During the regular season, the 24-year-old Doster led the league with 63 extra-base hits, including 39 doubles and 21 homers. He also committed just 12 errors in 139 games, but he was left off the official Rawlings Eastern League All-Star team, an omission that shocked Macha because he had voted for Doster as the league MVP. "I love his approach to the game," the Thunder manager said. "He plays hard all the time, and he has some pop in his bat."

Trailing 5-2, the Thunder frustration reached a boiling point in the eighth inning. After an infield pop out, Selby stormed into the dugout and began smashing the bat rack with his Louisville Slugger. Throughout the season, Macha had sought to temper the rage that boiled within his hard-hitting infielder, but the pressure of a do-or-die playoff situation had summoned the monster within the stocky Mississippi native once again. As his player seethed, Macha turned a disgusted eye to the tirade. It wasn't his idea of postseason leadership. "I told him if he did that again, he was out of the lineup; I didn't care," Macha said. "I think he has the potential to be a big-league hitter. Not if he acts that way, though. He's got to learn to get control of his emotions."

Reading closer Blake Doolan ended the game with a double-play ball to Merloni and a hard liner by Shelton that Sefcik gloved for the final out of a 5-2 Reading win. Delgado, who produced two of Trenton's six hits, had been stranded on third in the final frame. After the obligatory 10-minute cooling-off period, the cozy visitor's clubhouse was opened for interviews. There were the blank stares from losing players with thin white towels hugging their waists. Macha welcomed the usual interrogative contingent of five reporters into his cramped office. "There's no pressure on us," he insisted. "If you go out there with pressure, you can't play. We have to relax. What are we playing for here, a ring? Pressure is when you get to the big leagues, playing for the World Series, for 150,000 bucks. This should be fun."

As for Mitchell, everyone in the hushed Thunder clubhouse knew they had wasted a critical opportunity to break the Reading pitcher's spell over them. "At the beginning of the game, our approach to him was not good," Macha critiqued. "We were chasing a lot of balls in the dirt. Our approach improved, but he's 2-11 against the rest of the league, so maybe the rest of the league is more patient against him."

Added Delgado, "I think he thinks he's Cy Young against us."

Down the corridor in the considerably louder Reading clubhouse, "Cy Young" was fielding another round of questions about his mastery of Trenton.

"I can't answer it," he said with an impish facial gesture, as if to imply the whole thing was a dark secret. "The only explanation that I can come up with is that those guys are a free-swinging team. I lay the breaking ball on the ground, and they're a straight fastball hitting team. But there's always this little thing in the back of my mind, 'I've done it to them so many times before, maybe they might do it to me.'"

With Game 1 in Reading's column, the Phillies' nightly ritual of beer and cards at the Municipal Stadium RBI (Runs Batted "Inn") Room was just shifting into gear. While Reading was taking the playoff opener, 35-year-old Baltimore Orioles' shortstop Cal Ripken, Jr., was tying the Major League Baseball consecutive-games-played record of 2130 established by New York Yankees' first baseman Lou Gehrig between 1925 and 1939. The festivities from Oriole Park at Camden Yards were broadcast live on two televisions placed at opposite sides of the RBI Room. Dancy accepted the well-wishes of Reading staff members; during the season, he had won his 1200th game as a minor-league manager. As he weaved in and out of conversations, he looked quite comfortable about his team's chances of winning Reading's first Eastern League championship since 1973.

Hodes and Mahoney also stopped by the RBI Room for a few cold Yuenglings. They seemed pleasantly surprised to see the Thunder qualify for the playoffs in just their second year. "I didn't think we'd contend for the title until the third season," Hodes said. While Hodes sat at the bar, Phillies' pitching coach Larry Andersen (the same Andersen who started against the Thunder in Wilmington during the transplanted home opener on April 17, 1994) entertained an audience on the other side of the room. Generally acknowledged as one of baseball's premier pranksters during a major-league career that spanned almost two decades, Andersen brought his comedy routine to the Eastern League on a full-time basis in 1995. In early May, he had tripped the sprinkler system at Waterfront and caused an unscheduled natural disaster during one of Nipper's visits to the mound. At the time, Andersen denied involvement, but he proudly fessed up to the deed in the cozy environs of the RBI Room. "It wasn't that hard to get into," he said of the Waterfront sprinkler control box. "Just turn a few knobs like this," he added with a few hand gestures. The next time Reading played at Waterfront, the sprinkler box was locked.

Later in the season, Andersen pulled one of the all-time minor-league tricks on one of his star pitchers, righty Wayne Gomes. As television cameras chronicled the entire ruse, Andersen told Gomes that he had been traded to Japan. Buying into the story, Gomes called his mother, packed up all of his belongings, and even began to cry. To seal the authenticity of the caper, Andersen had an impostor imitate a Japanese television reporter by asking the pitcher if he liked sushi. "I don't want no fucking sushi," he replied. Gomes went so far as to return his spikes to Reading trainer Brent Leiby before Andersen finally called off the fun and let the bewildered pitcher in on the secret.

While the RBI Room keg slowly disappeared into the night, Macha enjoyed a late-night supper with Rick Peterson and Steve Braun at T.G.I. Friday's. The No. 1 topic of conversation was Selby's temper. Macha contemplated removing him from the Game 2 line-up, but after discussing the matter with his colleagues, he decided what the player needed was further exposure to the pressure that was affecting him. Selby would play after all. Before Game 2, manager and player would discuss the situation further, however.

GAME TWO

Wednesday, September 6 was a cloudless carbon copy of the previous week in Canton and Reading, with the mercury poking its head even higher on the thermometer. The Thunder conducted a crisp, upbeat batting practice. "Whoever wins this game is going to win the series," Bennett predicted behind the batting cage. The pitching match-up featured Orellano against 20-year-old Reading righty Rich Hunter. At three levels during the '95 season, Hunter was 19-2. Orellano, as Peterson pointed out, "was out of gas." During batting practice, Schofield escorted David Doster down the third-base line to snap a picture with Nomar that easily could have been captioned, "Eastern League Dream Double Play Combination." As team photographer for both Trenton and Reading, Schofield was the brunt of several jokes. Observers called the series "The Schofield Cup." Said others, "Regardless of who wins, he will be drinking somewhere after the last game."

A crowd of 2889 had barely settled into its seats when Nomar deposited the first pitch of the game—a fastball—386 feet over the left-field wall for a 1-0 Thunder lead. Clearly, he didn't intend for the Thunder to bow out of the series without a fight. Doster responded in the bottom half of the inning with a 404-foot solo homer off Orellano, who bowed his head and searched his soul for one more strong outing.

The Thunder countered with four runs in the second as two Reading errors opened the door for a 5-1 advantage. Merloni, Nixon, new outfielder J.J. Johnson, and Nomar each scored in this inning, Johnson after reaching base on a fielding miscue by Phillies third-base phenom Scott Rolen. In most instances, a four-run lead would have been enough for Orellano, but the cushion quickly evaporated. Phils' first baseman Tommy Eason smoked a one-out homer in the second to cut the margin to 5-2. After escaping the inning, Orellano disappeared into the clubhouse for a brief motivational chat with Peterson. Nothing worked, and the lefty was pulled after three-plus innings, by far his shortest outing of the year. He left behind a 5-4 lead for Ciccarella, who held the Phillies scoreless for three innings. "That was a bad day," Orellano said later. "I can throw better than that." The look on his face told otherwise. Clearly, he was tired following 5 months of consistent excellence against Double-A hitters.

With Trenton leading 6-4 in the seventh, Ciccarella gave way to righty Todd Ingram in the seventh. Ingram inherited one runner—Doster—whom he allowed to score to make it a one-run game at 6-5. Sefcik's RBI single in the eighth knotted the score at six. Acquitting himself quite nicely while making Macha look like a genius for leaving him in the lineup, Selby opened the top of the ninth with a double to right field off Blake Doolan. Hardge replaced Selby as a pinch runner, and McGuire walked on four pitches, bringing Delgado to the plate with runners on first and second. The catcher's first sacrifice bunt attempt caromed off the plate into foul territory. His second effort looped off the

bat into foul territory on the right side—but high into the air—where first baseman Dan Held gloved it for the critical first out. There was a collective groan in
the Thunder dugout. Shelton, pinch hitting for Blosser, grounded Doolan's
fourth delivery to Rolen, who flipped to Doster for the apparent force-out. The
usually sure-handed Doster dropped the ball, however, as McGuire slid into the
bag. At the same time that Doster lost his grip, second-base umpire Hunter
Wendelstedt mistakenly thumbed McGuire out. Macha went ballistic almost instantaneously, sprinting across the infield to protest the obvious miscall.

According to Merloni and McGuire, Doster later admitted it was the worst
call he had ever seen. Rolen even commented on the "brutal" call as Hardge
chugged into third base. Macha hammered away at Wendelstedt for a few moments as McGuire shook his head in disbelief and gestured toward second. The
umpire wasn't about to toss the Trenton manager from the game at such a critical juncture, but he wasn't going to change the pivotal call, either. Instead of
having the bases loaded with one out, the Thunder had first and third with two
away. Macha pointed to the scoreboard in protest before finally walking back to
the third-base coaching box. Throughout the 1996 season, he would refer to
the play as "the night Wendelstedt stuck it up our ass." Merloni, the next batter,
chased an outside slider with a 3-2 count for the final out of the inning, but in
spite of Wendelstedt's mistake, the real theatrics were soon to follow.

Facing Sullivan to lead off the bottom of the ninth, Reading left fielder Rob
Grable took a ball on the first pitch. On the second delivery, a fastball, Grable
unloaded for a game-winning solo homer that tailed away from Nixon and
over the center-field fence. The homer was the sixth of the game, but the first to
exit the park anywhere other than left field. Grable was mobbed by his teammates as he touched the plate with the winning run. The swing game belonged
to Reading. The Thunder fan contingent, on hand for the second consecutive
night, fell silent and hurriedly descended to the exits. Sullivan stalked off the
mound in a fury, and downturned heads in gray uniforms told Trenton's story.
The Phillies' jubilance stood in marked contrast. "I really wasn't trying to hit a
homer there," Grable explained in the euphoria of the Phillies' clubhouse.
Could the Thunder rebound from such a swift, devastating defeat? Not likely,
according to the parties involved. "Yeah, their backs are against the wall,"
Grable said solemnly.

Inside the Thunder clubhouse, Sullivan karate-kicked the wooden partition
on the outside of his locker. During the '94 season, he had pitched 11 games for
Reading, compiling an 0-1 record and a 5.14 ERA. He had subsequently been
traded to Boston as part of a four-player deal. Now, in the Thunder's most important game of the season, he had been victimized by his former team. The
foot-wide crater now in the visitor's clubhouse was testimony to his considerable frustration. Macha had to help the enraged pitcher remove his foot from
the hole. Nearby, Delgado cursed aloud in both Spanish and English, lament-
ing his failed bunt attempt to anyone who cared to listen. Merloni stood forlornly by the toilet stalls. "It's going to be real tough to come back," he said,
"but I don't know anybody on this team who's going to lay down. That's not
the way we are."

Inside his office, Macha struggled to explain his team's third consecutive loss in a pressure situation. He commented that the small crowd "had received its money's worth," and he explained his approach to the Thunder's 2-0 deficit. "It's not like it's the fourth quarter and we're down 28-0 and we're just going to run the clock out. We've got nothing to lose. If we come back, it's a great comeback."

Down the corridor, Reading's confidence level was thick and tangible. Said Eason, "This club showed me all the guts in the world tonight." He admitted the win was even more gratifying because the winning homer came against Sullivan. "We've hit him hard every time since his trade," he added.

As the Thunder players trundled into the bus for the short ride back to Waterfront, there was every reason to think they were a beaten team—both physically and emotionally. Dancy and Andersen dressed and made another appearance in the RBI Room to watch another night of Ripken ceremonies from Camden Yards. The Reading manager wanted to finish the best-of-five series the next night in Trenton.

GAME THREE

During the early afternoon hours of Thursday, September 7, the Trenton players began arriving at Waterfront in familiar clumps of two and three. Hardge and Shelton. Merloni and Garciaparra. McGuire and Selby. Bennett and Cederblad. Each group knew that this could be their last evening together during the '95 season. Macha relaxed in his office, discussing all of the post-season paperwork that remained. He had to file written evaluations of every player in the league for Duquette and Schaefer. He talked about Nomar's future and about the talent level of the Reading team. "Speed, defense, power; they've got it," he praised. In some ways, it sounded like a concession speech before the fact.

Plumeri strolled into the office dressed to the hilt in a black suit and tie. "Sam is so gracious to come in whether we win or lose," Macha offered in a genuine burst of admiration for the 81-year-old owner. "Last night, after the toughest loss of the season, he gave me a pat on the back. Not only that, but I've gotta make sure I have a cup on tonight because he's throwing out the first pitch." Everyone in the room broke into laughter.

During batting practice, a pair of female fans presented Macha with a large bag of 5-cent bubble gum tethered to a silver mylar "THUNDER" balloon. The bag was placed atop the bat rack in the home dugout for everyone to share. The manager conducted several television interviews as Comcast cable crews readied for the first-ever Waterfront playoff broadcast. Orellano played table tennis in the weight room across the hall from the clubhouse. Cederblad relaxed at his locker, pondering his ability to throw a third-straight complete-game victory. The season depended on it.

After Plumeri threw out the ceremonial first pitch—a ball low and outside—the game started ominously for the Thunder as Doster's RBI double scored Wendell Magee and a pair of errors (on Selby and Merloni) led to an RBI single by Tommy Eason. The first half-inning ended with the Phillies on top 2-0 and a crowd of 5349 wondering what Trenton could do to slow the Reading express.

Nomar led off the Thunder first against lefty Matt Beech with a double and scored on a McGuire single. The Thunder tied it at 2-2 on a walk to Hardge that plated Selby. Johnson, however, grounded out with the bases loaded to end what could have been a breakthrough inning.

Taking charge against Cederblad, the Phillies scored a run in the top of the second and added two apiece in the third and fourth as Fred McNair and Doster each slammed two-run homers to left. Cederblad lasted just four innings, having allowed seven runs on six hits. His curveball had failed him at a most inopportune time. The final score was 12-5, with Reading advancing to the best-of-five Eastern League Championship Series against New Haven, which had defeated Portland in four games in the Northern Division playoff series. While the Phillies exchanged high fives on the field, Macha enjoyed one last stroll across the diamond. He doffed his green cap several times for the crowd, which stood and applauded. Nomar and Merloni embraced and presented Schofield with an autographed bat. "We want you to have this for all you've done for us this season," Nomar said. There was no remorse on his face. The Thunder had been beaten by a surging team, one that was playing its best baseball of the season. In the deciding Game 3, the Phillies hit four homers and three doubles. In the last two games, they had sent eight balls over the fence.

In the Trenton clubhouse, Merloni lit up a cigar and leaned back on his stool. Around him, belongings were hastily packed in red-and-blue Boston equipment bags. Through the concrete walls of the training room, the whoops and hollers of the Reading celebration were audible. Cederblad sat at his stall with a can of orange soda cradled in his long, thin fingers. Blosser dressed as his blond toddler son played in the corner—and he left without paying his clubhouse dues, one final slap at the Boston organization that had given up on him. He signed with Baltimore during the off-season.

Down the hall, in the very room where Runnells' '94 Thunder team had dressed and suffered almost daily, Dancy stood and addressed his Southern Division champions. At roughly the same spot 15 months earlier, Runnells had played sock ball with Clark and Mashore. "You guys are halfway there," Dancy shouted above the din as he shook a champagne bottle back and forth, readying it for his contribution to the postgame party. "I want you to enjoy this. This is for you." And spraying the room with a circular twist, he laughed gleefully as the Reading players flesh-piled each other. Sefcik, who would be summoned to the big-league club the following day, conducted an interview at his locker. Doster—the clear series MVP—joined in the mayhem. One of the Reading relievers picked up a jar of peanut butter and began tossing it in clumps. On the perimeter of the celebration, Schofield snapped pictures. Upstairs in the Thunder luxury box, Philadelphia General Manager Lee Thomas was toasted by Thunder officials. Moments later, he headed to the ground level to congratulate Dancy and his players.

After completing his speech, the champagne-soaked Dancy wiped his eyes and walked down the short corridor to speak to Macha. Knocking on the office door, he extended his hand to the Thunder skipper, saying simply, "You take care. You did a hell of a job this season."

Macha replied, "You, too."

As he prepared for his final office shower of the year, however, Macha had something other than baseball to ponder. "I'm thinking about driving home tonight. I told Sam [Plumeri] I need to get laid."

Goodbyes completed, that's exactly what he did.

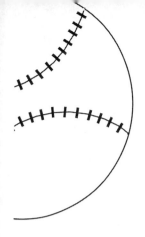

CHAPTER 19

Streaking Into 1996

"This is obviously a team the fans love very much. These people have all been very nice, and I just can't wait to see what it's all about here in Trenton. I'm just dying to know what it feels like to pitch in front of 6000 people all screaming for you."

—THUNDER PITCHER BRIAN ROSE AT THE 1996 "WELCOME NORTH DINNER"

While pondering his team's playoff loss, Thunder manager Ken Macha headed to Arizona for 2 1/2 weeks to serve as interim manager of the Arizona Fall League's (AFL) Phoenix Firebirds. Thunder players on the Phoenix roster included Lou Merloni and Trot Nixon as well as former pitchers Scott Bakkum and Brent Hansen. Macha filled in while Boston first-base coach Frank White completed his major-league duties (the Red Sox were swept by eventual American League Champion Cleveland in the best-of-five AL Divisional Playoffs). By mid-October, Macha returned home to Export, eager to learn what his 1996 assignment would be. After leading the Thunder to a 73-69 record and a first-place Eastern League Southern Division tie with Reading, he was hoping for at least a shot at managing Triple-A Pawtucket. Like his players, he was ready to move up the ladder; however, Schaefer and the Red Sox had other ideas. They wanted him to return to Trenton specifically to shepherd the development of four of their top prospects—pitchers Brian Rose and Carl Pavano, outfielder Nixon, and shortstop Donnie Sadler. "We're very happy with the job Kenny's done, but we feel like he's most valuable to the organization at the Double-A level—in Trenton," Schaefer said in late October. Macha sent out several résumés to other teams, and he was briefly considered for the Phillies' Triple-A job that eventually went to former Boston manager Butch Hobson (who, ironically, was forced to resign during the '96 season when he was arrested for cocaine possession in a Rhode Island motel).

Gradually accepting that he would spend another season in the Eastern League, Macha settled in for the long winter. He coached sandlot basketball. He shoveled snow. He completed projects around the house. He spent treasured time with his wife, Carolyn Virginia, and his two children, Eric and Kristin. His disappointment had very little to do with the Thunder franchise, which had proven that it could fill Waterfront Park on a nightly basis, creating a big-league atmosphere for the players. For Macha the pragmatist, another year in Double-A meant another salary in the $40,000 range—or approximately half what he had earned as third-base coach for California during the '94 season. Although he had already qualified for his major-league pension, he was dealing with economic reality. If he returned to Trenton, he wanted a living allowance to help defray the cost of his Bensalem, Pennsylvania, apartment. He also wanted a raise, but his plea to Schaefer was only marginally successful. "They gave me a little bit, but I'm not getting rich doing this," he said.

With Macha in place for a second tour of duty, Boston's next order of business was assigning Trenton's hitting and pitching coaches. The name Harold "Gomer" Hodge quickly surfaced for the hitting position. The 51-year-old Hodge was a career minor-league coach who spent the '95 season with the Montreal organization at Single-A West Palm Beach and Triple-A Ottawa. Although Ottawa won the International League title, Macha had serious concerns about North Carolina native Hodge, whom he later called "the laziest man in baseball" on several occasions during the '96 campaign. After laboring through most of the '95 season without a full-time hitting coach, Macha's arm was fatigued from the extra batting practice he had been forced to throw. He needed Hodge to pick up some of the slack, and he was worried that Hodge would break down during a 142-game journey. Nonetheless, Hodge was awarded the hitting coach job in late November.

Soon thereafter, the Red Sox hired the 40-year-old Ralph Treuel as Macha's pitching coach. No stranger to Waterfront Park, he had been Detroit's roving pitching instructor during the '94 season. During the '95 season, he had been the Tigers' big-league pitching coach, serving alongside manager Sparky Anderson during his final season in Motown. For 12 years, Treuel had dedicated his services to the Detroit organization. Suddenly, he was part of Boston's plans. Adapting to a new organization—and the sheer volume of deciphering a team's worth of new personalities—would take him a few months. "There weren't a lot of jobs out there," Treuel said of his difficult job search after Detroit officials told him his contract would not be renewed. "I feel very lucky to have this opportunity." Furthermore, during his first 1996 visit to Trenton, Treuel was pleasantly surprised to see the many improvements at Waterfront since the inaugural season. In addition, he and Hodge took up residence in the Chambersburg section of town, a short 5-minute drive from the stadium. Their rented home—which was owned by Trenton lawyer Buck LaFerrara—soon became known affectionately as the "Hodge Lodge." (One evening, Treuel heard the sounds of Frank Sinatra being played on the loudspeaker at the adjacent Chambersburg Little League complex. "It was so beautiful I had to come out on the porch and listen," he recalled.)

While Macha was disheartened by his '96 Trenton assignment, Thunder management and fans were elated about his return. McCarthy was particularly pleased. The manager's presence in the dugout for the second consecutive season would provide continuity for everyone involved with the franchise. There would be no feeling-out period during the spring of '96. In Macha, the Thunder knew that they had an unflappable leader. His fairness and analytic approach ensured that the 1996 team would be a solid product. "I don't think I was bummed out about coming back too much," Macha said. "I was looking more at starting the season over at page one, starting over fundamentally with a new group of guys."

A FAVORITE SON RETURNS

At 1:30 PM on Saturday, December 16, 1995, Tony Clark stepped out of a white van in front of Waterfront Park. Resplendent in dark slacks, cream sweater, and a large gold necklace with the Detroit Tigers' trademark "D" cursive logo, he walked toward the South Trenton stadium for the first time since he had been promoted to Triple-A Toledo on August 8, 1994. Viewing the facility's handsome brick facade, he smiled nostalgically. He had rearranged his entire holiday schedule to attend the Thunder's second-annual "Winterfest" as a guest of the franchise. He returned to Trenton as a big leaguer—a Trenton-bred big leaguer.

After playing the entire '95 season with Toledo, Clark was called to Detroit in early September when the active major-league rosters expanded from 25 to 40 players. In 27 games for manager Sparky Anderson's Tigers, he hit .238, with five doubles, three homers, and 11 RBIs. He doubled in his first major-league game—against Cleveland. One of the homers took place at Yankee Stadium on a hanging slider from New York reliever Steve Howe. Ironically, Clark remembered facing Howe during the left-hander's May 18, 1994, Waterfront rehab appearance. "I knew that he liked to work me inside," the former Thunder slugger recalled. "I was waiting for it."

Big Tony exhibited an unmistakable air of confidence as he returned to Trenton for the Winterfest. Just as he had during his Thunder days, he tirelessly signed autographs and shared baseball stories with those who had packed Waterfront during the '94 season to watch him blossom as a professional baseball player. Many of the Trenton admirers offered congratulations on his daughter, Kiara Maree, who was born during the fall of '94. "They came bearing gifts, too," Lipsman said. "It was really incredible."

"When people respect you and your ability enough to make a sacrifice out of their day to come say, 'Hi,' you can't put a price tag on that," Clark said. "The least I could do was come out for the weekend just to say, 'Thanks.' I won't forget Trenton because of the people that were here. That's the easiest way to put it."

Also during December 1995 at the Major League Baseball Winter Meetings in Los Angeles, Hodes was honored as the 1995 Eastern League Executive of the Year. The award was the culmination of a 2-year effort that had produced phenomenal results. By that time, preparations for the 1996 Double-A All-Star Game, July 8 at Waterfront Park, were well underway. On Tuesday, November 21, 1995, the Thunder unveiled the All-Star logo, a four-color circular design that featured Waterfront's red brick facade, the Thunder logo, and the words "All-Star Game" in blue-and-yellow script. Knowing that the All-Star effort would be a monumental task, Hodes decided to hire eight new staff interns for the '96 season.

In mid-December, 1 day before Clark's Trenton reunion, Macha made the first of two off-season Trenton public appearances, signing autographs in the

Waterfront Dugout Shop with Joe Hudson, Shawn Senior and Todd Carey. Outside the store's large, picture-frame window, snow flakes formed a scenic backdrop along the Delaware. By late February, the manager was back for the Winter Warm-up Dinner, which was held for the second consecutive year at the Hyatt Regency Princeton. A nostalgic crowd of 400 paid $30 each to dine with the manager, AL President Gene Budig, former Cleveland Indian Larry Doby, and the guest of honor—Jeff Suppan. The 21-year-old "Soup" was flown in from Fort Myers (where he was preparing for spring training) to deliver a speech about his '95 big-league experience. After the dinner, as Macha sped home in his pick-up, Soup treated Carey, Merloni, and Blais to several rounds of beer at T.G.I. Friday's. He proudly paid the tab with his brand-new American Express Card. The next morning, he departed for an autograph show in New England.

The off-season produced the usual complement of trades and player moves. On January 10, 1996, McGuire and Bennett were part of a four-player deal that sent them to Montreal along with left-handed pitcher Rheal Cormier. In exchange, the Red Sox received Expos' infielder Wil Cordero and lefty Bryan Eversgerd. While McGuire expressed surprise about the deal, Schaefer was particularly upset to part with the charismatic former UCLA star. "I spent a lot of time with him, and he's a great kid," the Red Sox coordinator said.

Also during the winter, the Thunder announced concrete plans for All-Star Week. As expected, on July 5, the U.S. Olympic team was scheduled make a Waterfront appearance against Korea as part of the NationsBank Tour. In addition, the stadium would be used for a July 3 business exposition, a July 4 fireworks show and concert, and a 2-day "ThunderFest" on July 6-7. According to Lipsman, the ThunderFest marked "the first time anyone on the minor-league level has attempted a 2-day event" designed to let patrons experience everything from live pitching and hitting on the Waterfront field to a simulated radio broadcast. A committee of local business leaders was established to brainstorm All-Star ideas, and five presenting corporate sponsors were lined up to bankroll much of the event's publicity. That corporate nucleus included Trenton's Helene Fuld Medical Center, Budweiser, CoreStates, AmeriHealth, and Comcast-Metrophone. The entire All-Star effort was coordinated by Mahoney, who was asked to pull all of the organizational aspects together into one smooth, well-run plan. Hodes wanted to make sure that the many visitors to Trenton and Waterfront Park enjoyed an unforgettable experience.

STARTING OVER

By early March, Macha and his prospects reported to Fort Myers, eager to prepare for the '96 season. The manager checked into his room at the major league hotel, the Sheraton Harbor Place, which is situated 4 miles from the Boston minor-league complex. As uncharacteristically strong winds whipped across the playing fields, Macha and Schaefer began the task of molding the '96 Thunder roster. From the outset, it was obvious the team would have more speed than its '95 predecessor. Sadler—Boston's No. 1 prospect according to *Baseball America*—had been clocked running from home to first in 3.75 seconds by a major league scout. (The scout noted that an average major leaguer runs that distance from the right side of the plate in approximately 4.1 seconds.) In 1995 at Single-A Michigan, Sadler hit .283 with 41 steals. He also led the Midwest League with 103 runs scored in 118 games. Macha also was assigned center fielder Rick Holifield, who hit .247 for Reading in 1995. The 26-year-old Holifield, who was acquired by the Red Sox in an off-season trade with Philadelphia that sent closer Heathcliff Slocumb to Boston, had stolen 143 bases in eight minor-league seasons. His range as an outfielder was another extremely valuable asset. In fact, his sprinting catch of a Garciaparra fly ball in the eighth inning of Game 2 of the '95 Southern Division Playoffs against the Thunder had been a thing of beauty. Said Hodge, "That's the kind of guy who'll come to the park and help win you the championship."

A second Thunder season as a Boston affiliate meant that certain players would return to the New Jersey capital for an encore. Relationships fostered during the '95 campaign would be resumed. Among those penciled onto Macha's roster for a second tour were Nixon, Carey, McKeel, Blais, Cederblad, Senior, Fernandez, and possibly, Merloni. The '95 Fan Favorite, Merloni tried everything he could during spring training to fight his way onto the Pawtucket roster. During exhibition play, he hit over .600 with much-improved power. His 1995 AFL stint had paid off. On one memorable morning, he homered off Boston ace Roger Clemens, who was making a rare appearance at the minor-league complex. The ball was retrieved by Nixon's high-school baseball coach. In 93 Double-A games during the '95 season, Merloni had homered just once. After taking Clemens' two-seam fastball offering over the fence in front of Boston Red Sox General Manager Dan Duquette, Kevin Kennedy and Al Nipper, the Thunder infielder quipped, "I wanted to keep running right into Schaefer's office to renegotiate my contract. It was pretty awesome."

Spring heroics aside, Merloni was caught in a numbers crunch. Like Macha, the second-year manager who wanted to be in Triple-A, or even the majors, he was forced to accept his Trenton assignment. "Louie knows we'll get him up to Triple-A as soon as we can," Schaefer said. "I'd rather have him playing every day in Double-A."

By the end of spring training, it was apparent that the Thunder's five-man pitching rotation would include three 20-year-olds—righties Brian Rose and Carl Pavano and lefty Brian Barkley. The other two starters would be holdovers Senior and Fernandez. "You're gonna have a hell of a pitching staff in Trenton," Schaefer promised. "I'll take my chances with those guys." All three youngsters had been selected in the June 1994 draft—Rose in the third round, Barkley in the fifth, and Pavano in the thirteenth. All three had turned down college scholarships to sign with Boston—Rose from the University of Michigan, Barkley from the University of Texas, and Pavano from Louisiana State University. All three prospects were indicative of the aggressive approach the Red Sox scouting department had taken under Duquette. Rose received a $365,000 bonus to forego college, and Pavano was paid $175,000. Furthermore, both righties were New England natives—Rose from South Dartmouth, Massachusetts; and Pavano from Southington, Connecticut. In fact, Rose had been to opening day at Fenway Park on many occasions with his father, Lenny. During spring training, both Rose and Pavano were invited to speak at a meeting of the BoSox club, the Red Sox fan club. Everyone associated with Boston wanted to see them succeed because they were homegrown prospects. In 1995 at Single-A Michigan, Rose was 8-5 with a 3.44 ERA and 105 strikeouts in 136 innings. Also with Michigan, Pavano was 6-6 with a 3.44 ERA and 138 strikeouts in 141 1/3 innings. At Single-A Sarasota in 1995, Barkley was 8-10 with a 3.25 ERA. During spring training, Macha and Treuel enjoyed their first glimpse of all three pitchers. The manager asked around the organization, inviting their former coaches to assess their abilities. He was particularly curious about Rose and Pavano. Who was more developed at the age of 20? "Some say Rose; some say Pavano," the manager reported, and he was anxious to find out for himself.

In Pavano, the Red Sox had found a true diamond in the rough. At times, the 6-foot-5, 230-pounder seemed like a happy-go-lucky kid. Said one '96 season Thunder player, "Thank God he can pitch every fifth day, because if he couldn't, he'd be dangerous to society. But every fifth day, he's a genius." During spring training, Pavano talked about meeting women and all of the other things any college sophomore might enjoy. He charted pitches during exhibition games, spitting tobacco and cracking jokes. In high school, he had been a self-admitted hothead who dominated opponents with sheer overpowering stuff while leading his team to the 1993 Connecticut state championship. "I used to lose my cool a lot," he said. "If I threw a strike and the umpire didn't call it, I didn't care. If he wanted a 3-hour game, I'd give it to him." While several organizations lost interest in him because he was overweight and had a few bad outings during his senior season at Southington High, Boston recognized his raw potential. He was signed by Buzz Bowers and Ray Fagnant on June 30, 1994. With a huge frame and enormous, webbed hands, his upside potential far outweighed any perceived drawbacks. As the '96 season unfolded, it was amazing to watch his growth—both as a pitcher and as a person. As a way of focusing his development, Treuel limited his repertoire to three pitches—a 92- to 95-mph fastball, a change-up and a slider. In high school, Pavano also had thrown a curveball, but Treuel wanted him to concentrate on the slider as his Double-A breaking ball. Said Treuel, "Right now, Carl is more of a thrower than a pitcher. He's still learning his craft."

Rose, on the other hand, was a fierce competitor who generally was regarded as a more polished pitcher than Pavano at the outset of the '96 season. He had four pitches—a fastball, a curve, a change-up, and a slider. From a facial standpoint, the 6-foot-3, 215-pound Rose looked older than the baby-faced Pavano. Pavano commented several times that his Trenton headshot made him "look like Elvis." Together, they would complement each other extremely well. In many ways, theirs was a rivalry that was good for both individuals. Said Rose, "Baseball's my life, and I want to get to the big leagues as fast as I possibly can. Hopefully, I can put a lot of zeros on the scoreboard and take this thing step-by-step."

With three 20-year-old starters instead of one (Suppan in 1995), Macha knew that he would need some veteran bullpen help to provide a buffer if the youngsters faltered. During final roster cutdowns, he pleaded with Schaefer and Duquette for that support. As a result, returnees Cederblad and Blais were surrounded by righties Brent Knackert and Erik Schullstrom and lefties Bryan

Eversgerd and Ken Grundt. All four were at least 26 years old and had extensive Double-A experience. As Schaefer told each pitcher that he would be starting the season in Trenton, Macha had serious concerns that at least one of them would refuse the assignment. Knackert, who had pitched for Seattle in the major leagues way back in 1990, was foremost on that list. His look of disgust after talking to Schaefer was followed by a night of soul-searching, but after a great deal of thought, he decided to play for Macha and Treuel. One by one, the others agreed to don the funny Thunderbird logo. At least for a while. On arriving in Trenton, they would nickname themselves "the Grumpy Old Men." Together, their clubhouse pranks would provide a backdrop of comedy for the first month of the '96 season.

With the bullpen in place, Macha's other primary concern was where his team would find home-run power. Carey and Merloni both cleared the fences several times during spring training, but the Thunder roster that Boston sent north in April 1996 was devoid of any raw sluggers like Tony Clark and Pork Chop Pough. Trenton acquired free-agent, left-handed outfielder Kevin Coughlin at the last minute, but although Coughlin led the Southern League with a .385 batting average in 1995 as a Birmingham Baron, he had hit only six homers during his 7-year minor-league career. Outfielder Dan Collier was a 6-foot-3, 230-pound man nicknamed "Conan," but the 25-year-old Collier's career was checkered by a strikeout-to-at-bat ratio of almost 40 percent—much too high, Macha felt. As a result, it appeared the Thunder would have to rely on speed and pitching to carry the early part of the season.

During a late March intrasquad game, however, a new player arrived in the Thunder dugout. Wearing the red spikes of the Cincinnati Reds organization, he was unable to introduce himself formally before Macha sent him into the action. "Hi, I'm Adam Hyz . . ." the newcomer stammered.

"Get out there. You're in left field," the manager barked.

On the player list posted on a nearby chain-link fence, the new arrival's name was spelled HYZDLL. His real name was Adam Hyzdu, and he had just been released from the Reds' Triple-A Indianapolis roster. Following the release, he had driven straight to Fort Myers. "He's just a guy we want to take a look at," Schaefer explained. Who could have known that by late August Hyzdu would be chasing Clark and Pough's Thunder franchise home-run record of 21? In late March, Hyzdu asked a pair of reporters what the Red Sox planned for him. Informed that he was slated to start the year in extended spring training (in Fort Myers), he replied, "That's interesting." It wouldn't be long before he was headed to Waterfront.

Two days before heading north, Macha dined on a filet mignon at Fort Myers' Chart House restaurant. Between bites, he candidly assessed his 1996 club's Eastern League prospects. The season broke down into four specific questions. They were, in no particular order:

1) Could the 20-year-old pitchers thrive against more-experienced Double-A hitters?

2) Who would provide the power hitting—Nixon, Carey, McKeel, Collier, Merloni . . . Hyzdu?

3) Would the veteran bullpen—the Grumpy Old Men—be able to protect late-inning leads while the young arms adapted to the Eastern League?

4) Would the Thunder be able to capitalize on the raw, physical speed of Sadler, Holifield and second baseman Chris Allison (who was successful on 35 of 40 steal attempts at Michigan in 1995)?

At any rate, Macha felt he knew what to expect from the league during his second go-round. Pitching and defense were the keys to success in the Eastern League. With the Grumpy Old Men aboard to help him through April, he felt much more comfortable about his roster than he had at the same point in 1995. As the Thunder embarked on the franchise's third season, Macha and Treuel planned to send Rose to the hill to pitch the opener against Harrisburg. "I've worked my butt off for this," the pitcher said during the third annual "Welcome North Dinner" at Angeloni's Cedar Gardens on Thursday, April 4. "This is a big jump for me, but it's special, for sure."

The '96 season also marked a change in the radio broadcasting booth. McCarthy returned despite an inviting offer from Pawtucket, but Simonetta was replaced by 25-year-old Maryland native Andy Freed, a diehard Baltimore Orioles fan who prepped for his Thunder assignment by calling the Port St. Lucie Mets of the Florida State League. The 6-foot-5 Freed brought a refreshing brand of professionalism to the WTTM booth, quickly distinguishing himself as an ambitious student of the game. His daily pregame preparation included informal discussions with Macha, Treuel, and Hodge. His style was thorough and intense. Together, he and McCarthy blended their approaches and learned each other's strengths and weaknesses during an early season symbiosis.

THE THIRD SEASON BEGINS

On Friday, April 5, 1996—a brisk, early spring evening—the third Thunder season opened with a 2-1 victory over the Senators at Waterfront. For Freed, that game will always be memorable. "I was just so anxious to get started," he admitted. A sellout crowd of just over 6500 watched Rose work seven innings, allowing one run on six hits. McKeel was 2-for-3 with the game-winning RBI, authoring a prelude to what would be a season of consistent improvement. Eversgerd made the Grumpy Old Men proud by picking up the victory with two innings of scoreless relief. The win marked the first time Trenton had opened the year with a 1-0 record. It also foreshadowed things to come.

Game two of the three-game opening series against Harrisburg was a 15-inning, 3-2 loss that was decided by a solo homer from Senators' veteran outfielder Tony Barron. A crowd of 4923 snapped the Thunder's string of 33 consecutive sellouts. Like Merloni and the Grumpy Old Men, Barron had been caught in a numbers crunch and forced to start the season at Double-A. Senior, making his 1996 debut, was long gone by the time the outcome was decided 4 hours and 27 minutes after his first pitch. He worked five innings and gave up one run on six hits, walking one and striking out three. Before the game, he had expressed disappointment about returning to Double-A. He also admitted that he had started to doubt himself for the first time. "I never thought it would happen to me," he said. "The 1995 season was a huge learning experience for me because—at this level—you can't afford to question your ability. If you do, you'll go out there and get hurt . . . and I did."

The pressures that came to bear on Shawn Senior during the '96 season included more than just throwing a baseball and the accompanying drive that is required to make it to the big leagues. He was mulling the decision to become engaged to his long-time girlfriend. He was pitching under the watchful eye of his parents each time he took the mound at Waterfront. He was watching jealously as most of the attention was focused on Rose and Pavano. In many ways, the fun of the game of baseball gradually began to erode for the brown-haired, ruddy Senior. He even began to make self-deprecating comments. When presented with a card from his '94 season in Single-A Lynchburg, he quipped cryptically, "Yeah, that was when I was good-looking." Unlike McKeel and Carey— even the Grumpy Old Men, who seemed determined to make the most of their '96 season opportunity— Senior approached it as a sentence. He said all the right things, but his heart didn't seem to be synchronized with his mouth. During an April 3 interview, he explained that "for the guys who had a shot at going to Triple-A and are here, the worst thing we can do is come back and bitch about it. We need to lead, to step it up and not feel sorry for ourselves. It's just a matter of getting it done here." For Shawn Senior, however, getting it done would ultimately become an emotional impossibility.

On the other hand, the Grumpy Old Men injected a clubhouse character that sparked the Thunder from the season's outset. On arriving in the Trenton dressing room, they moved into locker stalls in the front corner of the rectangular clubhouse. Pointing down the row to Rose and Pavano, they added, "Those guys are the young guns." When Knackert began pitching professionally in 1987, Pavano was in sixth grade. On the name plates above their lockers, the Grumpy Old Men wrote "OLD (Grundt)," "OLDER (Schullstrom)," "EVEN OLDER (Eversgerd)," and "OLDEST (Knackert)." Not surprisingly, the pranks began almost immediately. Schullstrom, the most artistic member of the quartet, made three copies of Grundt's media-guide headshot, enlarged them, and distributed them to Knackert and Eversgerd. Later that night, they wore the masks into the dugout. Everyone was in stitches. The Grumpy Old Men also chipped in $30 each and bought a radio/CD boombox for the clubhouse. The purchase was accompanied by a promise: "Whoever is the last one playing here gets to keep the boombox."

Before each game, the Grumpy Old Men conducted a ritual game of "flip it," which was the equivalent of volleyball played with a baseball. Wearing miniature baseball gloves, they swatted the ball around in a circle—much like the old black-and-white films of baseball clowns. Their incessant antics kept Pavano, Rose, Sadler, and the other first-year Double-A players extremely loose. Knackert, who bore a striking facial resemblance to comic figure Bart Simpson, was the most amusing member of the group. During an early season trip to Canton, the Thunder was snowed out on back-to-back days as a rare, late April storm moved through the Stark County region. Knackert used the free time to do a little shopping at Belden Village Mall. His prized purchase was a red baseball cap with fake brown hair attached to the inside. Inscribed on the front of the hat was the caption, "Still Wild and Crazy at 50." Donning the new headwear, he walked toward several unsuspecting teammates and began bumping into them randomly. Fernandez, not realizing it was Knackert, almost started a fight with the pitcher. After things were smoothed over and the game called off due to inclement conditions, Knackert wore the hat back to Trenton throughout the 8-hour bus ride. Several days later, he even conducted a television interview behind his new disguise.

Another Grumpy Old Men creation was the "Wall of Shame" that decorated the hallway entrance to the training room. This area gradually was adorned with photocopies of various Thunder players' heads superimposed atop other people or things. Schullstrom—the artist of the group—was the true inspiration behind the Wall of Shame. Each day, it seemed, another entry was added to the impromptu gallery. One of the first was a picture of McKeel atop a bikini-clad woman. "Walteena—Miss April, 1996," read the caption. Other entries that accrued included a list of pitcher Rick Betti's top 10 pick-up lines; Fernandez atop a Buddha statue, hitting coach Hodge sliding between a donkey's legs with the caption "I was safe, ya asshole"; and Rose with dollar signs floating above his head.

In high school, Knackert had been voted the class clown. "All of my pranks are small," he explained. "I'm a spur of the moment kind of guy. The biggest thing that shocks people, I guess, is that I'm not afraid to do things." On April 26, he and Schullstrom donned yellow Thunder Game Day Staff jackets and tore tickets outside the stadium entrance. Like most relief pitchers, Knackert had plenty of free time on his hands to think of ways to amuse himself and those around him, but the flip side of his comedic personality was his effectiveness as a pitcher.

"The Grumpy Old Men were good for us," Hodge said. "The biggest thing was that the young pitchers knew that if they got to the sixth or seventh inning with a lead, the game was over. They were old, and they had been around the minor leagues for a long time. They threw strikes, and you didn't have to worry about them."

After splitting the first two games, the Thunder arrived at Waterfront on Easter Sunday, April 6, to a backdrop of cold, persistent rain. An announced crowd of 2912 braved the elements for the early season date, marking the second smallest "tickets sold" figure of the first three Thunder seasons. With such miserable conditions, it would have been logical—and practical—for Macha to want a rainout. Just the opposite was true, however. With a sinkerball pitcher like Pavano on the mound, he liked his chances all the more. "I had a feeling about Carl," he said after the precocious 20-year-old threw a five-inning, 6-0 shutout victory that marked Waterfront date No. 86 in a row without a weather-related cancellation. Pavano actually set the tone for the abbreviated win with a nifty defensive play on the game's first pitch. Harrisburg center fielder DaRond Stovall laid down a bunt attempt, and the Thunder pitcher ranged off the mound to his left, fielded the ball with a slide, and retired the Senators' outfielder with a perfect throw to first. "Carl's not exactly Baryshnikov out there," Macha observed. "But he made that play, and it was beautiful. He even fired me up."

The Thunder scored five runs in their half of the first on a Holifield triple, a

Coughlin sacrifice fly, a Carey double, a two-run single by Nixon, and a two-run double by the streaking McKeel. Exhibiting pinpoint control in his Double-A debut, Pavano threw first-pitch strikes to 14 of the 17 batters he faced. Of his 66 deliveries, 50 were strikes. "He was a strike-throwing machine," praised Macha. "After one inning, I said to him, 'You're throwing too many strikes.' " Disappointed that action was halted prematurely when the umpires decided it was simply too wet to continue, Pavano took his work-out inside to the treadmill. As he ran 20 minutes at a 7.5-mph clip, he talked about his maiden Eastern League experience. "I wanted to get out there. My change-up was good today, and I was able to work fastballs in and out." Down the hall in the Senators' clubhouse, Barron assessed Pavano's truncated masterpiece. "I would never have thought he's only 20 years old," the Harrisburg veteran said.

With a 2-1 record after three games, the '96 Thunder season was off to a promising start. The Grumpy Old Men helped to keep things loose in the Trenton clubhouse. Schullstrom made daily visits to the photocopier, creating fresh and humorous entries for the training room Hall of Shame. Everyone seemed comfortable in the new atmosphere. In the opening series, catcher McKeel was 4-for-6, with three RBIs. More significantly, he had handled both Rose and Pavano with deft effectiveness from behind the plate. "They both kinda pitch the same," he said. "They're very easy to catch, and they've both got good arms that are very deceiving to the hitter. And, I think they both know this game better than most people think."

Following an off-day on April 8, the first road trip of the season was a four-game journey to Bowie's Prince George's Stadium. The first game of the series would be Barkley's debut; however, a rainstorm on April 9 postponed the Texas lefty's first Double-A appearance until the following night. (The April 9 game would be made up as a doubleheader later in the season.) One night later, Barkley's long-awaited Eastern League baptism was not a pretty sight. In just four innings, he served up three home runs and departed after giving up eight earned runs. His ERA after one start was 18.00, and the Thunder fell to 2-2 with a lopsided 10-1 loss. Fernandez lost his 1996 debut the following night by a 7-4 margin. "I'm ready to get out of here," Macha said of Prince George's. He had good reason. In the 11 games he had managed at the suburban Washington, D.C., facility, the Thunder had compiled a 2-9 record. He smiled broadly as Trenton boarded the bus with a narrow 7-6 win in the final game of the series, evening its record at 3-3.

On Sunday, April 14, Pavano was bombed by Reading, and the Thunder suffered an ugly 10-0 loss. Clearly, the Eastern League wasn't going to be as easy as he had made it look during his first start. In five innings, he allowed seven earned runs and walked four.

DRAMA IN THUNDERLAND

On April 16, 25-year-old shortstop Randy Brown joined Macha's roster from Pawtucket. A career minor leaguer, Brown had suffered through an extremely traumatic experience during the '94 season. As a member of the New Britain

Red Sox, he had watched helplessly as his father, Jim, suffered a fatal heart attack in the lobby of a West Hartford, Connecticut, restaurant. Ironically, they were in the establishment for an early evening meal only because a scheduled game against Runnells' Thunder club had been rained out. Following Jim's death, Brown took time away from the game to grieve. His season was shot. He wound up hitting .224, with eight homers and 30 RBIs. He struck out 102 times in 389 at-bats. He spent the '95 season at Pawtucket, batting .250 with 12 RBIs in 74 games as a reserve infielder. When he arrived in Trenton, he was perceived mainly as a back-up to Donnie Sadler. In his first game, against Canton-Akron, he struck out four times in four plate appearances and looked badly overmatched. A tanned, 6-foot Texan, Brown resembled actor Patrick Swayze. He kept largely to himself, and despite his inauspicious Trenton beginning, he would author one of the dramatic moments in the New Jersey capital's minor-league history.

Following Pavano's April 14 loss, Barkley and the Thunder rebounded for an 11-7 win over Canton-Akron that gave them a 5-4 record. The victory also was the beginning of an altogether-improbable streak of fortune that left many of the Boston prospects feeling invincible each time they took the field. Part of the chemistry involved the Grumpy Old Men, who kept everyone in stitches and entered games with one goal in mind—to slam the door on their opponents. Part of the success centered around Macha, who handled each win or loss like it was just another game. Never too high. Never too low. It's a requisite approach for sanity in any professional baseball season.

On April 17, consecutive win No. 3 was a 6-5 Waterfront Businessperson's Special triumph over the Indians, during which veteran outfielder Paul Rappoli hit two homers. Rappoli had missed the entire '95 season with a broken elbow—suffered the day he was supposed to join the Thunder in Binghamton. "This was big for me, maybe to my teammates and coaches, too, to let them know I'm still around," Rappoli said. Throughout the season, "Rap" would be a stabilizing force for the team, a class act who handled his diminishing role in the organization with dignity. McKeel also homered on the cool, gusty April 17 afternoon as a crowd of 3889 enjoyed the day game—one of five Businessperson's Specials during the '96 season. Rose pitched 7 2/3 innings for his first Double-A victory. Knackert strolled in from the bullpen to pick up his third save in as many opportunities. Explained McKeel, "Everybody in this clubhouse is learning about everybody else. We didn't have a chance to get to know each other during spring training because we didn't play together. As a result, we were battling through some things at the beginning of the season."

As for Knackert, Macha appreciated his professional approach to spending more time in Double-A, observing, "His chances of sticking around are probably slim. I think he can get people out in the big leagues right now. It wouldn't surprise me if they took him straight from here." Added Schaefer, "He's got much too good an arm to be in Double-A, but we put him here for a reason. We wanted him to help out with some of the younger guys." On April 18, Eversgerd became the first member of the Grumpy Old Men to depart. He was traded to Texas for outfielder Rudy Pemberton. A tearful round of goodbyes in front of his locker stall signaled the end of a short but unforgettable period of Thunder baseball. "That's one less guy I have to carry," Grundt said in classic understated style. Shouted Merloni from across the room, "Yeah, pretty soon it's going to be 'Grumpy Old Man.' " Added Grundt, "Yeah, or Grumpy Old Grundt."

Hours after Eversgerd departed, Trenton completed their first four-game Waterfront sweep in three seasons (or 132 home dates). Delgado's three-run homer in the eighth was the impetus. The Thunder trailed Canton-Akron righty Bartolo Colon 2-0 in the early going, but Colon's 98-mph fastball couldn't nail down the win. After Delgado's homer put the Thunder on top 5-3, Knackert earned his fourth save. With an 8-4 record (7-2 at Waterfront), Trenton was picking up momentum on a nightly basis.

Brown's presence in a Thunder uniform became much more significant—and understandable—on April 19, when Schaefer and Boston dropped a bombshell. The 5-foot-5 1/2 inch Sadler (an "official" height that was confirmed by the Grumpy Old Men, who measured him in the clubhouse shower) was sent to extended spring training in Fort Myers to learn to play center field. Macha was baffled. In 12 Double-A games at shortstop, Sadler had four errors (in 41 defensive chances). He was hitting .333, with six runs scored and six RBIs. Before his reassignment, he had hit in 10 of his last 17 at-bats. He was just getting comfortable in his new surroundings. From infielder to outfielder, he was being asked to entirely rearrange the way he thought about—and played—the game of baseball. Ironically, he missed the Thunder's 5-3 win over Canton-Akron on April 18 due to a bout of nausea. "We're not sure whether he got sick before or after the phone call [to report to Fort Myers]," Macha said. "This came out of the clear blue, but it's not something that hasn't been talked about. I think the Red Sox are just looking long range, and they want to take full advantage of his athleticism." The unspoken part of the move was the fact that Sadler was vastly inferior to Nomar as a defensive shortstop. Boston knew it. Macha knew it. Everyone but the cocky Sadler knew it. Said Macha, "I think he can play the outfield, but I would hope no one messes around with his swing. I wasn't happy that they took him, but what are you going to do? That's what the farm system is for."

While Sadler underwent a crash course in outfield skills from Dick Berardino in southwest Florida, the Thunder kept right on winning. During a 14-4 shellacking of Reading on April 20—win No. 6 in a row—they hit a season-high six homers. Merloni enjoyed a career day, smashing two balls out of Municipal Stadium. Joining in the long ball parade were Collier, Delgado, Nixon and Holifield. Barkley was the beneficiary of the outburst, improving to 2-1 for the season. The following afternoon, Fernandez completed a three-game sweep of the Phillies by outdueling Beech for a 5-4 victory. Knackert picked up his fifth save, and Curley packed up the bus for a short, two-game series at Canton. Neither game in eastern Ohio was played, however, due to a series of early-spring storms that included a rare April snowshower. The Grumpy Old Men passed the time in the mall. Returning to Waterfront to face New Haven on Wednesday, April 24, Rose showcased some of his best stuff during a 4-1 victory that extended the winning streak to eight. He improved to 2-0 with 6 2/3 innings of scoreless ball. Once again, Knackert recorded the final out of the game, moving within two saves of Joe Hudson and Glenn Carter's Thunder single-season record of eight.

Meanwhile, the mystery shrouding Sadler's status was clarified when he returned to Waterfront—as a center fielder—to face the Ravens. Clearly, he was not used to fielding balls under the lights of his new position. On his first defensive chance, he booted the ball, only to pick it up and throw out the New Haven runner at second base. "Pretty good arm," Macha observed. Back in his customary lead-off spot, Sadler was 2-for-4, raising his average to .347. Over the next 3 weeks, he demonstrated a surprisingly good ability to make throws from deep in the outfield, prompting Boston officials to say, "Now we know he can play two positions, and that makes him even more valuable to the organization." In truth, after Boston's disappointing 6-19 start to the 1996 season, Duquette was entertaining ideas of calling Sadler to the majors in a desperate attempt to spark Kevin Kennedy's sagging squad.

After three consecutive no-decisions to begin the year, Senior entered his April 25 date against the Ravens intent on extending the Thunder winning streak to nine. His problem was a balky stomach that necessitated several visits to the clubhouse washroom between his 5 2/3 innings. "I had stomach cramps, and in the third I almost called time out," he said with a laugh after notching the victory—a 5-4 win that was his twelfth in a Thunder uniform (giving him one more franchise win than Edmondson and Orellano). "I guess you could say Shawn sucked it up there," Macha added. Knackert was again the man on the hot seat, recording his seventh save with a game-ending double play and earning Macha's praise as his "100-percent man." The victory improved Trenton's record to 13-4. In addition, they were 7-1 in one-run ballgames (a tribute to the Grumpy Old Men) and 9-2 at Waterfront.

Consecutive win No. 10 followed on Friday, April 26, a 2-1 victory over Hardware City that lifted Pavano's record to 3-1. The big righty worked eight complete innings, scattering four hits, walking one and striking out 10. A Waterfront crowd of 5665 saw Brown score both of the Thunder's runs. Knackert wiggled out of a bases-loaded, one-out predicament in the top of the ninth just for dramatic effect. Nothing—it seemed—could thwart Trenton's torrid early season pace. At 14-4, Macha's club was running away from the Eastern League Southern Division in the early going.

Regardless of the Thunder's teflon bullpen, nothing that happened during the streak could compare to the ludicrous events of Saturday afternoon, April 27. As the Thunder fell behind in the early innings, Hyzdu arrived at the ballpark. Schaefer had finally assigned him to Double-A after 3 weeks in extended spring training. At first, the Cincinnati native couldn't get into the home clubhouse, which is locked during games. He had to convince Thunder officials he was a player. By the ninth inning, Trenton trailed hopelessly—by an 11-6 margin—but Hyzdu was dressed and in the dugout, ready for service. Surely, the Thunder streak had met its match. Behind by five runs with Hardware City reliever Sean Gavaghan needing just three outs, Trenton seemed destined to fall to a 14-5 record. "It was fun while it lasted," Macha thought to himself. In the middle of the dugout was a piece of masking tape atop one of the gold jacket hooks. Written on the tape were the words, "The Hook 31." Whenever the Thunder needed a late-inning rally, Macha hung his blue-and-green jacket on the peg. As he summoned Hyzdu to pinch hit at the beginning of the ninth, the hook rule was in effect. So was the Macha underwear principle. For each game of the winning streak, he had worn the same pair of long white briefs. Throughout the '96 season, he donned them for good luck. "Look at 'em, they're full of holes," he liked to tell reporters who visited his office.

During each Thunder broadcast, Freed conducted a live player-of-the-game radio interview. On this afternoon, he was in the Thunder dugout waiting for Hardware City to put the finishing touches on the apparent win. McKeel turned to the first-year Trenton announcer and said, "It ain't over yet." It was more of a promise than Freed ever could have known.

McKeel's dugout pledge was brought to life by the newcomer—Hyzdu. In his first Trenton at-bat, Hyzdu slammed a solo homer to left. All of a sudden it was a four-run game and the noose began to tighten around Gavaghan's neck. "You don't want to walk into a situation like this to be a jinx," Hyzdu said later. "This team was playing well and they see this new guy coming in to screw everything up . . ." Within moments, Brown came to the plate with the opportunity to draw his team within a run. The resulting three-run homer drew a standing ovation from the Waterfront crowd of 5556. The way Brown saw it, he owed his teammates something for a pair of errors that had cost the Thunder dearly in the middle innings. When Dan Collier's two-out double skittered to the center-field wall to score Coughlin, the Thunder had drawn even, 11-11, after nine innings. The streak had assumed a life—and a will—of its own. In baseball, momentum is a force not to be taken lightly.

Sure enough, Brown came up in the bottom of the tenth with the bases loaded—and sure enough, he homered for the second time in as many innings. As he crossed the plate to punctuate the miraculous 15-11 win and his first career grand slam, his Thunder teammates lifted him on their shoulders and paraded him back to the dugout. "Greatest moment of my career," Brown said. "I've never been a part of anything like this in my entire life." Added Macha, "Hell, I don't know what to say."

Brown finished with seven RBIs, and in the process, he had gained an unspoken respect from everyone in the Trenton clubhouse. Many of the players knew what kind of adversity he had been forced to endure with his father's passing. This was his moment to enjoy—and what a moment it had been.

"He was going nuts," Freed recalled of Brown's reaction to the game-winner. "For a guy to hit home runs in back-to-back innings in a situation like that . . . It was like being a kid again and hitting a tennis ball in the back yard. I remember him walking through the office after the game with a smile on his face that seemed to ask, "I DID THAT?"

The following afternoon, Barkley completed the Hardware City sweep with 6 1/3 innings of four-hit ball—easily his best outing of the month. The resulting 2-1 victory produced franchise-record save No. 9 for Knackert, who was rapidly wearing out his welcome in the Eastern League. As the Trenton closer retired the final Rock Cats' batter, a delirious Thunder season-ticket holder paraded around the concourse with a broom. Cardboard strips attached to the handle listed the four opponents that the Thunder had swept during their 12-game rush. CANTON-AKRON. READING. NEW HAVEN. HARDWARE CITY. Said Knackert, "I saw the guy in the stands with the broom, and I wasn't going to let him down." The five-game homestand ended with Trenton in possession of a 16-4 record, seven games ahead of second-place Canton-Akron.

STREAKING ONTO THE ROAD

Next up for the surging Boston farmhands was a four-game trip to Norwich's Dodd Stadium, where they were joined by rehabbing Boston third baseman Tim Naehring. The first game of the series was rained out and postponed until August, when the Thunder returned to eastern Connecticut. Naehring spent the evening at Foxwoods, pressing his luck at the gaming tables, and McKeel and several other players made their way to the casino as well during the rare off-night.

On Tuesday, April 30, the scheduled second game was halted by the weather after Rose threw two scoreless innings. Knowing that Pavano would take over when action was resumed the following day, Rose grumbled, "I guess he'll suck up another one of my wins." On May 1, before a contingent of family and friends who made the drive from Southington, Pavano extended the winning streak to 13 by striking out nine batters in six innings of relief. "I'll take it," he said when apprised of Rose's comment.

After 16 days of nothing but winning baseball, the most prosperous streak in Thunder baseball finally came to its inevitable conclusion during the second half of the May 1 doubleheader. Norwich's Ray Ricken slammed the door on the Thunder offense, outdueling Fernandez for a 3-0 shut-out win. Nonetheless, the 13-game winning streak was the longest in the Eastern League since 1943—when Scranton reeled off 17 straight. Nobody in the Trenton clubhouse seemed concerned about the loss except Naehring, who facetiously joked about "costing these guys their streak." In reality, however, the early season run had given the Thunder a cushion with which they could work for the balance of the '96 season. If they played .500 ball for the rest of the year, they would win more than 75 games—surely enough to qualify for the playoffs for the second straight year. The mood in the Trenton dugout remained light and unconcerned, as typified by one of Naehring's remarks to Macha. While struggling at the plate during the doubleheader, he looked over to the manager and inquired, "Are you impressed yet?" Macha just laughed and rolled his eyes. Later that night, Naehring purchased a rib dinner that was delivered to the Trenton clubhouse and devoured by the Double-A players.

"I hope they're not feeling too bad," Macha said. "Let's be realistic, not too many times are you going to put 13 in a row."

While the streak was history, Sadler had other pressing business. At 8 AM on Thursday, May 2, he traveled to Fenway Park to conduct a center-field audition for Dan Duquette and Kevin Kennedy. He shagged fly balls in the shadow of the Green Monster and left thinking that he had a legitimate shot at being called to Boston at any time. He also told the Red Sox press corps that he missed playing shortstop and that his outfield experiment didn't provide an adequate comfort level. "I just think they're doing what's best for me to get to the big leagues," he said matter-of-factly. Added Schaefer, "You won't find many center fielders with a better arm than Donnie. He's going to be a weapon out there." Returning from his Boston trip in time for the Thunder's 5-2 loss to Norwich, Sadler went 2-for-3 with a pair of stolen bases. Nonetheless, the call to the Show never came. He played 30 games in the outfield before pleading to be returned to shortstop, and by early June, he would become an infielder once again.

On Sunday, May 5, during a doubleheader split at Binghamton, Knackert made his final appearance in a Thunder uniform. As anticipated, he was promoted directly from Trenton to Boston. In 11 Thunder games, he amassed a franchise record of 10 saves and a 1.38 ERA. In 13 innings as of May 5, he allowed six hits and struck out 21 batters. During his farewell address, he recited lines from the movie *Bull Durham*. "I just play them one game at a time, and good Lord willing, everything will work out. Without my teammates, I never would have been in position to have those save opportunities," he said with a straight face before leaving Trenton behind for good.

Ironically, the final game of Knackert's stay was a no-hitter—for the Mets. Binghamton lefty Joe Crawford spun a seven-inning masterpiece to defeat Fernandez 1-0. He joined Bowie's Rick Forney as the second opposing thrower to no-hit Trenton in three seasons. Crawford had spent spring training as a reliever with the Boston organization before he was traded back to New York. During the second half of a doubleheader, he was making a rare start. In spite of their league-best 19-6 record, the Thunder couldn't touch him on a clear, sunny day in New York's Southern Tier. The loss emphasized baseball's uniquely unpredictable nature. On any given day, you just never know what kind of bizarre occurrences might unfold, when you might see something you've never witnessed before. It is a reality that has kept fans coming back to the ballpark for 150 years.

CHAPTER 20

A Trenton
All-Star Gala

"Really, it's amazing when you think what the first season was like, the problems that we had with the field and the team and everything. Now, look at it. The Thunder are in first place, seven games up. The field is in beautiful condition, and they can play under any circumstances here. We've got three Thunder players on the [American League All-Star] team and an All-Star manager. What more could you ask after only three seasons?"

—NEW JERSEY GOVERNOR CHRISTINE TODD WHITMAN BEFORE THE 1996 DOUBLE-A ALL-STAR GAME, PLAYED BEFORE A RECORD WATERFRONT CROWD OF 8369 FANS

Despite the Thunder's torrid 17-4 start, infielder Todd Carey was not enjoying his second tour of the Eastern League. Through his first 20 games, the left-hander was hitting just .200, with four doubles, one triple, two homers, and four RBIs. Not exactly the kind of production he—or Macha—had been anticipating. Still, the sluggish start was camouflaged by McKeel, Brown, the Young Guns, and the perfection of the Thunder bullpen. By early May, Carey was ready to break out of his funk, and the result was an unprecedented month of offense. Between May 1 and May 31, the 6-foot-1, 180-pound Carey drove in a league-best 30 runs—four more than Selby had driven in during July 1995 (Clark's single-month best in Thunder colors was 22 and Pough's 25). "My confidence level is so high, especially with runners in scoring position," Carey explained. Macha and Hodge worked diligently with him on driving the ball to the opposite field. The manager even bet his prospect that he couldn't get a hit to left field during a late May road trip. After losing the wager the first night in New Haven, Carey went double-or-nothing the following evening and promptly doubled down the left-field line in his first at-bat; however, he was unable to drop a second hit into the required area. "I guess he'll be delivering two cases of my favorite beverage—Mountain Dew," Macha crowed. Carey's onslaught included a five-RBI performance against the Ravens on May 13 and four-RBI outings at New Haven on May 20 and at New Britain on May 31. The Rhode Island native seemed to save his best games for New England trips.

After their 17-4 April start, the Thunder compiled a 15-12 record in May. On May 20, before a 12-1 Trenton victory at New Haven, Grundt was promoted to

Pawtucket. In 12 Thunder games, he did not allow a run, walking six and striking out 13. "I think he can pitch in the big leagues with the stuff he has right now," Macha predicted. Grundt's place in the bullpen was taken by the struggling Senior, who was asked to be a reliever for the first time in his career. "It's not necessarily a permanent thing," Macha insisted about the move. "I think he knows it's a different situation, and he'll approach it that way."

On Saturday, May 25, Brown hit his second grand slam at Waterfront in less than a month, creaming a two-strike fastball from Portland lefty Bryan Ward over the left-field fence. A sun-baked crowd of 6742 stood and applauded. Brown's homer broke a sixth-inning tie and sparked a 9-6 Trenton victory. "Yes, I'm having fun," Brown admitted, "but I couldn't believe he threw me a breaking ball in that situation." After 44 games, the Thunder had a 30-14 record, and it marked the first time in three seasons the franchise had been 16 games over .500. Furthermore, when Trenton had scored five or more runs, it was a perfect 21-0. Thanks to Brown's timely round-tripper, Senior (3-3) picked up his first-ever win out of the bullpen.

Meanwhile, Rose continued to distinguish himself with a 3-1 mark during the season's second month. More important, each time he took the hill, Trenton seemed to find a way to win. On May 26, at home against Portland, he authored his Double-A signature game, allowing just three hits in a complete-game, 2-0 shutout. He walked one and struck out 12, which was the third-best single-game effort in modern Trenton annals—behind Shannon Withem's 14 and Suppan's 13. As a result, Duquette began to monitor his progress even more closely—perhaps pondering a repeat of Suppan's 1995 promotion. Through his first 10 Eastern League appearances, Rose had a very Soup-like 6-1 record, with a 2.32 ERA, 17 walks, and 47 strike-outs. He was stamping himself as a candidate to start the '96 All-Star Game, which would be played before the partisan Trenton crowd. "The thing about both Brian and Carl is that they're very low maintenance for 20-year-olds," Treuel said. (By the end of May, Pavano was 6-4, with a 3.29 ERA, 16 walks, and 55 strikeouts, and he had earned a decision in all 10 of his starts.)

Knackert's place as the Thunder closer was taken by 27-year-old Reggie Harris, who, like Hyzdu, joined the team from extended spring training. Harris represented a tangible link to Boston's past. In 1987, he had been the Red Sox's first-round draft pick. In the interim, he had pitched for both Seattle and Oakland during the Athletics' 1990 World Series season. He had been hampered by nagging elbow problems, but his velocity had returned to the 97-mph range during a 1995 stint in Taiwan. Following his 1996 spring training release by the Colorado Rockies, he had an opportunity to sign with the Yankees. Instead, he chose Boston because "they gave me a chance." When he arrived in Trenton, Harris expected to be around for a couple weeks at the very most—he wound up spending almost 4 months and appearing in 33 games. His presence in the Thunder clubhouse was especially beneficial for Pavano, who seemed to soak up his knowledge and experience with great zest. "I picked his brain all year," Pavano admitted. "We became pretty close, and he took me under his wing. When I got to Trenton, I was acting like an asshole, but he always told me, 'I'm real happy for you.' It's great to know he cares."

On Saturday afternoon, May 11, following a 4-2 victory over Bowie at Waterfront, the Thunder players and coaching staff were invited to a party at the Trenton Polish-American Democratic Club on Olden Avenue. They showed up en masse to enjoy free beer and food and to play pool. While signing autographs and talking with the members, Macha genuinely seemed to enjoy himself. The manager was even convinced to dance a polka by an elderly woman. He whirled around the dance floor with a smile on his face as the players laughed. Rappoli stayed for several hours, but Harris was the last to leave. He sat at the bar and chatted until 9 PM.

While Harris' addition continued the Grumpy Old Men tradition—minus the constant clubhouse buffoonery—a pair of broken wrists sidelined two significant Thunder veterans. On May 9, Binghamton lefty Rafael Roque hit Merloni squarely on his right arm with an inside pitch, and on May 21, in New Haven, he was officially diagnosed with a fracture. When he was placed on the disabled list, the infielder was hitting .232, with three homers and 16 RBIs. The recovery time for the injury was diagnosed as 2 months. Merloni returned to his Massachusetts home and contemplated retirement, but Schaefer eventually convinced him that giving up on his career would be a big mistake. When Merloni was ready to return to action, he was shipped instead to Triple-A. He joined Pawtucket on July 5, hitting .252 in 38 games for manager Buddy Bailey. The other broken wrist was a fluke injury to Coughlin, who had raised his average to .287 when he fell rounding first base at Yale Field on May 20. He, too, would miss 2 months of the season and never regain his hitting form.

The late May trip to New Haven also was significant because Macha won his 100th game as Thunder manager on May 21 at Yale Field. Underwhelmed by his achievement, he observed, "If you're around for 2 years, you better win 100."

Meanwhile, the Thunder offense was bolstered further by designated hitter Tyrone Woods' May 24 arrival from extended spring training. With Hyzdu (who was 10-for-16 during a four-game late May span) and Woods (who played for Harrisburg during the '93 and '94 seasons and spent '95 at Triple-A) in the lineup and McKeel continuing to get on base with impressive regularity, the Trenton batting order had very few holes. In his first 71 Thunder at-bats, Hyzdu hit .310, with four homers and 12 RBIs. The 6-foot, 225-pound Woods hit four homers in his first seven Trenton games, serving notice to opposing pitchers that he didn't want to spend too much time toiling in Double-A. Like Harris, however, he became stuck in a Thunder uniform, gradually growing embittered and indifferent.

During a late May trip to Hardware City, the Rock Cats' front office took out an advertisement in the local paper. "Come see Southington's Carl Pavano pitch for the Trenton Thunder," read the ad. With Duquette in the audience, he was rocked for 10 hits in five innings (including two homers). "It doesn't matter that I pitched poorly," he said in the visitors' clubhouse after the Thunder lost a 10-7 decision. "My friends are still going to be my friends, and my family is still going to love me." Added Schaefer, "With Carl, it's been one step forward, two steps back, but that's why he's in the minor leagues." Also during the Hardware City series, the Thunder enjoyed the first of a series of pasta dinners at Pavano's nearby home, courtesy of "Momma Pavano." (Curley drove the bus to Southington and shared in the revelry.)

While Pavano sputtered briefly, Rose was battling tendinitis in his right shoulder. After allowing six runs on seven hits against Hardware City on May 31 as Duquette looked on intently from his box seat, he was removed from the rotation for 2 weeks. "We're not going to rush him," Macha cautioned, but added Rose, "I didn't feel the same." "I talked to [Duquette] after the game and he said, 'I heard you've been throwing well. What happened?' But that makes you want to come back harder."

The three-game series between the Thunder and the Rock Cats at brand-new New Britain Stadium was a slugfest. On May 31, Harris blew the first Trenton save opportunity of the season—after 18 successful conversions. During the weekend series, the Thunder (10) and Hardware City (six) combined for 16 homers and 49 runs. Trenton lost two of three to fall to 33-17. "There wasn't too much quality pitching in this series," Macha quipped.

MOVING TOWARD THE ALL-STAR BREAK

By June 18, the Thunder's lead over second-place Harrisburg had dwindled to three-and-a-half games. Trenton (39-27) had lost seven of its last 10 games, while the Senators (36-31) had won seven of their last 10. The once-invincible feeling that the Thunder players had carried into each game had begun to resemble a mid-season rut. On an overcast late spring evening at Bowie, Pavano took matters into his own hands, spinning 8 1/3 innings of two-hit ball before a rain delay halted action in the ninth inning. Following a 1-hour hiatus, Trenton closed out a pivotal 3-1 victory. It was Pavano's eighth win in 14 games. Also that evening, Harrisburg lost to Hardware City, moving the Thunder four-and-a-half games ahead.

Offensively, on June 19, McKeel was hitting .313, with six homers and 41 RBIs. Carey had cooled some from his May pace, but he was still hitting .276, with 12 homers and 45 RBIs. Brown was hitting .298, with 11 homers and 33 RBIs. Hyzdu, one of the big right-handed bats that Macha needed, was sizzling along at a .322 clip with 10 homers and 29 RBIs in his first 42 Thunder games. Holifield was hitting .285, with 20 stolen bases. Woods had filled in the clean-up spot quite nicely, with a .333 average and seven homers in his first 25 Trenton games. Nixon was hitting just .239, with seven homers in 59 games, but his defensive ability and his penchant for doing the little things that help win ballgames was impressive. As a team, Trenton was hitting .264 with a league-best 74 homers.

As the Thunder cruised toward 50 wins by the All-Star break, it became increasingly apparent that Macha would be the American League manager for the July 8 Waterfront Double-A All-Star Game. The honorary position went to the manager of the AL affiliate with the best record. Thanks to the 13-game winning streak and his team's level approach to each game, he was forced to rearrange his family's vacation plans. In reality, Macha didn't want to manage the All-Star Game. He planned to return to Atlantic City to have his palm read for the second straight year. He even went on the record as saying, "I might not manage the game." Of course, that didn't sit well with Thunder officials. By the

June 24 cut-off date, Trenton had a 44-28 record, good enough to secure Macha's place in the AL dugout. Duquette called him just to make sure he wasn't entertaining a change of plans. "This might be a dubious honor," the Thunder skipper confessed, "but these guys are going to be here because of their ability. They're here to show off. I'm simply going to tell them to go out and do what they do best." Hodge and Treuel also were invited to coach the game, while Thunder trainer Terry Smith would serve as official medic for the AL.

On Wednesday, June 19, the Thunder's improbable 2-year run of Waterfront games without a rain-out came to an end at No. 116. Hodes shrugged off the postponement. He knew that the end was inevitable—and that it didn't detract from nearly 2 years of baseball in South Trenton without a rain-out. The stadium's rain gauge read 2.7 inches following a violent late-afternoon storm. "We'll start another streak," the Thunder General Manager pledged. "After Joe DiMaggio ended his streak [56 straight games with a hit], he started another one, right?" Thankful for the night off, most of the Trenton players scurried out of the clubhouse.

Two days later, the Double-A Association announced its '96 All-Star team. Thunder officials knew that the Trenton franchise probably would have three players—the maximum allowed. The key decision involved pitching. Would it be Rose or Pavano? Macha and Treuel felt Rose deserved the nod. The managers and broadcasters who selected the team, however, felt otherwise. Pavano (8-4, 3.64 ERA) was named to the squad instead of Rose (7-2, 3.43 ERA). Said Macha, "Let's put it this way. I'm glad I didn't have to make that decision. Brian certainly deserves to be on that team." Pavano would be joined on the AL squad by McKeel and Carey, who had parlayed his magnificent May into All-Star status.

"Sure, it's a little disappointing; I wanted to make the team," Rose said candidly. Added Pavano, "Rosie's having a great year, and he's been the anchor. I thought we both deserved to be on it, but I guess their hands were tied only being able to take three guys. We had a few others that could have been picked, too." Most notable among them was Brown, who was enjoying the best season of his career.

McKeel and Carey were thrilled to be included in All-Star festivities. Both had been demoted from Trenton to Sarasota during the '95 season. McKeel had been berated by Boston officials during '96 spring training. They wanted to see him begin to achieve his potential. The resulting half-season of consistency and production was impressive. "I've been healthy, and that's the biggest thing," McKeel said of his .313 average through 240 at-bats. "I'm finding out what I can do in this league and liking the results." In April, the North Carolina native had hit .377, with four homers and 17 RBIs, prompting Macha to observe, "He carried us offensively that month." Carey was more philosophical about his selection. "It will be the highlight of my career, definitely," he said. "It's nice to be recognized. Any time you put together a good series or two, you open some eyes and it's good for your career. Then if it doesn't work out for you with one organization, you can always hook on with somebody else."

On Sunday, June 23, Nixon authored part two of the 1996 Thunder's incredible comeback story. After trailing Canton-Akron 10-1 in the fifth inning—in a seven-inning game!—Trenton scored 14 of the next 15 runs to win on Nixon's grand slam. It was an outrageous high that quickly was followed by an 18-1, game-two loss. During the nightcap, a vocal fan in the left-field seats shouted, "Hey [Indians' manager Jeff] Datz, how are you going to blow this one?" The loss dropped Trenton to 44-28. Still, nobody seemed to be worried. The Indians had perhaps the best offense in the league.

By June 27, Senior was back in the starting rotation. Against Portland, he threw his first complete game of the season during a 4-1 victory. He allowed just four hits in perhaps the best Double-A outing of his 2-year Thunder stint. In sixteen 1996 appearances, he was 5-6 with a 4.72 ERA, but Senior had grown very tired of toiling in the Eastern League. While he labored against the circuit's talented hitters, he continued to watch as young phenoms Rose and Pavano basked in the spotlight. All of his life—from Little League to his 11-7 '95 campaign with the Thunder—he had been a winner. Now, he was questioning his desire to pursue the major-league dream. As the Thunder bus departed for Canton after the June 27 win, Senior was nowhere to be found. He had returned home to Cherry Hill, searching his soul for the will to continue.

Senior was suspended by Boston and given until the July 8-9 All-Star break to make up his mind if he wanted to return to the team. On the afternoon of Wednesday, July 10, he arrived at Waterfront to break the news to Macha and Treuel that he wasn't coming back. He would be replaced in the starting rotation by left-handed reliever Rick Betti.

"I've definitely changed a lot since I signed with Boston in 1993," Senior said. "I still like playing the game, but I can't go back if I'm not satisfied with my performances. I know that I have no one to blame but myself for what's happened to me on the field, but there have been a lot of things that have caused me to have second thoughts on what I want my life to be like. My plan was to put some good numbers up this year and then re-evaluate myself, but I wasn't where I wanted to be. Before I got myself into an even deeper hole, I knew I had to step away."

Although the timing was somewhat bizarre, Senior's decision represented a rarity among modern minor-league players. Most have to be told when to walk away. The money at the end of the rainbow is simply too tempting to quit. Senior planned to continue pursuit of his college degree at Philadelphia's LaSalle University and work part-time at Merrill Lynch. The minor-league lifestyle of bus rides and idle afternoons cooped up in a motel had taken its toll on him.

Watching Senior's June 27 Thunder swansong was the one-millionth patron in the Trenton franchise's brief history—Ocean Township resident John McPherson. As a token of appreciation from the Thunder, he received a pair of 1997 season tickets and an official team jacket. In a way, it was fitting that the one-millionth patron came from a community 40 miles from the ballpark. It showed that Trenton's impact was more and more far-reaching in terms of geographical impact.

On Sunday, June 30, the Indians pounded Rose at Canton for nine earned runs in 3 2/3 innings on the way to a 17-3 victory. Before he boarded the team bus, the young pitcher patiently assessed his performance. Suddenly, the All-Star snub was the furthest thing from his mind. "It's kinda back to reality," he admitted after watching his ERA swell from 3.09 to 3.83. Added McKeel, "He didn't have control of his fastball, and he tried to overthrow some. Every pitch he missed, they hit." Said another Thunder player, "Yeah, it looked like they were swinging at a beach ball."

Despite the bumps in the road, the Thunder kept plugging away at the top of the standings as the All-Star break approached. A 6-4 Fourth of July victory at Hardware City was win No. 50. By comparison, the 1994 Detroit-affiliated Thunder squad didn't win its 50th game until August 21, and in 1995, Trenton reached the 50-win plateau on July 26. The Rock Cats left 14 runners on base, lefty Rick Betti worked 2 2/3 innings of scoreless relief, and Harris notched his ninth save. Back at shortstop, Sadler made one of the most athletic plays in Thunder history, leaping high to corral a line drive in shallow left field. A crowd of 2415 stood and applauded the acrobatic effort. During the series, the Thunder returned to Southington for another dinner courtesy of Momma Pavano. Her son, of course, was a Double-A All-Star at the tender age of 20.

AN ALL-STAR GALA

On Sunday afternoon, July 7, Carl Pavano returned to the Trenton area for that evening's Double-A All-Star banquet at the Hyatt Regency Princeton. Throughout the build-up to the game, Macha insisted that he would pick the AL starter "with the best numbers." He didn't know, however, who had pitched when, and Pavano was set up perfectly to start the All-Star Game because he hadn't worked in 5 days. It was his normal turn to take the ball. Furthermore, everyone associated with the Trenton franchise wanted to see the hometown prospect on the mound, but Macha had another immediate concern. On the morning of July 8, a Miami radio station erroneously reported that he was about to be named the manager of the Florida Marlins. Instead, the job went to Marlins minor-league director John Boles. Macha had been flattered by the attention but insisted "there was absolutely nothing to it." He arrived at the Marriott Forrestal Village for the annual Double-A All-Star luncheon as if nothing had happened. (Big league job. What job?) As they had been the two previous years in Binghamton and Shreveport, the Double-A All-Stars were introduced to the crowd of 500, this time in Hardison's inimitable style. The Waterfront public-address announcer saved the three Thunder players for last. Pavano smiled and waved to the gathering. Earlier that morning, a loud thunderstorm had passed through the New Jersey capital region, and many of the baseball executives in attendance for the luncheon thought that was altogether appropriate, given the significance of the day. Comedian and impersonator Joe Conklin entertained the huge banquet room with a number of off-color jokes—among them, "The Thunder franchise is a great thing to have in town. It used to be that if you wanted to see a minor-league team, you had to go to the Vet to watch the Phillies." Everyone enjoyed that zinger.

Before the luncheon, Macha told Pavano that he would be the AL starter. He would be opposed by Memphis' Heath Murray. Arriving at Waterfront Park at 3 PM, the Thunder contingent donned their blue All-Star batting practice tops and headed to right field for the AL team picture. Among the AL stars was '94 Thunder reliever Rick Greene, making a triumphant return to New Jersey as the closer for the Jacksonville Suns. He was as entertaining as ever, mimicking some of the Trenton players from the inaugural season. Outside the stadium, the famous Budweiser Clydesdales readied for their march down Cass Street. A giant hospitality tent was set up in the plaza leading into the park, and jumbo shrimp were served. Everywhere you looked in South Trenton, banners and signs trumpeted the All-Star festivities. The event's logo had been affixed to everything from T-shirts to caps to billboards.

The pregame festivities included the annual Double-A home run contest— from which Pork Chop had been so rudely slighted the previous year. This time, Carey was included in the event. Teaming with AL mates Bubba Smith of Tulsa, Mike Cameron of Birmingham, and Bubba Trammell of Jacksonville (who led all Double-A players at the break with 27 homers), Carey hit a fat batting practice pitch from Hamilton High baseball coach Jim Maher into the Delaware. Trammell paved the way for a 7-5 AL contest victory with four homers. The winners were awarded $100 each. The losing National League quartet included Memphis' Derrek Lee, San Antonio's Paul Konerko, Harrisburg's 20-year-old outfield phenom Vladimir Guerrero and Reading's Bobby Estalella.

Slowly, the record crowd filled every nook and cranny of Waterfront. Governor Whitman readied for her ceremonial first pitch; she was on hand to repeat her historic May 9, 1994, delivery. "I made it to the plate this time," she said later. Pavano took his final warm-up tosses in the home bullpen as Treuel looked over his shoulder. Macha decided to lead off with Jacksonville second baseman Frank Catalanotto, batting Trammell clean-up and Carey sixth. After 11-year-old Katie Kwelty sang the National Anthem, Pavano dug in his size-14 spikes to face Portland second baseman Luis Castillo. The Thunder ace needed just seven pitches to work a 1-2-3 first inning. The third out of the frame was the ever-dangerous Guerrero, who grounded out to Carey.

Pavano knew that he wasn't going to work more than two innings. He opened the second with a groundout and a strikeout before serving up a 1-1 delivery to Orlando third baseman Kevin Orie. Orie jumped on the pitch for a solo homer to left field as his family stood and squealed in the seats behind home plate. "It was a change-up, and I threw it a little too hard," Pavano explained after making 21 pitches (six balls and 15 strikes). "But I wanted to go after them with my best stuff. If they beat me, they beat me." The National League extended the lead to 2-0 on a solo, third-inning homer by Portland center fielder Todd Dunwoody, who added an eighth-inning single to earn the Howe Eastern League "Star of Stars" award that had been presented to Pork Chop in '95. The Southern League Star of Stars award went to Orie.

The AL managed just two runs, both in the fifth inning. Carey's one-out triple scooted past Guerrero to the right-field wall to score Trammell during the rally. New Haven first baseman Todd Helton responded in the sixth with a solo homer off losing pitcher Jonathan Johnson of Tulsa. McKeel entered the game and promptly stroked a sixth-inning single. He also made a perfect eighth-inning relay throw to second base to cut down would-be base-stealer Ray Brown of Chattanooga. Enjoying his Trenton homecoming, Greene struck out one in the ninth to complete the on-field festivities. In spite of the 6-2 National League victory in a very rapidly paced game, Carey was encouraged by his performance. "This is definitely a positive sign, especially in front of the home crowd," he said. "This is such a confidence builder."

Within minutes after the final pitch, another thunderstorm dumped thick pellets of rain on the empty stadium. The postgame party was just getting underway at the nearby Trent House, one of the New Jersey capital's historic landmarks. Fortunately, the outdoor affair—catered by the Chambersburg Restaurant Association—had been moved beneath several large tents. One by one, the All-Stars gathered in the courtyard to drink free beer and discuss their exploits. Double-A executives and Thunder corporate clients joined the revelry, which lasted well into the morning. A DJ played "The Macarena" over and over again as members of the Trenton front office let off steam in the aftermath of a superb All-Star show.

CHAPTER 21

Memories and Inspiration

"I could manage for another 20 years and not have another prospect like him."

—THUNDER MANAGER KEN MACHA REMINISCING ABOUT NOMAR GARCI-APARRA DURING THE '96 SEASON

As Macha struggled to get through to Donnie Sadler, his thoughts kept wandering back to Nomar. For the second-year manager, the memories of his former All-Star shortstop were like fine wine—they kept getting better with age. "It's not just about your ability to go out there and play," the manager explained. "It's your intensity. It's your focus. It's your desire to succeed. It's . . . balls. He had the whole package."

After missing much of the '96 season with a torn tendon behind his left knee, Nomar exploded onto the Triple-A scene in late July, hitting .343, with 16 homers and 46 RBIs in 43 games. He was promoted to Boston in late August, in the process becoming the thirteenth former Thunder player to make his major-league debut. He joined a distinguished list of Eastern League shortstop products who had come through the league during the '94-'95 seasons, including Albany-Colonie's Derek Jeter, Binghamton's Rey Ordonez, Harrisburg's Grudzielanek, Portland's Edgar Renteria, and New Haven's Nefei Perez. Hearing Macha's lavish praise, Nomar said, "That's incredible. When I hear that, it's a huge honor. It makes me blush."

In spite of his 1996 team's winning ways, Macha insisted that he wasn't having as much fun managing the team. He liked the 1995 club's approach to the game much better. Much of it had to do with fundamental execution and attitude. The '96 team wasn't very good at executing the hit-and-run. The '96 team didn't have as many flamboyant personalities—the Pork Chops, the Nomars, the McGuires. In Sadler, he didn't see as much progress as he would have liked. In Trot Nixon, he saw a fierce competitor who doubted himself at the wrong times. The standings said the '96 Thunder were something special, but in his heart, Macha felt that the numbers were a facade. After all, he was winning with veteran players and precious few real major-league prospects, at least from a non-pitching standpoint. In Pavano and Rose, he had a pair of bona fide major-league talents anchoring his staff.

"Statistics don't get you to the big leagues," Macha insisted. "They're not going to tell you everything you need to know about a player. I guess the biggest thing I have to do is exercise a little patience."

By July 12, 1996, Trenton (53-36) had put together a three-game, post-All-Star break winning streak to move nine games ahead of Harrisburg (44-45). Although talented, the Senators had been perhaps the most inconsistent team in the league. On July 11, a Waterfront crowd of 7069 had watched Rose improve to 8-4 with a 2-1 victory over New Haven. With Senior out of the mix, Macha and Treuel decided to insert Betti into the rotation. As the only member of the Thunder pitching staff who was on Boston's 40-man roster, Betti was something of an enigma. Everyone in the Thunder dugout knew he possessed a certain toughness, but a 4.80 ERA in his first 19 Double-A games told the story of a pitcher who was alternately dominant and ineffective. Red Sox officials hoped a move to the starting rotation would both give him more innings and build his confidence.

On Monday, July 15, Trenton traveled to Portland for a three-game series against the Sea Dogs, who were again leading the Northern Division. The Thunder arrived with a 55-37 record, while Portland was 55-36. Macha's old friend H. Allen Mapes—the lobster man—was unable to take the Trenton players to dinner because all of the games were played at night. Seeking to do something for the Red Sox farmhands, however, Mapes had brought several lobsters to Waterfront Park in late June. The Thunder players ate the feast in their clubhouse during a rain delay. During the Portland series, Hyzdu and several other members of the Trenton roster spent the day at Mapes' summer home on the Casco Bay. He was a true Thunder benefactor.

The first game of the Portland series was a blow-out for Trenton, as Carey went 2-for-4 with three runs scored, a homer and two RBIs. Holifield was 3-for-6, with three runs scored. Hyzdu hit his thirteenth homer. The Thunder won by a 15-4 margin, but the game also represented a major setback for Thunder infielder Randy Brown. Early in the game, he was hit in the left forearm by a 92-mph fastball from Cuban defector Livan Hernandez. The blow broke Brown's ulna bone, and the pain on his face was obvious as he was treated by team trainer Terry Smith. His season was over. In 72 games, he hit .298, with a career-high 11 homers and 38 RBIs. He was placed on the disabled list, and for the remainder of the Portland series, he hung out in the press box with a large cast protecting his injury.

On July 16, the Thunder suffered another injury when Rose was hit in the right forearm by a second-inning, infield smash hit by Sea Dogs' right fielder Pookie Wilson. The ball rocketed off Rose's pitching arm near the elbow. The pitcher tried to shake off the blow, but Macha, Treuel and Smith were taking no chances. Rose was pulled from the game almost immediately and he spent the rest of the evening icing his arm. "It hurt, a lot," he said. "More than likely, I'll miss one or two starts. I'm hoping it's just a contusion." Added Macha, "We've got to get out of here while we still have some healthy people." Fortunately for Trenton, Rose wound up missing just one start. His injury healed very quickly, which was undoubtedly one of the benefits of being 20 years old and relatively carefree.

With Rose in the training room, a Hadlock Field crowd of 6861 was treated to a virtuoso performance by Carey, who entered the three-game series in a miserable 4-for-50 slump. His 4-for-4 evening included a two-run homer, his twenty-fifth in a Thunder uniform. In his last six at-bats, he had six hits. The Thunder wound up winning 5-4 as Harris picked up his twelfth save, extending his franchise record in that category. "Todd 'Careyed' the team tonight," Macha said afterward. "Get it?"

On July 21 against Hardware City, Betti made his first start, working three innings and allowing two runs on four hits. He also walked five. It was an ominous beginning to his career as a member of the Thunder rotation; however, Trenton won the game 5-4 on a Nixon RBI. The victory was the Thunder's sixtieth in 109 games. They led second-place Harrisburg by eight games—with 33 games remaining. McCarthy predicted that Trenton would clinch the division and home-field advantage for the Southern Division playoffs by mid-August. The franchise-record of 73 wins was sure to fall by the wayside as well.

WATERFRONT WACKINESS

By Wednesday, July 24, the Centennial Olympic Games in Atlanta were well underway. Unbeknownst to the 7160 patrons who filed into Waterfront Park that evening, there was a bomb threat called in to the South Trenton stadium 2 1/2 hours before the first pitch of the Thunder's 2-1 victory over Harrisburg. The park was inspected by Trenton police and detectives—and no bomb was found. The game proceeded without a hitch. Macha maintained that no one from the Thunder front office informed him of the threat. Two days later, a bomb exploded in Atlanta's Centennial Park, killing one and injuring dozens in the midst of an Olympic-sponsored outdoor concert, and this incident prompted Macha to reflect on the Waterfront situation, which had highlighted the vulnerability of his staff and his players.

"Whether the threat is real or not real, we see now that you have to be a little more serious when something like that happens," the manager said. "To me, Atlanta is a big wake-up call. People should be informed so they can have the option of staying in the ballpark or not."

Thunder officials countered by explaining, "We felt, after a long conversation with the police officers who were on hand, that it would be better to take care of the situation without alarming everyone." Later in the season, another threat was called in, but police quickly determined that it was a prank.

"It's just very sad society has come to this," Macha added.

Bomb scares aside, July was an extremely successful month for the Thunder franchise. The Double-A All-Star Game had played to rave reviews. The team was running away with the Eastern League Southern Division pennant, and individual stars were emerging on Macha's roster. In 28 July games, the Thunder compiled a 19-9 record, completing the month with a 66-42 record overall. It was as if the team had gathered its second wind and was ready to make a push toward everyone's goal—the Eastern League championship. By August 2, Hyzdu was hitting .325, with 16 homers and 57 RBIs. He seemed to be gaining confidence with each at-bat as he enjoyed his best season as a professional. Woods was steady, hitting .332, with 17 homers and 48 RBIs, and Carey had added 18 homers and 71 RBIs, prompting the question, "Who would break Clark and Pork Chop's Thunder record of 21 homers first—Hyzdu, Woods, or Carey?" Clearly, the race made for some intriguing intrasquad drama.

Fernandez—the affable knuckleballer—had compiled an 8-6 record with a 5.22 ERA, but his value to the team went much deeper than his statistics. He gave Macha and Treuel a pitcher who could throw on 3 days of rest, breaking up the rotation for the other four members. "In some ways, Jared [Fernandez] might be our MVP," Macha praised.

In addition, reliever Mike Blais entered August with an 8-2 record, a remarkable accomplishment for a bullpen specialist. Each time he entered a close game in the late innings, the Thunder seemed to find a way to win. "They call me the Snake," Blais said. "I come in and pick up the victory, but the main thing is that the guys are giving me run support."

During a four-game early August trip to Binghamton, Doug Hecker became the first Trenton player to return to the Double-A level as a pitcher after failing as a position player. His minor-league odyssey had taken him to Single-A Sarasota for the first four months of the '96 season. In 26 Single-A games, he compiled a 2-2 record and a 4.97 ERA. He joined the Thunder on August 2, the same day Cederblad was placed on the disabled list. "My goal this season was to make it back to Trenton," Hecker explained.

In reality, his promotion was a story of perseverance and will. He had started the '95 season as Macha's everyday first baseman/left fielder. He had been demoted after 2 1/2 months of struggling against Double-A pitching. Then, he turned to pitching. And he succeeded. He chose Knackert's old uniform—No. 96—on his return.

On August 6, while the Thunder played a home game against Reading, Pork Chop's career as a Boston farmhand came to an abrupt end. His playing time had been severely diminished in Pawtucket, and he asked Red Sox officials for his release. It was granted before the PawSox boarded a plane at Boston's Logan Airport, signaling an ignominious end for a genuine Trenton folk hero. In 74 games with Pawtucket during the '96 season, Pork Chop never found a groove. He wound up hitting .236, with 12 homers and 40 RBIs. He also struck out 68 times in 242 at-bats.

As the Thunder inched their way toward the regular-season championship, they never really faced a pressure situation. There was a loose confidence that had permeated the entire season. Part of that attitude came from Gomer Hodge, whose sense of humor and slow North Carolina accent kept everyone laughing—some called it "The Gomer Factor." At the ballpark, he had a unique routine that included extra work in the batting cages and plenty of time for storytelling in the dugout. He also had a friendly relationship with several Eastern League umpires. During a mid-August series at Norwich, he continued a running wager with first-base ump Scott Nance. For every Trenton out, Hodge paid the umpire $1. For every Thunder hit, the umpire paid Hodge $3. For every Thunder run, the umpire paid Hodge $4. With Trenton playing well, the '96 season was a very profitable one for Gomer Hodge. At the end of the Norwich series, he announced, "He [Nance] owes me twenty bucks." (Hodge would give the umpire plenty of opportunity to win it back the next time he worked a Thunder series.)

Hodge's mannerisms also rubbed off on Sadler, who was struggling through the season as best he could. During an early August game, the diminutive short-stop was thrown out of a game for arguing a called third strike. The reason? He had borrowed one of Hodge's favorite sayings. Wheeling around to confront the umpire, Sadler barked, "[Fuck you], you dick." Added Hodge with an al-most parental smile, "Where do you think he learned that?"

Hodge also recalled a Mexican pitcher whom he managed during the 1980s. The player spoke no English, so naturally, the first thing he learned was one of Hodge's favorite expletive phrases, "What the [fuck's] going on?" Five years later, Hodge ran into the pitcher again during a Latin American winter league game. "He was walking across the field and I hear him shouting, 'What the [fuck]?' with a big smile on his face," Hodge remembered. That was just Gomer. Always laughing. Always keeping everybody loose. By mid-August, Macha was growing tired of the act—he didn't think Hodge was serious enough about his job. As a result, Gomer spent most of his social time with Treuel, driving in the passenger seat of the gold Saturn that was loaned to the Thunder staff. "You know the movie *Driving Miss Daisy?*" Treuel inquired. "Well, with Gomer, I'm driving Mr. Daisy."

On Sunday, August 11, Todd Carey broke Pork Chop's Thunder extra-base hit record of 49 with an RBI triple at Norwich. Hyzdu also homered, giving him 20. Woods—who had been nicknamed "Little Cecil" by Hodge for his re-semblance to Yankees' designated hitter Cecil Fielder—hit a solo homer, bring-ing his total to 19. While the Thunder sluggers were air-mailing balls to all por-tions of Dodd Stadium, Betti worked six innings to improve to 6-1 (and 3-0 as a starter). In the bottom of the fifth, with the bases loaded and 6170 patrons begging for the Navigators to blow the game open, Betti faced second baseman Pat Kelly. Kelly was in Norwich on a rehabilitation assignment. Working the count full, Kelly battled Betti for several pitches before popping out to the in-field and stranding three base runners. The at-bat typified Betti's bulldog style. "He's a street fighter," Treuel explained. "He's not going to back down to any-body. He takes it personally if you get a hit off him."

The Thunder went on to a 7-2 victory. With 22 games remaining, Trenton (72-48) was eight games ahead of Harrisburg (63-55), meaning the magic number to clinch home-field advantage for the playoffs was 15.

PAVANO THE MAGNIFICENT

For thousands of fans who enjoyed the '96 Thunder season, the virtuoso pitch-ing of Carl Pavano will be a lasting memory, particularly the second half of the season. It was as if the young pitcher blossomed right along the shadow of the Delaware River. Following the All-Star break, he began a roll of dominant pitching rarely seen in the minors—at any level. The string of excellence coin-cided with his discovery of a Chambersburg restaurant named Cesare's. Because

Pavano (and Sadler) lived in Trenton's Italian neighborhood, they were able to explore their surroundings. In Cesare's, Pavano found an inexpensive establishment that served great food in large quantities. His pregame meal consisted of pasta with marinara sauce and chicken. He stopped by Cesare's regularly to chat with the owner and staff. He was an Italian young man in an Italian setting. In short, he was home away from home, and his pitching numbers reflected that comfort level.

"I like pasta, and I don't cook," Pavano explained. "Cesare takes good care of us, but nothing compares to my mom's food. It wouldn't be fair to her for me to say anything like that."

Between July 13 and July 30, Pavano worked 24 consecutive scoreless innings, establishing a Trenton record in the process. On July 18, he threw a complete-game seven hitter against Hardware City, walking none and striking out 11 (a season high). On July 24 against Harrisburg, he scattered two hits over eight innings, walking one and striking out six while lowering his ERA from 3.51 to 3.30. By August 1, he was 11-5, tying Brian Edmondson, Shawn Senior, and Rafael Orellano for the Thunder single-season win record.

On August 3 at Binghamton, Pavano moved into sole possession of that mark with a complete-game, 4-1 victory over the Mets. He took the record in stride, however, knowing he wasn't finished piling up wins. "I want to win every time I'm out there," he said.

Pavano's winning streak wasn't just about throwing fastballs, change-ups, and sliders. During July, he had been introduced (by Thunder Director of Group Sales Geoff Brown) to a gentleman named Bernard R. Czyzewski. Czyzewski—whom Pavano referred to as "Mr. C"—had been a patient at Mercer Medical Center for 8 months when the pitcher first visited him. He was undergoing intensive treatment for muscle and nerve damage caused by an allergic reaction to a blood thinner.

"The guy was down on his luck," Pavano recalled. "His esteem wasn't up at all. He told me he liked the Thunder and that he had been to some games before he got sick. He told me he grew up near the park."

The first time Pavano visited Mr. C in the hospital, he presented the patient with a T-shirt, a ball, and a hat. He also offered some inspirational advice. "I told him to do his exercises so he could come to a game," Pavano said.

Without telling the pitcher, Mr. C calculated when Pavano's turn in the Thunder rotation would come up. In the meantime, he worked diligently on his rehabilitation exercises. Pavano visited again on August 7. Then, miraculously, on Thursday, August 8—the final Waterfront Businessperson's Special of the 1996 season—Bernard Czyzewski arrived at the stadium in a portable hospital bed. With several attendants surrounding him, he watched appreciatively as Pavano improved to 13-5 with a complete-game, 5-1 victory over Reading. The win lowered the pitcher's ERA to 2.92. More significantly, it lifted Mr. C's spirits to an unprecedented high.

"It felt so good to get out there," Czyzewski said. "Better than all the medicine in the world."

After the game, Mr. C waited patiently outside the stadium entrance until Pavano iced his right arm, showered, and dressed. He insisted, "I'm not leaving until Carl comes out." Moments later, he had an opportunity to congratulate the young pitcher in person.

At the time Bernard Czyzewski first met Carl Pavano, he had almost given up on life. The relationship brought hope back into his daily activities. Everyone who witnessed their special bond could see that much. More than anything, however, it meant something to Pavano. He was enjoying overwhelming success as a professional athlete, moving ever closer to his goal of pitching in the big leagues. Time spent in the hospital talking baseball with Mr. C was a reality check, an anchor in a sea of praise, autograph-signing, and back-slapping.

"I was really happy I made someone's day," Pavano said of Mr. C's unannounced visit to the stadium. "The nurses at the hospital told me he hasn't smiled in a while, so I don't feel like I'm going out of my way at all to help him."

When the 1996 season ended in September, one of Pavano's final stops was Mr. C's room. "It was an inspiration for me," the pitcher said. "I didn't realize the impact one of us Thunder players could have on someone."

CHAPTER 22

Icing on the Cake

> "It's not a hockey game. It's not like there's 5 minutes left and you can just dump the puck into the other team's zone. You've got to play—and play hard—every day."
>
> —THUNDER MANAGER KEN MACHA ON AUGUST 17, 1996, TALKING ABOUT TRENTON'S 11-GAME LEAD OVER HARRISBURG WITH 17 GAMES REMAINING IN THE REGULAR SEASON

Before a 7:05 PM game at New Haven on August 22, 1996, Macha gathered his players near the visitors' bullpen. Holding a copy of the 1996 Rawlings Eastern League All-Star team, he announced the Thunder selections to the group. Hyzdu had been chosen as one of the three outfielders, joining Harrisburg phenom Guerrero and Portland's Dunwoody. McKeel was named the All-Star catcher, a tribute to his season-long dedication and consistent improvement. Finally, Pavano was named the Eastern League Pitcher of the Year, joining a distinguished list of honorees that includes big leaguers Arthur Rhodes (Hagerstown, 1991), Bobby Jones (Binghamton, 1992), and Paul Wilson (Binghamton, 1995). As the Thunder players applauded the trio's achievements, Harris placed his arm around Pavano and walked him down the left-field line, adding a personal note of congratulations.

During batting practice, designated hitter Tyrone Woods also praised Pavano, claiming that he was "the best pitcher I've ever seen in the league." What made the 20-year-old so successful? "It's his fastball," Woods said. "Everything's at the knees, and his ball moves." Woods waved his hand from side-to-side to illustrate his point.

While sitting in the left-field bleachers, Macha discussed the Eastern League All-Star team, which had included a very personal snub. Carlos Tosca, Portland's third-year skipper, had been chosen the Eastern League Manager of the Year by the voting panel of league managers, broadcasters, and media. "That's not what's important," Macha claimed when asked if he was disappointed. In reality, though, he had a legitimate chance to become the first man to have been named both Eastern League Player of the Year and Manager of the Year. His team had the best record in the league and had been comfortably in first place for more than 4 months. What may have hurt Macha's chances was the large complement of veterans that had been assigned to his roster. Some Eastern League observers felt that guys like Knackert, Grundt, Schullstrom, Harris, Hzydu, and Woods made it easy for the second-year Thunder skipper. On the contrary, Macha's 1996 challenge was compounded by the wide range of experience that filled his clubhouse. Motivating a Double-A player who feels he should be playing at least one level higher is never an easy task.

Before arriving at Yale Field for the final game of the four-game series, Macha spent 2 hours on a Boston organizational conference call. "When I got out of bed afterwards, I was dizzy," he claimed. One of the items of discussion was Reggie Harris, who was on the verge of returning to the majors for the first time since 1991. Once at the ballpark, however, Macha was fuming—at Sadler. During the previous night's 6-0 victory over the Ravens, the moody shortstop had failed to run hard to first base on a couple of balls. Macha had seen enough. He unceremoniously benched the 21-year-old Texan—at least for one game. He also ripped Sadler for his lack of intensity.

"The guy has the maturity of a 15-year-old," Macha said. "That's why Nomar is going to be in the big leagues next year and this guy [Sadler] is going to be back in Double-A. If he does stuff like [not running balls out every at-bat] in Fenway Park, 35,000 people are going to boo him off the field."

One major-league scout took Macha's prediction even further. "If he does stuff like that in the major leagues, somebody's going to take him aside and kick his ass—especially if it costs the team a game. They play to win up there."

Throughout the season, Sadler continued to be a major disappointment for the manager. In many ways, Macha felt as if he had been unable to get through to the young speedster. Sadler had been stubborn and uncomfortable during his first Double-A assignment. "I think he's tired," Harris said. "And he's 21, so there's no reason for him to be tired. I think he needs to improve his diet, too. He eats a lot of junk food and drinks a lot of soda."

While Sadler brooded in the dugout, Rose worked eight innings, allowing two runs on seven hits before departing with the game tied 2-2. Hyzdu hit a two-run homer—his twenty-second—off Ravens' starter Brent Crowther to provide the Thunder offense. A crowd of 6433 watched New Haven win 3-2 on left fielder Derrick Gibson's one-out RBI single off Hecker in the bottom of the tenth. Inside the Thunder clubhouse, the champagne and Eastern League Southern Division championship T-shirts were quickly packed up and loaded back into McCarthy's Pontiac Grand Prix. In addition, Harrisburg had defeated Norwich, leaving the Thunder's magic number to clinch the division at two. The mood among the players was quiet as they showered and dressed. Macha was concerned about the lack of offense during the four-game series split, but he also was aware that his hitters had complained loudly about the poor lighting at Yale Field. Carey had experienced a particularly bad series, going 2-for-14; he had not homered since August 7. "We've got to get a few guys tuned up," said Macha between bites of a turkey sandwich. "Everything runs in cycles, and we're in a little bit of a down cycle right now."

As the final six-game, regular-season homestand began at Waterfront on Friday, August 23, the Thunder were eager to continue their dominant play in South Trenton. With a 44-21 home record (including wins in six of their last eight Waterfront dates) and Pavano on the mound, the team was feeling good about its chances against Canton-Akron. A victory would clinch at least a tie for the pennant. Another sellout crowd—this one numbering 7159—filled the stadium in time for the 7:11 PM first pitch. Among those patrons was the 400,000th of the season, Jackie O'Donnell of Mt. Holly, New Jersey. On the field, Boomer whipped the audience into a frenzy. Beyond the green center-field backdrop, a Comcast camera readied for the evening's cable broadcast; the station had taped a segment of Macha in the clubhouse, explaining the concept of a magic number to his players.

Throughout the second half of the season, Pavano had been virtually invincible, and through six batters that night, he looked untouchable again, working his two-seam fastball in and out to retire the Indians in order on one of the most humid evenings of the season. On a first-pitch delivery to left fielder Greg Thomas in the third, however, Pavano made a mistake. Thomas clubbed it over the left-center wall for a 1-0 lead. The Thunder countered with two runs off Canton-Akron starter Travis Driskill in the bottom of the inning as Nixon tripled and Abad homered to left. Pavano allowed a run apiece in the fourth and fifth, and the Indians edged ahead 3-2. The Thunder tied things in the bottom of the fifth on McKeel's RBI single, but Sadler's weak infield pop up with runners on first and third and nobody out sent the Thunder shortstop into a rage. He smashed his bat against the plate. In the third-base coaching box, Macha turned and shook his head in disgust. With the echoes of "Take Me Out to the Ballgame" still fresh, however, Abad drew a lead-off walk in the bottom of the seventh to set up a six-run Thunder inning. The key blows were a McKeel triple (his first three-base hit of the season) and a two-run homer by Hyzdu. "It was a slider, and I just ran into it," Hyzdu said after tying Woods for the team lead at 23 home runs. As he circled the bases, his trademark Mozart music played over the loudspeaker, and the Thunder faithful rose to their feet to applaud the opposite-field shot that landed just to the left of the scoreboard. The Thunder won, 9-4.

While Hardison announced that win No. 80 had clinched at least a tie for the Southern Division pennant, the Thunder players shook hands and received the news that Harrisburg also had won. Once again, the champagne was removed from the ice buckets. Everyone dressed hurriedly. Another day, another win. It was a business-as-usual atmosphere that had existed from the outset of the season.

After an 0-for-4, two-strikeout night, Sadler was one of the first out the door. McKeel stopped by Macha's office, and the manager chided him about two passed balls that he had committed during the game. "You owe me a couple bucks," the manager bellowed. "How about reaching up and catching the ball next time?" Elsewhere, Abad returned to the field for a television interview, and Pavano sat at his locker and patiently discussed his latest victory, which improved his league-best record to 15-5. During the 1990s, only three Eastern League pitchers had won 15 games—London's Rusty Meacham in 1990, New Haven's Juan Acevedo in 1994, and Pavano.

"I couldn't have done it without these guys," he said excitedly. "They get me runs, and I keep them in the game."

Despite his Double-A success—by late August he had certainly earned the right to try his luck at Triple-A or even the majors—Pavano seemed comfortable with his development. Macha and Treuel still considered him to be more of a thrower than a pitcher, although the manager admitted, "He's learning his craft."

"Right now, I want to stay here and win the league title," Pavano said. "I'm not concerned about anything else."

Macha arrived at the ballpark early the next afternoon to catch up on some paperwork. Soon thereafter, the bat phone rang. Boston needed a pitcher, and the Red Sox wanted Harris. Moments after the "order from headquarters" came down, trainer Terry Smith booked the pitcher's reservations for a 9:30 PM flight from Newark to Boston. After almost 4 months of living in Princeton's Novotel Hotel and earning $4000 a month, Harris was returning to the show, where he would earn almost four times that much. Macha's orders also included sending Cederblad back to Triple-A. The lanky Australian did not want to leave, however. He wanted to stay and join the inevitable pennant-clinching celebration.

"There go two of our best relievers," Macha lamented, "but in Reggie Harris' case, I try to be truthful to everyone, whether their time is coming or coming to an end. He stayed here and stuck it out. I'm sure there were a lot of times when he was frustrated. Boston was concerned about his command when he first got here. He was walking too many guys, but this might have been a growing-up experience. The other night, he hit 97 [mph] on the radar gun. There aren't too many pitchers in the big leagues who throw 97."

Harris' final meeting with the Trenton media was a mixture of relief and catharsis. On one hand, he had achieved his goal; on the other, it had taken much too long. Leaving behind a franchise-record 17 saves wasn't his idea of accomplishment. I don't have anything left to prove in Double-A," he had said repeatedly to anyone who would listen. Nonetheless, he was returning to Boston, which had drafted him in the first round when he was just 18 years old.

"This is a big relief off my shoulders," he said as he sat in front of his Waterfront locker for the final time. "I feel bad I have to leave these guys, but I've gotta take care of myself. Maybe I'm a little bitter that it didn't happen until now, but I can shrug that to the side."

Above Harris' head hung a "ROCK ON THUNDER" sign that Knackert had left behind when he vacated the locker. Of the six players to be promoted directly from Trenton to Boston during the '95 and '96 seasons, two had dressed in that stall. (Ironically, Harris' promotion meant that the Red Sox had to remove Knackert from the 40-man major-league roster.)

Somewhat incredibly, Harris missed his flight to Boston and was forced to make alternate travel plans. He arrived at Fenway Park on Sunday afternoon in time for the Red Sox's 8-5 victory over Seattle, a win that moved Boston one game over .500 (66-65) for the first time all season.

THE CLINCHER?

Short two pitchers, Macha and Treuel held their breath and hoped for a solid effort from Brian Barkley, who had struggled mightily at times during the season. The 20-year-old Texan was up to the task, however. Needing one victory to sew up the division and Trenton's first unshared minor-league pennant since Tommy Heath's 1947 Trenton Giants won 52 of their last 62 games to finish 88-50 in the Class B Interstate League, the Thunder offense wasted no time providing Barkley all the cushion he would need. Hyzdu homered for the third consecutive day, hitting a solo shot to center field off Canton-Akron lefty Steve Kline. A two-out error on Indians' third baseman Todd Betts in the third set up Woods' twenty-fourth homer, a 420-foot line drive that caromed off the green hitting backdrop in straightaway center. With a 3-0 lead in the fourth, the Thunder added five runs on five hits to assume a commanding 8-0 advantage. Sadler's two-run double was the key blow in that inning, and a festive crowd of 7185 sensed the significance of the evening. As Barkley completed seven innings—matching his longest outing of the year—the Thunder led 9-1. Doug Hecker then came on and finished off the Indians, striking out designated hitter Luis Raven for the final out as everyone remaining in the stadium stood and applauded. From hitter to pitcher, Hecker's unique personal story punctuated the moment. Indians' left fielder Alex Ramirez finished the game 4-for-4 with a pair of doubles, but his perfect night had done little to thwart Trenton's title plans.

Knowing that Harrisburg had lost to Norwich and they had clinched the division, the Thunder's on-field celebration was brief and uneventful. Lipsman passed out white championship T-shirts to the players as they walked back to the dugout, and announcer Brandon Hardison trumpeted the "Eastern League Southern Division champions, your Trenton Thunder!" Macha and Hyzdu headed to the first-base camera box for a television interview. Barkley iced his arm after throwing 118 pitches. Inside the clubhouse, the champagne was chilled and ready, and the lockers were covered with brown plastic sheets.

A minor-league clubhouse pennant celebration is a unique experience. From the instant the bubbly is passed around and the cigars lit, it becomes unorchestrated mayhem. Young men who have been thrust together for months, most of them living paycheck to paycheck, behave like unbridled children. All of the hours on the bus, in the training room, and in the dugout suddenly seem worth the sacrifice.

It also is a rare time when outsiders are allowed to enter the ballplayer's domain for a few moments of borrowed joy. Among those in the room as Macha delivered his congratulatory speech were Plumeri Sr., Hodes, and Prunetti. Wearing a black knit shirt, the county executive soaked in the significance of the evening while dodging champagne corks. In the scramble to open bottles, reliever Scott Emerson cut his middle finger on a loose metal tab-top; fortunately, it was his right (non-pitching) hand. Within moments, Macha was drenched and thick smoke filled the room. Photographers captured the scene, protecting their expensive equipment from the spray.

"We've worked hard for this," Macha shouted above the din. "Let's enjoy it."

As he toweled off for his nightly press briefing, the manager admitted the impromptu champagne bath had been a strange sensation, "My eyes were stinging, and my balls were freezing."

From behind his desk, Macha summarized his team's nearly wire-to-wire first-place 1996 performance. They had led the division for 4 1/2 months. "Whatever we do from here on out is icing on the cake," he said. "When over the course of 142 games you've won as many games as we have, it's a hell of an accomplishment. Barkley was huge tonight. We just lost a couple of relievers, and he went out there and pitched his ass off."

"I don't know what it was about him tonight," Treuel added as he punched the nightly game report into his laptop computer. "He had a look on his face that told me he was locked in. That showed me a lot."

"This is awesome," Barkley exclaimed, cigar in hand. "The last inning, I went out there and I had an adrenaline rush."

As the celebration escalated, several players began digging their hands into a large white sheet cake that was inscribed with the green-and-blue lettering "Congratulations Thunder." Within moments, a full-scale cake fight ensued. Colored stains decorated the clubhouse rug for days following the unrehearsed pastry battle. ("I guess the cake was a bad idea," Hodes said later.)

On one side of the room, Pavano and Rose puffed their cigars. On the other, Nixon offered his best impression of "Ace Ventura, Pet Detective." Macha rejoined the fray only to find himself decorated by caesar salad from the postgame spread. "That was the only thing left," said Blais. Hodge was assaulted by champagne, beer, and food so many times that he was forced to take four showers; Macha settled for "one double cleaning." Before the revelry was complete, the shower floor was covered with lasagna.

Conspicuously absent from the jubilant scene were Woods and Sadler. Big Tyrone had celebrated Eastern League pennants before, and he ripped the plastic from the front of his locker and dressed in disgust. "I don't get any respect. I'm not going anywhere in this organization. I'm going to go home and go to fireman's school and get on with my life." Down the row, Sadler also dressed hurriedly and headed out the stadium's back door. His girlfriend was in town, so the celebration held little attraction for him.

The Thunder front office was the next target of celebration ringleaders Blais, Pavano, Nixon, and Abad. "No Rain Wayne. No Rain Wayne," echoed the cry as the players summoned Hodes back to the clubhouse. He was doused and followed shortly by Lipsman, who also was covered with beer. "I'm glad we brought them in there," Emerson said. "It makes them feel like they're a part of us winning, which they are."

Macha dressed and headed to the Corner Inn for a few beers with groundskeeper Migliaccio. Because all of the clubhouse food had been turned into projectiles, the manager took home a pizza for late-night snacking. By late morning the next day, he was back at the stadium. "I received a lot of congratulatory phone calls, including Bill and Hillary [Clinton]. I told them I'm voting for Dole."

The Sunday afternoon game, however, was a disaster for the newly crowned divisional champs. Fernandez was bombed for 10 runs in four innings, and Ramirez extended his incredible string of consecutive hits to nine before he was finally retired on a ground-out in the eighth. Using a lineup written by Hodge that did not include Hyzdu, Woods, or Sadler, the Thunder rallied from a 12-2, sixth-inning deficit to make the final score a respectable 12-8. Carey also hit his twentieth homer, a two-run shot that bounced on the riverbank over the right-field fence. In the three-game series, however, Ramirez was 9-for-13, giving him 19 hits in his last 29 at-bats against the Thunder. In four Sunday afternoon games against the Indians, Trenton pitchers had allowed 58 runs.

"That's exactly why we don't want to face them [the Indians] in the playoffs," Blais said. "We'll take our chances with Harrisburg."

CHAPTER 23

The World Ahead
of Them

> "We want to win the championship very badly. We're not going to go into this thing nonchalantly."
>
> —1996 THUNDER PITCHER AND 1996 EASTERN LEAGUE SOUTHERN DIVISION PLAYOFFS GAME 1 STARTER CARL PAVANO

On Wednesday, August 28, a Waterfront crowd of 7327 watched Pavano improve to 16-5 with a 3-1 victory over Harrisburg (the Senators' fifth consecutive loss overall). "The biggest thing for me was to end on a good note here tonight," Pavano said. "This is definitely special to me. You don't make a career in the minor leagues—but you've gotta start somewhere."

Before the game, McKeel was awarded the coveted watch as Thunder Fan Favorite, joining Perona and Merloni as members of the first trio to be awarded that distinction. After the game, the Thunder players tossed their green caps into the stands, now a Trenton tradition on "Fan Appreciation Night." Macha chose to hand-deliver his cap to 3-year-old fan Alicia Laureti, who was seated in the first row behind home plate. It was typical Macha—classy, stoic, and even-handed. The final 69-date Waterfront Park 1996 attendance total was 437,446. The Thunder's average of 6340 patrons was well ahead of Eastern League competitors Bowie (6094) and Portland (6007), Southern League leader Birmingham (4292 for 69 games), and Texas League leader San Antonio (5522 for 69 games). In its first three seasons, the Thunder had drawn 1,209,613 patrons—a staggering testimony to minor-league baseball's popularity in the 1990s.

With five regular-season games remaining in Canton-Akron, the Thunder owned an 84-53 record. The final series in eastern Ohio also represented the last Eastern League series for Canton-Akron at Thurman Munson Memorial Stadium. The Indians, who had failed to catch slumping Harrisburg for the second Southern Division playoff spot, closed out the facility in style, taking three of five games from the Thunder. Trenton appeared to be more interested in resting for the playoffs than winning. Hyzdu suffered a lower back injury that required a few days off. Mahay—who like Hecker had been converted to pitching—made his Double-A debut and was shelled for 13 runs in 3 2/3 innings; as a result, his Thunder ERA was an unsightly 29.45.

Unfortunately for Macha, the Thunder also suffered a pair of devastating personnel losses while the team was in Canton. Said Schaefer, "In baseball, you never know when the call is going to come. That's why you have to be ready at all times." On the eve of the Eastern League playoffs, pitchers Betti (9-1, 3.67 ERA) and Blais (10-3, 3.94 ERA) were promoted to Triple-A Pawtucket, which was about to begin its International League playoff series against Rochester. Since his insertion into the Thunder starting rotation in late July, Betti was 6-0. He had exhibited an uncanny ability to pitch out of trouble.

Meanwhile, Blais had established a reputation as a winner. With 10 victories out of the bullpen, he had bailed the Thunder out of many predicaments during the season, and like Betti, he also was disappointed with the timing of his promotion. Quite simply, he wanted to stay and help the Thunder win an Eastern League championship ring. Following the slew of late-season changes, Macha tried to rally the troops, to bolster their flagging spirits for the playoff run. "I told them we've got to have the right attitude and be upbeat about those guys leaving," he said. "I knew some of my players were down about it, but they have to know that the whole thing about the minor leagues is you want to help the major-league club. And that's what we did. Regardless of these guys getting called up, we still have a good team."

"I hope the best for this team," Blais said before he boarded the Trenton bus for the final time. "It's hard to leave a team you've been a part of all year, especially now."

The last game of the regular season was a 5-2 loss to the Indians, who completed their campaign with a 71-71 record. Sadler sat out the action. Carey extended his single-season record for doubles to 34, and Nixon made the final out at Thurman Munson Stadium. A pair of youngsters walked through the stands with a sign that read, "Thanks Canton-Akron Indians. See you in Akron." Everyone in the Thunder clubhouse seemed lifeless. The long ride back to the Delaware Valley awaited, and Macha insisted, "We've got to come out tomorrow with a little more intensity."

PLAYOFF GAME 1

During the regular season, Macha's club had beaten Harrisburg 12 of 18 times, including a three-game sweep at Waterfront Park on August 26-28. The Thunder rolled behind 1996 Eastern League and Howe Sportsdata Minor League Pitcher of the Year Pavano, a veteran bullpen, and a bold team spirit that more often than not prevailed in close games. Pavano finished the regular season with a 16-5 record and a league-best 2.63 ERA. In one meteoric year, the 6-foot-5, 230-pound right-hander tied Senior for the Thunder franchise career victory mark, a remarkable accomplishment considering that Senior had pitched the entire '95 season and half of the '96 campaign before mysteriously taking his leave of absence. Rose—the scheduled Game 2 playoff starter—finished the regular season 12-7 with a 4.01 ERA.

Offensively, the Thunder led the Eastern League with 150 home runs. Woods and Hyzdu accounted for one-third of that total, with 25 each. Hyzdu established a Thunder record .337 batting average and drove in 80 runs (six short of

Clark's record 86). In 128 games, McKeel hit .302, with 16 homers, 78 RBIs, and a Thunder record 86 runs scored. Carey chipped in with 20 homers, 34 doubles, and 78 RBIs. He also struck out 123 times in 125 games—an alarming ratio for any major-league prospect. In a season-long journey of feast or famine, Carey, a Brown University graduate, had experienced dramatic emotional extremes.

At 12:30 PM on September 3, just hours before Pavano took the mound for the pivotal Game 1 against the Senators, McKeel was unexpectedly summoned to the Show. As his former Double-A teammates prepared for the postseason, the 24-year-old catcher was flown to Seattle to join the Boston Red Sox. He took with him the catcher's glove that had been given to him by New York Yankees catcher Jim Leyritz. The glove had provided constant inspiration during the '96 season.

"I hope that big-league uniform fits him better than his Double-A one," Macha chided in the wake of McKeel's departure. "He was a little slack in the pants." After laughing for a moment, the manager admitted that his team was in deep trouble without its catcher. "To me, the guy really showed what this club was all about. He's not the greatest physical specimen, doesn't have the greatest arm or the greatest physical tools, but he gave everything he had and helped us win. Certainly, I'd like to have him now." Many Thunder fans felt the same way—why couldn't Boston wait a couple days to summon McKeel?

Nonetheless, McKeel's big-league promotion was one of the most heartwarming stories of the first three Thunder seasons. From a light-hitting 6-year minor leaguer to team leader, his '96 transformation was a clear illustration that baseball's grueling minor-league system worked. During the '95 Thunder campaign, he had been demoted to Single-A Sarasota 2 months into the season. The following year, during spring training, Boston officials threatened to start him in Single-A again if he didn't shape up. "I told him that he was ticking me off," Schaefer recalled. Beginning in the spring of 1994, Schaefer had built the Boston farm system from the ground level. He was a no-nonsense baseball administrator who demanded maximum effort from his players; he had been known to release young men simply because "I was tired of looking at them." In McKeel's case, Schaefer observed, "He didn't realize what he was doing, but he was kind of going through the motions. But Walt's a tough kid, and I knew he had the ability." Nonetheless, at Boston's Fort Myers, Florida Minor League Complex, a heckling fan peppered McKeel with insults. "You'll never hit in Double-A," he insisted loudly from the bleachers during an exhibition game. "You're a bum."

McKeel was a genuine, down-to-earth minor-league baseball farmhand, however. During the summer of 1990, he signed with Boston directly out of Greene Central High School in tiny Snowhill, North Carolina. He was the kind of of guy who asked Thunder officials to tape NASCAR races during Sunday afternoon games. He liked to drink Crown Royal and Coke in bars around the league, and he was a gritty player who didn't feel he had given 100 percent unless his uniform was coated with dirt. "My biggest goal this season was to play as hard as I could," he said matter-of-factly. "Temperamental-wise, I think it's paid off." Privately, McKeel was thrilled to have hit better than .300 for the '96 Thunder. ("As long as it started with three," he said of his batting average.)

"Every time we thought McKeel wasn't going to hit, he kept hitting," Mc-Carthy added. "It was just a high that he was on all season."

McKeel's place was taken by 23-year-old Philadelphia native Joe Depastino, while Betti and Blais were replaced by 21-year-old righty Peter Munro and 24-year-old righty Brad Tweedlie. All three had been successful at Single-A Sarasota, but their Double-A baptisms would take place in the heightened intensity of the Eastern League playoffs. The irony of that situation wasn't lost on Carey or any other Thunder veteran. "When you get to Double-A, you're only a phone call away from the major leagues," Carey said. "When you're in Single-A, you don't understand that. So once you get here, it's something to think about."

As the playoffs began on Tuesday, September 3 before a Waterfront sell-out crowd of 6886, Pavano was on a magnificent roll. For the season, opponents hit just .230 against him. In preparation for his Game 1 playoff start, the Thunder had flown him from Canton to Trenton 2 days early. On the afternoon of September 3, he ate his normal pregame meal of pasta and chicken at Cesare's Cafe. As Pavano dug his cleats into the rubber for the first pitch to Harrisburg designated hitter Jon Saffer, the momentum appeared to be clearly in the Thunder's favor.

After a strong first inning, however, Pavano's streak of dominance was shattered. The Senators scored three runs in the second and five more in the fifth. A pair of errors by Sadler helped to open the floodgates for Harrisburg. Pavano departed after 5 1/3 innings, having allowed eight runs—five of them earned. Sadler homered in the fourth, but the two-run shot wasn't nearly enough to rally the Thunder. Had Pavano missed McKeel? Was he simply due for an "off" night? The silent search for answers permeated the Thunder clubhouse.

During the third inning, Pavano also had made a youthful mistake that incensed Senators' first baseman Dan Masteller. The 28-year-old Masteller, who played 79 games with the Minnesota Twins in 1995, had argued a called strike with home-plate umpire Mark Wegner. On the next pitch, Masteller hit a line drive to Thunder second baseman Nick Ortiz for the final out of the inning. As he walked off the field, Pavano looked in Masteller's direction and shouted, "Swing the bat, pussy." The exchange served as powerful motivation for Harrisburg—who went on to win the game.

Before the game, Senators' second-year manager Pat Kelly had gathered his team for a brief conversation. He told the players that nobody expected them to win the series. He also reminded them that the Thunder players had said repeatedly—and publicly—that they wanted to face Harrisburg instead of hard-hitting Canton-Akron, Cleveland's Double-A affiliate. The Harrisburg team meeting was another turning point in the series.

The Game 1 loss cast a pall over the Thunder clubhouse. Their ace had been rocked at a most inopportune time. "Pavano got hit pretty hard tonight," Macha said in his office as reporters circled his desk. "He's not a machine. He's 20 years old, and they put it to him pretty good. He didn't have the fastball he normally does."

As he iced his shoulder, Pavano expressed hope that he would get another crack at Harrisburg. "I'm not really worried. One bad start doesn't mean it's over. There's some payback out there for us."

Sadler showered and dressed in a hurry, but not quickly enough to avoid being cornered by reporters. His effort had been an embarrassment, and both of his defensive miscues had led to big Harrisburg innings. "For me in the field tonight, it was just a total lack of concentration," he said. "I wasn't real focused. It was just a lack of effort. I wasn't giving 100 percent. I don't know where I was out there. I was in the middle of nowhere."

Macha's approach to all of the 107 players he managed during the '95-'96 seasons was honest and forthright. By and large, that calm, professional treatment was appreciated by the players. Whether they were summoned to the office to be released, promoted, or reprimanded, they found a man who handled them with equanimity.

At one point late in the '96 season, Sadler had asked to be left out of the line-up. Macha inquired why, and the shortstop responded that he was dejected about his play. The following day, Sadler reconsidered and took the field—only to play one of his finest games of the season. "I guess I made the right decision," he told reporters, but the dark, brooding side of his nature seemed to counterbalance his moments of brilliance. On the road, he kept largely to himself, eating fast food in his hotel room. "He's in a league of his own," said one Thunder veteran. Added another, "That's a hard-headed little guy." "Look at him. He's 21 and he's got the whole world ahead of him, but he doesn't seem like he's enjoying himself."

GAME 2

Following his self-deprecating admissions after Game 1, Sadler (accompanied by Woods) showed up several minutes late for a team meeting before Game 2. Strolling into the clubhouse with a bag of Kentucky Fried Chicken in their hands, they scurried to dress and hit the field in time to appease Macha, but nobody in a Thunder uniform was impressed with their tardiness.

"He [Sadler] had all day to get here after a game like the one he played last night and he arrives at 4:11. That's incredible," said Boston Minor League Hitting Coordinator Steve Braun.

Added reserve outfielder Paul Rappoli, who had continued to be one of the Thunder's emotional leaders during the '96 season, "If you don't try to succeed in baseball, you're not going to succeed in life. I mean, what are you going to do when it really matters. You're not going to make it. You'll give up." All Rappoli wanted from Sadler was a maximum effort. He felt that had been lacking in Game 1.

As Woods circled the field in a slow jog before Game 2, Macha called him aside. At a time when the Thunder needed his leadership, he had come up short. For several minutes, the pair argued about Woods' status in the Boston organization. After his powerful contribution to the Thunder success, the 27-year-old player felt that he should be in Triple-A. "I don't make those decisions," Macha replied. "I just try to make you as good a player as you can be while you're here."

In the dugout, Braun summed up one of the great truths of professional baseball, applying it directly to Woods' predicament. "As soon as you realize that there isn't anybody who's been in this game who didn't get screwed over at one point or another, then you can deal with it," said Braun, a 15-year major-league veteran with Minnesota, Seattle, Kansas City, Toronto, and St. Louis.

In spite of the turbulence in the Thunder clubhouse, Trenton played well in Game 2, breathing life back into their championship hopes. Right on cue, Rose threw a eight-hit, complete-game gem, and solo homers by Carey and outfielder Andy Abad provided the impetus for a 6-2 victory. Carey's right-field blast landed in the Delaware River as an overflow crowd of 6702 marveled at the accomplishment. "That lifted our team," Rose said, and added Carey, "They've taken a lot of guys up to Pawtucket, so we kinda knew going into tonight that we had to go out and let it roll."

The series headed to Harrisburg for Game 3 tied at one apiece.

GAME 3

On a humid central Pennsylvania evening—September 5— two busloads of Thunder fans arrived at Harrisburg's RiverSide Stadium. They cheered robustly from the third-base grandstand as Sadler led off with a single against Senators lefty Tommy Phelps and scored on Woods' single to right. Bolstered by the crowd, Woods looked ready to give his best effort. In the bottom of the first, however, Barkley—the epitome of a control pitcher with an average fastball— was unable to protect the early 1-0 lead. Laboring through a 36-pitch inning, Barkley allowed three runs in the frame. Back-to-back two-out hits by first base-man Scott Talanoa, left fielder Brad Fullmer, and shortstop Geoff Blum intensi-fied Barkley's nightmare. Despite Woods' towering two-run homer in the sixth, the Thunder were pushed to the edge of elimination by a 5-3 loss.

In 5 1/3 innings of the most important start of his professional career, Barkley gave up 12 hits, walking one and striking out two. In the postgame pall, he was disconsolate—and disgusted with himself. "I just didn't have anything tonight, to be honest with you," he said. "I didn't do my job. We needed a bet-ter outing from me than that."

Added Macha about his team's predicament, "We've won more than two in a row before, right?"

GAME 4

Game 4 was postponed for one night as the remnants of Hurricane Fran plowed through central Pennsylvania, and during that rare off-night, the Thun-der players stewed over their rapidly fading opportunity. Some watched cable television in their rooms as Baltimore's Eddie Murray hit his 500th home run, becoming the third player in major-league history to collect both 500 homers and 3000 hits. No one of the Thunder players was more pensive than knuckle-baller Fernandez, who had won 14 games for the Thunder over the last season-and-a-half. A unique pitcher who carried a custom-made fastpitch softball glove for his catchers to use behind the plate, Fernandez had been alternately brilliant and terrible during the '96 season. You never knew which. With a 9-9 record and a 5.08 ERA, he had started a team-high 29 games. During the August 25 loss to Canton-Akron, he had been torched for 10 earned runs in four innings, and during eight innings against Binghamton on August 15, he had allowed just two hits—and no runs. One of the most insightful players of the first three Thunder seasons, he was intent on prolonging the season. "This is exactly where I wanted to be," he insisted.

With Hurricane Fran finally out of the way, the Thunder and Fernandez went to work against Harrisburg lefty Scott Forster. Back on August 28, Forster had taken a no-hitter into the seventh inning at Waterfront Park only to lose a 3-1 decision to Pavano. Opening Game 4 with a flourish, the Senators struck for a run in the first on Brad Fullmer's double. On the play, the Thunder committed a defensive lapse—missing the cut-off man—that allowed Saffer to score. The hole grew to 2-0 in the third on third baseman Jose Vidro's sacrifice fly. In the top of the fourth, Forster briefly lost control of the strike zone, walking Nixon, Hyzdu, and Woods to load the bases for Carey, and on Forster's fourth delivery, the third baseman lifted a shallow fly ball to right fielder Guerrero, the '96 Eastern League MVP who hit .360 to earn one big-league scout's acclaim as "the best prospect in this league for 20 years." At third, Nixon tagged the base and headed for home. Simultaneously, Macha screamed for him to hold—Carey's hit wasn't deep enough to challenge Guerrero's major-league arm. Hearing the manager too late, Nixon slipped in the basepath and was tagged for the second out. The Thunder later tied the game on catcher Ricky Borrero's two-run single, but the big inning had been thwarted by Nixon's blunder.

"I didn't hear anything, honest," Nixon said later. "I stopped, lost my footing, and then all hell broke loose."

"I told him to hold," Macha said solemnly during his postgame press conference. "In the dugout, he said he couldn't hear me."

Fernandez kept the Thunder in the game as long as he could, but with the bases loaded in the sixth, Macha pulled him in favor of the untested Brad Tweedlie. The reliever threw eight fastballs among his nine deliveries. One of them was a towering triple by DaRond Stovall that eluded Nixon's grasp and caromed off the center-field wall. The three ensuing runs drove the final nails in the Thunder coffin. A season of achievement had come to an end by a 5-2 margin. Trenton's Eastern League championship would have to wait for at least another year.

Suddenly, unexpectedly, the season was over. A group of 50 or so Trenton fans stood outside the visiting clubhouse cheering the players one by one as they dejectedly hauled their equipment to the bus. Nobody had expected the season to end this way, not without at least one more victory celebration. "We'll get 'em next year," promised Curley, who had driven more than 100,000 miles with the team over the first three seasons. "I've gotta do this whole thing again if I want a championship ring."

"I felt frustrated watching them," added McCarthy. "Everybody could have lived with the loss because Harrisburg was playing well, but it was the mental and physical mistakes that made it tough to take. All year, this team was the best team in the league, but they labored through the playoffs. They hadn't done that all year. They just sleepwalked."

Macha's slow trek to the parking lot might as well have been accompanied by a funeral march. Less than 100 yards from where the first pitch in Thunder history had been thrown on April 8, 1994, the beaten manager pondered what might have been. "Who was the better team this series?" he mused quietly before climbing behind the wheel of his green-and-brown pick-up for the 4-hour drive to Export, but the question didn't need an answer. In two seasons as a minor-league manager, he had compiled a 159-125 regular season record—a .560 winning percentage. In the playoffs, however, he was 1-6—a .143 winning percentage.

Approximately 1 hour later, the Thunder bus stopped at a rest area on the Pennsylvania Turnpike. Together, 25 players enjoyed their last supper of the '96 season. It was the final official act of a 146-game season that had begun on the spring training fields of Fort Myers, Florida, some 6 months earlier.

"We felt like we were on top of the mountain all year," McCarthy said. "Then it came crashing down."

Harrisburg advanced to the best-of-five Eastern League Championship Series against Northern Division champion Portland, and the Senators prevailed in four games, winning the franchise's third championship in 10 years. Kelly and his players celebrated with five cases of champagne in the visitor's clubhouse at Portland's Hadlock Field. Harrisburg had won 10 of its last 13 games. Trenton, on the other hand, had dropped six of its last seven.

In spite of the disappointing finish, there was no doubt the Thunder franchise had come full circle. From a 55-85 record—30 games under .500—in 1994 to an 86-56 ledger—30 games over .500—in 1996, Trenton had exceeded everyone's expectations. The cozy ballpark nestled along the Delaware River had been a springboard for scores of major-league players. It had hosted a Double-A All-Star Game and the U.S. Olympic team. It had found a giant niche in the community, one that would be perpetuated by more than 300,000 preseason ticket orders for the 1997 campaign.

By early September 1996, minor-league baseball was still alive and well— waiting for the next generation of families to sing "Take Me Out to the Ballgame." Nowhere was that truth more evident than in Mercer County Waterfront Park.

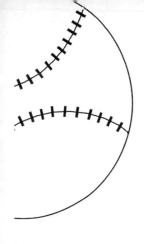

Glossary of Names

Andy Abad - 1995/96 Thunder outfielder; involved in July 20, 1995, Soho bar fight

Pat Ahearne - 1994 Thunder pitcher; made major-league debut with Detroit in 1995

Chris Allison - 1996 Thunder second baseman who played 109 games

Scott Bakkum - 1995 Thunder relief pitcher

Brian Barkley - 20-year-old 1996 Thunder pitcher; started 22 games

Matt Bauer - 1994 Thunder relief pitcher

Shayne Bennett - 1995 Thunder relief pitcher; native of Australia

Rick Betti - 1996 Thunder pitcher; compiled 9-1 record

Mike Blais - 1995/96 Thunder reliever; 10-3 record, five saves in 1996

Greg Blosser - 1995 Thunder outfielder

Rich Bombard - 1994 Thunder pitching coach

Boomer - Thunder mascot

Kevin Bradshaw - 1994 Thunder coach

Steve Braun - Boston Minor League Hitting Coordinator; Mercer County native

Tarrik Brock - 1994 Thunder outfielder

Wes Brooks - 1995 Thunder pitcher

Randy Brown - 1996 Thunder infielder; hit .298 in 72 games before breaking wrist

Donald Burris - Mercer County Waterfront Park contractor

Tim Cain - 1995 Thunder reliever

Todd Carey - 1995/96 Thunder infielder; 1996 Double-A All-Star

Ken Carlyle - 1994 Thunder pitcher; 1994 Double-A All-Star

Glenn Carter - 1995 Thunder reliever; nicknamed "Whiskey"

Joe Caruso - Thunder co-owner; founder of Omnifirst Capital

Joe Caruso - 1995 Thunder relief pitcher

Blas Cedeno - 1994 Thunder relief pitcher; native of Venezuela

Brett Cederblad - 1995/96 Thunder pitcher; native of Australia, nicknamed "Thunder from Down Under"

Joe Ciccarella - 1995 Thunder relief pitcher

Ray Cipperly - Waterfront Park groundskeeping consultant

Tony Clark - 1994 Thunder infielder; Eastern League All-Star; made major-league debut for Detroit Tigers in September 1995 and set Thunder single-season RBI record of 86

John Clarke - Mercer County Waterfront Park architect

Chris Correnti - 1995 Thunder trainer
Bill Dancy - 1994/95 Reading Phillies manager
Dean Decillis - 1994 Thunder infielder
Alex Delgado - 1995/96 Thunder catcher; made 1996 major-league debut with Boston
Joe Delli Carri - 1994 Thunder infielder; New Jersey native
Brian DuBose - 1994 Thunder outfielder; nicknamed "Doobie"
Dan Duquette - 1995/96 Boston Red Sox General Manager
Brian Edmondson - 1994 Thunder pitcher; first-ever Thunder starter
Bill Evers - 1994 Albany-Colonie Yankees manager
Bryan Eversgerd - 1996 Thunder relief pitcher; one of the four "Grumpy Old Men"
Jared Fernandez - 1995/96 Thunder knuckleball pitcher
Rob Fitzpatrick - 1994/95 Harrisburg catcher
Andy Freed - 1996 Thunder radio broadcaster
Aaron Fuller - 1995 Thunder outfielder
Nomar Garciaparra - 1995 Thunder shortstop; 1995 Double-A All-Star; 1995 Eastern League All-Star; made major-league debut in August 1996
Gary Goldsmith - 1994 Thunder pitcher
Pete Gonzalez - 1994 Thunder catcher
Rick Greene - 1994 Thunder relief pitcher; 1996 Double-A All-Star for Jacksonville
Mike Guilfoyle - 1994 Thunder relief pitcher; New Jersey native
Ken Grundt - 1996 Thunder relief pitcher; one of the four "Grumpy Old Men"
Brent Hansen - 1995 Thunder starting pitcher
Mike Hardge - 1995 Thunder infielder
Brandon Hardison - Waterfront Park public address announcer
Doug Hecker - 1995 Thunder infielder; 1996 Thunder relief pitcher
Wayne Hodes - Thunder General Manager; 1995 Eastern League Executive of the Year; 1996 *Sporting News* Minor League Executive of the Year
Rick Holifield- 1996 Thunder outfielder
Joe Hudson - 1995 Thunder relief pitcher; made major-league debut for Boston in June 1995; New Jersey native
Adam Hyzdu - 1996 Thunder outfielder; 1996 Eastern League All-Star; set Thunder single-season batting record with a .337 average; hit 25 home runs
J.J. Johnson - 1995 Thunder outfielder
Rich Kelley - 1994 Thunder relief pitcher; noted for his pick-off move to first base
Brent Knackert - 1996 Thunder relief pitcher; one of the four "Grumpy Old Men"
Alex Ladnyk - President of Excalibur Graphics; designed Thunder logo
Pat Lennon - 1995 Thunder outfielder; set franchise record with 18-game hitting streak
Dana Levangie - 1995/96 Thunder catcher
John Levenda - 1993/96 Eastern League President
Eric Lipsman - Thunder Director of Marketing and Merchandising; nicknamed "Pookie"

Ken Macha - 1995/96 Thunder manager, nicknamed "Mock"

Ron Mahay - 1995 Thunder outfielder; 1996 Thunder relief pitcher; made major-league debut in May 1995 with Boston; first former Trenton player to record a major-league hit and home run

Brian Mahoney - 1994/96 Thunder Assistant General Manager; named Norwich General Manager in August 1996

Jim Maloney - 1994 Thunder partner and legal counsel; died of a heart attack in September 1994

Jeff Martin - 1995 Thunder catcher

Justin Mashore - 1994 Thunder outfielder; nicknamed "Mayshe"

Brian Maxcy - 1994 Thunder relief pitcher; first former Trenton pitcher to win a major-league game (with Detroit) in 1995

Tom McCarthy - Thunder radio/television broadcaster; Thunder Director of Public and Media Relations

Tom McGraw - 1996 Thunder relief pitcher

Ryan McGuire - 1995 Thunder first baseman/outfielder; hit .333 in 109 games

Walt McKeel - 1995/96 Thunder catcher; 1996 Double-A All-Star; 1996 Eastern League All-Star; voted 1996 "Fan Favorite"

Kirk Mendenhall - 1994 Thunder shortstop; holds franchise record for errors with 35

Lou Merloni - 1995/96 Thunder infielder; voted 1995 "Fan Favorite"

Jeff Migliaccio - Waterfront Park groundskeeper; named 1995 Eastern League Groundskeeper of the Year

Dave Miller - 1994 Detroit Director of Minor League Operations

Trever Miller - 1994 Thunder starting pitcher; threw first pitch at Waterfront Park

Bart Mix - Waterfront Park sound operator

Pat Murphy - 1995 Thunder infielder

Dave Mysel - 1994 Thunder starting pitcher

Al Nipper - 1995 Thunder pitching coach; 1995 Boston Red Sox pitching coach

Trot Nixon - 1995/96 Thunder outfielder

Kelley O'Neal - 1994 Thunder second baseman; first batter in Thunder history

Rafael Orellano - 1995 Thunder starting pitcher; 1995 Double-A All-Star; holds Thunder records for most strikeouts in a season, with 160, and most innings pitched, with 186 2/3

Bill Pae - Artist who designed Boomer's costume

Todd Pae - Thunder Director of Business Operations

Carl Pavano - 1996 Thunder starting pitcher; 1996 Howe Sportsdata Minor League Pitcher of the Year; 1996 Eastern League Pitcher of the Year; holds Thunder record for most wins in a season with 16

Bobby Perna - 1994 Thunder infielder

Joe Perona - 1994 Thunder catcher; 1994 Thunder "Fan Favorite"

Dean Peterson - 1995 Thunder starting pitcher

Rick Peterson - 1995 Thunder pitching coach

Rico Petrocelli - 1995 Thunder coach

Cecil Pettiford - 1994 Thunder reliever

Sam Plumeri, Sr. - Thunder co-owner

Clyde "Pork Chop" Pough - 1995 Thunder infielder; 1995 Double-A All-Star Game MVP; 1995 Eastern League All-Star

Evan Pratte - 1994 Thunder infielder

Bob Prunetti - Mercer County Executive; threw out the first pitch at the first Thunder game; responsible for masterminding Waterfront Park construction

Frank Ragazzo - Executive Director of Mercer County Park Commission; Prunetti's right-hand man

Dan Raley - 1994 Thunder coach

Paul Rappoli - 1996 Thunder outfielder

Mike Rendina - 1994 Thunder infielder

Brian Rose - 1996 Thunder pitcher; compiled a record of 12-7

John Rosengren - 1994 Thunder pitcher

Tom Runnells - 1994 Thunder manager; former Montreal Expos manager

Donnie Sadler - 1996 Thunder shortstop and center fielder

Brian Saltzgaber - 1994 Thunder outfielder; first Thunder player to record a hit at Waterfront Park

Bob Schaefer - Boston Minor League Field Coordinator

Dave Schofield - Thunder team photographer

Erik Schullstrom - 1996 Thunder relief pitcher; one of the four "Grumpy Old Men"

Bill Selby - 1995 Thunder infielder; made major-league debut with Boston in 1996

Shawn Senior - 1995/96 Thunder starting pitcher; won 16 games over a 2-year span; New Jersey native

Ben Shelton - 1995 Thunder infielder

Nick Simonetta - 1994/95 Thunder radio broadcaster

Phil Stidham - 1994 Thunder relief pitcher; nicknamed "Red"; first Thunder player to make major-league debut (with Detroit) in June 1994

Mike Sullivan - 1995 Thunder relief pitcher

Jeff Suppan - 1995 Thunder starting pitcher; nicknamed "Soup"; made major-league debut with Boston in July 1995

Lee Tinsley - 1995 Boston outfielder; made brief rehab appearance with Thunder

Ralph Treuel - 1994 Detroit Minor League Pitching Coordinator; 1996 Thunder pitching coach

Brad Tweedlie - 1996 Thunder reliever

Sean Whiteside - 1994 Thunder reliever

Shannon Withem - 1994 Thunder starting pitcher; established Thunder single-game strikeout record with 14

Tyrone Woods - 1996 Thunder designated hitter; shares Thunder record for most home runs in a season with 25

Jose Zambrano - 1995 Thunder outfielder

1994 BATTING & PITCHING STATISTICS

BATTING

Player	G	AB	R	H	2B	3B	HR	RBI	SB-CS	SO	BB	BA	SA	OBP	E
*Brock, Tarrik	34	115	12	16	1	4	2	11	3-3	43	13	.139	.270	.238	1
#Clark, Tony	107	394	50	110	25	0	21	86	0-4	113	40	.279	.503	.346	13
Decillis, Dean	88	295	33	76	18	2	6	32	2-2	40	27	.258	.393	.321	13
Delli Carri, Joe	116	316	36	71	16	3	1	26	8-5	61	34	.225	.304	.304	15
*DuBose, Brian	108	378	48	85	10	3	9	41	12-10	96	32	.225	.339	.295	5
Gonzalez, Pete	16	55	3	15	3	0	0	8	2-1	7	4	.273	.327	.333	5
Mashore, Justin	131	450	63	100	13	5	7	45	31-7	120	36	.222	.320	.283	3
McConnell, Tim	42	118	16	29	6	0	2	13	1-1	17	12	.246	.347	.321	5
Mendenhall, Kirk	115	384	56	83	17	3	8	35	24-3	89	47	.216	.339	.308	35
Milne, Darren	113	364	38	89	11	2	6	36	11-5	71	27	.245	.335	.307	5
*O'Neal, Kelley	43	129	12	25	5	1	0	13	4-4	32	13	.194	.248	.264	7
#Perna, Bobby	18	58	4	6	2	0	0	3	0-1	18	5	.103	.138	.172	4
Perona, Joe	107	359	39	79	24	3	5	26	0-5	50	31	.220	.345	.293	16
#Pratte, Evan	87	319	38	83	19	1	4	34	2-3	55	27	.260	.364	.330	13
*Rendina, Mike	116	387	46	88	15	0	11	46	2-1	77	29	.227	.351	.283	5
*Rojas, Roberto	62	167	20	32	1	2	1	12	19-8	49	17	.192	.240	.266	5
Saltzgaber, Brian	26	71	6	12	3	0	1	4	3-4	18	7	.169	.254	.250	1
*Sanchez, Yuri	28	78	7	16	2	2	0	2	4-1	25	11	.205	.282	.303	11

*Left-hander

#Switch-hitter

PITCHING

Pitcher	W-L	ERA	G	GS	CG	ShO	SV	IP	H	R	ER	HR	HB	BB	SO	WP	AVG.
Ahearne, Pat	7-5	3.98	30	13	2	0	0	108.2	126	55	48	8	5	25	57	5	.293
*Bauer, Matt	2-0	1.07	14	0	0	0	3	25.1	17	4	3	0	0	13	30	0	.198
Carlyle, Kenny	3-9	4.10	19	19	5	1	0	116.1	125	75	53	6	3	47	69	5	.271
Cedeno, Blas	1-3	2.58	34	0	0	0	3	52.1	50	18	15	5	2	27	40	4	.256
Edmondson, Brian	11-9	4.56	26	26	2	0	0	162.0	171	89	82	12	6	61	90	11	.272
Goldsmith, Gary	0-4	3.86	4	4	2	0	0	25.2	23	12	11	3	0	9	27	3	.247
Greene, Rick	1-1	7.91	20	0	0	0	3	19.1	17	17	17	0	0	21	5	2	.258
*Guilfoyle, Mike	7-8	4.47	42	0	0	0	5	50.1	60	27	25	4	1	25	36	1	.308
*Kelley, Rich	1-2	5.74	16	4	0	0	5	42.1	46	28	27	8	0	20	29	3	.295
Maxcy, Brian	0-0	0.00	5	0	0	0	1	10.2	6	1	0	0	1	4	5	0	.150
*Miller, Trever	7-16	4.39	26	26	6	0	0	174.1	198	95	85	9	3	51	73	3	.290
Mysel, David	5-10	4.58	20	20	2	0	0	108.0	122	72	55	14	4	52	64	5	.284
Pettiford, Cecil	1-2	5.05	29	0	0	0	0	41.0	39	23	23	2	1	32	33	3	.247
*Rosengren, John	0-2	7.27	3	3	0	0	0	17.1	21	15	14	2	0	11	7	0	.318
Stidham, Phil	0-0	0.00	6	0	0	0	3	6.0	4	0	0	0	0	0	6	2	.182
*Whiteside, Sean	2-2	2.45	25	0	0	0	5	36.2	26	13	10	2	1	15	31	4	.193
Withem, Shannon	7-12	3.44	25	25	5	1	0	178.0	190	80	68	10	4	37	135	5	.277

*Left-hander

1995 BATTING & PITCHING STATISTICS

BATTING

Player	G	AB	R	H	2B	3B	HR	RBI	SB-CS	SO	BB	BA	SA	OBP	E
*Abad, Andy	89	287	29	69	14	3	4	32	5-7	58	36	.240	.352	.328	2
*Blosser, Greg	49	179	25	44	13	0	11	34	3-2	42	13	.246	.503	.292	0
Brown, Matt	4	11	1	2	0	0	0	0	0-0	2	1	.182	.182	.250	0
*Carey, Todd	76	228	30	62	11	1	8	36	3-4	44	28	.272	.434	.359	9
Delgado, Alex	23	72	13	24	1	0	3	14	0-0	8	9	.333	.472	.424	3
#Fuller, Aaron	58	204	27	40	7	4	0	10	15-4	45	15	.196	.270	.257	3
Garciaparra, Nomar	125	513	77	137	20	8	8	47	24-12	42	50	.267	.384	.338	23
*Graham, Tim	8	25	2	4	1	0	0	0	0-1	5	1	.160	.200	.192	0
Hardge, Mike	40	127	18	31	4	1	0	12	3-4	26	11	.244	.291	.300	9
Hecker, Doug	61	221	20	45	16	0	5	32	2-0	43	18	.204	.344	.266	4
Johnson, J.J.	2	6	1	3	0	0	0	1	0-0	0	0	.500	.500	.500	0
#Juday, Rob	3	10	0	1	0	0	0	0	0-0	4	2	.100	.100	.250	0
Lennon, Pat	27	98	19	39	7	0	1	8	7-2	22	14	.398	.500	.478	3
Levangie, Dana	42	129	10	23	3	1	0	7	1-3	30	11	.178	.217	.246	1
*Mahay, Ron	93	310	37	73	12	3	5	28	5-6	90	44	.235	.342	.332	6
Martin, Jeff	78	254	25	55	10	1	4	30	3-3	83	16	.217	.311	.273	6
McGuire, Ryan	109	414	59	138	29	1	7	59	11-8	51	58	.333	.459	.414	10
McKeel, Walt	30	84	11	20	3	1	2	11	2-1	15	8	.238	.369	.298	2
Merloni, Lou	93	318	42	88	16	1	1	30	7-7	50	39	.277	.343	.373	20
*Murphy, Pat	35	114	17	26	4	0	0	11	10-6	21	6	.228	.263	.270	6
Nava, Lipso	20	51	7	11	3	0	1	7	1-0	5	1	.216	.333	.268	0
*Nixon, Trot	25	94	9	15	3	1	2	8	2-1	20	7	.160	.277	.214	0
Pough, "Pork Chop"	97	363	68	101	23	5	21	69	11-5	101	0	.278	.543	.373	8
*Selby, Bill	117	451	64	129	29	2	13	68	4-7	52	46	.286	.446	.350	29
Shelton, Ben	35	118	23	22	2	0	4	13	1-1	31	27	.186	.305	.349	1
#Tinsley, Lee	4	18	3	7	1	0	0	3	1-0	5	1	.389	.444	.421	0
Zambrano, Eddie	20	69	5	10	1	0	1	7	0-0	25	6	.145	.203	.221	0
Zambrano, Jose	22	62	7	15	6	0	2	7	2-1	15	11	.242	.435	.382	1

*Left-hander
#Switch-hitter

PITCHING

Pitcher	W-L	ERA	G	GS	CG	ShO	SV	IP	H	R	ER	HR	HB	BB	SO	WP
Amos, Chad	0-0	12.6	6	0	0	0	0	5.0	10	8	7	2	0	3	1	2
Bakkum, Scott	6-4	1.34	28	0	0	0	0	47.0	31	12	7	4	2	9	24	1
Bennett, Shayne	0-1	5.06	10	0	0	0	3	10.2	16	6	6	0	0	3	6	1
Blais, Mike	2-0	2.52	13	0	0	0	0	25.0	19	8	7	1	1	7	20	0
*Bogott, Kurt	0-1	2.70	2	0	0	0	0	3.1	3	1	1	1	0	1	2	5
Brooks, Wes	5-11	4.12	29	23	5	0	0	161.2	149	87	74	17	11	43	85	5
Cain, Tim	4-3	3.73	29	1	0	0	4	50.2	46	25	21	1	6	17	45	3
Carter, Glenn	1-1	3.07	14	0	0	0	8	14.2	15	8	5	0	1	4	10	1
Caruso, Joe	1-1	11.3	11	0	0	0	5	12.2	21	16	16	1	2	8	8	2
Cederblad, Brett	3-2	3.63	8	5	2	1	0	44.2	43	19	18	4	2	11	36	2
*Ciccarella, Joe	2-1	2.73	22	2	0	0	0	33.0	31	13	10	3	0	12	33	0
*Emerson, Scott	0-0	4.76	4	0	0	0	0	5.2	9	3	3	0	0	2	5	1
*Eshelman, Vaughn	0-1	0.00	2	2	0	0	0	7.0	3	1	0	0	1	0	7	0
*Faino, Jeff	1-1	2.35	5	0	0	0	0	7.2	9	3	2	1	0	1	5	0
Fernandez, Jared	5-4	3.90	11	10	1	0	0	67.0	64	32	29	4	5	28	40	2
Hansen, Brent	4-5	3.26	11	11	3	1	0	77.1	70	32	28	5	12	17	52	1
*Hill, Chris	0-0	9.00	7	0	0	0	0	6.0	7	6	6	0	0	6	10	1
Hoeme, Steve	2-0	3.33	20	0	0	0	6	24.1	23	9	9	1	3	8	17	3
Hudson, Joe	0-1	1.71	22	0	0	0	8	31.2	20	8	6	0	1	17	24	2
Ingram, Todd	1-1	5.84	18	0	0	0	0	24.2	27	19	16	2	2	21	16	1
Johnson, Dom	1-2	9.42	5	2	0	0	0	14.1	19	16	15	2	1	12	11	2
Langbehn, Gregg	0-1	5.40	14	0	0	0	1	13.1	9	9	8	0	1	9	11	0
Malloy, Chuck	0-0	4.76	1	1	0	0	0	5.2	9	5	3	0	2	1	1	1
*Orellano, Rafael	11-7	2.99	27	27	2	0	0	186.2	146	68	62	18	11	72	160	9
Peterson, Dean	4-8	5.38	20	14	1	0	0	88.2	96	57	53	7	4	27	47	3
Riley, Ed	0-0	2.76	16	0	0	0	1	16.1	14	6	5	1	4	9	10	0
Ryan, Ken	0-2	5.82	11	0	0	0	2	17.0	23	13	11	1	0	5	16	0
Sele, Aaron	0-1	3.38	2	2	0	0	0	8.0	8	3	3	0	2	2	9	0
*Senior, Shawn	11-7	4.52	27	27	0	0	0	151.1	154	91	76	15	9	68	90	10
Sullivan, Mike	3-1	1.37	15	0	0	0	2	19.2	17	5	3	1	2	3	16	0
Suppan, Jeff	6-2	2.36	15	15	1	1	0	99.0	86	35	26	5	8	26	88	4

*Left-hander

1996 BATTING & PITCHING STATISTICS

BATTING

Player	G	AB	R	H	2B	3B	HR	RBI	SB-CS	SO	BB	BA	SA	OBP	E
*Abad, Andy	65	213	33	59	22	1	4	39	5-3	41	33	.277	.446	.369	1
Allison, Chris	109	357	49	82	7	1	0	22	14-11	61	28	.230	.255	.291	21
Borrero, Richie	26	71	12	22	5	2	3	26	2-1	16	8	.310	.563	.380	3
Brown, Randy	72	245	46	73	15	2	11	38	9-4	56	27	.298	.510	.379	19
*Carey, Todd	125	440	78	110	34	3	20	78	4-4	123	48	.250	.477	.326	24
Collier, Dan	28	94	12	20	3	0	4	9	2-1	36	9	.213	.372	.282	0
*Coughlin, Kevin	52	170	24	46	2	1	0	18	5-4	24	22	.271	.294	.359	1
Delgado, Alex	21	81	7	18	4	0	0	14	1-0	8	9	.222	.383	.304	0
*Holifield, Rick	109	375	73	100	20	4	1	38	35-18	98	52	.267	.421	.367	4
Hyzdu, Adam	109	374	71	126	24	3	25	80	1-8	75	56	.337	.618	.424	3
Jackson, Gavin	6	20	2	5	2	0	0	3	0-1	3	2	.250	.350	.318	1
Levangie, Dana	23	55	5	12	3	0	2	7	2-2	11	12	.218	.382	.358	1
Manto, Jeff	6	21	3	6	0	0	0	5	0-0	5	1	.286	.286	.333	3
McKeel, Walt	128	464	86	140	19	1	16	78	2-5	52	60	.302	.450	.385	10
Merloni, Lou	28	95	11	22	6	1	3	16	0-2	18	9	.232	.411	.330	8
Naehring, Tim	3	9	2	2	1	0	1	2	0-0	3	1	.222	.667	.300	1
*Nixon, Trot	123	438	55	110	11	4	11	63	7-9	65	50	.251	.370	.329	5
Ortiz, Nick	38	130	20	29	4	0	3	13	2-2	28	13	.223	.323	.294	4
Patton, Greg	6	16	3	3	1	0	0	1	0-1	4	4	.188	.250	.350	1
*Rappoli, Paul	69	193	16	41	8	0	3	22	4-4	54	27	.212	.301	.313	0
Romano, Scott	1	6	0	1	1	0	0	0	0-0	2	1	.167	.333	.286	0
Sadler, Donnie	115	454	68	121	20	8	6	46	34-8	75	38	.267	.385	.329	27
Woods, Tyrone	99	356	75	111	16	2	25	71	5-4	66	56	.312	.579	.403	0

*Left-hander

PITCHING

Pitcher	W-L	ERA	G	GS	CG	ShO	SV	IP	H	R	ER	HR	HB	BB	SO	WP
*Barkley, Brian	8-8	5.72	22	21	0	0	0	119.2	126	79	76	17	5	56	89	7
Bennett, Joel	1-0	8.31	3	0	0	0	0	4.1	3	4	4	2	0	2	8	0
*Betti, Rick	9-1	3.67	31	8	0	0	1	81.0	70	39	33	7	3	44	65	5
Blais, Mike	10-3	3.94	53	0	0	0	5	77.2	74	37	34	10	2	23	52	3
Cederblad, Brett	1-3	3.72	27	3	0	0	2	58.0	59	27	24	8	3	16	49	5
Doherty, John	1-1	1.85	4	4	0	0	0	24.1	20	8	5	0	3	2	14	0
*Emerson, Scott	1-0	5.85	19	0	0	0	0	32.1	34	24	21	4	1	26	23	7
*Eversgerd, Bryan	1-0	2.57	4	0	0	0	0	7.0	6	2	2	0	1	4	2	0
Fernandez, Jared	9-9	5.08	30	29	3	0	0	179.0	185	115	101	19	10	83	94	10
*Grundt, Ken	1-0	0.00	12	0	0	0	0	12.2	6	0	0	0	0	6	13	1
Harris, Reggie	2-1	1.46	33	0	0	0	17	37.0	17	6	6	2	0	19	43	1
Hecker, Doug	0-1	2.25	13	0	0	0	2	20.0	18	5	5	1	1	5	12	2
Knackert, Brent	0-0	1.38	11	0	0	0	10	13.0	6	2	2	0	0	6	21	2
*Mahay, Ron	0-1	29.5	1	1	0	0	0	3.2	12	13	12	1	0	6	0	1
*McGraw, Tom	3-4	3.18	30	0	0	0	1	34.0	34	15	12	1	0	19	32	1
*Merrill, Ethan	3-6	7.05	13	10	1	0	0	60.0	71	55	47	12	3	26	42	5
Pavano, Carl	16-5	2.63	27	26	6	2	0	185.0	154	66	54	16	11	47	146	7
Pierce, Jeff	0-0	1.00	4	0	0	0	0	9.0	6	1	1	0	1	4	5	1
Rose, Brian	12-7	4.01	27	27	4	2	0	163.2	157	82	73	21	13	45	115	3
Schullstrom, Erik	3-0	2.54	19	0	0	0	1	28.1	23	11	8	1	4	13	22	1
*Senior, Shawn	5-6	4.72	16	13	1	0	0	82.0	89	53	43	13	6	42	49	1

*Left-hander